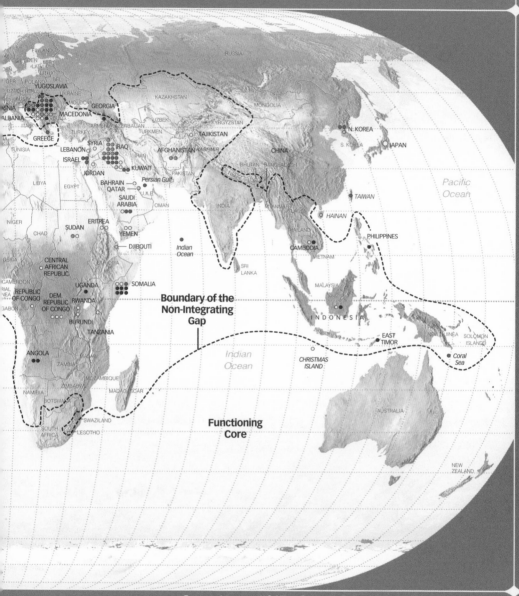

Boundary of the
Non-Integrating
Gap

Functioning
Core

Response data source: U.S. Military Services via Dr. Henry Gaffney Jr. / The CNA Corporation

THE PENTAGON'S NEW MAP

THE PENTAGON'S NEW MAP

*War and Peace in
the Twenty-first Century*

THOMAS P. M. BARNETT

G. P. PUTNAM'S SONS
NEW YORK

While the author has made every effort to provide accurate Internet addresses at the time of publication, neither the publisher nor the author assumes any responsibility for errors, or for changes that occur after publication.

G. P. Putnam's Sons
Publishers Since 1838
a member of
Penguin Group (USA) Inc.
375 Hudson Street
New York, NY 10014

Library of Congress Cataloging-in-Publication Data

Barnett, Thomas P. M.
The Pentagon's new map : war and peace in the twenty-first century /
Thomas P. M. Barnett
p.   cm
ISBN 0-399-15175-3
1. United States—Military policy.   2. World politics—1989–   I. Title
UA23.B337   2004   2003070695
355'.033073—dc22

Printed in the United States of America
1   3   5   7   9   10   8   6   4   2

This book is printed on acid-free paper. ∞

Book design by Brian Mulligan/Lovedog Studios

To Vonne,

A dream worth pursuing
A poet worth knowing
A love worth living

And to John,

A life worth emulating

CONTENTS

AN OPERATING
THEORY OF
THE WORLD

WHEN THE COLD WAR ENDED, we thought the world had changed. It had—but not in the way we thought.

When the Cold War ended, our real challenge began.

The United States had spent so much energy during those years trying to prevent the horror of global war that it forgot the dream of global peace. As far as most Pentagon strategists were concerned, America's status as the world's sole military superpower was something to preserve, not something to exploit, and because the future was unknowable, they assumed we needed to hedge against all possibilities, all threats, and all futures. America was better served adopting a wait-and-see strategy, they decided, one that assumed some grand enemy would arise in the distant future. It was better than wasting precious resources trying to manage a messy world in the near term. The grand strategy . . . was to avoid grand strategies.

I know that sounds incredible, because most people assume there are all sorts of "master plans" being pursued throughout the U.S. Government. But, amazingly, we are still searching for a vision to replace the decades-long containment strategy that America pursued to counter the Soviet threat. Until September 11, 2001, the closest thing the Pentagon had to a comprehensive view of the world was simply to call it "chaos" and "uncertainty," two words that implied the impossibility of capturing a big-picture perspective of the world's potential futures. Since September 11, at least we have an enemy to attach to all this "chaos" and "uncertainty," but that still leaves us describing horrible futures to be prevented, not positive ones to be created.

Today the role of the Defense Department in U.S. national security is being radically reshaped by new missions arising in response to a new international security environment. It is tempting to view this radical redefinition of the use of U.S. military power around the world as merely the work of senior officials in the Bush Administration, but that is to confuse the midwife with the miracle of birth. This Administration is only doing what any other administration would eventually have had to do: recast America's national security strategy from its Cold War, balance-of-power mind-set to one that reflects the new strategic environment. The terrorist attacks of 9/11 simply revealed the yawning gap between the military we built to win the Cold War and the different one we *need* to build in order to secure globalization's ultimate goal—the end of war as we know it.

America stands at the peak of a world historical arc that marks globalization's tipping point. When we chose to resurrect the global economy following the end of World War II, our ambitions were at first quite limited: we sought to rebuild globalization on only three key pillars—North America, Western Europe, and Japan. After the Cold War moved beyond nuclear brinkmanship to peaceful coexistence, we saw that global economy begin to expand across the 1980s to include the so-called emerging markets of South America and Developing Asia. When the Berlin Wall fell in 1989, we had a sense that a new world order actually was in the making, although we lacked both the words and the vision to enunciate what could be meant by that phrase, other than that the East-West divide no longer seemed to matter. Instead of identifying new rule sets in security, we chose to recognize the complete lack of one, and therefore, as regional security issues arose in the post–Cold War era, America responded without any global principles to guide its choices. Sometimes we felt others' pain and responded, sometimes we simply ignored it.

America could behave in this fashion because the boom times of the new economy suggested that security issues could take a backseat to the enormous changes being inflicted by the Information Revolution. If we were looking for a new operating theory of the world, surely this was it. Connectivity would trump all, erasing the business cycle, erasing national borders, erasing the very utility of the state in managing a global security order that seemed more virtual than real. What was the great global danger as the new millennium approached? It was a software bug that might bring down the global information grid. What role did the Pentagon play in this first-ever, absolutely worldwide security event—this defining moment of the postindustrial age? Virtually none.

So America drifted through the roaring nineties, blissfully unaware that globalization was speeding ahead with no one at the wheel. The Clinton Administration spent its time tending to the emerging financial and technological architecture of the global economy, pushing worldwide connectivity for all it was worth in those heady days, assuming that eventually it would reach even the most disconnected societies. Did we as a nation truly understand the political and security ramifications of encouraging all this connectivity? Could we understand how some people might view this process of cultural assimilation as a mortal threat? As something worth fighting against? Was a clash of civilizations inevitable?

Amazingly, the U.S. military engaged in more crisis-response activity around the world in the 1990s than in any previous decade of the Cold War, yet no national vision arose to explain our expanding role. Globalization seemed to be remaking the world, but meanwhile the U.S. military seemed to be doing nothing more than babysitting chronic security situations on the margin. Inside the Pentagon, these crisis responses were exclusively filed under the new rubric "military operations other than war," as if to signify their lack of strategic meaning. The Defense Department spent the 1990s ignoring its own workload, preferring to plot out its future transformation for future wars against future opponents. America was not a global cop, but at best a global fireman pointing his hose at whichever blaze seemed most eye-catching at the moment. We were not trying to make the world safe for anything; we just worked to keep these nasty little blazes under control. America was hurtling forward without looking forward. In nautical terms, we were steering by our wake.

Yet a pattern did emerge with each American crisis response in the 1990s. These deployments turned out to be overwhelmingly concentrated in the regions of the world that were effectively excluded from globalization's Functioning Core—namely, the Caribbean Rim, Africa, the Balkans, the Caucasus, Central Asia, the Middle East and Southwest Asia, and much of Southeast Asia. These regions constitute globalization's "ozone hole," or what I call its Non-Integrating Gap, where connectivity remains thin or absent. Simply put, if a country was losing out to globalization or rejecting much of its cultural content flows, there was a far greater chance that the United States would end up sending troops there at some point across the 1990s. But because the Pentagon viewed all these situations as "lesser includeds," there was virtually no rebalancing of the U.S. military to reflect the increased load. We knew we needed a greater capacity within the ranks for nation building, peacekeeping, and the like, but instead of beefing up those assets to improve our capacity for managing the world as we found it, the Pentagon spent the nineties buying a far different military—one best suited for a high-tech war against a large, very sophisticated military opponent. In short, our military strategists dreamed of an opponent that would not arise for a war that no longer existed.

That dilemma is at the heart of the work that I have been doing since the end of the Cold War. How do we describe this threat environment? How did we fail to heed all the warning signs leading up to 9/11? How do we prepare for future war? Where will those wars be? How might they be prevented? What should America's role be in both war and peace?

I believe I have found some answers.

Now might be an appropriate time for me to tell you who I am.

I grew up—quite literally—as a child of the sixties, somehow maintaining my midwestern optimism in America's future through the dark eras of Vietnam and Watergate. Captivated by the superpower summitry of the early 1970s, I set my sights on a career in international security studies, believing there I would locate the grand strategic choices of our age. Trained as an expert on the Soviets, only to be abandoned by history, I spent the post–Cold War years forging an eclectic career as a national security analyst, splitting my time between the worlds of Washington think tanks and government service. Though I worked primarily for the U.S. military, my research during these years focused on everything but actual warfare. Instead, I found myself instinctively exploring the seam between war and peace, locating it first in U.S. military crisis responses and then America's foreign aid, and finally focusing on its leading edge—the spread of the global economy itself. What I found there in the late 1990s was neither "chaos" nor "uncertainty" but the defining conflict of our age—a historical struggle that screamed out for a new American vision of *a future worth creating*.

And so I began a multiyear search for such a grand strategy, one that would capture the governing dynamics of this new era. Working as a senior strategic researcher at the Naval War College in Newport, Rhode Island, I first led a long research project on the Year 2000 Problem and its potential for generating global crises—or "system perturbations," as I called them. Early in the year 2000, I was approached by senior executives of the Wall Street bond firm Cantor Fitzgerald. They asked me to oversee a unique research partnership between the firm and the college that would later yield a series of high-powered war games involving national security policymakers, Wall Street heavyweights, and academic experts. Our shared goal was to explore how globalization was remaking the global security environment—in other words, the Pentagon's new map.

Those war games were conducted atop World Trade Center One; the resulting briefings were offered throughout the Pentagon. When both buildings came under attack on 9/11, my research immediately shifted from grand theory to grand strategy. Within weeks, I found myself elevated to the position of Assistant for Strategic Futures in the Office of Force Transformation, a new planning element created within the Office of the Secretary of Defense. Our task was as ambitious as it was direct: refocus the Pentagon's strategic vision of future war. As the "vision guy," my job was to generate and deliver a compelling brief that would mobilize the Defense Department toward generating the future fighting force demanded by the post-9/11 strategic environment. Over the next two years I gave that brief well over a hundred times to several thousand Defense Department officials. Through this intense give-and-take, my material grew far beyond my original inputs to include the insider logic driving all of the major policy decisions promulgated by the department's senior leadership. Over time, senior military officials began citing the brief as a Rosetta stone for the Bush Administration's new national security strategy.

But the brief was not a partisan document, and the Defense Department was not the only audience hungry for this strategic vision. Within months, I was fielding requests from the National Security Council, Congress, the Department of State, and the Department of Homeland Security. When *Esquire* magazine named me one of their "best and brightest" thinkers in December 2002, I began getting more requests, this time to brief in the private sector, concentrating in the field of finance and information technology. After I then published an article in the March 2003 issue of *Esquire*, called "The Pentagon's New Map," which summarized the strategic thrust of the brief, invitations from both the public and private sectors skyrocketed. The article was republished many times over in Europe and Asia, and e-mailed to generals and diplomats and policymakers worldwide, and when I found myself in London one fall evening speaking in the House of Commons, I knew the material's appeal had vastly outgrown my ability to deliver it on a room-by-room basis.

Thanks to this book, I am finally able to deliver the brief to you. I was once asked by a visiting delegation of security officials

from Singapore how my vision of future war differs from traditional Pentagon perspectives. My answer was, "Pentagon strategists
typically view war within the context of war. I view war within the
context of everything else." This book will be mostly about the
"everything else" associated with war in the twenty-first century, or
that essential connectivity between war and peace that defines globalization's advance.

This vision constitutes a seismic shift in how we think of the military's place in American society, in how our military functions in
the world, and in how we think of America's relationship to the
world. All such "contracts" are currently being renegotiated, whether
we realize it or not. As citizens of this American union, we all need
to understand better the stakes at hand, for it is not the danger just
ahead that we underestimate, but the opportunity that lies beyond—the opportunity to make globalization truly global.

This book will describe that future worth creating. It will explain why America is the linchpin to the entire process, not because
of its unparalleled capacity to wage war but because of its unique
capacity to export security around the planet. It will provide a way
to understand not only what is happening now, but also what will
happen in matters of war and peace across this century. It will explain where and why conflicts will arise, and how we can prevent
them. It will explain why this new strategy of preemption and this
new global war on terrorism must be subordinated to the larger
goal of spreading economic globalization around the planet. My
purpose here must be clear from the outset: I am proposing a new
grand strategy on a par with the Cold War strategy of containment—in effect, its historical successor. I seek to provide a new language, or a new context within which to explain strategic choices
that America now faces. By design, it will be a language of promise
and hope, not danger and fear. Some will interpret this as naïveté,
others as unbridled ambition. I choose to see it as a moral responsibility—a duty to leave our children a better world.

Thanks to 9/11 and the two wars it has so far spawned, Americans now understand that there is no other great power like the

United States. Instead, we begin to see the world for what it truly is: divided into societies that are actively integrating themselves into globalization's Functioning Core and those that remain trapped in its Non-Integrating Gap—that is, largely disconnected from the global economy and the rule sets that define its stability.

In this century, it is disconnectedness that defines danger. Disconnectedness allows bad actors to flourish by keeping entire societies detached from the global community and under their control. Eradicating disconnectedness, therefore, becomes the defining security task of our age. Just as important, however, is the result that by expanding the connectivity of globalization, we increase peace and prosperity planet-wide.

This is the ultimate expression of American optimism, which right now is undoubtedly the rarest and most valuable commodity on earth. The simple fact is, an optimistic belief in the future is quite frightening for a lot of people. If I were to paint a future beyond hope, more would find satisfaction in the description, for it would leave us all more easily off the hook. My business—the business of national security strategy—is the business of fear, but it need not be. My colleagues far too often market that fear to the public, demanding trust in return. By doing so, they extort the public's sense of hope in the future, and this is wrong. It is wrong because America's hope in the future is what has for well over two centuries driven this amazing experiment we call the United States. I believe life consistently improves for humanity over time, but it does so only because individuals, communities, and nations take it upon themselves not only to imagine a future worth creating but actually try to build it.

Despite our tumultuous times, I remain wholly optimistic that it can be done. My hope is that this book may help convince you of the same.

—Thomas P. M. Barnett
January 2004

Chapter 1

NEW RULE SETS

HAVE YOU EVER TRIED to explain a sport to someone who doesn't know anything about it? It is amazingly hard, especially with kids, who tend to ask the most direct—and therefore the hardest—questions. Recently, I've spent a lot of time trying to explain football to my two oldest kids, neither of whom play (blame it on soccer). I wouldn't bother trying to teach them the game except for the fact that I have two season tickets to the Green Bay Packers at Lambeau Field, so every fall I take both back to Wisconsin to see one game each. Because they have to sit with 72,000 screaming fans for more than three hours of grand spectacle, my kids naturally want to learn what the yelling is all about. So each game we attend together becomes a tutorial of sorts, and what that mostly consists of is explaining the rules of the game.

That is all I mean when I use the phrase "rule sets"—a collection of rules that delineates how some activity normally unfolds. Football has a rule set; so does baseball, and basketball, and hockey. These rules tell you how to keep score in the game, what constitutes unfair play, and how everyone is supposed to behave when they're on the field or court. These rule sets are distinct; you can't start playing baseball by football rules or vice versa. So playing by the appropriate rule set is how we keep any game from collapsing into chaos. It's why we have referees and umpires; they enforce the rules so everyone playing gets roughly the same chance to succeed.

What I'm going to do in this book is talk a great deal about the rules concerning conflict and violence in international affairs—or under what conditions governments decide it makes sense to switch from the rule set that defines peace to the set that defines war. The field of national security, like any field of endeavor, is chock-full of rules that are distinct and can be described. But as with any complex subject matter, experts tend to dominate the public debate. In general, this is good, because the public wants to hear from people who know what they're talking about when it comes to making difficult decisions like "Should we invade this country?" But it can also be bad, because experts love to use jargon, vague language that obscures rather than illuminates the issues at hand—like "national interest" and "strategic threat."

Since September 11, 2001, it has gotten a lot harder for even experts to speak authoritatively about the rule sets governing war and peace, primarily because it seems as if the world has left one era behind and entered another that feels very different and unfamiliar. It is almost as if we were playing football one minute and then the game suddenly switched to soccer—the two sides in this conflict do not seem to be keeping score in the same way, or even playing by similar rule sets. If this "global war on terrorism" is something new, then it will naturally generate a new rule set concerning war and peace, or one that replaces the old rule set that governed America's Cold War with the Soviet Union.

My purpose in writing this book is to explain how I think these new rule sets for war and peace will actually work in the years ahead, not just from America's perspective but from that of the entire world. To do that, I will need to take you inside the game that is U.S. national security planning, because America is the biggest rule maker in the business of global security affairs. As I explain these rules, I will have to decode a lot of jargon, and explain the many long-running, insider debates that have shaped how the Pentagon views this new "global war." That means I will be exploring a lot of past history before I can walk you into the future; I have to make you a student of the game so you can appreciate just how much the rule sets have changed since 9/11.

The easiest way to start explaining the new rule sets in national security is to share a story or two about what it has been like to work as a ground-floor analyst in and around the Department of Defense since the end of the Cold War in 1990, which is basically when my career began.

What does a national security analyst do? I directed research projects, meaning I would spend several months looking into a specific question or issue that some higher-up in the Pentagon food chain decided needed addressing, because either it was a new problem or it was an old one for which new answers were desired. At the end of this research—which consisted mostly of reading other experts' similar reports, reviewing any real-world data from past military operations, speaking to former policymakers with lots of experience, and sometimes simply brainstorming new approaches with fellow analysts—I would write up my findings in a formal report and deliver that document to the sponsor of the project along with a set of recommendations for future action. This formal reporting process usually included a face-to-face meeting with the sponsor, during which the project director would summarize the research team's analysis in a briefing, meaning I would deliver an oral presentation of the report organized around a series of slides projected onto a screen.

Since I was a specialist in political-military issues, a lot of times what I did in these projects was simply to review existing Department of Defense policy to see if it still made sense as the world outside continued to change and evolve. As you might imagine, many such "policy reviews" were conducted in the early 1990s, following the collapse of the Soviet threat. It was here that I realized how hard it was going to be to get the Pentagon out of the Cold War mind-set and start adapting to a radically different *world*.

PLAYING JACK RYAN

My sister Maggie has always suspected I really work for the Central Intelligence Agency, and that my pretense of being a "national security analyst" is just a cover. Like most people I know, she simply doesn't believe that the military pays me just to sit around and think about the future of the world. But that is basically what I do: I worry about everything.

In the movies, anyway, lowly analysts are constantly cracking codes or discovering huge plots to launch a global war. Then the soundtrack kicks in, our normally mild-mannered hero grabs a weapon, and it's off to the exciting if improbable climax, where he gets to shoot the foreign spy, recover the stolen computer disk, or maybe defuse the weapon of mass destruction just as the counter hits 0:01.

In *The Hunt for Red October,* Tom Clancy's hero, Jack Ryan, a mere Naval Academy professor with good connectivity inside the intelligence community, pulls off what every real pol-mil analyst dreams of: the briefing of a lifetime to senior decision makers confronting a major international crisis. But more than just narrating slides in front of some principals, Ryan convinces a room of Cold Warriors that now is the time to extend an olive branch to a renegade Soviet submarine captain seemingly hell-bent on starting World War III. Of course, there's gunplay and all sorts of close calls as the story unfolds, but in the end Ryan actually brings an entire Soviet submarine crew in from the cold. It's a wonderfully hopeful ending, and you walk out of the theater thinking maybe—just maybe—we've turned a corner with this "evil empire."

Well, I actually played a similar role in making peace with the Russian Navy following the end of the Cold War. I didn't shoot anyone or pound my fist on the table in front of the President, but I basically got to play the Jack Ryan role in the way it actually happens in the real world. In doing so, I got my first great exposure to the shifting global rule sets that would come to define the 1990s.

The story begins in the winter of 1990. I was just starting my first professional job as an analyst within a tiny think tank working directly for the Chief of Naval Operations (CNO). This group of select analysts and naval officers, called the Strategic Policy Analysis Group (SPAG), was—like everything else in the defense community—undergoing serious transformation following the fall of the Berlin Wall. SPAG had been set up in the late 1980s to help the CNO brainstorm new nuclear warfighting strategies. But when the Soviet Union collapsed, the group lost much of its luster and was passed off to the Navy's prime operations research contractor, the Center for Naval Analyses (CNA).

My first assignment with SPAG was to review the Navy's options for potential upcoming naval arms control negotiations with the successor Russian Navy. The official U.S. Government position on naval arms control had long been "just say no!" Frankly, my implied task was simply to rebless that conventional wisdom. So I made the rounds in Washington, D.C., interviewing all the usual suspects (the so-called Formers, or individuals who previously held high national security positions in the government) and visiting various Western embassies. When it came time to write the report, I was paralyzed by the illogic of the starting premise: that arms control still mattered with an enemy whose military forces stood on the cusp of an unprecedented peacetime decline. I mean, their economy was collapsing, so certainly their military would shrink dramatically over the 1990s. If that was true, why bother with arms control?

Enlisting the help of one maverick naval intelligence expert by the name of Ken Kennedy, I ginned up a series of alternative future scenarios for the Russian Navy, ranging from an "Ugly" one, in which their warfighting capabilities improved even as their fleet shrank, to a "Good" one, in which their entire fleet withered away by the century's end. Our calculations were exceedingly simple, back-of-the-envelope stuff: figuring out the composite age of their existing fleet, how much it would cost to keep those ships up and running, and what new ships and subs they would logically build across the nineties as budgets were radically slashed. It was not the usual way intel experts went about their business of forecasting the future Soviet military. In fact, Ken confessed that this approach pretty much went against his entire career up to that point.

The bottom line, which I packaged into a PowerPoint brief, was quite direct: since the Soviet Navy was going away, the U.S. Navy should immediately ditch arms control and instead dramatically ramp up its military-to-military cooperation with the Russian Navy. In effect, I argued that we should make immediate peace with the Russians and become their mentors as they transformed their fleet from a threatening blue-water navy with global reach to a minor, Coast Guard–like force.

My first-ever professional brief came in the spring of 1991 in a large conference room at the Center for Naval Analyses. The event was a regular quarterly meeting of one- and two-star admirals in charge of implementing Navy policy, a meeting in which they reviewed our think tank's latest research. It was a big deal to have my work showcased in this manner, since I was not the project director on this one but only a lowly analyst. I was nervous as hell, because I had never delivered a brief before to the top brass, and I had been forewarned by colleagues that if they did not like what they heard, I would know it immediately.

In that presentation I made my impassioned, Jack Ryan–like plea to immediately embrace the Russian Navy as a new ally. What these guys were expecting was that I would say it still made sense to stonewall those devious Russians on naval arms control, but instead here I was going on and on about rapidly increasing all our cooperation with our former enemy—guys against whom these admirals had spent a lifetime planning for war. It went over like a lead balloon. Several of the admirals openly questioned my sanity. One admiral wondered aloud if I was a "pinko," or "just plain stupid." That got a lot of laughs around the room, and immediately my credibility was shot.

Another announced gravely that he had "joined this navy to fight the Soviets, not to be their mentor." Pretty soon the room was simply buzzing with all these negative rejoinders and I knew I had lost control of the situation, which is just about as bad as it gets during a brief. Usually at that moment, someone senior will pipe up, "Let's let the man finish his brief before we start taking it apart," but this time no one did. The senior-most admiral just stared at me like I was a complete waste of his time.

My immediate superior, a Navy captain, had no choice. He walked up to my overhead projector and flicked off the lamp, pulling me offstage before I could do any more harm—something I have yet to see occur again in all my years in this business. He later called it a "mercy killing." Needless to say, I was embarrassed beyond belief.

Right after the brief, one of my colleagues, a newly minted Navy captain named Phil Voss, came up to me and opened my regulation dark-blue sports jacket, looking for "smoking holes." Then he put his arm around me and said something I'll never forget: "Tom, a year from now, no one in this room today will remember a word of what you said. What they will remember is that you did not lose your cool under fire."

About six weeks later, communist hard-liners in Moscow staged the infamous August coup that culminated with Boris Yeltsin standing on a tank, exhorting the masses to take back the government. Naturally, once word of the coup hit the airwaves, I felt about three feet tall. How could I have been so naïve? So stupid? I was actually afraid to walk down office hallways, the snickering was so loud. I thought I was finished in the business. I mean, if this was my first strategic call, how was I ever going to live it down?

All's well that ends well. The coup collapsed within three days, and a whole new dialogue immediately opened up between Moscow and Washington. In an unprecedented twist for a novice analyst, I began giving the brief over and over again throughout the intelligence community, pushing my argument for expanded military cooperation with the Russians more aggressively with each audience.

I was the only guy in the business with a detailed vision for this unexpected moment in history, so every time I briefed, someone in the audience would decide that So-and-so somewhere higher up the policy food chain "absolutely needs to see this immediately!"

The words every analyst longs to hear from the "principal" (the senior-most audience member) during a brief are "Who has seen this brief?" When you hear that, you know you have just passed through another gate and someone higher up awaits. Eventually, I made it all the way up to the three-star admiral in charge of Navy policymaking, Vice Admiral Leighton (Snuffy) Smith. It had taken me six months of delivering the brief well over a dozen times, virtually unheard of for a lowly CNA analyst.

Then came the real payoff. About six months after the failed August coup, the White House called over to the Pentagon to ask Admiral Smith what the Navy's plans were for expanding navy-to-navy ties with the Russians. According to his deputy at the time, Rear Admiral Jim Cossey, Snuffy turned to him and barked, "Well, where's that plan for making nice with the Russians?" Cossey blurted, "Give me a minute, sir," and walked back to his desk, where he had a copy of my report. In it, on page 19, was a chart detailing sixteen ways the U.S. Navy could expand cooperation with the Russian Navy. As Admiral Cossey told me later, "I simply ripped out that page and handed it to him, saying, 'Got it right here, Admiral!'"

Not exactly a Tom Clancy novel, but it's how things actually work inside the Pentagon. That report was on the admiral's desk because someone close to him had made sure it got there. That someone got it there because word had gotten around the Pentagon that this report was worth reading. That word got around because I gave all those briefs—winning battles one briefing room at a time. It's one thing to have the right answer, but it's another thing to have it in the right person's hand at the right time. In the movies, that's just one dramatic scene, but in real life it is more a matter of plugging away month after month, even when a lot of people think you have a screw loose.

Admiral Smith ended up proposing most of the list to his Russian counterpart in a subsequent summit. Only about half of the ideas came to fruition in the 1990s, primarily because the decline of the Russian Navy was as profound as we had predicted in the "Good" scenario. Naturally, back in 1991 most knowledgeable security experts considered that scenario to be the least plausible and therefore most fantastic. To these die-hard Cold Warriors, the idea that the Soviet military would simply melt away in a few short years was simply too bizarre to entertain.

As for me, I walked away from the experience convinced that the old rules no longer applied and that dramatic new rules were coming to the business of national security.

When I gave my "let's-make-peace" brief time and time again into the fall of 1991, I often noticed that while the admirals around the table vigorously shook their heads in disagreement, the younger officers lining the back walls nodded their heads in assent. This was a huge lesson for me: if one was going to change things, one needed to focus on the mid-level officers, or the commanders and the captains. Because in just a few short years, they would be running the Navy, and they realized, intuitively, that the future threat environment they would be dealing with would not revolve around the Soviets but around something or *somebody* else. I didn't pretend to have a good description of that new world order back in 1991, but many of those junior officers (lieutenant commanders and below) were roughly my age (late twenties) and must have seen me as someone who would be seriously working that case in the coming years—someone not trapped in the past.

Breaking from the Cold War wasn't exactly easy for me, not after spending ten years in college preparing to do analytic battle with the "evil empire." Hell, I expected to spend my life helping to end the Cold War! I wasn't even thirty years old, for crying out loud, and already I was a former Soviet expert on the former Soviet Union.

Much like the U.S. military, I felt the need to reinvent myself. The only thing I was certain of was that if we did our jobs right, we wouldn't be calling it the "post–Cold War era" for long. The new rule sets were already coming at us from all angles—from technology, international trade, generational demographics, and the damaged global environment.

The trick, as I saw it, was simply to sharpen my listening skills, for all the clues were already appearing in the emerging strategic environment, waiting for all of us to connect the dots. To do that, I knew I needed to spend most of my time talking to smart people outside the military. In short, I needed to focus my career on helping the military reconnect to that larger world outside the Pentagon.

NEW RULES FOR A NEW ERA

Across the first half of the 1990s, the Defense Department ordered think tanks like CNA to conduct major research projects examining how U.S. military forces should change in response to the "emerging environment"—one not dominated by the old Soviet threat. I participated in several of these studies, serving as a deputy project director to a senior CNA manager.

One feeling I never could shake as I worked with the Pentagon during these years was that the defense community was becoming increasingly irrelevant to the process of global change. So much seemed to be going on that had almost nothing to do with the employment of U.S. military power. In fact, whenever we did send our forces around the world, it always seemed as though we were babysitting chronic "bad boys" (e.g., Saddam Hussein) or basket cases (e.g., Haiti, Somalia) on the margin. As the millennium neared its end, it seemed as if it were the Pentagon itself being left behind by the great sweep of history. It seemed as though the military was becoming increasingly divorced from this amazing world of rapid integration and increasing flows of trade, capital, ideas, and people. When the planet collectively decided to name that phenomenon "globalization," the Pentagon instinctively distanced itself further. I began using the term widely in my work in the mid-1990s, only to be chastised for my "globaloney" by more than a few colleagues.

My attempt to focus on globalization proved very hard for me as an analyst, because I was working in one of the world's premier operations research facilities, the Center for Naval Analyses. CNA attracts a lot of logical engineer types who like to crush large process problems down to manageable (and countable) tasks. Brilliant as many of these analysts are, they don't spend much time pondering the imponderables. To them, the phrase "big picture" is more epithet than illumination. Nonetheless, CNA was almost a perfect finishing school for someone who had spent years at Harvard learning how to think abstractly about international relations. Surrounded by all these hard, or physical, scientists (I being a soft, or social, scientist), I was forced to introduce a lot more rigor into my thinking, to link my strategic concepts more clearly to real-world statistics, and—most important—to constantly pursue that holy grail of operations research: reproducibility.

A good strategic concept is reproducible, meaning as you share it with others, you replicate that same, undeniable understanding of the crux of the issue—in mind after mind after mind. The Cold War strategy of containment was quite reproducible in the fifties and early sixties, when it seemed exceedingly clear what we had to do to keep the Soviets from extending their Iron Curtain any farther across Europe. Later, when the threat became more multifaceted, to include national liberation movements and alternative Third World development models, containment lost much of its reproducibility. It simply started meaning different things to different people. The rule sets were shifting.

This is an important thing to remember, because we as a nation have spent the last decade trying to decipher the post–Cold War era, trying to figure out what's the essential task or fundamental struggle. Until September 11, 2001, we basically had no reproducible strategic concepts to guide our use of military power. In fact, the closest thing we had to a reproducible strategic concept was really the opposite of one, or the notion that the post–Cold War strategic environment was defined by chaos and complete uncertainty, hence we needed to defend all against all.

Why did the defense analytic community perform so poorly across the 1990s in terms of generating reproducible strategic concepts? Being bottom-up thinkers, most security analysts believe it's only right to leave the big questions for the policymakers up on top. But as I learned each and every time I walked into a Pentagon briefing room, most of those policymakers are neck-deep in day-to-day management issues and are rarely able to step back from their never-ending schedule of fifteen-minute office calls to actually contemplate the big-picture question of *Why?*

So much of the defense analytic community—not to mention the intelligence community—assumes that as all the worker bee analysts toil in their individual cubbyholes, someone up top fits all the disparate efforts into some logical, strategic whole. In truth, that rarely happens in the Pentagon—or elsewhere in the government. Most senior and mid-level policymakers spend their days putting out bureaucratic fires, and when someone like me comes into the room to brief them on the view from 30,000 feet, I'm typically welcomed like a fabulous diversion from their daily grind.

I've given a lot of briefs over the years to special groups embedded throughout the U.S. Government that are dedicated to "strategic issues," "strategic assessment," "long-range planning," and so forth, suggesting that all they do is focus on the big picture, only to have them exclaim at the end of my presentation that "nobody focuses on the big picture like you do!" This always leaves me wondering, "What the heck do *you guys* do all day?"

The answer, of course, is that all these "strategic studies" groups are trapped in the production cycle of reports, quadrennial reviews, annual estimates, and long-range plans. In effect, they're too busy cranking out big-picture material to ever spend any serious time actually thinking about the big picture. They focus on "what" and "how" but almost never ask "why?" Having put in time in some of these groups over the years, I know that the drill is meeting upon meeting until every single word on every single page (or slide) has been massaged to death. In the end, these assignments are like crack for strategic thinkers: highly addictive, providing you with delusions of grandeur, but ultimately leaving your brains fried. Do enough of these stints and you'll start rapping Armageddon like Nostradamus.

Why is this? These planning efforts almost universally focus on preventing horrific future scenarios rather than building positive outcomes. Despite the fact that these blue-ribbon groups and commissions enjoy the participation of some of the brightest people and generate some of the most fascinating operational concepts, I have yet to see any one of them ever come up with a compelling vision of a future worth creating. Instead, their reports mostly decry all the nasty futures that must be avoided. The only place where I've found positive long-range planning in the U.S. foreign policy agencies is, oddly enough, the U.S. Agency for International Development (USAID), where I worked for close to two years as a CNA consultant in the mid-1990s. I've long daydreamed about what it would be like to combine the USAID's eternal optimism with the Defense Department's rigorous worst-case planning procedures.

So how does a hungry pol-mil analyst go about generating the big picture?

Besides avoiding every staff meeting possible, the first rule to becoming a truly long-range thinker is to do whatever it takes to weasel out of every assignment you are ever offered to actually join some official long-range planning effort. Don't worry, you'll actually be trapped into enough of them to check that box on your résumé.

The second rule is to read everything you can get your hands on that seriously explores future trends, meaning you almost never read any official Defense Department reports or projections. Those documents are crammed from stem to stern with fear and loathing of the future, and if they were ever correct in their projections, this planet would have self-destructed decades ago and fallen to those *damn dirty apes!*

The third and most important rule is to interact with as wide a group of experts as possible while avoiding like-minded thinkers. For me, this meant spending the 1990s talking with technologists, business leaders, Wall Street heavyweights, mass media gurus, grassroots activists, social psychologists, and economic development experts, to name just a few. I have come up in the world of "military strategy," and I spend almost none of my time with fellow strategists. Frankly, many of them are okay with that.

In the early 1990s, the conventional wisdom around the Pentagon said we were living in a "more dangerous world" than the one we had just left behind in the Cold War. That's right. Even though the threat of global nuclear war had basically passed, many national security strategists were touting the notion that the world was a far more chaotic place, because the Cold War's "bipolar order" had collapsed. Because Washington and Moscow were no longer able to manage their respective camps, the global security environment was devolving into "chaos," the new Pentagon buzzword to describe the lack of a global security rule set to replace the one that had defined the "stable" Cold War standoff between America and the Soviet Union—you know, the good old days.

I have a lot of problems with the notion of chaos as a guiding strategic principle. It just seems like such a cop-out. So like any good Roman Catholic, I obsess instead about "rules," or all the procedures, laws, treaties, rules of thumb, and conventional wisdom that seem to guide the actions of individuals, corporations, governments, and the international community at large. I focus on rules because wherever I find them in healthy abundance (*read* quality, not quantity), I know the U.S. military's role in enforcing them will be small, because once you have rules, you typically find rule enforcers already built into the system (e.g., our very robust and distributed U.S. law enforcement network of federal, state, and local police). Likewise, wherever rules are clear because most players in that system agree they're good, there's not as much enforcement required, because most participants simply decide on their own that playing by the rules is the best course of action. But where you don't find generally agreed-upon rules, or where rules are out of whack or misaligned across social sectors, then you're talking about the future of instability, the potential for misperceptions leading to conflicts, and the clash of competing rule sets.

It's as simple as that: The fewer the rules, the more war you have. Back in the early 1990s, it was becoming clear to me that the world was not a more dangerous place, just one in which the rules concerning war and peace were not as clearly defined as they had been during the Cold War. So, yes, the Pentagon's security blanket (the Soviet threat) may have been torn to shreds, but a new global security order was clearly in the works—just not one defined by a military superpower rivalry. Figuring out what the new global security rule set was and what larger forces were shaping it would determine the future strategic posture of the U.S. military.

I knew it would not be easy to convince anyone in the Pentagon that there was some underlying method to the seeming madness of U.S. military crisis responses in this yet-unnamed "post–Cold War era." Containment was coherent. Chaos is not. Throughout the 1990s, the Pentagon lurched from Somalia to Haiti to Bosnia to Kosovo, and it did so without the slightest understanding *why*. Each engagement had its merits, but taken as a whole, they did seem to spell chaos, and chaos is no one's idea of a strategic paradigm, especially if you are the world's only superpower.

According to most people in the defense community, if you want to understand the future of conflict, you figure out the future of weapons technologies. Then you plot out who's likely to get their hands on these technologies. Then all you need to do is assume that anyone who wants to get their hands on those technologies must inevitably fear or hate America and thus seek to do her harm and— *presto!* You've identified the future threat! Unless, of course, they are already allies and it was you who sold them the weapons in the first place.

An even easier calculation is, Who's an ally? Answer: Basically anyone who agrees with your definition of the future threat, or anyone to whom you've already sold weapons.

See, it may look like rocket science, but it really isn't.

Admittedly, that sort of step-by-step threat-identification process is easy to follow, spy upon, or track in intelligence estimates. In short, you follow the technology and assume the worst about everything and everyone. It's a lot like being a suspicious parent: "What have you got there, son? Oh, really, and what do you intend to do with that, mister? All right, then, hand it over now or you're going to be in big trouble!"

This sort of approach is the reason the defense community was so flabbergasted by the rise of globalization in the 1990s. As far as most security experts were concerned, it was a complete negative, for all it did was facilitate the spread of dangerous military technologies around the world. So if you described globalization as a good thing leading to the integration of economies, the development of emerging markets, and the "shrinking" of the world, you were almost immediately labeled naïve or a wide-eyed optimist. As far as the Pentagon was concerned, the post–Cold War era was one in which constant warfare raged around the planet and dangers to U.S. security grew at every turn. So what if the nineties marked the biggest peacetime expansion of the U.S. economy or a huge growth in the spread of a truly integrated global economy? Most national security doomsayers knew full well that America was heading for a nasty fall, and these genetically predisposed pessimists felt fully vindicated by the terrorist attacks of September 11, 2001.

Of course, these same fearmongers had been touting these dangers for years and years, so if they're right only every decade or so, then damn it, even a broken clock is right twice a day! I've been reading Pentagon and CIA projections about future threats for years, and each report I've ever perused has always said the same thing: anything is possible and eventually *everything will happen.* That sort of brave futurology means you'll never take one in the rear end, but it doesn't mean you'll be pointed in the right direction or that you'll be able to move any faster than the flow of current events. You'll always end up being reactive, even as the inevitable, *ex post facto* congressional hearings "prove," yet again, the "disturbing" and "alarming" failures of your intelligence community to predict the unpredictable—like a 9/11. Doesn't it seem weird that the same senators who prattle on during Sunday news programs about how the world is a chaotic, unpredictable place still always seem to show up on C-SPAN following some security disaster to decry yet another "intelligence failure"? Who are these people kidding?

Rather than dwell on the unpredictability of future threats or attacks, our strategic vision for national security needs to focus on growing the community of states that recognize a stable set of rules regarding war and peace, as in "These are the conditions under which it is reasonable to wage war against identifiable enemies to our collective order." Growing that community of like-minded states is simply a matter of identifying the difference between "good" and "bad" regimes, and rallying the former to work collectively to encourage the latter to change their ways, applying military power when diplomacy alone does not do the trick. But changing "bad" states to "good" ones requires that we generate some broadly accepted definition of what a "good state" is, meaning a government that plays by the security rules we hold dear—like "Don't harbor transnational terrorists within your territory" and "Don't seek weapons of mass destruction." Enunciating that rule set is the most immediate task in this global war on terrorism, and promoting the global spread of that security rule set through our use of military force overseas (e.g., preemptive war against regimes that openly transgress the rule set) is our most important long-term goal in this struggle.

But the growth of any global security rule set reflects the underlying economic reality of the world at large. In the Cold War, that security rule set reflected the bifurcation of the global economy into capitalist and socialist camps. So where do we draw a similar line today? In the era of globalization, we draw that line between those parts of the world that are actively integrating their national economies into a global economy, or what I call globalization's Functioning Core, and those that are failing to integrate themselves into that larger economic community and all the rule sets it generates, or those states I identify as constituting the Non-Integrating Gap. Simply put, when we see countries moving toward the acceptance of globalization's economic rule sets, we should expect to see commensurate acceptance of an emerging global security rule set—in effect, agreement on why, and under what conditions, war makes sense.

Where this global security rule set spreads and finds mass acceptance, the threat—by definition—will diminish. Because if the economic rule sets are fair and equitably applied, "losers" or "unhappy" players will find sufficient political opportunities, within the rules, to press their cases for adjustment, restitution, and the like (like Canada going to the World Trade Organization to protest U.S. tariffs on lumber—no soldiers, just lawyers). Moreover, as political and military cooperation grows among the states within the Functioning Core, their collective ability to absorb the disruptive blows unleashed by terrorists and other bad events will inevitably grow. In effect, that which does not kill globalization makes it stronger: the world gets blindsided by AIDS, wakes up a bit, and then handles SARS better, which in turn only makes us smarter and more prepared for the SARS-after-next. The preparations for Y2K had the same positive effect on our recovery from 9/11.

If we apply that sort of approach to the global security system, then we break out of the Pentagon's tendency to view U.S. national security as somehow divorced from—or worse, exacerbated by—the spread of economic globalization. Instead, we begin to understand the threat less in terms of anyone, anywhere getting his hands on dangerous technology and more in terms of which players, governments, and even entire regions count themselves either in or out of the expanding global rule set we call globalization. Up to now, the U.S. Government has tended to identify globalization primarily as an economic rule set, but thanks to 9/11, we now understand that it likewise demands the clear enunciation and enforcement of a security rule set as well.

When we view the global security environment as divided between those states that adhere to globalization's emerging security rule set (the Core) and those that do not (the Gap), we begin to understand that the real sources of instability in our world are not only concentrated in those "off-grid" areas but are likewise found anywhere that rule sets are out of whack—even at home.

What I mean by rule sets "out of whack" is when one aspect of life (say, security) seems to have fallen behind some other aspect of life (say, technology) in terms of providing sufficient rules to account for an unexpected turn of events. Identity theft is a good example: The technology of communications and finance simply leapfrogged ahead of the legal system to the point where criminals were committing crimes that we didn't even have names for not too long ago. Eventually enough people got burned by this new form of crime that the political system responded, passing new security rule sets that allow the police to prosecute the offenders. But until that happened, the rule sets were out of whack—too many rules in one sector but not enough in another.

Think about 9/11 for a minute. It told us that we didn't have enough rule sets in certain areas of our lives (e.g., airport security, visa policies), and that those rule-set gaps could easily be exploited by those who not only don't adhere to our general rule sets but actually prefer to see them overthrown or at least kept out of their neck of the woods (e.g., Muslim extremists who dream of a Middle East greatly isolated from the "infidel" West). This kind of diagnostic approach isn't about assigning blame or pointing fingers; that's what Congress is for. What this sort of rule-set focus is really good for is understanding where we are in history, what the main security tasks of the era truly are, and how we can forge a comprehensive strategy for not only protecting America but likewise making the world a better place for everyone over the long haul.

I believe that history will judge the 1990s much like the Roaring Twenties—just a little too good to be true. Both decades threw the major rule sets out of whack: new forms of behavior, activity, and connectivity arose among individuals, companies, and countries, but the rule sets that normally guide such interactions were overwhelmed. These traditional rule sets simply could not keep up with all that change happening so quickly. People were doing new things, both good and bad, for which we had to invent not just new names but entirely new rule sets to make clear to everyone what was acceptable and unacceptable behavior in this new era. That tumultuous situation of rule sets being disjointed existed within families, communities, nations—even the international security order itself.

Eventually the situation spins out of control and nobody really knows what to do. Economic crashes effectively marked the end of both tumultuous decades, followed by the rise of seemingly new sorts of security threats to the international order. In the 1930s, it was fascism and Nazi Germany, while today most security experts will tell you it is radical Islam and transnational terrorism. In both instances, the community of states committed to maintaining global order was deeply torn over what to do about these new security threats—try to accommodate them or fight them head-on in war? Most of the time we cannot even agree on what to call these threats—for example, what makes a government a "rogue regime," and when are terrorists legitimately viewed as "enemy combatants"? If there are no easy answers, then there are no common definitions, and that means rule sets are out of whack.

Meanwhile, the global economic order will inevitably grow brittle if there is widespread confusion over what constitutes legitimate threats to international stability and order (e.g., al Qaeda? America the out-of-control hyperpower?). Everyone becomes more worried about the future, and so trust decreases across the system, making compromises all the harder to achieve. If it gets really bad, states stop cooperating on economic rule sets altogether, and start turning on one another in security matters. In the 1930s, the global economy basically collapsed in on itself, as the major players put up walls around their economies in the form of tariffs and other restrictions on trade. Today, we face similar temptations as the Core and Gap fight over the former's high agricultural subsidies and the latter's high tariffs against industrial imports. In the 1930s, the world drifted toward global war, while today many around the world speak ominously of America's growing "empire" and the prospect of "per-petual war."

My shorthand for rule-set divergence in the 1990s is roughly the same as the one I would offer for the 1920s: economics got ahead of politics, and technology got ahead of security. In effect, we let the world get too connected too fast. Not that connectivity itself is bad, for I'm a huge believer in the free flow of mass media, ideas, capital, goods, technology, and people. Rather, we didn't construct sufficient political and security rule sets to keep pace with all this growing connectivity. In some ways, we got lazy, counted a little too much on the market to sort it all out, and then woke up shocked and amazed on 9/11 to find ourselves apparently invited to a global war.

The question that now stands before us is whether or not this decade ends up being a repeat of the 1930s, when, by God, we really did end up in a global, *total* war. World Wars I and II, in combina-tion with the self-destructive economic nationalism of the 1930s, completely wiped out all the gains in global economic integration achieved by that first great globalization era of 1870 to 1914.

Taking to heart the lesson of the demise of Globalization I, the United States decided to institute a new global rule set following World War II, or one that restored some sense of balance to the eco-nomic, political, and security rule sets that defined what later be-came known as the West. I'm talking about the resource flows (Marshall Plan), the massive reorganization of the U.S. Government (Defense Act of 1947, which created the Defense Department, the CIA, and other entities), the creation of a slew of international or-ganizations (United Nations, International Monetary Fund, World Bank), new economic rule sets (General Agreement on Trade and Tariffs, Bretton Woods agreement on a currency stabilization regime), and the forging of new military alliances (the most impor-tant being the North Atlantic Treaty Organization). This period of rule-set "reset" took the better part of a decade, consuming U.S. diplo-matic and military efforts deep into the 1950s. This Rome wasn't built in a day.

Nor was it promulgated without a significant amount of long-range planning, or the sort we seem to have forgotten in the Pentagon, perhaps because the bulk of that historic planning occurred in the State Department. Here we had the so-called wise men, most notably George Kennan, who looked around the world and decided it wasn't hard to identify the main sources of mass violence in the system over the previous quarter-century: basically a militarist Germany, an expansionist Soviet Union, and an imperialist Japan. So they did the logical thing: they created a long-term strategy to buy off the two losers from World War II while waiting out the third.

Their dream was simple enough, but amazingly bold: perhaps by the end of the century both Germany and Japan would be so pacified and economically integrated into a resurgent West that they would never again pose a threat to global peace, and maybe—just maybe—the Soviet Union would collapse of its own accord and join the dominant Western rule set in perpetual peace. Now, of course, this is basically history. But step back to 1946, and that simple plan looks less like a strategic vision and more like a daydream. To many security experts of that era, the notion that we could rehabilitate Nazi Germany and imperial Japan while simultaneously standing up to the Reds was simply ludicrous. We had neither the will nor the wallet after fighting World War II, and our experience in the Korean War made it seem like this new world would feature lots of U.S. casualties for very uncertain and unsatisfactory outcomes.

Sound familiar? This is why I prefer comparing George W. Bush to Harry Truman rather than Ronald Reagan. Reagan didn't win the Cold War but had it handed to him on a silver platter. Truman really got the ball rolling, just like Bush, who—if he plays his cards right—may yet set in motion a new strategic security paradigm that will far outlive his presidency. But that will happen only if the Bush Administration generates reproducible strategic concepts, or a compelling containment-like vision that other, successor administrations can also champion. Reproducible here means both Republicans and Democrats can understand them in the same basic way. Not identical, mind you, but we can't be forever arguing about definitions. Trust me, the military wants this sort of bipartisan consensus in the worst way.

This outcome, obviously, is far from certain. If I compare Bush favorably with Truman in terms of action, I'd be forced to give him a failing grade to date in terms of strategic vision, which is just a fancy way of saying how he explains his foreign policy to the public and the world. No doubt Bush has a far tougher task than Truman, because Truman's enemy was more clearly defined by its military threat, whereas Bush's enemy is characterized less by a direct threat to our way of life than a sheer rejection of it. The Soviets were really out to get us, whereas the antiglobalization forces—represented in their most violent form by an al Qaeda—don't seek our historical destruction so much as a sort of permanent civilizational apartheid.

Because we called the post–World War II period the Cold War, history remembers those decades mostly as a scary, strategic standoff between the United States and the Soviet Union. In reality, that was the sideshow of the containment strategy. The real goal of that visionary strategy was to resurrect globalization on three key pillars: the United States, Western Europe, and Japan. Between 1950 and 1980, we succeeded beyond our wildest dreams, as roughly 10 percent of the global population controlled the vast wealth of the resurgent global economy. But around 1980 it got even better, if you listen to the World Bank, which notes the emergence across the 1980s of roughly two dozen globalizing economies, to include such current globalization welterweights as South Korea, Brazil, and India, not to mention the emerging heavyweight of that class China.

That wondrous story of Globalization II (1945–1980) is the buried lead of all Cold War histories yet written. Truth be told, Globalization II was the Cold War's *raison d'être,* whereas Globalization III (1980 and counting) is its "peace dividend," the pot of gold we spent the 1990s fruitlessly searching for in the U.S. federal budget. But you know what? It was completely worth it, because globalization, with an assist from the spectre of nuclear weapons, has effectively killed the idea of great-power war—all-out conventional (nonnuclear) war among the world's most powerful states that concludes only when one side is completely defeated. But even better than that, Globalization II and III have lifted hundreds of millions out of poverty over the second half of the twentieth century. While the world's population has doubled since 1960, the percentage living in poverty has been cut in half.

For those of you who thought that globalization was invented in the 1990s, let me tell you why all this talk about rule sets is important. We let economic nationalism outpace political reason in the 1930s and we got a Great Depression for our failings. We let the technology of killing get ahead of our ability to manage security relationships among great powers in the 1930s and we got the Second World War and the Holocaust for our failings. We stand at a similar point in history now, having just gone through the "roaring" nineties only to wake up with a four-aspirin hangover called the Asian flu, the tech crash, 9/11, and the global war on terrorism. How we move ahead depends greatly on how we view our world and the rule sets that define it.

Despite being the world's sole military superpower, America needs to understand that it stands on the cusp of a new multipolar era defined by globalization's progressive advance. It also needs to realize that the emerging global conflict lies between those who want to see the world grow ever more connected and rule-bound and those who want to isolate large chunks of humanity from the globalization process so as to pursue very particular paths to "happiness." If we as a nation, through our diplomatic and security strategies, succeed in closing the rule-set gaps that currently exist, we will do far more than make our nation more secure or wealthier, we'll finally succeed in making globalization truly global.

The task that lies before us is no less historic or heroic than that surmounted by the so-called greatest generation over the course of the twentieth century. And, yes, this task will consume a similar length of time.

In retrospect, what was scariest about the rule-set misalignment of the 1990s was that the world was trying to administer a very complex system using tools designed for another era. The package of new rule sets America forged after WWII was designed to prevent the collapse of Globalization I, not necessarily to advance the far more complex and comprehensive Globalization III. They were designed to prevent war among great powers, not necessarily to deal with rogue regimes and transnational terrorist networks.

The rule sets we put in place in the late 1940s and early 1950s have not aged well in most instances. Some, like the International Monetary Fund, have morphed dramatically over the decades, leaving behind their original functions (currency stabilization) and taking on new roles (lender of last resort) as globalization expanded and matured. Other rule sets, like having World War II's winning coalition constitute the permanent, veto-wielding members of the UN Security Council, are seriously out-of-date. Even NATO is at great risk of losing its identity as it struggles to admit former socialist states, much less pursue combat operations somewhere other than Europe.

When 9/11 exploded into the global consciousness, it crystallized that sense of rule-set misalignment, not just for grand strategists but for average citizens too. Much as at the end of World War II, America simply wasn't ready to deal with its own success at the end of the Cold War, and so it spent much of the 1990s letting the international security environment run on cruise control— defined as lobbing a few cruise missiles every time some bad boy like Saddam or Osama got seriously out of line. Collectively, we became too enamored with free markets and too suspicious of government, assuming that "hidden hands" would keep us secure, along with rent-a-cops and gated communities. Much of this self-delusion was based on the notion that the new economy obviated much of what might be called the normal upkeep of various political and security rule sets. I mean, if the Internet was simply going to remake all aspects of society and repeal the business cycle, then the political and security realms were simply going to have to take a backseat to this technologically driven global revolution.

In reality, the rise of this new economy meant we needed more stringent, not more relaxed political and security rule sets. Simply put, in the rush to connect the world up to the grid, we forgot to make sure we kept things safe for the average person. So, yeah, global nuclear war deservedly became a nostalgic notion, but the "democratization of violence," as Fareed Zakaria calls it, moved the planet into a new era of dominant threats. Instead of an almost abstract, all-consuming Armageddon that everyone could push to the back of his or her consciousness, now we all go through a litany of personal exercises—raising arms, spreading legs, surrendering watches and shoes—every time we want to fly a commercial airline. With the terrorist attacks of 9/11, the strategic threat morphed into something far more up-close and personal, in a shockingly abrupt transition from one era to the next.

That is what I call a "rule-set reset." It is when you realize that your world is woefully lacking certain types of rules and so you start making up those new rules with a vengeance because—by God—we simply cannot ever let something like *that* ever happen again! Such a rule-set reset can be a very good thing—putting your house in order, so to speak. But it can also be a very dangerous time, because in your rush to fill in all the rule-set gaps, your cure may end up being worse than the disease. No government that tried to deal with the Great Depression of the 1930s set about purposefully to destroy the global economy of that era, and yet they did—with the best of intentions.

To me, 9/11 was an amazing gift—as twisted and cruel as that sounds. It was an invitation from history, albeit one with a horrific price tag. But 9/11 the world-historical event must ultimately yield far more hope than fear, far more love than hatred, and—most important—far more understanding than pain. But that will happen only if America *chooses* to see it for what it was: feedback from a world in significant distress. On that morning, America was forced to wake up from the dreamlike nineties. We were compelled to recognize the great rule-set gaps that afflicted the world order, leaving so many trapped in significant pain and suffering. That these heinous terrorist acts were perpetrated by those committed to destroying Globalization III should only strengthen our resolve to deny them the outcome they so desperately seek: that of condemning some portion of the global population to isolating deprivation.

But it's not enough simply to cram our political system with a plethora of poorly thought-out rule sets. That's not to say that the Patriot Act is all bad, or that the Bush Administration's new policy of preemption necessarily represents a dangerous turn in our nation's history. These new rule sets were both inevitable and much needed. Fortunately, within the U.S. political system we have the judicial branch to fine-tune the Patriot Act and every other domestic rule set that follows. But on the world stage, the global community is the court in which our appeals for new rule sets must find eventual acceptance if we are to be successful in extending Globalization III to its logical ends. The global rule set's real reach is not defined by this superpower's ability to project military power, but by the progressive reduction of those global trouble spots to which U.S. military power must consistently deploy.

Have no doubt, new global rule sets are being forged all over this planet as a result of 9/11 and our self-proclaimed global war on terrorism. The only questions that remain are, Which rule sets will find the widest acceptance? And how far will America go—or change—to make sure its preferred rule sets prevail?

PRESENT AT THE CREATION

Growing up as a kid in the sixties, I found myself inexorably drawn to the national nostalgia for the 1940s. Part of that was the two-decades-back recycling the mass media typically engage in, but a lot of it had to do with the sharp contrasts between the Vietnam War and World War II—or the "bad" versus the "good" war.

Like most kids in the sixties, I played "war" a lot, and our enemies were always the Nazis, who were a splendid, iconic sort of enemy. Beating them explained the good life we were living in the

1960s. So just as my daily Catholic mass celebrated Christ's victory over death in a ritualistic fashion, I and my friends routinely triumphed over the Nazi evil in my backyard. It just made sense in a way that the evening news coverage from Southeast Asia never could. It was reassuring. It seemed right. Heck, even the Russians had been our friends back then.

My mom's father collected World War II newsreels, and these 16-millimeter archives became my time machine for visiting that simpler, more understandable past. Like the heroes in most time-travel stories, I wanted so much to live back in the days when my entire world seemed to have been born. Those early postwar years marked the beginning of everything that dominated the Cold War era: all the rule sets, institutions, rivalries, alliances, strategies— even nuclear weapons. As I went off to college in 1980, determined to become a Soviet expert and join the struggle of our age, I couldn't help but curse my generational timing. I wanted to be Dean Acheson or Paul Nitze. I wanted to become one of the "wise men." I wanted to be present at the creation.

Instead I was present at the demise, although that certainly looked a long way off in 1980. In fact, it looked like we'd be stuck, strategy-wise, in almost suspended animation for my entire career. All the big rule sets seemed carved in concrete. I was reading text-books that were often a decade old, and that wasn't a problem, because nothing much had really changed in our understanding of the superpower struggle.

Then I moved on to graduate studies at Harvard, where I got to learn directly from the giants in the field, like the Russian historian Richard Pipes and the Soviet foreign policy expert Adam Ulam, heavy hitters who advised presidents. Imagine entering an academic discipline in which you knew full well you would never come close to achieving what these masters had accomplished, because, frankly, they were the originals in the field who wrote all the pathbreaking books.

Of course, what was neat about the field of Soviet studies was the same thing that was neat about *Star Trek:* Much as in the short-run TV show encompassing only seventy-nine episodes, there were only so many "stories" in the Cold War you needed to master in order to be considered professionally trained. As with the show, you could memorize most of the dialogue ("We will bury you!" "Beam us up, Scotty!") and all of the main characters (Andrei Gromyko, Pavel Chekhov). But while such mastery gave one the confidence to enter any classroom or graduate seminar, I couldn't help feeling as if my fledgling academic career in the late 1980s were one big game of Trivial Pursuit. I wasn't creating anything, I was just rearranging *matryoshka* dolls ("Gorbachev fits inside Andropov, who fits inside Brezhnev, who fits inside Khrushchev, who . . .").

Looking back on it now, I curse myself for not paying more attention to the world around me. I read newspapers and journals by the boxload, but I wasn't really trying to parse events out against some larger arc of history that, if I had been more imaginative in my reasoning, I would have realized was there all along. Because, like everyone else, I viewed the world through this bipolar prism, I couldn't see the forest for the trees.

In retrospect, the entire Cold War effectively ended around 1973. For all practical purposes, the whole conclusion to the struggle had been predetermined by that point. The rest of the Cold War was simply waiting around for the inevitable. No wonder it all seemed so stultifying.

What I mean by the entire Cold War effectively ending in the early 1970s is that the historical arc of that superpower rivalry basically peaked at that point. In essence, everyone on both sides fundamentally made their peace with the bipolar order, meaning from then on, the Soviets could have their chunk of the world and we weren't going to hassle them much, and the West could have its chunk of the world and they weren't going to hassle us much. Sure, we'd both keep sticking it to each other with spies, proxy wars in exotic Third World locales, and cheating at the Olympics (on their side only), but the chance for significant changes in the "correlation of forces," much less for global nuclear war, basically evaporated around that time.

On the Soviet side, President Leonid Brezhnev made his peace with both his own public and Eastern Europe, saying, in effect, *pretend to obey me and I'll pretend to rule you.* On the U.S. side, having gone through the self-destructive effort of trying to capture the Cold War "bridge too far" called Vietnam, we basically retired the whole anti-Communist hysteria of the past and started—thanks to President Richard Nixon and eventual Secretary of State Henry Kissinger—looking at the Soviets more like a global mafia we could tolerate rather than Nazis we needed to exterminate. Thanks also to Nixon and Kissinger, most of the serious hatchets were buried not only between Moscow and Washington (détente), but between Peking and Washington (and "Nixon goes to China" entered our political lexicon). We signed all sorts of agreements with Moscow that made them feel legitimate in Europe in a way they never felt before. We gave Taiwan's seat on the UN Security Council to the People's Republic. We let Russian ballerinas tour the United States and we sent Ping-Pong players to China. We even started calling Peking *Beijing* to make them happy.

Why is it important to realize that the Cold War really ended in 1973 and not in 1989? Because the world we are dealing with today largely emerged between those two dates. Between 1973 and 1989 the world evolved dramatically. We just did not notice it because America was still so focused on the superpower rivalry with the Soviets. During these years the Middle East shifted from being a strategic backwater to the main focus of U.S. military responses around the world, China began its amazing evolution from Mao Zedong's isolated society to Deng Xiaoping's emerging market, and globalization expanded beyond the Old Core of the United States, Western Europe, and Japan to include the "new globalizers" in Latin America and Developing Asia. By staying so fixated on the Soviet threat for so long, we missed a new global security order long in the making. When America finally woke up from the Cold War, we found that new strategic environment so unfamiliar that we experienced brain-lock, retreating from the grand strategy of containment to a fearful reliance on "chaos" as our guiding principle.

A good way to capture the rise and fall of the Cold War is to examine the rule sets that defined the strategic nuclear rivalry between the United States and the Soviet Union across the decades. Think of a long historical arc that started with our first use of nuclear weapons in 1945 and extended until the Soviet Union formally disbanded at the end of 1991. At the beginning of that arc, there were essentially no rule sets to guide our use of nukes or our defense against the Soviet weapons that soon followed. This was the truly scary time that extended deep into the 1950s—the time of "duck and cover" that my eldest siblings remember from their parochial school days. During this rising phase, we were constantly being caught unaware by "gaps," or dramatic unbalances that seem to suggest the nascent nuclear rule set could collapse in a sneak attack at any moment. There were "bomber gaps" and "missile gaps" that dominated our security agenda for significant stretches. This stressful period wore heavily on the minds of many Americans, who inwardly debated the question of "Better Red than dead?"

That unstable strategic relationship hit a spike with the Cuban missile crisis in 1962. Fortunately for the planet, key people on both sides stepped back and took a deep breath before doing anything disastrously stupid. At that point, our side had a serious heart-to-heart with itself, asking if there wasn't a better way to manage this volatile relationship that had the potential to evaporate the planet thanks to a moment of careless misperception. There was an overwhelming sense that we needed a better rule set, and so, as we so often have done in American history, we simply invented one—Mutual Assured Destruction, or MAD.

The story of how this came about is instructive for today's contentious debates over the new strategy of preemptive war. The notion that nuclear war was effectively unwinnable, and therefore the strategic standoff between us and the Soviets was far more stable than most people realized, had been voiced by plenty of experts prior to the Cuban missile crisis. But after that close call, Defense

Secretary Robert McNamara took the bold step of elevating it to a permanent cornerstone of U.S. strategic nuclear planning. To a lot of Americans at that time, the acronym MAD was descriptive in more ways than one—it just seemed plain crazy to believe neither side would ever use these weapons against the other in the future. Humanity had never before created a weapon it did not use, and so it seemed inconceivable that Hiroshima and Nagasaki would be the only times the world would ever see nuclear weapons fired in anger.

Yet that is exactly what has happened—to date. But nuclear weapons did a whole lot more than hold the superpower rivalry in check, they basically ended war among great powers, the definition of which, over time, merged with that of "nuclear power." In other words, to have nukes meant you were a great power, and to be a great power meant you never went to war with other great powers, thanks to nukes. When the United States created the new rule set called Mutually Assured Destruction, it did nothing less than kill great-power war for all time. It is no coincidence that no two great powers have ever gone to war with each other since 1945, the year America invented nuclear weapons. It took us almost two decades to come to that understanding—to recognize that essential rule-set change. But when we did, and successfully exported that rule set to other great powers, the threat of global war basically ended in human history.

That is how powerful a new security rule set can be in terms of shaping world history, which is why it is so very crucial that today, as America seeks to export this new security rule set called preemptive war, we are very careful in making sure this strategic concept is correctly understood. In short, preemptive war is not a tool for reordering the Core's security structure, as some fear. Rather, it is an instrument by which the Core should collectively seek to extend its stable security rule set into the essentially lawless Gap. Our goal should be nothing less than effectively killing transnational terrorism for all time.

MAD was a stroke of sheer brilliance on McNamara's part, for he recognized the existential deterrence that already existed between the United States and the Soviet Union—if only we had the courage and common sense to realize it. By existential deterrence I mean simply that nuclear weapons aren't for the *using* but for the *having*. By having them in sufficient number to assure the Soviet Union's demise following any first strike they might launch, we maintained the conditions for unwinnable war—and that's all the Cold War required in the end. So whatever crimes some believe McNamara later committed during the Vietnam War, in my mind they're greatly overshadowed by this one great act of securing global peace.

Of course, it wasn't enough for just the United States to understand and adhere to the notions of MAD; we had to convince the Soviets of this wisdom. That effort to educate the Soviets took several years, but graduation came finally in the signing of the first Strategic Arms Limitation Talks (SALT) agreement in 1972 at the Moscow summit between Nixon and Brezhnev. That summit, plus two additional ones between these leaders in subsequent years, effectively concluded the Cold War by greatly diminishing the threat of global nuclear war and implicitly codifying the rules of the rivalry from here on out (e.g., unlimited conventional arms sales to client state—okay; Third World proxy wars—okay; nuclear brinkmanship anywhere—not okay; conventional brinkmanship in Europe—not okay).

Sure, there would still be arms races, double-crossing moles, and all sorts of heated rhetoric right up to the very end, but this was just history playing itself out. Like a marriage that dies long before divorce papers are filed, this bipolar relationship, despite all its attendant mood swings, effectively entered its predetermined decline in the early 1970s. The Soviets would engage in one last gasp of ideologically driven optimism in the late 1970s, when they began supporting the "countries of socialist orientation," clustered mostly in the Middle East and sub-Saharan Africa. But once Moscow encountered its own bridge too far in Afghanistan, the grand and inexorable socialist retreat began.

Again, why this story is of crucial importance to us today is that while the superpower rivalry peaked in the early 1970s, a new grand historical arc began—that of the "world-historical relationship," as Michael Vlahos calls it, between America and Islam. Kissinger and Nixon were the giants present at that creation, and we have lived ever since with the rule sets then put in motion. If the rule set of NATO has historically been characterized as "keep the Americans in, keep the Germans down, and keep the Russians out," then the American rule set for the Middle East over the past three decades could be described as "keep the Israelis strong, keep the House of Saud safe, and keep the fundamentalist radicals down."

In 1967, the decades-long war between Israel and Islam began, slowly pulling the United States into the fray. Our involvement jumped dramatically with the 1973 war (Kissinger's "shuttle diplomacy") and the simultaneous rise of OPEC's willingness to use oil as a strategic economic weapon. From there it's been all uphill: through the fall of the Shah of Iran, the Teheran embassy hostages and the failed *Desert One* rescue attempt, the bombing of the Marines barracks in Lebanon, the creation of Central Command, the 1980s Iran-Iraq war and America's escorting of endangered tankers in the Gulf, right on to *Desert Storm* and our twelve-year war with Saddam that ended in 2003, only to be replaced by a long-term military occupation. It has been a stunning escalation over the decades, one that was almost completely obscured to the American public until the Berlin Wall fell in 1989.

The grand historical arc of our relationship with Islam is clearly peaking with the Bush Administration's decision to topple Saddam Hussein's regime—and to rehabilitate Ba'athist Iraq, much as we did with Nazi Germany and Imperial Japan following World War II. It is an understatement to say that the time for a clear enunciation of new rule sets is at hand. The strategy of preemption is one such rule set, but it obviously doesn't go far enough to set in motion the sort of sweeping historical change envisioned by those who argued that removing Saddam would trigger a Big Bang of positive political-military developments across the region. Running this historical arc to ground over the coming years will be the great focus of U.S. foreign policy, and that will require the State Department to supplant the Defense Department as the guiding force in U.S. decision making, rule making, and deal brokering in the region. We need a Kissinger for the Middle East—not the Kissinger we actually had there in the mid-1970s but the Kissinger we sent to Moscow and Beijing in the early 1970s. We need a visionary who understands that we've already reached the mountaintop.

My concerns for U.S. national security strategy go far beyond peace in the Middle East, or even the Defense Department's mistaken assumption that it can bring stability to that region simply by taking down enough "bad guys." It is not enough for the Bush Administration to say that our new strategic focus is an "arc of instability" that stretches across the Muslim-dominated regions of North Africa, the Persian Gulf, Central Asia, and Southeast Asia. America needs to understand the larger global conflict we join when we seek to transform Iraq from "rogue regime" to model Arab democracy. It is an enduring conflict between those who want to see disconnected societies like Saddam's Iraq join the global community defined by globalization's Functioning Core and others who will do whatever it takes in terms of violence to prevent these societies from being—in their minds—assimilated into a "sacrilegious global economic empire" lorded over by the United States. The most frightening form this violence takes in the current age is religious-inspired transnational terrorism, or what Daniel Benjamin and Steven Simon dub "the age of sacred terror." Over the long run, the real danger we face in this era is more than just the attempts by terrorists to drive the United States out of the Middle East; rather, it is their increasingly desperate attempts to drive the Middle East out of the world.

Most experts will tell you that modern terrorism began in the late 1960s, roughly corresponding to the youthquake that rocked many advanced industrial societies at that time. From its origins in the late 1960s, politically inspired or ideologically driven terrorist groups slowly ramped up their attacks worldwide, in no small measure because of systematic support from the Soviet bloc. When that aid disappeared in the late 1980s, global terrorism nosedived, leading many experts (including me) to surmise it would no longer constitute a significant security threat for the international community as a whole.

What really happened in the 1990s is that many of these terrorist groups, cut off from Soviet material and ideological support, fundamentally reinvented themselves as religiously motivated terror movements. This is not to say that religious motivations weren't present prior to the nineties—they were just sublimated to accommodate their Soviet sponsors. Worldwide, the number of casualties from terrorist acts skyrocketed starting in the mid-1990s, with almost a tripling of average annual casualties. The eight-year period 1987–1994 saw 9,575 global casualties from terrorism, but over the next nine years (1995–2003), the total jumped to 27,608.

If we date the origins of the historical arc of "sacred terror" somewhere in the early 1990s, then it's clear that we as a country are still riding this learning curve upward at a dramatic rate. Compared with our progress along the extended learning curve we traveled on nuclear weapons, we're not even out of the 1950s yet. Not surprisingly, our collective domestic responses to the dangers posed by catastrophic terrorism look an awful lot like the silly season of "duck and cover" from the atomic-crazed 1950s—only now it's duct tape and plastic sheets for cover. I won't even mention some of the wackiest ideas, like the military consulting with scriptwriters of Hollywood thrillers, or the Pentagon's notion of setting up a betting parlor for predicting terrorist strikes.

Should we be embarrassed by our current fumbling toward enunciating robust rule sets to guide future responses? Absolutely not. We should do what we always do in such situations: throw government money at the problem, enlist the aid of the private sector wherever possible, and inspire this country's entrepreneurs, inventors, and grand strategists to fill in the rule-set gaps as quickly as possible. But for now, keep one eye on the terrorist-threat index and one arm around your common sense. Reaching the summit of this historical arc will take time, but by my standards the Pentagon is showing all the right signs of taking this grand challenge as seriously as they took the nuclear age that preceded it. As a people Americans are easily spooked, but no enemy should ever bet against our boundless capacity for resourcefulness. We are a nation of MacGyvers.

This is not the first time a period of expansive globalization has pitted the advanced states against an ideological menace hell-bent on splitting the world in two. Globalization I generated its own frictions, many of which came together in the Bolshevik movement under Vladimir I. Lenin, another charismatic leader with a stomach for indiscriminate violence and great skill at leading a transnational terrorist network. Like Osama bin Laden, Lenin also dreamed of taking a vast swath of the planet offline, creating a kind of alternative universe where our rules didn't apply, where our money found no purchase, and where our power had no reach. And like bin Laden, Lenin taught adherents that their "way of life" was endangered. His terrorist movement succeeded beyond our wildest fears, eventually enslaving roughly one-third of humanity in an isolating, politically repressed existence that yielded a frightening legacy of shorter life spans and widespread environmental devastation. There's a reason most international adoptions today involve Western families importing babies from former socialist states.

Can a bin Laden, or perhaps a bin-Laden-after-next, possibly succeed in the same manner as Lenin's Bolsheviks? As U.S. Trade Representative Robert Zoellick likes to say about the current era of globalization, "No future is inevitable." That is true for only so long as America and the world remain trapped by the rule sets of the past. If we as a nation are able to surmount the rule-set gaps that plague both our "world-historical relationship" with Islam and our—until recently—feeble responses to the rise of "sacred terror," I believe a very positive long-term scenario for Globalization III is ours for the taking. But only if Americans remember that while typically this country follows the rules, sometimes history—1776, 1861, 1945, 1962, 2001—calls upon this nation to *create new rules*.

Whether we realize it or not, we are all—right now—standing present at the creation of a new international security order. You might think that the global war on terrorism is nothing more than the twisted creation of a warmongering Bush Administration, but you would be wrong. The global conflict between the forces of connectedness and disconnectedness is here and it is not going away anytime soon. Either America steps up to the challenge of defining this new global security rule set, or we will see those rules established by people who dream of a very different tomorrow.

A FUTURE WORTH CREATING

I felt absolutely crushed watching the televised picture of World Trade Center One's collapse on September 11, 2001. I had been inside the building a couple of dozen times over the previous three years as part of the Naval War College's ongoing research partnership with Cantor Fitzgerald, the Wall Street broker-dealer firm that lost several hundred of its employees on that terrible day. I had led several daylong workshops on the 107th floor at the Windows on the World restaurant and had come to know a significant number of the amazingly talented people who worked at Cantor Fitzgerald.

The research project I was conducting with Cantor's help involved exploring how globalization was altering America's definitions of national security—in effect, altering our calculus of risk management. The workshops we conducted jointly brought together Wall Street heavyweights, senior national security officials, and leading experts from academia and think tanks. These were amazing conversations for everyone involved, primarily because of the novelty of having all these people in the same room discussing globalization's future and the threats that could derail it.

Our joint venture was called the New Rule Sets Project. As director, I regularly visited two places: the World Trade Center and the Pentagon. This only made sense, since the project sought to facilitate America's understanding of the growing nexus between national security and globalization, and that meant getting Wall Street and the Pentagon talking to each other on a regular basis. On 9/11,

I was gearing up for another Pentagon briefing the following week. It would have occurred in the Navy's command center facilities that were destroyed that day. The week following that canceled trip, I was scheduled for another round of planning meetings at Cantor's headquarters on the 105th floor.

This steady stream of briefings and meetings gave me a new, far broader sense of how globalization was shrinking the world, not just geographically but also pulling together seemingly disparate sectors. Individuals on both sides of this unprecedented dialogue—security and financial—often said that this was the first time they had genre-hopping conversations like this since college. I took that as a real compliment, meaning we were crossing policy boundaries at will and getting decision makers out of their usual mind-sets. A great example of this was the debates we had about China. When the full panoply of Beijing's interactions with the outside world was put on the table, the country seemed a whole lot less inscrutable all of a sudden—less threatening. The deeper we plunged into how the worlds of finance and national security overlapped, the more the phrase "unintended consequences" kept cropping up, along with "spillover," "tipping points," and "pathway dependencies." What had looked like "chaos" from the Pentagon's perspective appeared a lot more orderly once you knew how to track globalization's causes and effects.

In this unique dialogue, Wall Street executives helped my research team connect the dots in ways the Pentagon never does in its long-range planning. It was like we were drawing a new map of the world and the great currents of activity that defined the mixing bowl that is globalization. A lot of times I felt like some explorer, going where no man has gone before. It was very exciting. It popped me out of bed in the morning. It made me feel that my work had meaning—I was doing something important to make the world a better place. Like everyone else, I needed that feeling, because it gave me hope for the future.

When the terrorists struck both the World Trade Center and the Pentagon on 9/11, the New Rule Sets Project essentially ended because of Cantor Fitzgerald's catastrophic losses. Like most people, I felt a sense of outrage over the many lives cut short, but I also felt a new sense of urgency in my work. A lot of my colleagues confessed that 9/11 made them feel that their work was somehow trivial, that they had been studying the wrong issues. This was only natural, because everyone in this business feels a bit responsible when America takes a body blow like 9/11—we feel bad we did not see it coming. That feeling was, of course, eventually overwhelmed by all the new assignments that the global war on terrorism generated throughout the Defense Department.

But in those days immediately following 9/11, I must confess that I was at a loss about what I should do with my career, which at that point seemed completely defined by this pathbreaking project. At one point, I even considered leaving the college and offering to work for Cantor Fitzgerald. But that felt as if I was reaching for straws. Deep down, I knew I had been on the trail of something truly important in the New Rule Sets Project—something that would frame what was really at stake in this hastily declared "global war." That realization helped me get my feet back on the ground in my career, but it also forced me to think more clearly about that global future I had long assumed was inevitable.

September 11 told me that globalization's uneven spread around the planet delineated more than just a frontier separating the connected from the disconnected—it marked the front lines in a struggle of historic proportions. The combatants in this conflict harbor very different dreams about the future, and if 9/11 alerted us to the asymmetry of will regarding the use of violence to achieve desired ends, then that asymmetry—that rule-set gap—would have to be eliminated. Revenge was pointless, and even killing the killers smacked of treating symptoms rather than the disease. America's use of military power in this war has to be guided toward strategic ends: the destruction of those who would wage war against global connectivity and the freedoms it unleashes.

America cannot really join this war until it can define the enemy, and it has had difficulty doing so out of the fear of appearing racist or intolerant. But here is where our fixation on quick fixes and "big bangs" undermine our ability to keep our eyes on the prize, because identifying that goal leads us to identifying the true enemy. That enemy is neither a religion (Islam) nor a place (the Middle East), but a condition—disconnectedness.

To be disconnected in this world is to be kept isolated, deprived, repressed, and uneducated. For young women, it means being kept—quite literally in many instances—barefoot and pregnant. For young men, it means being kept ignorant and bored and malleable. For the masses, being disconnected means a lack of choice and scarce access to ideas, capital, travel, entertainment, and loved ones overseas. For the elite, maintaining disconnectedness means control and the ability to hoard wealth, especially that generated by the exportation of valued raw materials.

If disconnectedness is the real enemy, then the combatants we target in this war are those who promote it, enforce it, and terrorize those who seek to overcome it by reaching out to the larger world. Our strategic goals, therefore, are to extend connectivity in every way possible, but only in a manner that promotes justice as much as order. Because when we sacrifice, when we suffer, and when we die in this war, we must know that the good we promote is both immediate and lasting. Americans need the confidence of knowing that every difficult step we take represents forward progress on some level.

To that end, we need to understand what is really at stake here, which is nothing less than the future of globalization itself. You may say that globalization is not a goal or a strategy but simply a condition of the world we live in, and you would be right on many levels. But globalization is also a historical process, or something that is defined by a sense of momentum and purpose. Globalization has a past, which defines its limits, but likewise a future whose promise it must fulfill, otherwise it will become a spent notion in the minds of political leaders whose determined actions are required for its continued advance. In short, once globalization is "done" as far as most leaders are concerned, the willingness of states to continue compromising with one another to further its growth will evaporate. Everyone in this world will lose if this hopeless situation comes to pass, but more saliently, the historic window of opportunity will close on a major portion of humanity currently living outside globalization's Functioning Core. That is not just a sad or unjust scenario, it is one fraught with danger for America—the world's biggest economy and the political ideal most closely associated with globalization's promise and peril.

Whether we realize it or not, America serves as the ideological wellspring for globalization. These *united states* still stand as its first concrete expression. We are the only country in the world purposely built around the ideals that animate globalization's advance: freedom of choice, freedom of movement, freedom of expression. We are connectivity personified. Globalization is this country's gift to history—the most perfectly flawed projection of the American Dream onto the global landscape. To deny our parentage of globalization is to deny our country's profound role as world leader over the second half of the twentieth century. More important, to abandon globalization's future to those violent forces hell-bent on keeping this world divided between the connected and disconnected is to admit that we no longer hold these truths to be self-evident: that *all* are created equal, and that *all* desire life, liberty, and a chance to pursue happiness. In short, *we the people* needs to become *we the planet*.

There are essentially two big questions for the future of globalization. The first question is, "What will constitute the great dividing line between who's in and who's out of globalization's Functioning Core?" Another way of saying this is, "How big will the Non-Integrating Gap end up being?" The answer here is crucial, because the size and composition of the Gap will determine the nature of warfare in the twenty-first century.

The second big question is, "Do new rules emerge globally that erase—or at least ease—the misalignment of rule sets that emerged across the 1990s?" In other words, "Do political and security rule sets catch up to all the connectivity fostered by the economic and technological advances we have witnessed in this current era of globalization? Or does globalization keep feeling like a runaway train that must eventually jump the track, as its previous version did in the tumultuous 1930s?"

With regard to the first question, I offer two possibilities: We live either in a world divided by competency or one divided by culture. A world divided by competency corresponds to Thomas Friedman's description of the differences between the "Lexus world" and the "olive tree world." In his seminal 1999 volume exploring the globalization phenomenon of the 1990s, Friedman divided the world into those people who seem to "get" globalization and all that it promises (e.g., the ability to manufacture high-tech goods like Lexus automobiles) and those people who don't seem to "get it" and thus prefer to remain trapped in a simpler world where groups fight over little chunks of "sacred lands" (like this olive tree grove, or that mountaintop).

At the other end of that spectrum is someone like Samuel P. Huntington, whose controversial 1996 volume *The Clash of Civilizations* posited that the future of global conflict would be defined by where the world's major civilizations bump up against one another (the concept of "fault-line wars"). In his mind, it's not so much a matter of who is good or bad at globalization as it is the sheer reality that different cultures value globalization's resulting connectivity and content flows in very different ways. For example, not every culture is going to welcome the Internet (connectivity) if it means easy access to pornography (content flow).

Those are basically the two great choices in terms of how the world ends up defining globalization's frontier: either it is just a matter of bringing countries "up to speed" to participate in the global economy, or we have to admit that some cultures simply will never be able to join our not-so-global economy.

Turning to the second question of rules, I posit two potential pathways: Either the world develops new rule sets to meet the challenges of the age or the rule-set misalignment that emerged in the 1990s persists, meaning economic rule sets are always outpacing political ones, and security rule sets never quite catch up to all that technologically driven connectivity. Another way to express this danger of misalignment is to say that America itself may come up with a host of new rules (e.g., preemption strategy, global war on terrorism, the Patriot Act) to bridge this divide, but that these new rule sets will have a divisive effect on globalization's Functioning Core. Simply put, other advanced societies will reject the new rules we propose, leading to a situation where America's security rule sets are seriously out of sync with that of other great powers—like France, Germany, Russia, and China. In this pathway, we do not really accomplish anything worthwhile in terms of advancing globalization: old divisions are simply replaced with new ones.

If, in waging war against the forces of disconnectedness, the United States ends up dividing the West, or the heart of the Core, then our cure ends up being worse than the disease. This is what Robert Kagan really speaks to when he talks about the "West"—as we have historically defined the trans-Atlantic security bond between North America and Western Europe—coming undone. His 2003 book *Of Paradise and Power: America and Europe in the New World Order* is frequently shorthanded by the quote, "It is time to stop pretending that Europeans and Americans share a common view of the world, or even that they occupy the same world." In other words, Europe and America tend to view rule sets very differently. Our willingness to use military power against Saddam Hussein's regime, for example, proves that America believes new rules are required in security (preemption), whereas most in Europe see no such misalignment between the rule sets of technology (weapons of mass destruction) and security (war should remain purely a defensive option). Clearly, that gap in perception had long existed between the United States and Europe, only to grow truly dysfunctional when the unifying Soviet threat disappeared. So it is not just a matter of recognizing the rule-set misalignments that emerged in the 1990s, but also of agreeing on what constitutes the right rule-set reset, and here America and Europe appear to disagree strongly—for now.

Of course, others will say that America cannot be afraid to forge these provocative new security rule sets, that we simply must admit that "dangerous times" call for "dangerous measures." Admittedly, the U.S. defense community is very partial to such arguments, although most officers I know worry about the long-term repercussions for American society as much as my wife, Vonne—a card-carrying member of the ACLU—does. So when I hear journalist Robert Kaplan—a real Pentagon favorite—admonish America to adopt a form of "warrior politics" suitable for managing an explicit "empire," I get more than a little nervous. In my mind, if the Pentagon does its job right, the rest of the country gets to go about its business with as little change as possible. I am not interested in "toughening up" America for the big bad world outside; I am far more interested in taming that part of the world that currently lies outside the Core's firm security rule sets, rules that have given this country a very peaceful previous quarter-century. The "good war" is a won war, not a war forever waged.

Let's not kid ourselves, most of the rule-set changes proposed since 9/11 focus on war and the military management of "empire." But that just reflects our habit of thinking about war solely within the context of war instead of approaching war as something that occurs within the context of everything else. Yes, you can bomb terrorist-haven countries back into the Stone Age (usually a very short trip), but that hardly constitutes promoting connectivity in and of itself. Yes, invasions and regime changes facilitate the removal of our enemies in this war, or those who endeavor to keep entire societies trapped in splendid isolation (the Taliban, Saddam). But as we've seen in both postwar Afghanistan and Iraq, that is not even half the battle. If all we do—for lack of effort—is simply replace one "disconnecting" leadership with another, then the countries in question will inevitably lapse back into problem status. So clearly, the rule-set reset we seek is far larger than simply keeping the barbarians at the gate, which—frankly—is what virtually every discussion of "American empire" is really about. In effect, America's avowed goal should be extending our culturally neutral, rules-based "civilization" called globalization, because if we do not all live under the same basic rule set, there will always be a global hierarchy by which some rule and others are ruled. *Until there are equal rules, we are not all equal.*

You want a future worth creating? It is called making globalization truly global. If we shoot for anything less in this global war on terrorism, we simply shoot ourselves in the foot, condemning globalization to futures worth debating. If globalization is permanently hampered by rule sets being out of whack, the Core will remain seriously vulnerable to damaging "shocks to the system" like 9/11, outbreaks of contagious diseases, future "electronic Pearl Harbors," or rapidly emerging environmental catastrophes of global proportions. Worse still, the progressive division of the world economy into cultural or regional camps diminishes the overall potential for international cooperation—meaning, in effect, that no one is minding the store on such big issues as the proliferation of weapons of mass destruction, global warming, and the spread of AIDS. In this far darker scenario, we all seem to live in a dog-eat-dog world, where every major power looks out for number one. Over time, globalization's advance is invariably reversed by increased economic nationalism, arms races, and—eventually—conflict among great powers. You could describe this scenario as a rerun of the 1930s. Flash points might include Europe versus America over genetically modified organisms, China versus America over a solution to the North Korea problem, and Russia versus America over the latter's growing military presence in Central Asia.

You might say, "That's being awfully pessimistic. Surely there is no reason to expect America to part ways with its oldest friends, even if our new, tougher foreign policy alienates old foes like Russia and China." It is true that it is extremely difficult to posit global futures in which America so angers our old Cold War allies that we no longer seek similar ends, even as we often argue about the choice of means. The real danger, in my mind, lies in potential splits not among the Old Core but between the original pillars of Globalization II (North America, Western/Old Europe, and Japan) and the emerging pillars of Globalization III, such as China, India, Brazil, Chile, Argentina, South Korea, and Russia. In some ways, you could call this scenario the "West versus the rest"—sort of a division between Old School and New School globalization.

What signs do we see of this occurring? If the United States has trouble attracting peacekeeping forces from New Core states like India, Russia, and China, and we can only get our staunchest military allies to help out whenever we topple a rogue regime in the Gap, that is a bad sign. Another bad sign is when New Core economies band together against Old Core economies in trade negotiations, because that signals that globalization's emerging markets still feel somewhat shut out of its "inner sanctum." So when China, India, and Brazil come together to lead a new movement of emerging markets—the so-called Group of 20-plus—in the current negotiating round of the World Trade Organization, that is a bad sign.

Looking more broadly, we may note that a good example of a future intra-Core wedge might be the environment: the Old School globalizers push hard for more stringent environmental controls that hamper the New School globalizers in their efforts to further develop their economies and catch up to the West. Another might be the still-unfolding AIDS crisis. According to the National Intelligence Council's excellent study on the epidemic, most of the growth in cases in the coming years will be centered in the New School globalizers—India, China, Brazil, and Russia. Not surprisingly, one of the most divisive current issues in WTO negotiations is the question of loosening patent restrictions on AIDS-treatment drugs so that these states can stem this rising tide without bankrupting themselves.

Say the Old and New Core do not turn on each other, is it enough simply to keep these two great communities together while making sure the Gap doesn't grow in size? In my opinion, the main danger in having the world divide into the "Best versus the Rest" (or a pure division by competency) is that the Best (Old and New School globalizers) will invariably be tempted to engage in knee-

jerk reactions to perceived threats emanating from the less connected parts of the global economy—globalization's losers. This
global pathway could be shorthanded as "I've got mine so to hell
with you!" It is a world full of walls between the functioning and
nonfunctioning regions of the global economy, or a long-term acceptance of the current status quo. These barriers are mostly about
keeping bad things from flowing from the Gap to the Core. What is
so scary about this outcome is that it effectively means that connectivity—and thus globalization—will not spread beyond its current frontiers. In effect, the club stops admitting new members, like
a European Union that continues to find Turkey "too different" and
likewise stonewalls former (Slavic) Soviet republics.

But worse than that, if all the Core does is maintain itself while
telling the Gap to fend for itself, eventually all that pain and suffering
trapped inside the Gap will seek release, much as we saw on 9/11. In
short, we cannot simply put a long fence around the Gap and assume
that it can be contained, as the old Soviet threat was.

To reiterate, the only global future truly worth creating involves
nothing less than eliminating the Gap altogether. America can only
increase its security when it extends connectivity or expands globalization's reach, and by doing so, progressively reduces those trouble
spots or off-grid locations where security problems and instability
tend to concentrate. In sum, the best-case scenario for Globalization III must be its continued expansion. It is not enough for the
Core to survive. It must grow. Conversely, the best-case scenario involves not just growing the Core but shrinking the Gap as well.
Keeping with the theme of this opening chapter, the only way to
accomplish Core expansion and Gap shrinkage is to extend the
reach of rule sets. That means not only must Old and New School
globalizers reach agreement on the rule-set reset for trade (i.e., better alignment of economic and political rule sets in the ongoing
Doha Round negotiations of the WTO), but they must also come to
a clear understanding on what the reset between technological and
security rule sets must be.

Right now, the biggest proposal out on the table is the U.S. strategy of preemption, which, in effect, argues that whenever known rule breakers get close to obtaining weapons of mass destruction, it is only normal and right for great powers to strike preemptively for the avowed purposes of regime change. But again, focusing solely on that strategy does a great disservice to the task at hand. In many ways, the breadth of the rule-set reset on security is far wider than just the question of how we deal with bad actors in the system. In reality, it encompasses the far larger question of how we deal with all this rising connectivity in ways that do not hamper globalization's continued expansion.

Remembering that the rule-set reset following the Second World War took a decade or longer, we can see that some patience is clearly in order. Moreover, to get to that best-case outcome, America needs to understand that getting the rest of the Core to accept its new security rule set will require significant compromises along the way. This is crucial, because if the United States is viewed by the rest of the great powers as going off the deep end in its idiosyncratic quest for what other cultures consider to be unacceptable new rule sets, then America may well find itself belonging to a Core of one. That means the quickest route from the best- to worst-case scenarios runs right through the White House. No matter how logical or necessary our new rule sets may appear to us, if we cannot sell them to a large chunk of the planet, we lose our credibility as a competent superpower, and our rules will invariably be dismissed by other cultures as reflecting an American bias, not universal truths.

In many ways, nudging globalization in the direction of that best-case scenario is the ultimate example of global risk management: the quickest way to secure America absolutely is to run hog-wild with preemptive strikes against the most dangerously disconnected states like Iran, North Korea, Syria—or basically, the "who's next?" strategy. But a mindless pursuit of America's short-term security is likely to damage globalization's capacity for expansion, and therein lies our best hope for increasing our security over the long haul.

Scaring the rest of the world to death with some half-cocked "World War IV" to-do list will divide up the planet pronto, not to mention send our own society into anguished upheaval.

America faced a similar situation during the Second World War, when President Franklin Delano Roosevelt and Supreme Allied Commander General Dwight D. Eisenhower were both pressured by public opinion, allies, and world events to end the war as quickly as possible. But instead of winning that war quickly only to lose the peace, they made a series of calculated compromises that not only kept the alliance intact but kept the American public firmly supportive of an activist postwar strategy as well. The global war on terrorism cannot be a multileg sprint from one "Berlin" to the next, because the United States simply cannot shrink the Gap by itself.

Ultimately, to shrink the Gap over the coming decades, the United States will need the combined assets of the entire Core. To bring that much of the world along as we seek to test out and propagate new rule sets in international security, America must carefully but forcefully enunciate a comprehensive vision of a future worth creating. That vision will have to sell on both Main Street and Wall Street, in both Berlin and Beijing, and in both the Core and the Gap. Anything less is a waste of our servicemen and -women.

Chapter 2

THE RISE
OF THE "LESSER
INCLUDEDS"

THE U.S. MILITARY HAS always done well in responding to defeats. It has never done as well responding to victories. America won a huge victory across the Cold War: we stood down the world's only other military superpower while simultaneously setting in motion globalization's great advance around the planet. A new era was born with the collapse of the Soviet Union, but our being present at its creation was not nearly enough. America needed to embrace the new security environment in which it faced no peers, through its clear redefinition of both an enemy worth fighting and a future military worth building.

The Pentagon failed dramatically on both counts, and it did so primarily out of fear for its own institutional standing within the U.S. political system—or, to put it more bluntly, its share of the federal budget. That fear drove the military to cling to the dream of a "near-peer" which would justify its desire to retain a military fashioned primarily for great-power war, when the new era not only did not generate such a threat but instead challenged America's definition of a "New World Order" by producing its exact opposite: the rise of the so-called lesser includeds.

Pentagon long-range planning in the Cold War had been very simple: figure out what the Soviets had and then build a roughly similar mix of ships, aircraft, and heavy armor (e.g., tanks), always keeping our forces ahead of *their* curve by pursuing the best technological advances. World War III, therefore, constituted the Big One against which all long-range planning proceeded. Everything else the U.S. military did in terms of operations around the world was bundled together in the concept of the lesser includeds. Lesser includeds were not situations the military shaped itself around. Instead, by "force sizing" according to the Big One, it was assumed that the resulting military would be able to handle all the smaller-sized contingencies—hence the diminutive phrase "lesser includeds." Even though the U.S. military spent over 90 percent of the Cold War engaged in such lesser includeds, its force-sizing principle remained the Big One with the Soviets, because—quite naturally—that one was for all the marbles.

When the Red Army went away, the Pentagon lost its measuring stick. The U.S. military had two choices: it could find some new enemy, or combination of enemies, to size itself against, or it could try to prepare more broadly for the future by planning for a wide range of capabilities that were not necessarily linked to any one enemy, or any one threat. In the latter path, called capabilities-based planning, the Pentagon would have logically scanned the strategic environment as a whole for the skill sets required to manage it effectively, but it chose not to do so, instead focusing on identifiable threats. Military leaders did so out of fear for their institutions' future in the post–Cold War era: they were afraid they would lose this great Army, Air Force, Navy, and Marine Corps they had re-created out of the debacle that was the Vietnam War.

So the Pentagon clung desperately to the definition of a big bad threat out there to justify a continued focus on great-power war, when in reality none was in the offing. In the early 1990s, this first took the form of "reconstitution" for any reemergent Soviet threat. In short, the military could not change too much because the Soviets might reappear. That concept faded as quickly as the Red Army.

Then the incoming Clinton Administration came up with a new force-sizing principle called the Two-Major Regional Conflicts scenario under Secretary of Defense Les Aspin. It was a two-for-one deal, substituting two regional threats (Iraq and North Korea) for the old Soviet threat. That concept mutated repeatedly over the mid- and late 1990s, as the Pentagon kept coming up with new twists (typically involving the sequencing of events between the two theaters of operation, the Persian Gulf and Northeast Asia) to make the scenario seem as stressing as possible to its budgetary masters in Congress.

But neither half-scenario nor the combined dual scenario sufficed for Pentagon strategists committed to "transforming" the U.S. military into the next-generation, warfighting machine without peer. But here was the conundrum: The Pentagon wanted this fabulous military force in order to defeat any future foe, and yet—over time—it became convinced that the only way it could achieve that future force, because of budgetary constraints, was to retreat from the present world, where it kept being dragged into all these lesser-included situations. With the Clinton Administration apparently focused on constructing a new world financial order, the Pentagon felt as if it were left holding the bag in a series of lesser includeds (e.g., Somalia, Haiti, Yugoslavia, Iraq), none of which was going to propel the military toward any future "transformation," because in combination they constituted a huge drain on resources.

In short, the Pentagon feared this new world disorder would ruin the military it had spent the previous two decades resurrecting after Vietnam. It would turn our fighting forces into a "9-1-1" emergency response force tending to the world's bad neighborhoods. The U.S. military would end up pulling guard duty for the International Red Cross and other humanitarian relief organizations, finding itself trapped in Third World hellholes where ethnic tribes wanted nothing more than the freedom to hack their enemies to death *en masse*.

Most military leaders wanted little to do with trying to manage this messy world, preferring instead to plan brilliant high-tech wars against brilliant high-tech opponents. The Soviets were clearly gone, and if the Iraq–North Korea combo was not doing the trick, something more frightening would need to be invented—some future, down-the-road threat that would justify "transformation" budgetary requirements for the long run. That future threat, it was decided in 1995, would be China. In that year China fired off several missiles in the general direction of Taiwan, ostensibly to test them but in fact to scare the hell out of an increasingly assertive Taiwanese political leadership. A year later, during Taiwan's national elections, the United States sent naval forces into neighboring waters as a "show of force" in the face of similar threats (aka the Taiwan Straits crisis of 1996), and the strategic die was cast—the new, future "peer competitor" had been found.

The Pentagon's unwillingness to embrace the emerging reality of the post–Cold War strategic environment reflected America's general ambivalence about playing security guard to any "new world order." We told ourselves that if we tried to manage that world, all we would end up doing was making the rest of the planet mad at us, so better that we accept the economic "multipolarity" of this new era, one in which a united Europe, Japan, and eventually other rising economic powerhouses would become our equals in diplomatic strength. So we let the international security environment largely run itself, committing ourselves piecemeal to its management. Meanwhile, the Pentagon dreamed of a future force worth building to wage war against a future enemy worth defeating—rising China.

As the 1990s ended, all the contradictions that we now face in our post-Saddam military occupation of Iraq were in place: We continued to build a military that could wage war without peer, but one that could not wage the peace that necessarily followed. Our continued focus on the Big One left us with a force that can topple rogue regimes at will, without the assistance of allies, but cannot manage all the lesser includeds that arise in the aftermath—even with the help of our closest allies. In effect, we spent the 1990s buying one sort of military, only to realize after 9/11 that we needed another to wage this global war on terrorism, a threat that until recently was routinely considered the least of the lesser includeds.

This chapter is about a deep fear that gripped the Pentagon throughout the 1990s. This fear was not about the world outside but about what was happening within the Defense Department itself following the disappearance of the Soviet threat. The Pentagon spent the decade denying the rise of the lesser includeds, or the growing importance of small threats, small enemies, and small wars. Pentagon leaders feared that if the U.S. military lost its Cold War unifying focus on the Big One, it would suffer ruination—it would not be ready when America needed it most.

In the end they were right, but for all the wrong reasons. It is easy today to look back on this time and say it was all about the money, but it was all about the money only because America lacked the vision—and the visionaries—to define the 1990s as anything beyond a mere addendum to the Cold War. America simply assumed that a better future was there for the taking, when in reality it was there for the creating. This country—through Democrat and Republican administrations alike—just waited a dozen years to take up the challenge.

Examining the roots of that fear allows us today to understand the nature of the challenge that lies ahead for U.S. military forces as they rapidly transform themselves for this global war on terrorism—as America finally steps up to the task of managing the strategic security environment that is globalization's Gap.

THE MANTHORPE CURVE

In the early 1990s, William Manthorpe was Deputy Director of the Office of Naval Intelligence. He came to CNA one morning in the fall of 1991 to brief a select group of Navy admirals and Marine generals on his view of the future of the world. This group of "flags," as they are collectively known in the military, had been handpicked by the Chief of Naval Operations and the Commandant of the Marine Corps to lead a several-month effort by the Department of Navy's best and brightest to enunciate a new strategic naval vision for the post–Cold War era. Their end product was to be nothing less than the first major naval White Paper on grand strategy since World War II. In short, they were asked to play Mahan for the twenty-first century.

U.S. Navy Captain Alfred Thayer Mahan is generally considered the greatest naval grand strategist the world has ever known. In the latter years of the nineteenth century, he laid out the strategic principle for the employment of U.S. naval power around the world that focused on first capturing and then exploiting "command of the sea," or simply the ability of your navy to rule the waves and deny that capacity to opposing fleets. Without that resulting sea power, no great power could hope to dominate or even seriously influence the course of wars on land.

During the Cold War, Mahan's precepts were fairly easy to follow, because the U.S. Navy faced a somewhat symmetrical opponent in the Soviet Navy. But now that the Soviet Navy seemed to be disappearing, naval leaders were becoming nervous about their role in U.S. grand strategy. Added to that growing unease was the sense that the Navy had been badly outclassed by the U.S. Air Force in the just-concluded *Desert Storm*. The Air Force had all those wonderful cameras in the noses of all those smart bombs that seem to dominate the combat, along with General Norman Schwarzkopf's famous "left hook"—tanks that encircled most of the Iraqi forces, trapping them for rapid decimation.

Meanwhile, the Navy felt as though no one much appreciated all the aircraft sorties they flew off of carriers or all those Marines that were used to feint an amphibious assault on Kuwait City. Naval leaders were concerned that the wrong lessons were being learned from *Desert Storm,* meaning lessons that made it seem like you needed a smaller navy or Marine Corps. Everyone in the Pentagon knew that force-structure cuts were coming, meaning both personnel and equipment would be reduced. After all, the American public expected a peace dividend, and the Defense Department's budget was the logical place to start.

So the naval leadership decided now was the time for a new naval strategic vision, or one that would reassert the utility of naval power as Mahan had a century earlier. Besides the handpicked flags, who later became known as the "Gang of Five," the real work of this effort would be performed by thirty or so captains and colonels brought together at CNA for several weeks of visioneering. It was going to be a sort of constitutional convention for the U.S. Navy and Marine Corps. We were going to figure out "the way ahead."

Every captain and colonel assembled must have harbored dreams of being the next Mahan. That was completely by design, for these guys really were the best and brightest—an amazing array of talent, intelligence, and experience.

I was assigned by CNA to assist the leader of the Gang of Five, a charismatic two-star admiral named Ted Baker. Baker, in turn, worked for the three-star admiral in charge of the whole affair, Vice Admiral Snuffy Smith. The Marines had similarly impressive flags attached, but as usual, as the bigger naval service, the Navy took the lead.

Just days after this historic effort was convened, Bill Manthorpe was brought in to deliver the official view of the Office of Naval Intelligence on the future of the world. To everyone's amazement, Manthorpe laid it all out on one overhead vugraph. Like all great slides, it was quite simple in form—almost iconic. But what it did was nothing short of profound, for it captured the essence of the emerging debate within the U.S. military regarding the future security environment and the choices we faced as a nation.

Before I go any further, I need to explain the almighty cult of the briefing in Pentagon culture, and in particular the power of the right "slide" in steering important intellectual debates throughout the U.S. military.

The brief is the dominant form of idea transmission in the world of the Pentagon, far more than in any other part of the government and far more than in the business world. Inside the Pentagon, the "killer brief" is *everything,* and so an amazing amount of effort goes into the construction of slides, which back in 1991 still consisted of hard-copy vugraphs printed out on acetate sheets slapped onto an overhead projector. Today of course they are presented directly off laptops via state-of-the-art projectors.

The killer brief can do wonders for one's career. It is just that simple inside the defense community: good briefers do what they will, and bad briefers do what they must. Every battle I have won in my career began with a brief that outperformed the ideas presented by competitors. Inside the Pentagon, that is how bureaucratic wars are essentially waged—one briefing room at a time. If you want to get to someone high up in the Administration, you will have to go through a plethora of gatekeepers, or lower officials whose goal in life is nothing less than to spare their "principal" from the proverbial "briefer from hell." On the other hand, these gatekeepers want nothing more than to deliver the brief "that must be seen." Many of them are quite explicit when you start your brief. They will say, "Do you know why you are giving me this brief?" If you say yes, then every comment they will offer you during your presentation will be explicit advice on how to reshape your material for presentation to their principal. For example, I was told once by an Assistant Secretary of Defense to remove the phrase "shit happens" from one of my slides prior to delivering the brief to the Deputy Secretary of Defense, who at that time was a man notorious for his dislike of profanity of any sort. I was also told which slides I should dwell on, and where I should expect a rude question or two.

As an analyst, you want nothing more than to produce that killer brief and run it up the chain, because, frankly, that is just about the only way you ever get into the offices of the senior-most officials. A killer article will not do it, because the official can simply peruse a summary prepared by his staff. Only the killer brief can get you that most valued of Washington commodities—face time with a senior government official. Get your ideas to the right senior official (members of Congress can be especially good conduits), and you might find your ideas being briefed to the Secretary of Defense or the Secretary of State, or passed along to the President himself. If your timing is right, you can change U.S. policy or help to redefine its expression. In short, the right brief can change history.

A killer brief or slide can be especially powerful when delivered as a lead-in to some officially convened decision-making event involving senior leaders. These are the briefs most pol-mil analysts would give their eyeteeth for—the "briefing up" of top military brass as they begin some exclusive workshop or retreat where "straphangers" (or nonvoting aides and other lackeys) are not allowed and discussions are "off the record." These no-holds-barred insider forums are where the biggest decisions are made, the ultimate one being "the Tank," where the Joint Chiefs of Staff meet regularly. What they produce tends to be the most important steering policy documents, to include—in this historic instance—the precedent-setting publication known as the "white paper" signed out by the Secretary of Navy himself, along with the Chief of Naval Operations and the Commandant of the Marine Corps.

Now, to hear Mr. Manthorpe present the slide, there really wasn't any choice to be had, because, like all talented grand strategists, he had a particular vision in mind. I disagreed with that vision, yet I couldn't take my eyes off the slide as he talked his way through it. The visual image was simply that arresting.

The chart featured two axes: the horizontal one displaying time, or the unfolding post–Cold War era, and the vertical one displaying threat, gauged from low to high. Manthorpe's argument was straightforward: The great Soviet threat that had dominated all strategic planning for decades was rapidly dissipating, but no matter how much it declined, it was unlikely to be surpassed by that of the aggregate rest-of-world (or ROW) threat. In effect, the ROW threat was the Pentagon's way of expressing the cumulative total of lesser-included scenarios, meaning those non-great-power threats not big enough to size and shape your forces around. Instead, the normal practice at that time was deciding how many armored divisions or aircraft carriers America needed based on the biggest high-end threat you could identify—the Big One *du jour*. The assumption at the time was that if we built for the Big One, then that same mix of forces would adequately handle all the smaller threats, but not vice versa—hence the hierarchy.

As far as Manthorpe was concerned, the U.S. military needed to stay focused on the Big One. The Russians might have exited stage right for now, he cautioned, but if history was a guide, and Manthorpe believed it was, then the Russians would probably become resurgent within a twenty-year time frame—just as the Germans had following their defeat in World War I. Manthorpe also held out the notion that China could replace Russia as the source of that resurgent long-term threat, but his money was on Russia.

I absolutely disagreed with Manthorpe's judgment, though I recognized the power of his argument. As a Soviet expert, I knew the Big Red Machine was kaput not just for the 1990s but for all time, and as a political scientist tracking Deng Xiaoping's amazing reforms in China, I saw a country that was finally joining the world, not setting itself up for confrontation. That did not mean I saw no need for employing U.S. military power around the world—far from it. I just believed the time for focusing on the Big One had passed, and that now it was time to adjust to a world of lesser includeds. That is what I advised every chance I got with Ted Baker and all the other flags involved in the process.

What was so immensely daring about Manthorpe's slide was that it outlined the major choices we had as a nation, and then made a bold call regarding the correct choice—at least in Bill's mind. I was stunned by his presentation. I had never seen anything so strategically audacious in my life. Every brief I had ever seen on the "strategic environment" since arriving in Washington had consisted of slide upon slide cataloging every "cat and dog" threat the briefer could dream up. You never put all your eggs in one basket in the carefully hedging environment that was Pentagon planning in the early 1990s.

But Manthorpe was not interested in covering his rear end. He had a call to make and he made it—unequivocally. I respected the courage of his brief immensely. While intuitively I knew I disagreed with his final judgment, I had to marvel at his analysis. The guy became my hero on the spot, because I knew someday I wanted a visual just like that—one that would make everything clear in one

THE MANTHORPE CURVE

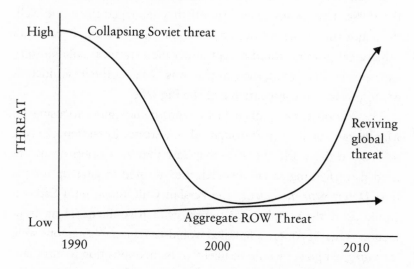

sweeping glance of both history and the strategic environment. I just wanted mine to prove the opposite point: The future was not about dealing with the biggest threat in the environment, but dealing with the environment of threats. Over time, that meant weaning the Pentagon off China and refocusing it on those parts of the world being left behind by globalization.

Manthorpe's slide became, in many ways, the Rorschach test upon which all future visions could be tested. As such, the participants in this vision effort, known prosaically as the Naval Forces Capabilities Planning Effort (or NFCPE), debated it endlessly. You could basically divide all those captains and colonels into three camps.

The camps and their corresponding visions were differentiated by how far down the Manthorpe Curve they sought to peer in search of the "compelling" national security task. The first camp I dubbed the Transitioneers, because they focused on the near term. They saw a world minus the Soviets as quite chaotic, and so they believed U.S. forces needed to be out in the world, dealing with as many of those lesser includeds as possible so as to assure the transition to a safer era. In the naval community, this camp was primarily the surface fleet officers and the Marines, both of whom were ready to embrace the sort of other-than-war operations that would dominate the 1990s. This group figured that if they managed the world well, the major threat curve would never again turn upward, because all other great powers would accept our benign status as sole military superpower. In essence, their notion was "Master the lesser includeds to preclude the appearance of the Big One."

The second camp looked farther down the curve, focusing on Manthorpe's major-threat trough. They were not interested in trying to manage the world, because they saw that as a drain on much-needed warfighting assets. Instead, they wanted to gear up for the next *Desert Storm,* figuring the Persian Gulf tussle with Saddam would prove the template for future regional conflicts. Their argument was that if America handled would-be regional hegemons well, then no great power would be likely to rise in opposition to our management of the global security environment. This camp was populated by the naval air, or carrier, community, whose vision was, in effect, to walk softly and carry a big stick. Hence I named this camp the Big Sticks. While the Big Sticks agreed with the Transitioneers' logic of mastering lesser includeds, they parted ways over the choice of which lesser includeds we should focus on. Their motto might be described as "Not all lesser includeds are created equal."

The final camp rejected both the near-term and mid-term foci of the other camps, and instead looked the farthest down the Manthorpe Curve. By doing so, they effectively rejected any focus on the lesser includeds, preferring instead to wait for signs of the Big One—no matter how long that took. This group, populated mostly by the submarine community, fretted over a resurgent Russia as much as Manthorpe did, so I called them the Cold Worriers. But to be fair, their real argument was that America needed to keep its powder dry and stay technologically ahead of any great power that might sneak up on us in coming decades. Like Manthorpe, they figured the United States was living in a rerun of the 1920s, so we might as well start planning for the next world war, however it was going to unfold.

The opportunity to participate in these historic discussions was the chance of a lifetime. The atmosphere was incredibly tense, though, because the room was full of would-be Mahans, each trying to be the one whose brilliance would be imprinted on new strategic doctrine. As the weeks dragged on without resolution, each of the Gang of Five would anoint his own personal best boy to go off on his own and try writing the magnum opus all of us knew would eventually have to be written. In each and every painful incident, the resulting personal vision was summarily rejected by the congress as a whole.

Over time, the divisions of thought manifested themselves in the self-selection of the officers into various working groups, with the most iconoclastic of the quartet calling themselves the F Troop, led by a serving air wing commander named Howard "Rusty" Petrea. The lead thinker there was a brilliant, dry-witted captain who flew helicopters for a living, Bradd Hayes. Bradd was an enigma to just about everyone. A devout Mormon, he routinely had us in stitches with his shockingly bawdy sense of humor. More amazing, given all the brass hanging around, he started writing a daily parody of the Pentagon's news-clipping service, known as the *Early Bird,* in which he not only made fun of the Gang of Five but also mercilessly lampooned the many national security "giants" we regularly hosted to brief the group as a whole. Bradd was a fearless sort of figure in those days—a captain who knew he would never become admiral and so had nothing to lose by speaking his mind. His influence over the group was enormous, because he was willing to state truths in an uncompromising fashion—a skill he retains today as a professor at the Naval War College.

As with all such efforts, we focused our daily grind on generating the master brief that would eventually spell out our vision to the Secretary of the Navy, so at the end of each day the various working groups would present their competing concepts, and then overnight a special "Integrators" group would merge those concepts for review by everyone the following morning. Those sessions were brutal. A small fire extinguisher was kept on hand during these debates. If anyone thought a particularly stupid statement had been made, they were allowed to take the extinguisher and present it to the offending party. It started out as a funny way to avoiding having people yell out "bullshit" when someone else was talking, but after a few weeks officers were angrily slamming that heavy metal canister down on tables with enough force to make most of us jump.

I was part of that Integrators group, working for probably the most able leader I have ever met, then Brigadier General–select Tom Wilkerson of the Marine Corps. Wilkerson's great gift was that he could lead people toward decisions they did not want to make. He did it with humor (he sounded amazingly like comedian Dana Carvey), grace, and a natural sense of command. Wilkerson assigned me to write a script to go along with the PowerPoint slides as we built them. In effect, I became the group's historian, because my text had to reflect all the debate that went into the tortuously agreed-upon bullets. Despite the eighteen-hour days during my wife's first pregnancy, I loved this assignment. Sure, I left Vonne eating alone on Thanksgiving, but I was part of history!

Our work came to a head after close to two months of nonstop debate. Tensions ran high, because the effort was dragging on too long, plus the Department of Navy was simultaneously being rocked by the infamous Tailhook scandal, in which a host of officers had been accused of sexual assault at an annual aviators' conference. As the scandal migrated up the ranks in search of heads to roll, fuses grew shorter at our meetings. In one memorable incident, a member of the Gang of Five, Rear Admiral Dave Oliver, jumped over a table during a brief, yanked the acetate vugraph off the overhead projector, and destroyed it on the spot. Oliver had previously warned the captain giving the brief about one bullet that he found particularly offensive (the idea of refitting nuclear missile submarines with cruise missiles), declaring that if he ever saw it again, he would tear it off with his bare teeth (which he did). This minor brouhaha was descriptive of the debates we were having at the time: the so-called rag-top option (the resulting sub was described as a "convertible") spoke to moving away from the Big One, where nu-

clear missiles occupied the top roost of the force-structure pan-
theon, to a world of lesser includeds, in which America's typical
military strikes would involve conventional missiles. In 1992, the
idea seemed sacrilegious to an old nuke submariner like Oliver, but
Charlie Schaefer's then–"crazy idea" is being implemented by the
Navy today.

One stormy Saturday night, our band of brothers finally presented the completed brief to the Gang of Five. It was a do-or-die
moment for us all, because the CNO and Commandant were scheduled to review the material within days. Either the ideas we encap-
sulated in this long brief would strike the flags as the new "great
story" the Navy and Marine Corps would use to sell themselves to
Congress and the American public, or we would have failed in our
mission—something no one wanted on his personnel record. The
presentation went very badly, and when the Gang of Five moved
next door for a closed executive session, we could hear the yelling
through the office walls. The next Monday Admiral Ted Baker was
out as head of the working group, and General Wilkerson took over
day-to-day operations of a much smaller collection of captains and
colonels, since the bulk of them had to return to their various commands around the world according to a predetermined schedule.
We had blown our deadline, and heads were beginning to roll. But
worse than the fear that careers might get cut short (and some ultimately were), everyone knew there were strong institutional forces
that worked against the Navy's being able to adjust to the strategic
environment that was emerging. The old joke went, "The U.S.
Navy—200 years of tradition unimpeded by progress!" The Secretary had given us a free hand to come up with the right vision, but
there was an overwhelming sense that we had fumbled this historic
opportunity to do the right thing.

At that point, we were down to fewer than twenty officers, all of
whom were already assigned to the Washington area. We were told
by the Gang of Five that we had two weeks to come to some consensus—or else. Then, a breakthrough. Going back over the brief,
Wilkerson located the stumbling block that was keeping us from

reaching agreement. It was actually on the first substantive slide, which laid out the "the strategic concept of the naval service." And it all came down to one word in the first bullet.

The bullet had begun, "The fundamental purpose of naval forces is to *achieve* command of the seas," followed by a series of sub-bullets that listed some goals: "To protect U.S. citizens and territory . . . demonstrate U.S. commitment overseas and promote our interests . . ." and so on. In the final version, that bullet read: "The fundamental purpose of naval forces is to *use* command of the seas." Changing that verb made all the difference in the world, because in the first rendering, the United States still needed to secure command of the seas *before* anything else could be achieved. In the final version, command of the seas was simply assumed, and that breakthrough meant naval forces could revolutionize the way they thought about projecting U.S. combat power ashore.

That may not sound like much of a difference at first blush, but it actually describes a turning point in human history. Think about it: Great military powers throughout history have staked their ability to wage war far from home on the power of their navies. Stretching all the way back to ancient Greece, the ability to rule the seas has essentially defined which powers *are* great powers.

What the Navy was coming to grips with in 1992, as the Soviet Navy continued its decade-long collapse, was an unprecedented moment in world history: America possessed the planet's *only* blue-water navy. By "blue water," I mean a navy capable of projecting military power across all the world's open oceans. In contrast, the rest of the world's major states subsist largely on "green" (littoral) or "brown" (inland) fleets, meaning they have no effective reach beyond their region. Sure, a Russia today can send a few capital (or large) ships to distant waters, but they are not capable of operating on their own for any length of time. They cannot rule the waves, just ply them now and then. Frankly, the same is true for every other navy in the world today, including China's. While that country may harbor dreams of global naval power in some distant future, let me assure you that China's ruling Communist Party will not survive to see that day.

Again, what is amazing about this period of history is not only that America possesses the world's dominant navy, something that previous imperial powers have achieved—like England in the nineteenth century. What is amazing is that we own the world's *only* navy with a global reach, and no other power is making any serious attempt to catch up. If you look around the world today, you see countries that have armies and air forces and what can charitably be called the equivalent of the U.S. Coast Guard. The world has effectively surrendered the seas to the U.S. Navy, and it has done so out of immense trust that America will not abuse that unprecedented power. That is the end of one great arc of human history, and the beginning of something completely different.

Accepting this stunning reality was incredibly difficult for the U.S. Navy back in 1992. *Achieving* command of the seas has been the driving goal of the U.S. Navy throughout most of its existence. Saying that it was just ours for the taking was like telling a boxer that his opponent in the ring no longer had the use of his arms— the historical contest that had defined the Navy's warrior ethos no longer existed. This is why the Navy desperately needed a new operating theory of the world once the Soviet Navy began its disappearing act. Simply put, the Navy needed to move beyond its history into something completely unprecedented. It needed to decipher the new security rule set (let's not forget about the boxer's ability to kick, for example) or risk becoming irrelevant to the projection of America's air and ground forces, which no longer relied on its ability to secure the "sea lines of communication" during war. The U.S. Navy needed a new *raison d'être*.

This is where Manthorpe and Mahan met in our debates over the Navy's new, post–Cold War vision, because it was on this point that the Navy and Marines finally admitted to themselves that a fundamental aspect of their operational rule set had changed. Not surprisingly, many of the officers had a very hard time surrendering that verb (*achieve*), because once they did, they knew serious force structure changes would result. In other words, certain ship categories (like submarines) would be cut more than others (the sacred carriers that define our Navy) in the coming years.

So it was not simply semantics, because those words (*to achieve command of the seas*) had to remain if the submarine community had any hope of limiting its losses in coming years. Careers were on the line, because opportunities for future command were on the line. Simply put, fewer subs meant fewer commands, and fewer commands meant fewer captains making it all the way to admiral over time. The dominance of the submarine community within the Navy, which stretched back several decades thanks to the dominant role of ballistic-missile submarines (read, the Big One with the Soviet Union), was coming to an end. Institutionally, this was a tectonic shift within the Department of Navy, and the Cold Worriers were not going to take this lying down.

Wilkerson knew how hard it would be to get this group of officers to let go of that past, but unless they did, the new naval vision of focusing more directly on "influencing events ashore" could never be truly embraced. At its core, then, it was a resource issue. But it was also a question of the needs of the many (the Navy as a whole) overcoming the needs of a few (the submarine community). It was *all ashore that are going ashore!* You knew the Marines were champing at the bit to project power ashore, as were the fighter jocks that flew off the "big decks," as carriers are known. The one force that would be left behind historically in the blue waters was the submarine fleet, which has struggled ever since to redefine itself as a littorally focused land-attack force.

So here is where you begin to see how one slide—even one bullet item on one slide—can change history. I will not pretend that everything changed overnight with this brief. The naval community has suffered infighting ever since over the meaning of the white paper that ultimately resulted from our work. But substituting that one word on that one slide represented nothing less than a sea change for the U.S. Navy. Once we stated that America owned the seas and was without peer, the new naval vision—or the new rule set on war—could be pursued. The Navy was the first of the major services to recognize this massive rule-set shift because it suffered the greatest threat loss when the Soviet Union disappeared. Both the Army and the Air Force have other armies and air forces they can and will occasionally fight against—as in our recent wars in Iraq. But the Navy fundamentally has no other navy left to fight anymore—unless you cling to the chimera of naval war in the Taiwan Straits.

General Wilkerson's genius was that he never forced the issue with the group in these highly charged debates. Instead, every time the group came to some sticking point somewhere else in the brief, he would gently bring us all back to that first slide and remind us of where the crux of the matter lay. Finally, one morning, the group voted to change that first slide's first bullet, and the rest was history.

Well, almost. Now that we had our story ready to tell, we had to sell it to the Gang of Five. Here I thought my moment of personal glory was coming. As the captain who was preparing to give the final brief to the flags readied his slide package, I presented him with the script I had so diligently constructed over the previous weeks. To my shock, this Captain Charlie Schaefer, a good friend and colleague of mine in SPAG, refused to use my script. He was very kind in his rejection, saying he needed to be able to say what he felt needed to be said at this culminating moment. Charlie, as a submariner, had great difficulty delivering the final package to the Gang of Five, and so he planned to use that moment to raise some objections he still had to the vision as completed.

I was crushed. All those weeks of eighteen-hour days had been— in my mind, at least—leading up to this payoff. My secret hope was that the briefing script would serve as the basis for the resulting white paper. Instead, I felt completely shut out of the moment. Angry beyond words at Charlie, I threw my text down on the floor and stormed out of the building. I did not return until the final brief occurred. The new vision was very warmly received by the Gang of Five, and orders were given to immediately put together the final written report that would serve—months later—as the basis for the historic Department of Navy white paper entitled . . . *From the Sea.*

Now for the end of the story.

A couple of days later I wandered into the group's office spaces at CNA, looking to gather up my working papers. It was the day the final written report was due, and as I walked in I bumped into one of the two Marine colonels in charge of putting the document together. Rick "Sterno" Stearns greeted me with a great big grin. "Hey," he said. "We used a bunch of your stuff in the final report!" I was stunned. Then Sterno told me how he and his partner, Colonel Mike Strickland, had pulled an all-nighter to get the final report stitched together. When they got stuck about halfway through the process, they found my papers strewn across the floor.

Well, after reading some of them, they decided to include much of my material in the final report. In the end, the report consisted of a first section on grand strategy built primarily with writings from Captain Bradd Hayes, a middle section on operational concepts that utilized my write-up of the group's debates, and a final third on future changes that the two colonels themselves had collected together from various other participants' contributions. Colonel Stearns joked that the final document was a "real Frankenstein," confessing, "It took us most of the night just trying to hide all the zippers."

. . . *From the Sea* represented a genuine turning point in the history of the U.S. Navy and Marine Corps. By admitting to themselves that the old Mahanian rule set of focusing on sea control first and foremost had been overtaken by events, the Department of Navy began a decade-long search for a new strategic map that would guide their application of this new operational vision of "influencing events ashore." But as the new Clinton Administration took the reins in 1993, major questions still remained, such as what the dominant threat of this new era would turn out to be.

Should America focus on influencing events ashore primarily in Asia, to deter possible rising competitors in a China or—God forbid—a Japan? Or should our focus remain centered in the Persian Gulf or the Korean peninsula, where dangerous regional hegemons needed careful watching? Or should America seek more vigorously to deal with all this rising ethnic conflict and this new category of "failing states"? To many observers in the early 1990s, the world appeared to be coming apart at the seams, making the choice difficult indeed. Would the Pentagon help build a "new world order" in this fractured security environment crammed full of lesser includeds, or would it retreat from this fractious world to focus ahead on the Big One?

The answer is, the Pentagon tried to do both.

THE FRACTURING OF THE SECURITY MARKET

It is always interesting to go back and see what people in the past were predicting would happen in the future. Since seers typically predict bad things, such reviews are like chicken soup for this optimist's soul. Things never really turn out as bad as predicted, and yet reviewing the fears behind such predictions is usually quite illuminating, because the unease underlying these fearful prognostications is invariably warranted on some level. People have an innate sense for detecting when rule sets are out of whack, or for when all your procedures and contingency responses seem built for one type of emergency and suddenly you find yourself dealing with something completely different.

Working with the Pentagon during the changeover from the Bush to the Clinton Administration, I picked up a lot of that unease in various working briefs I saw. Working briefs, or draft briefs, are the equivalent of the Pentagon's subconscious. They consist of a universe of PowerPoint presentations that explore—in a preliminary fashion—the strategic issues at hand. They are generated by the boatload as part of the Pentagon's never-ending stream of annual planning. Most never leave the building, and they are not meant for public consumption, even though few of them are ever classified. These briefs are sort of the pillow talk within and among the military services—stuff they confess to one another and worry about ceaselessly, but not something for polite conversation.

The U.S. military was a mass of conflicting fears and impulses at this point in history. The security rule set it had grown so comfortable with over the past couple of decades was evaporating. Once the United States and the Soviets had basically figured out the relationship in the early 1970s, the struggle became almost completely internalized on each side—a pure balancing act of military capabilities that each knew they would never really use against the other in war. Yes, each side would practice and prepare for such warfare as though their lives depended on it, but as an officer, you were not going to earn your "stars" (or flag rank as an admiral or general) actually fighting the Soviets anywhere.

At least through the mid-1970s, there was an alternative to the grand conflict: the lesser-included proxy wars we fought in the Third World—Korea and Vietnam being the two great examples. But when Vietnam ended, even that option for real-world combat seemed to disappear for the U.S. military, and the Pentagon entered into a long period (1975–1990) of internal rebuilding that featured no real wars. As we began to emerge across the 1980s from the cocoon of the Vietnam Syndrome—or the fear of quagmire and body bags—the pickings were pretty slim. The Soviets seemed to be pulling out of everywhere: first the Third World in general, then out of Afghanistan in particular, then Eastern Europe, and finally out of the Soviet republics themselves.

The Persian Gulf War definitely gave the military a renewed sense of confidence and purpose exactly when it needed one, but the effect was not long-lasting. The static quo of the Cold War was gone and—for the first time in our history—we had to figure out how much responsibility we felt for the world at large, not just as a military power but as a nation. In the Cold War you worried about your friends and your enemies, and everyone else was pretty much on their own. But now it seemed that the entire world comprised *everyone else.* This was a pretty scary thing to contemplate for an institution genetically predisposed to worry about everything in a worst-case sort of way. There seemed to be no logical boundaries to the problem sets we might be called upon to deal with, and there was simply no compelling rule set to guide our choices. George H. W. Bush had offered up the phrase "new world order," but that hardly narrowed anything down.

The Pentagon's unease with this new world order simply jumped out at me in those working briefs. Scared—not scary—sentiments abounded. The U.S. military worried about not having allies in the future, that Soviet military technology would flood the world, and that it would get left holding the bag in failed states around the world. Worse, military leaders feared that the American public expected casualty-less wars after *Desert Storm,* a fear that later seemed vindicated after eighteen servicemen were killed in Mogadishu in October 1993 (the *Black Hawk Down* incident), leading to our subsequent pullout from warlord-dominated Somalia.

It was in this nervous environment that the concept of "mission creep" began to be discussed more and more, and the U.S. military's unease on this subject spoke volumes about what they sensed was emerging in the international security environment. "Mission creep" is an old concept that many experts used to describe the process of the military's incremental assumption of tasks in the Vietnam War that were—by most soldiers' standards—beyond their normal purview. The concept of "nation building" is often viewed as a result of mission creep. You go into a country like Somalia in late 1992 and all you are supposed to do is settle things down enough so the relief supplies can flow again, and before long you find yourself drawn into remaking a nation from the bottom up.

The fear of mission creep was justified, but it was just a microcosm of what the U.S. military really feared about the post–Cold War era: interest creep. "Interest" here refers to "national interest," which is one of those great phrases constantly used in Pentagon publications, even though nobody really knows what it means. The Pentagon just knows it needs to protect American interests, promote them when possible, and never step beyond their logical boundaries—whatever those are. There is no list of "national interests" to be found anywhere throughout the U.S. Government, much less the Pentagon. You either know them or you don't. Raising your hand during a Pentagon brief to ask what exactly these interests are is considered impolitic in the extreme.

What drove the military nuts across the 1990s and still does today is that unlike the static quo of the Cold War, where our security interests seemed clear enough (Hold that line!), definitions of U.S. national interests now seem incredibly fluid. Pick up the *New York Times* or the *Washington Post* and you can find half a dozen different interpretations in the op-ed pages alone—day after day after day. If I had a nickel for every time I heard a mid-level military officer exclaim how nice it would be if the politicians simply got together and decided what those "national interests" were, I could have bankrolled the peace dividend myself.

To put it most simply, America's national interest in the era of globalization lies primarily in the extension of global economic connectivity. Global connectivity benefits America economically by increasing our access to the world's goods and services while promoting our exports of the same. With that growing connectivity around the planet, we see the rising need for political and security rule sets that define fair play among nations, firms, and even individuals, not just in trade but in terms of war, which—as we have seen with 9/11 and the resulting war on terrorism—is no longer restricted to just organized violence between nation-states. That global system of security rules is the most important peace dividend of the Cold War; these rule sets allow globalization to flourish and advance, and by doing so, they have effectively killed great-power war, a destructive force that haunted the international community for close to two centuries (dating all the way back to Europe's Napoleonic Wars of the early 1800s).

Reiterating the theme of chapter 1: more rules means less war. So extending globalization's rule set leads ultimately to less violence in the system, and that is definitely in America's national interest.

Today, nations and societies that desire greater economic connectivity with the outside world understand that it comes with a price—adherence to a wider array of political and security rule sets. Not every regime accepts that essential transaction easily, and a few display a firm willfulness to play outside the rules. We call these governments "rogue regimes," and we seek to change their behavior and—at the very least—constrain their ability to engage in any rule-breaking (or -bending) behavior. Ultimately, their need to transgress the emerging global rule set on security stems from their fear of losing control over their own populations, whose disconnectedness from the outside world is seen as a prerequisite of their continued subordination to the state's authoritarian grip over their daily lives.

But as we have seen with al Qaeda, there are also groups of individuals within societies that reject the notion that their "homeland" should join this larger community of states that define globalization's Functioning Core. They fear that by joining this modern—or "Western"—system of rules, their traditional society will be forever damaged and ultimately perverted. They are willing to wage warfare against individuals, states, and even the system itself to prevent that outcome. Increasingly, as the number of rogue regimes shrinks around the world, thanks both to time (dictators never fade away, but they do die) and the occasionally coherent efforts of the Core (prodded primarily by the United States), these nonstate actors committed to hijacking their societies from globalization's creeping embrace will come to define the dominant security threat across the system as a whole. In a nutshell, this is the rise of the lesser includeds: violent individuals fighting the system of globalization, with disconnected states as the prize.

In my career, I have found it very useful to view the international security environment across these three separate perspectives: the system or community of states, individual nation-states (both "good" and "bad"), and individuals operating both within societies and across them (e.g., evil leaders abusing their own populations, transnational terrorists). Applying this tripartite perspective (system, states, individuals) to the question of where big violence may be sourced in the international security environment, I break down the universe of traditional military contingencies as follows: there is system-level violence of the sort we feared would occur in the Cold War, otherwise known as World War III; then there is the classic sort of interstate war like Saddam's Iraq (the quintessential rogue state) invading Kuwait in 1990; and finally, there is the sort of violence that occurs not between states but within them, like the ethnic cleansing of Serbia's Slobodan Milosevic in the 1990s and the terrorism that afflicts Israel on a daily basis. I basically include "transnational" terrorism in this category, because like all politics, all terrorism is ultimately local: it occurs within states and it typically involves specific grievances even as it rages against the system—be it an oppressive regime, the "hegemonic" United States, or the "polluting" forces of globalization.

Despite the fact that the Cold War era was defined by the superpowers' nuclear standoff or the threat of system-level war, the military mind is far more comfortably located at the level of the nation-state, where the paradigm is one of my-army-against-your-army. In reality, most military officers thought of the Soviets in this way, which made the whole process of strategic planning for war so oddly antiseptic and pristine: in effect, you could plan for it all you wanted because the overarching reality of nuclear weapons and Mutually Assured Destruction meant you would never get the chance to try it out for real. But you nonetheless had to gin up and maintain a huge conventional military force, because no one was comfortable with the notion of relying solely on nukes to keep the Red Army at bay in Europe.

When the Soviets went away at the end of the Cold War, the military mind's natural tendency to view the world through the prism of the nation-state was subtly reinforced. System-level conflict became a complete abstraction, but in a world seemingly populated by rogues and regional hegemons like Iraq, Iran, and North Korea, it made even more sense to have your strategic planning—not to mention your intelligence community—focus heavily on what other states were buying, building, or developing for their militaries.

This tendency to focus on nation-states has made it hard for the

Pentagon to decipher the new security rule sets generated by globalization's progressive advance. As globalization has spread dramatically over the past two decades, two huge changes have unfolded across the international security environment. First, the sources of mass violence have migrated *downward,* or from the state to the individual. To put it somewhat facetiously, in the current age, states don't kill people, people kill people. Second, while nation-states still "compete" with one another, that competition has left the military realm, where governments are the dominant actor, and moved on to the economic realm, where increasingly international organizations become the dominant venue of coordination and negotiation, such as the G-7/8 group of advanced economies or the World Trade Organization. What that means is traditional economic power and competition have migrated *upward,* or from the state to the system.

These two developments help explain the progressive rise of the lesser includeds in U.S. national security planning.

The migration of violence downward, or below the level of the nation-state, is fairly easy to express and track. Basically, wars between states have disappeared over the past half century, but especially since the end of the Cold War. Nukes effectively ended great-power war following the Second World War, giving the world as a whole a wonderfully long respite from system-level war that I believe will never end. Meanwhile, state-on-state wars have effectively gone the way of the dinosaur in recent decades. When wars occur now, they are almost exclusively internal wars, where some subsection of a state wishes to break off from the whole or where social violence between groups within a state erupts into full-blown civil war. In fact, the only real wars that have occurred between sovereign states since the end of the Cold War have involved United States–led multinational coalitions to either reverse an act of overt interstate aggression (kicking Iraq out of Kuwait in 1991) or to effect regime change (Afghanistan in 2001 and Iraq in 2003). In my mind, describing these three wars as interstate conflicts is entirely misleading, because in each instance the conflict was initiated by a

United States–led coalition on behalf of the international community—albeit with varying levels of support. In effect, these are wars between the system and renegade states, with the United States–led coalition serving as the system's proxy or representative. The goal of each war was not to conquer a state for particularistic gain but rather to readmit that disconnected state back to the system—or community—of peaceful states.

If the threat of system-level war ended with the Cold War and interstate wars are virtually extinct, then where is all the violence in this "chaotic" world? It lies overwhelmingly within nation-states, or those lesser includeds to which the Pentagon had developed an aversion during the Cold War. Not surprisingly, the spending associated with all that violence has likewise begun migrating from the level of the state to the individual. State-to-state arms transfers may have declined significantly with the Cold War's end, but the traffic in small arms has increased dramatically, by all credible accounts fueling the endemic societal wars that afflict many backward states in the Gap. According to the Small Arms Survey, an independent research project of the Graduate Institute of International Studies in Geneva, the trade in civilian small arms recently surpassed that of military small arms. Factor in the growth in private security firms in both the advanced and underdeveloped portions of the global economy, and it becomes clear that both individuals and corporations have begun self-financing a good portion of their security needs in the post–Cold War era.

A good share of that security spending by corporations is likewise designed to protect the growing connectivity between states and regions that we define as globalization. This brings us to the other great security trend of the last two decades, the migration upward to the system level of the sort of power and competition long associated with states. Who conducts this competition and exercises this power? A certain amount of regulatory oversight is maintained by the international organizations that have sprung up over the decades to facilitate all the growing connectivity we now associate with globalization's advance. These largely faceless international bodies regulate all manner of trade, along with such obscure efforts as the codification of Internet protocols, protection of patents, and harmonization of global pharmaceutical testing. The international regulatory organizations probably best known to most Americans today are the World Trade Organization, the World Bank, and the International Monetary Fund.

This system-level competition is largely economic now. Instead of military superpowers jostling over desired client states, we now have supranational entities such as the European Union and NAFTA (the North American Free Trade Agreement zone encompassing the United States, Canada, and Mexico) jostling over candidates for free-trade agreements. Of course, most global economic activity is conducted by corporations and individuals on their own, because in many ways globalization is all about expanded connectivity between nonstate actors and the system, with states largely getting out of way except for regulating activity on the margins (i.e., policing the rule breakers and rule benders).

So if competition is migrating above the level of the nation-state and violence is migrating below it, how does a military that largely views the world in terms of nation-states keep current with global change? It begins to understand that the global market for its security "service" is fracturing. Yes, the world still needs a Leviathan-like military superpower to come into regional security situations and dispatch the rule-breaking regime in question, so certain state-on-state military capabilities will always be required. But the world is also suffering a significant amount of subnational violence, overwhelmingly concentrated in the states with the least connectivity to the globalization process. Then there are those nations we need to rebuild once we have decapitated their rogue leadership.

But where is the global Leviathan for nation building? It sure does not look like the U.S. military, based on our historical track record. And where is the global Leviathan for stopping transnational terrorists from pulling off the next 9/11, whatever form that takes? Can the U.S. military aspire to that role in any form, or do we specialize solely in regime change in response to catastrophic acts of terrorism? If so, maybe the United States might want to reconsider spending more than ten times as much on the Defense Department as it does for the Department of Homeland Security. Because who knows? Maybe the American public believes it should be protected—as individuals—from transnational terrorists hell-bent on their mass murder, and not just see the bulk of security dollars go toward securing America's "national interests" abroad.

The essential rule-set gap that defined U.S. national security in the 1990s was that we had a military that was fundamentally designed to protect our nation from other nations, when in reality the biggest *direct* threats we now face are from nonstate actors waging war against a global system to which we are strongly connected and with which we are intimately identified. Where do those nonstate actors find sanctuary? Primarily in failed states located inside the Gap, which means those states are *indirectly* a source of threat to the United States, whether they are ruled by authoritarian leaders such as Liberia's Charles Taylor (now deposed, in large part because of his support to terrorist groups) or divided up by warlords (meaning no one's really in charge).

What did the Pentagon spend the nineties planning for? Wars with Iraq, Iran, North Korea, and China—all nation-states. What have been the Pentagon's biggest successes in the global war on terrorism since 9/11? Our invasions of Afghanistan and Iraq.

There is an old saying that if all you have is a hammer, the entire world begins to look like nails. The terrorist attacks of 9/11 revealed a global security environment far more fractured than any the Pentagon had previously been able to visualize in its constantly churning production of quadrennial reviews, annual posture statements, and technology road maps. That is because all those strategic planning documents focused first and foremost on nation-states, and the Pentagon continues that focus primarily because the nation-state is the "image" it most comfortably recognizes.

The Rise of Asymmetrical Warfare

I was both unwittingly and unwillingly introduced to the concept of asymmetrical warfare as a young child growing up in my small hometown of Boscobel, Wisconsin. My dear father was the city attorney, which meant he sometimes had to enforce city ordinances with townsfolk who, for example, saw no reason why raising pigs in their backyard might disturb their neighbors. I sometimes found myself standing up to fairly sizable bullies who were determined to make me pay for the fact that my dad had made their dad lose the livestock.

Like anyone smaller facing someone larger, I engaged in asymmetrical warfare to defend myself. In other words, I pulled every dirty trick on them that I could think of, always trying to exploit their weakest points. While I got roughed up now and then, I never really ever got beat up, because I was willing to pull out all the stops to defend myself. I knew I would never survive a straight-up fight, so I would run because they were slower, hit them below the belt because they were taller, or joke my way out of the situation. But I never did try to punch them out, because punching was their strength, and it simply made no sense for me to fight their way.

When the Red Army disappeared across the 1990s, the U.S. military not only stood alone among the world's militaries, nobody else even hailed from the same zip code. So all of a sudden we went from bipolar standoff to nobody left worth fighting in a straight-up contest. In effect, we became the global military bully by default. We became Casey Stengel's New York Yankees or Vince Lombardi's Green Bay Packers, at once admired and feared.

Well, the U.S. military knew it was basically unbeatable, especially in a straight-up fight, and so it spent a lot of time and mental energy in the nineties thinking about how smaller opponents would seek to negate its strengths by being clever and "dirty" in any combat with us. It is not that the Pentagon feared any state initiating a war directly with the United States, but rather that State A would attack State B and we would have to rush in to defend State B and send State A packing. Of course, that scenario sounded suspiciously like a rerun of Iraq's 1990 invasion of Kuwait, raising the old charge that the military prefers to plan for the last war, not the next one. But there were other handy situations that fit this profile, like North Korea trying to invade South Korea, or China targeting Taiwan (the emerging favorite). This trio of scenarios was the preferred mix, by and large, for the Pentagon's planning across the nineties on this new concept of asymmetrical warfare.

When you were explaining to Congress what you felt you needed in force structure, or your overall array of ships, aircraft, tanks, and the like, it was a whole lot easier to simply point to a chart that listed everything the Soviets had and say, "We'd like that in green, some of those in navy blue . . ." But we would never trade our force structure for Iraq's or China's, and so convincing Congress not to cut the defense budget any deeper across the nineties became quite a song and dance on the part of Pentagon officials, as asymmetrical warfare became a tune every analyst knew by heart.

But what strategists did in the nineties was to elevate the concept of asymmetrical war even further. Our enemies would not simply avoid fair fights, the Pentagon contended, but they would do so in such a way as to "deny" our "access" to conflicts involving our "national interests." So when State A attacked State B, A would seek to conquer B quickly so it could present the world with a *fait accompli* that the U.S. military could reverse only if it was able to overcome A's ability to "deny access" to the battlefield through their "asymmetrical, anti-access strategies." Basically, State A's hope would be that America would look at the situation as too far gone, meaning likely to cost too many U.S. casualties to reverse, and we would simply choose to accept the new status quo.

Now, when Pentagon staffers briefed these concepts, they were masters at making this outcome seem downright insulting to American pride. *And are we going to let this little pissant dictatorship disrespect Uncle Sam like that?* But when you stood back and thought about it for a while, the level of assumed U.S. responsibility for global order suggested by this pairing of concepts was nothing less than staggering. In effect, our national interest was limitless.

In the Cold War we had our friends to worry about and the Soviets had theirs. Then there was the occasional tug-of-war over client states in the Third World. It may have seemed like a lot, and it was, but the level of responsibility for the status quo was fairly manageable: hold the line against the Soviets in Europe and Asia, and if they got too friendly with anybody else around the world, you got even friendlier with that country's next-door neighbor. I mean, it wasn't like we had a standing order to reverse any act of aggression around the planet, at least not after we ditched the "domino theory" in Southeast Asia and realized that losing a Vietnam or Cambodia did not exactly signal the fall of Western civilization.

But even stranger was the notion that now that the East had actually fallen, the Pentagon somehow felt so responsible for global security that it wanted to be able to reverse any significant act of aggression anywhere in the world. Not a bad thing in and of itself, but you'd better be able to explain your choices to the American people, and that is where the lack of a guiding vision came into play. Of course, the Pentagon had no such desire to play global cop—far from it. They were simply searching for the toughest list of tasks they could come up with to justify the largest and niftiest package of military capabilities possible. That is the budget game in a nutshell. So if you want to play that game well, you gin up a host of strategic concepts like "access denial" and asymmetrical warfare, and then tell the senators that in a world of chaos and complete uncertainty, we need to be able to overcome these devious opponents wherever they are found.

In retrospect, where we should have been applying this concept of asymmetrical warfare was not so much to regional rogues but to transnational terrorist networks like al Qaeda. Here, just about everyone involved in national security planning missed the boat. By focusing on nation-states as the great source of violence and threat in the system, we ignored the rising role of transnational terrorism.

Simply put, we refused to realize just how successful America had become in deterring both global and interstate war, but we refused to move off that dime until something bigger—and frankly, more compelling in a budgetary sense—came along. That something turned out to be 9/11, which has progressively altered funding priorities not only across the defense budget but across the federal budget as a whole.

The defense community, however, should have seen this change coming long before 9/11. The evidence had grown with each passing year. The history of U.S. crisis response over the past three decades indicated a progressive downshifting of our focus from system-level threats to state-level threats, and finally to threats that arise from failing states—or what I call the disconnected states. In short, history was telling us that we were moving progressively away from warfare against states or even blocs of states and toward a new era of warfare against individuals.

This downshifting of U.S. crisis-response patterns can be tracked decade by decade. As far back as the 1970s, much of our crisis response was focused on countering the perceived Soviet advance into the Third World, such as their growing support for "countries of socialist orientation" in the Middle East and sub-Saharan Africa. So our crisis-response pattern in the seventies looked like a long "arc" of containment that ran from the Mediterranean through the Persian Gulf, wrapping around the underbelly of Asia all the way up to the Korean peninsula. In effect, we had spent the fifties and sixties largely focused on keeping the Soviets from expanding their influence east or west, but by the seventies we were more concerned about their heading south.

In the 1980s, we downshifted from this system-level perspective and focused more openly on a series of interstate conflicts or wars concentrated in the Middle East, or what the Pentagon likes to call Southwest Asia. Two key events helped focus our attention at the end of the seventies: the Soviets invaded Afghanistan and the Shah fell in Iran. At that point, our crisis-response pattern became very tight, as the bulk of our activity focused in and around the Persian Gulf (Iran-Iraq War) and the Eastern Mediterranean (Israel's invasion of Lebanon and a spiking of radical Islamic terrorism across the region).

In the 1990s our pattern of crisis response seemed to drill down even further on a cluster of mini-containment situations involving failed states (Somalia, Haiti) and rogues (Serbia's Slobodan Milosevic and Iraq's Saddam Hussein) who needed to be kept in their boxes lest they commit too much violence against their own people. So in the 1970s we were still dealing with the "evil empire," while in the 1980s we downshifted to "evil states," and in the 1990s we downshifted further to "evil leaders."

This downshifting was not a sign of the world coming apart but rather an indicator of where big violence was heading. By the end of the 1980s it became clear to everyone that system-level war had long since departed the scene, and by the end of the century it became clear that interstate wars had similarly disappeared. All that really leaves in the international system today is mass violence within states and the terrorists that tend to emerge from those endemic conflicts over time, like all those al Qaeda operatives who cut their teeth on Afghanistan's internal violence.

On 9/11 America got a real dose of what asymmetrical warfare is going to be in the twenty-first century. It isn't going to come from rising near-peers like China, who are rapidly integrating into the global economy, nor is it going to come from rogue regimes, whose fixed position we can surround at our leisure and attack at will. The real asymmetrical challenge we will face will come from globalization's disenfranchised, or the losers largely left behind in the states most disconnected from globalization's advance. The main thrust of this challenge will be led by educated elites, like an Osama bin Laden, who dream of disconnecting societies from globalization's grasp and—by extension—from America's "empire." Like the intellectual Lenin and his Bolsheviks a century before, these transnational terrorists will use every dirty trick in the book against the powers that be, and they will grow more perverse in their violence over time because they know, deep down, that time is not on their side. Over time, globalization's advance will rob the al Qaedas of the world of the opportunity to seize control of societies and turn back the clock.

Al Qaeda's victims were not going to be our soldiers but our citizens. We lost more Americans in combat on 9/11 than on any day since the Civil War, and it was completely by design. Bin Laden fears what globalization and U.S. military hegemony are doing to his people, and so to personalize the danger he sees in this historical process, he brings his violence directly to American citizens in a war he believes he is fighting quite symmetrically—even if the U.S. government does not.

Put these two images together and the asymmetrical outline of bin Laden and al Qaeda's strategy seems far more logical. The United States cannot be defeated on the nation-state level, but it can be humbled on an individual level if enough Americans are murdered, and even defeated on the system level if we are induced as a nation to withdraw militarily from the Persian Gulf.

You could say that America pursued the knee-jerk reaction in response to 9/11. Since we could not easily track down the individual terrorists spread across this global network, we did the one thing we know how to do well: we invaded a nation-state. Of course, al Qaeda was largely concentrated in Afghanistan in terms of its senior leadership and its training camps, but the notion that we could destroy their global network of individual operatives by eliminating their main hideout is a little like assuming you could disable all McDonald's franchises around the world by taking out Hamburger U.

The fact that we did invade Afghanistan should tell us plenty about the ultimate enemy that we face—disconnectedness. When Vladimir Lenin wanted to create the world's first socialist state in defiance of the capitalist world system, he ended up in Russia, a nation whose economic development was significantly retarded— or precapitalist. Correspondingly, when bin Laden and al Qaeda sought to launch their worldwide resistance to the United States–led globalization process, they invariably settled in a nation whose economic connectivity to the outside world was severely retarded—or preglobalized.

The task that the Pentagon and the rest of the U.S. Government woke up to on September 12 reflected the very fracturing of the global security environment we had spent a decade or longer ignoring. This global war on terrorism is simultaneously fought across all three of the levels I cited earlier: network war across the global system to disrupt terrorist financing, communications, and logistics; state-based war against rogue regimes that harbor or support such terrorist groups; and special operations that target individuals for either capture or—when dictated by circumstances—serial assassination.

What immediately became apparent in late 2001 as America's multilevel response to terrorism unfolded was that this war was going to involve a whole lot more than just the Defense Department. Since the system-level response is largely financial, the Treasury Department plays a huge role in a new form of war that involves lawyers, banking officials, data-mining experts, and customs agents. Since our war against individuals will occur not only in disconnected states where Special Operations forces lead the way, but likewise in advanced states where law enforcement agencies typically take control, the Justice Department commingles its efforts with that of the U.S. military to a degree that has never been seen before. Even on the level of state-based war, where the Pentagon will clearly lead any efforts at regime change or preemptive strikes, the bulk of any follow-up will naturally revert to the State Department, as we increasingly witness in postwar Iraq. In short, the Pentagon can no longer plan for war solely within the context of war but increasingly must plan for prosecuting such war within the context of everything else.

I had spent the 1990s trying vainly to reconnect the military to the world outside the Pentagon: to the fracturing of the security market, to the rise of the lesser includeds, to the reality that wars now occur within the context of everything else. I readily admit that despite my considerable briefing skills, I mostly entertained but did not inform my military audiences, which found my strategic concepts truly fascinating but not applicable to the world they recognized. In short, I expanded minds but did not change them.

I am not going to kid you: I was not the lone visionary trying to reconnect the Pentagon to the larger world of globalization. It was simply the case that my superior briefing skills gave me far more opportunities than anyone else to pitch that product and make that sale. In the end, all such efforts were overtaken by the events of 9/11. In one blinding flash, the U.S. defense establishment was taught a lesson about needing to broaden its perspective beyond its historically myopic focus on nation-states. Moreover, the Pentagon learned that its long-held assumptions regarding the so-called lesser includeds had grown dangerously out-of-date. We were completely unprepared for this new form of multilayered war, and it was our own damn fault.

As our nation continues in this rule-set reset, we must be careful not to view 9/11 as a historical aberration or a onetime event. As far as the Pentagon must be concerned, there can be no such thing as lesser includeds anymore.

How 9/11 Saved the Pentagon from Itself

As the Pentagon entered the new century, it was clear to many national security experts that the Defense Department had basically spent the nineties buying one type of military while operating another. Sound hard? It was. But the weirdest thing was, the Pentagon did this to itself and knew it was doing so all along, in large part thanks to the light leadership touch displayed by the Clinton Administration for eight years. After starting off on the wrong foot by picking Les Aspin as Defense Secretary and then leading with a fight over gays in the military, the Clinton White House quietly backed off from trying to run the Pentagon about halfway through its first term, yielding two of the quietest secretaries the Pentagon has ever had: William Perry and William Cohen. In the second half of the 1990s, it often felt as though the military was "home alone" in the Pentagon, which is why the Bush Administration felt that they had to reestablish civilian control over the military when they came into power in 2001.

If the Clinton secretaries had displayed a better leadership capability, would it have made a difference? Probably not, because the military itself was basically coming apart at the seams, splitting into two rival camps over the decade: one that had to deal with the international security environment as it was and another that preferred to dream of one that "should be." The result was that the Pentagon kept building a military for some distant, downstream threat that they were convinced would eventually appear, only to leave the current military on its own to deal with a messy "here and now" collection of lesser includeds. So when the military tells you they were treated badly by the Democrats over the nineties, don't believe them. The military treated itself badly over the 1990s; the Clinton Administration simply let them do it.

What happened to let this split emerge within the military? All the services experienced the same sort of inner crisis that drove the Navy and Marines to gin up . . . *From the Sea*—that search for a new enemy or new standard against which to measure themselves. The Army's self-doubts were the worst, because after the Cold War it was the service immediately targeted for the cruelest cuts in force structure. Later, in the mid-1990s, as the concept of "transforming" the military took root, the Army got even more nervous, fearing that this next-generation military would do without ground forces altogether. That suited the Air Force just fine, because its leadership was under the distinct impression that air power had won the first Persian Gulf War all by itself, and later the Kosovo campaign to boot.

By the end of the Clinton Administration, all the services eventually came to realize that they were buying one sort of military for the future while the present demanded something dramatically different, primarily because the extensive overseas operations of the 1990s had worn down, or "hollowed out," the forces somewhat. In essence, the misalignment of strategy and operations had become painfully obvious to most observers by 2000, as each service was cannibalizing platforms like aircraft for spare parts, and military families were stressing out from the high rates of overseas deployments by their loved ones.

Watching this unfold over the years, I was reminded of the old joke about the guy who goes to the doctor complaining that every time he twists his arms far behind his back and then jumps up and down on the floor, he feels a stabbing pain in his spine. So he complains, "It hurts so bad when I do that, doc!" To which his physician replies, "Then don't do that!"

I was one of those doctors telling the Pentagon to knock it off over the nineties, to no avail. Our message was a simple one: You cannot keep buying these expensive, high-tech platforms for some distant future war and expect the military to have enough resources left over to deal with all of today's operations. Following my experience with the Navy's White Paper . . . *From the Sea,* I participated in a CNA study that looked at how the U.S. Navy should plan to alter its "force structure" (i.e., the mix of ships, submarines, aircraft, etc.) over the coming years in response to the "emerging strategic environment" (strategic environments are always "emerging" in the Pentagon's vernacular).

I reunited with my longtime CNA mentor Hank Gaffney in this study. Hank and I had written up a celebrated article that described the intra-Navy debates that had raged during the creation of the white paper, or the three camps I had dubbed the Transitioneers, Big Sticks, and Cold Worriers. In this force structure study, we wanted to see what would happen if the Navy actually pursued the specific advice of those three camps in deciding which ships and aircraft it should buy over the coming generation. By showing naval leaders the different fleets they could end up with twenty years later, depending on which vision they followed, we hoped to open some eyes regarding the big trade-offs we knew eventually had to be made given budgetary constraints. Let me just describe the two extreme cases here: the Transitioneers, who wanted to manage the here-and-now world of lesser includeds, and the Cold Worriers, who wanted to wait for the Big One down the road. I will focus on these two arguments because they essentially capture what actually happened across the nineties. In effect, the Pentagon split the difference between the two opposing visions, buying the military favored by the Cold Worriers while trying to manage the world in the manner advocated by the Transitioneers.

Because the Transitioneers wanted to manage the messy world as they found it, they argued that America needed a force with lots of platforms (e.g., ships, aircraft, personnel vehicles). This is basically what happened across the 1990s: the U.S. military was involved with operations all over the Gap, often engaging in multiple situations at the same time. If the Transitioneer advice had been followed, the Pentagon would have bought high numbers of relatively cheap platforms, or ships and aircraft full of technology we already had and therefore did not have to spend a lot of money developing. Could we have spent less on technology? Yes, because the opponents we faced in all these lesser includeds were not of the high-end variety we associated with the Big One. Somalia was a quagmire, all right, but it was not World War III in terms of technology requirements.

In contrast to that particular vision, the Cold Worriers argued that America needed a force that emphasized high tech above all else as the key to staying prepared for the Big One. Because all that high technology is supremely expensive, you needed to sacrifice *numbers* of platforms for *quality* of platforms. You would end up with fewer ships and aircraft, or a smaller force structure, but your military force would rock 'n' roll like nobody else's on the planet.

Now, those are two very different choices, so the Pentagon split the difference: buying the Cold Worrier force but operating it according to the Transitioneers' code. By building one sort of military for some imagined future while operating another sort of military in the here and now, the Pentagon stressed itself out far more than the Clinton Administration, Congress, or "global chaos" ever could.

More than once in the mid-1990s, I had the opportunity to brief senior admirals in charge of force-structure planning, and I was quite blunt in my diagnosis that they were buying one navy and operating another. Their response carried the ring of bureaucratic fatalism: "You're absolutely right, Dr. Barnett. Can you come back next year and remind us again?"

Why did the Pentagon feel it had to argue for the high-tech strategy even as it put the squeeze on the number of platforms and personnel so desperately needed to manage this messy world? The military knew that it was still running itself largely on an industrial-era model that said you defeated your opponents by overwhelming them with stuff (ships, aircraft, tanks, bombs, etc.). But the military also realized that this type of warfare was disappearing, because great powers, including the United States, simply could not afford that sort of massive military establishment anymore.

It is awfully hard to argue against the U.S. military embracing new technologies as they emerge, because we all want our forces to be the best equipped in the world—that is how we win. But the trade-off with numbers is no small matter, either, especially if it meant—as it did across the 1990s—that our military was stretched hard to respond to all the lesser includeds the White House chose to engage. So it was not a case of the Pentagon ignoring either the present or the long-term future but of its trying too hard to cover both bases—albeit in different ways. In effect, by trying to prepare for the long run while simultaneously managing so much in the here and now, it was the mid-term that got lost in the shuffle. Of course, the mid-term always gets lost in strategic planning, which itself represents a constant struggle to disengage yourself sufficiently from the here and now to prepare adequately for things beyond the foreseeable future.

But if one remembers back to Manthorpe's Curve, it was that mid-term outlook where all those lesser includeds came closest to matching the threat from the peer competitor—as Russia continued its collapse and China continued its rise. To listen to the Cold Worriers, there was simply no chance all those lesser includeds would ever replace the fabled "near-peer competitor" as a worthy target for a "transformed," or next-generation, U.S. military. I mean, all this sexy, high-tech military capability that we were buying across the nineties really needed a sexy, high-tech enemy to fight against, right? Absolutely, said the Cold Worriers, and if Russia looked more feeble as the decade unfolded, then, damn it, we would make do with China.

When China and the U.S. Navy seemed to square off during what became known as the Taiwan Straits crisis of 1996, the Cold Worriers fell in love at first sight. China provided them everything they needed: an emerging great power that was building up its military for what looked suspiciously like an anti-access asymmetrical strategy for an invasion of Taiwan—a key ally of the United States that logically fell within the purview of our national interests. Best yet, China's military buildup was relatively slow, meaning Cold Worriers could make their case for transforming the U.S. military *ad infinitum,* because we would always need to stay one step ahead of those tricky Communists.

Talk about old times!

The only problem with this whole approach was that China spent the same decade joining the global economy, sucking up foreign direct investment from Europe, Japan, and the United States, and rapidly becoming one of America's biggest trade partners and the largest source of its trade deficit. I mean, for a future "near-peer competitor," this was almost unseemly. Didn't Beijing realize they were supposed to be our strategic opponent down the road? If they weren't careful, they were going to screw it up faster than the Russians did!

As the new Bush Administration entered office in 2001, the schizophrenic atmosphere of the Pentagon's strategic planning process was heading for a breaking point, or at least a complete loss of credibility. We were buying this fabulous "transformational" force for our distant-but-splendid conflict with China, which instead kept insisting on integrating its economy with ours, while at the same time our military seemed stretched around the planet, dealing with all these lesser includeds. The result was like having our cake, but putting it in the freezer to eat—maybe, just maybe—in a couple of decades. What suffered in the meantime? Our military personnel, especially in the National Guard and Reserves. These long overseas deployments represented a fundamental renegotiation of the Pentagon's contract with its own personnel—in effect, a greater workload for the same pay.

This misalignment of strategic vision and strategic environment was turning brother against brother inside the Pentagon in the second Clinton Administration. Simply put, there was not enough money to go around for all the services to pursue transformation (read, lots of new, high-end platforms), plus engage in all these overseas operations. Something had to give, and without a great single enemy to point at, that something was not going to be the defense budget's top line.

So the services did what they always do in times of peace: they turned on each other. The Air Force wanted transformation in the worst way, because they worship technology above all. Naturally, the fighter jocks felt the best way to advance their cause was for the Pentagon to shortchange the Army, which—after all—was not really needed in a world where smart bombs alone won entire wars. Of course, the Army is pretty nice to have around once you have decapitated that rogue leadership and end up having to run a country, as we found out in Iraq. Similar tensions were brewing both within the Navy itself (carriers versus the rest of the fleet) and between the Navy and the Marines.

The upshot of all this interservice competition was a heightening of the Pentagon's desire to trump up the Chinese threat, because arguing that the Big One was being neglected was the tried-and-true method to get Congress to plus-up the budget. It also increased arguments within the Pentagon to withdraw from trying to manage the world. In many ways, the military spent the second half of the 1990s waiting out the Clinton Administration, openly voicing the assumption that a return of the Republicans would mean less nation building and more budget for high-tech acquisitions, and George W. Bush was sending all the right signals as he geared up his run for the presidency.

As the Clinton Administration came to a close, this insiders' debate over short-term responsibilities versus long-term requirements had not changed much from the arguments I witnessed during the Department of Navy's effort to define the future a decade earlier, except that the participants now spoke in updated tongues. The Cold Worriers now spoke the complex language of "network-centric warfare," or the notion that the rise of computing technology now made communication networks the locus around which all operational planning would revolve, as opposed to the military's "platform-centric" past, in which we developed doctrine around the dominant ships, aircraft, and heavy armor in our arsenal. Naturally, all this high-tech focus on digital power was going to cost plenty, so the basic tune had not changed (we need a high-end opponent to plan against), even if the lyrics had (we will overwhelm *him* with information dominance!).

Meanwhile, the Transitioneers, who had no desire to retreat from the world but instead sought to manage it day in and day out, were condemned to a sort of pig Latin known as Military Operations Other Than War, or MOOTW (pronounced "moo-twah"). In the macho world of the military, it wasn't difficult to see who would lose this doctrinal fight: obviously the guy who's only talking about things "other than war." Who, after all, joins the military to do things other than war? I mean, isn't that called the Peace Corps?

As the 1990s came to a close, the split in the Pentagon between those who wanted to focus on the high-tech wars of the future and those who were stuck wrangling the lesser includeds of today was widening to the point where, if some solution was not soon found, the military's strategic planning process would collapse under the weight of all the contradictions. Inside the Pentagon, this much-feared crash was called the "coming train wreck" between "future requirements" and "current operational realities." Everyone knew it was just around the corner, but the only thing that could break the bureaucratic logjam was a significant defeat at the hands of an enemy, or something that would throw all the conventional wisdom and the rule set it generates right out the window.

The terrorist attacks of 9/11 were just such a defeat. That terrible day did more than just bring Americans together, it effectively healed the rift between the Pentagon's competing strategic visions. It did so by pulling all those advocates of transformation out of the clouds and back down to the earth, telling them that if their dreams of future warfare made sense for some distant "near-peer competitor," then they had better decide what is ready *now* for this global war on terrorism. As Secretary of Defense Donald Rumsfeld declared in the fall of 2001, the 9/11 attacks provided the Pentagon with a new "sense of urgency" regarding a transformation that "cannot wait." It was not simply that a new Big One had been found, the concept itself had been completely redefined. Overnight, China dropped off the radar, to be replaced by terrorist groups "with global reach" and any rogue nation suspected of supporting them.

But if Rumsfeld saw transformation energized by 9/11, by the spring of 2002 plenty of other reformers were already declaring it a "casualty of 9/11." In a well-read *New York Times Magazine* article, Bill Keller declared that the first post-9/11 defense budget "drenches all the old status-quo programs that keep the military pretty much the way it is." In effect, 9/11 signaled transformation's death knell, because it allowed the Pentagon to put off the tough budgetary choices between long-term desires and near-term realities. The flaw in that logic was the assumption that the budgetary plus-up for this war on terrorism would be permanent, when in reality there will never be enough money to put off these difficult choices, especially with the return of gargantuan federal deficits.

On the contrary, this war on terrorism only sharpened the budgetary struggle between the advocates of transformation and the practitioners of MOOTW, because it called in the former's promise to "do more with less" while elevating the latter from doctrinal stepchild to grand strategy. As America is learning in this global war on terrorism, it is one thing to topple the Taliban or Saddam Hussein with our highly lethal, highly maneuverable force, but quite another to actually transform those battered societies into something better—to reconnect them to the larger, globalizing world outside. As *Washington Post* columnist David Ignatius quickly pointed out, that sort of social transformation is an up-close-and-personal effort, requiring not just lots of boots on the ground but well-trained, well-versed, and well-motivated boots on the ground. September 11 did not merely substitute al Qaeda for China, it knocked the concept of the Big One right off its doctrinal pedestal. The rise of the lesser includeds was complete, and new military rule sets were in the making.

My claim that 9/11 elevated Military Operations Other Than War to grand strategy is something I know many national security strategists will vehemently deny. Plenty will argue that America is still better off focusing on China as our inevitable opponent in the future Big One, and if that scenario becomes politically unpalatable in the new security era, we should simply invent someone else. Their dogmatic contention is that if the United States becomes obsessed with managing this messy "empire," we will commit the same mistake the Romans and the British made during their imperial heyday: we will focus so much on administering our system that we will miss the great threat rising in the distance.

It is an interesting argument, but ultimately a false dichotomy. As author Max Boot points out in his recent history of America's "small wars," Britain did not lose its empire for simply trying to run it well, but because it was forced to fight two world wars in rapid succession. America will not lose globalization for simply trying too hard to facilitate its advance, but rather by administering the global security system so badly that emerging economic superpowers like China feel they have no choice but to redirect resources desperately needed for economic development toward a senseless military confrontation with us.

The pragmatic advocates for transformation realize that the Global War on Terrorism, or GWOT, has become a permanent fixture in Washington's ongoing budget debates. But the GWOT is far more than just a meal ticket, for this struggle must lead to a consensus within the Pentagon that a never-ending search for the Big One cannot be allowed to blind us to changes in the strategic environment, much less the crucial military tasks they generate. The future worth creating is the globalization that is truly global. That is the Big One we seek, and if it takes a Pentagon obsessed with mastering a universe of messy lesser includeds, then I say, let the real transformation begin.

Chapter 3

DISCONNECTEDNESS DEFINES DANGER

IF THE 1990S WITNESSED the death of the old rule sets in international security, none of the new ones seemed readily apparent inside the Pentagon as the century came to a close. The U.S. military continued to buy one sort of military while operating another, planning for war strictly within the context of war. "Transformation," or the push to modernize the U.S. military for future threats, was more rhetoric than reality. Old Cold War habits died hard, if at all. Defense contractors continued to offer their big-ticket wares for great-power war, declaring with complete confidence that these high-tech ships, aircraft, and tanks were wholly suited for the strategic environment at hand.

> DEFENSE CONTRACTOR: This billion-dollar platform is exactly what the U.S. military needs for the future!
> PENTAGON OFFICIAL: How can we be sure?
> DEFENSE CONTRACTOR: Because this is exactly what we're selling right now!

During the second Clinton Administration, I ran across this mock "personals ad" taped to a wall in a Pentagon office:

ENEMY WANTED

Mature North American Superpower seeks hostile partner for arms-racing, Third World conflicts, and general antagonism. Must be sufficiently menacing to convince Congress of military financial requirements. Nuclear capability is preferred; however, nonnuclear candidates possessing significant bio-chemical warfare resources will be considered. Send note with pictures of fleet and air squadrons to:

CHAIRMAN JOINT CHIEFS OF STAFF

THE PENTAGON

WASHINGTON, DC

UNITED STATES OF AMERICA

The rise of the lesser includeds found few, if any champions inside the Pentagon as the new century dawned. Military Operations Other Than War, where later almost all of the "global war on terrorism" would be found, remained a bastard doctrine. Meanwhile, the incoming Bush Administration seemed hell-bent on depicting China as the rising near-peer threat—the new measuring stick for great-power war. The emerging strategic environment I was charting in my New Rule Sets Project with Cantor Fitzgerald could not be found on any maps being used in the Pentagon in 2001. Instead, the Defense Department rank and file were told by our new civilian masters that there would be no nation building on their watch, no wasting of U.S. forces in meaningless peacekeeping operations in remote countries, and no Third World quagmires of any sort. America would focus on the "big pieces" in the security environment. The Pentagon's new map looked an awful lot like the old one.

I began drawing my new map for the Pentagon in the mid-1990s—1996, to be exact. At that point, I was so unhappy with the state of strategic planning within the Pentagon that I began generating "alternative global futures," or scenarios of future international security environments based *solely* on the premise that the world was progressively integrating itself economically. I tried to insert these ideas into a prominent "strategic vision" study that the

Center for Naval Analyses was conducting for the commander of U.S. naval forces in Europe, but they were summarily rejected by the senior project director as being so much globaloney. I was told, "This isn't a study about global economics, but about the future security environment."

Nonetheless, I continued to work on these strategic concepts on my own time, eventually generating a huge PowerPoint briefing that I offered to anyone who would listen. Lacking an official Pentagon sponsor for the work, I finally found refuge under my longtime mentor, Hank Gaffney, who let me bill my hours as a "self-initiated study" as long as I spent most of my time toiling on officially sponsored research projects. That was fairly embarrassing for someone who prides himself on always having ideas that sell, but either you believe in the material or you don't, and I did.

My strategic vision centered on a best-case scenario in which North America, South America, Europe, and most of Asia came together in a vast, nearly global economy, with only Central Asia, the Middle East, and Africa trapped on the outside, noses pressed to the glass. Lacking a clear great-power enemy in this scenario, I posited that radical Islam itself would ultimately be labeled the main threat. Intuitively, I knew this was a poor sales job on my part, because the Islamic world would remain far too fractured to constitute a coherent threat. Simply put, my enemy just wasn't "sexy" enough. Still, I did not want to give up on the brief, because it felt like my best work, if only I could understand its true ordering principle, which I was pretty sure was not radical Islam but something larger.

I spent the next half-decade figuring out just what that larger ordering principle was, and in the process I finally found my version of the Manthorpe slide. This chapter is devoted to explaining how that *eureka* moment ultimately came about, or how I came to draw the Pentagon's new map.

Whatever happened to that original brief, you ask? I still use it. In fact, it became the basis for an elective course recently offered at the Naval War College called "Thinking Systematically About Alternative Global Futures." In the class, I teach the next generation of military leaders that they must abandon the Pentagon's tendency to view the world "vertically" through the lens of intermittent wars ("Look, another bolt from the blue!"). Instead, they need to think more "horizontally," seeing history for what it was and the future for what it will be: the periodic ebb and flow of economic globalization. In my mind, this is how you place war within the context of everything else.

How I Learned to Think Horizontally

When I left Harvard in the summer of 1990 with my spanking-new Ph.D. from the Government Department, I was pretty sure I had all the intellectual tools to cut it as a policy analyst in Washington, D.C. I knew a lot of my fellow students and professors looked unfavorably on the choice, believing it was quite a step down from a career in academia, but I was eager to find out how things worked in the real world.

Washington, D.C., is a lot different from rural Wisconsin, where I grew up. In Wisconsin, people ask you what you do because they are really interested and—if possible—they would like to help you get ahead in life. But in Washington, people ask you what you do because they want to check your status relative to theirs, and getting down your particulars proves handy if they ever need to bring you down a peg or two.

Naturally, career types there will tell you what a wonderful place the capital is, and how it is full of such diversity ("We have both kinds of people here—Democrats and Republicans!"), but let me put it to you this way: it is very hard to live in a society built entirely around your most aggressive personality traits. Sometimes I felt like I was Dr. Jekyll at home and Mr. Hyde at work, with my hellacious morning commute serving as my daily potion.

What always disturbed me about my graduate years at Harvard was how as students we spent most of our time in seminars trashing all the giants in the field. It always reminded me of the scene in the movie *The Princess Bride,* in which the despicable villain, Vizzini, played by Wallace Shawn, brags of his intelligence by exclaiming, "Have you ever heard of Plato? Aristotle? Socrates? *Morons!*"

Harvard, as it happens, is the perfect finishing school when it comes to working for the government. Because in Washington, the only way to stand out when you are surrounded by thousands of people just like you is to tear down their ideas. The problem is, in that vision-hostile environment it is almost impossible to come up with any stories with happy endings—as I like to call strategic visions. That is because no one in Washington is really interested in your happy ending; all they obsess about is preventing what they are certain will be the disastrous outcome of your ill-conceived plan. So if you want to get ahead or get noticed, you learn to excel at this pack-dog mentality, and you bury whatever dreams you had of proposing something different or better. This is why we do not have any real leaders in Washington anymore, just investigations.

I got my job at the Center for Naval Analyses the old-fashioned way: I convinced an older version of myself that I was a younger version of him. It was pretty easy actually: he had gone to Harvard as an undergraduate, and I had as a graduate student. He had had my old boss, Professor Adam Ulam, as his government tutor at Eliot House, and I had been a government tutor at Eliot House. He had written his dissertation on West Africa, and mine had involved Soviet-bloc relations with Southern Africa. He was someone who thrived on generating grand strategic visions, but subordinated that love by and large to his amazing skill at dissecting the flaccid reasoning of Pentagon strategists, and I . . . was smart enough to spend the bulk of my eight years at CNA learning everything I could from the man. Eventually, of course, I would have had to use that knowledge to discredit him thoroughly and steal his job from him, but I took the high road and left Washington for the Naval War College, and so we have remained good friends.

Henry H. Gaffney Jr., or Hank, as everyone calls him, is probably the smartest man alive when it comes to understanding how the

Pentagon and national security decision making actually work. But what really marks Hank as unique in the defense community is the combination of his wide-ranging but detailed knowledge of security issues, his innate ability to ferret out weak assumptions in strategic logic, and his crankiness and lack of respect for authority. It is his encyclopedic knowledge of both global security issues and Pentagon history that allows Hank to spin off dozens of brilliant, big-picture observations about U.S. national security planning every time he stands up to give one of his own infamous briefs, which, frankly, feature such complex conceptual visuals that you could spend a lifetime trying to figure out what they all mean.

During my eight years in Washington, Hank Gaffney and I did a lot of research together and coauthored a number of significant reports, and most of the big ideas I have hatched over my career either began in or were intimately shaped by my time with him. But what Hank really taught me was how to think horizontally. By that I mean thinking broadly across subject matters versus drilling down deep into a particular subject, which I call vertical thinking. In both the Pentagon and Washington in general, the system of debates awards points almost exclusively to those who think vertically, because intense subject-matter expertise allows you to poke holes in everyone else's thinking. Inside the Beltway, vertical thinkers are expert at telling why something will never succeed, and little else. Horizontal thinkers tend to be the exact opposite. They often argue by analogy and are quick to borrow concepts from other fields. They are usually synergists, meaning they combine disparate concepts in new and unusual combinations. For example, in my Ph.D. dissertation I borrowed from the field of interpersonal psychology to explain how the relative "weakling" Romania stood up to Soviet bullying tactics within the Warsaw Treaty Organization, ultimately achieving a certain degree of foreign policy independence.

The most important advantage of horizontal thinking is the ability to see a future unfolding in realistic stages, never becoming too invested in any one particular pathway. Most of what passes for strategic planning in the Pentagon involves the acquisition (or buying) of future technologies in the form of weapons systems and platforms (e.g., ships, aircraft, tanks). Within those narrow confines, most vertical thinkers do well. But these same vertical thinkers are incapable of making similar forecasts about the messy world lying outside the Pentagon. Here their tendency to define the future as straight-line projections of current trends consistently betrays them, because you can never mechanistically extrapolate tomorrow from today.

Change in that real world outside the Pentagon's five-year planning cycles is far from linear. Instead, it arrives in irregular clumps, like growth spurts in a teenager. Moreover, when tipping points are reached in any historical process, previously incremental rates of change can quickly segue into profound transformations. My daughter Emily is currently twelve years old. In 2016, she will be twice as old as she is today, but she will not automatically be twice as smart, or twice as tall, or twice as lovable. She will be something else altogether, and her journey from preteen to woman will feature more zigzags than this father can possibly anticipate from his current perspective. I can project a range of pathways for her life's unfolding, but if I become unduly fixated on one particular downstream outcome (e.g., a Ph.D. from Harvard in political science by 2020), I could end up very disappointed—even shocked—at this seemingly unanticipated turn of events!

Such a mechanistic approach to predicting the future would seem ludicrous when discussing an entity as complex as a teenage girl, and yet the Pentagon displays the same tendency time and time again with far more complex entities, such as China. In twelve years, China's economy may well be twice as large as it is today, but does that mean China will automatically be twice as "powerful"? Twice as "Communist"? Twice the "threat"? Sounds nutty, doesn't it? Yet you can discern this logic throughout a lot of the Pentagon's long-range projections concerning China, as if you can simply transport today's China to some point in the future where all capacities are somehow "doubled" and yet the country's political-military establishment remains essentially unchanged.

Most vertical thinkers hate having to deal with that sort of real-world messiness. They like their models to be clean, so they "control" for that sort of messiness, or declare those sorts of factors to be extraneous to their model and thus simply delete them from their thinking. This is why, when vertical thinkers engage in strategic planning outside of the technical fields in which they are both comfortable and competent, they tend to jump right to the punch line. By that I mean, when they think about future scenarios for the global security environment, they need a scary future point that satisfies all their needs and culminates logically in their advocating some fabulous new weapon or platform technology. One of their great tricks for doing this is what I call the "absurdly isolated conflict scenario." These are used all the time to justify amazing force levels (e.g., number of ships in a particular category) that have almost nothing to do with reality.

My all-time favorite in this regard was a Navy brief I saw in the mid-1990s that projected how many surface combatants (noncarrier ships with warfighting capabilities) the Pentagon would need twenty years down the road. The scenario chosen was a rerun of the start of the Korean War. Okay, fair enough. But then the briefer started adding on absurdly isolating characteristics, such as having the entire Army, Air Force, and Marine Corps simultaneously involved with another distant war. Then the briefer posited that the United States would have—by that future date—almost completely eliminated its ground forces within South Korea. Moreover, we would have no allies to help us deflect the North Korea invasion—none whatsoever. Plus, the Navy would have no carriers or submarines in the region at the time of the invasion, so only surface combatants would be used to help South Korea, which naturally had let its own military decline dramatically in the meantime, to fend off a huge, amazingly high-tech invasion force streaming over the border from North Korea. Guess what the end result of the analysis was. The U.S. Navy *clearly* needed almost twice the number of surface combatants as the budgeters projected the Navy could afford. The analysis was impeccable in terms of the internal logic of the scenario itself. The ludicrous part was imagining a pathway that led America to this simply unbelievable point in future history.

This type of thinking also explains how budgetary train wrecks are preprogrammed into the Pentagon's long-range acquisition plans. By that I mean it is impossible—politically and economically—to both retire the required numbers and types of platforms and build the required numbers and types of platforms in a year-to-year fashion to actually make the desired force structure appear by the projected date. This is an acute consequence of vertical thinking applied to fundamentally horizontal processes.

The Pentagon's penchant for applying vertical thinking to force structure planning reflects the harsh realities of trying to plan against downstream threats, or the Big One mentality too many strategists still retain from the Cold War. For example, it takes several years to build a modern aircraft carrier, and that ship's life may span more than half a century. To justify that sort of expenditure, you need to project an awfully big threat deep into the future. The more you do that, budget cycle after budget cycle, the more that sketchy forecast takes on the air of an immutable truth. After a while, it is simply so engrained in the budgetary system that not even an event like 9/11 can easily dislodge it. If you don't believe me, check out the Pentagon's current long-range budgetary planning document, known as the POM (for Program Objective Memorandum). If you look deeply enough, you will see China looming throughout as the dominant planning assumption.

What is the horizontal alternative to such thinking? The best example would be "evolutionary acquisition" or "spiral development" of military technologies. In this approach, new capabilities are introduced to the force prior to their perfection, thus giving the military personnel in the field opportunities for testing and experimentation. Improvements are achieved in an iterative fashion, allowing for adaptation over time to changes in the strategic environment. In theory, this is how the Defense Department currently acquires all its new capabilities, but the focus in these efforts is not so much on staying responsive to a changing global security environment as in speeding up the time between the creation of a new technology and its insertion into the field of battle. In effect, horizontal thinking is currently applied to the scheduling of individual technologies, but it is not applied to strategic planning as a whole, where the Pentagon still displays the need for placing big bets on singularly large future threats.

This bias for vertical thinking is especially crucial in determining how the Pentagon thinks about conflict scenarios, because rather than concentrating on how to manage complex, real-world situations as they unfold, Pentagon strategists typically want to bypass all that mess and jump right to the punch line—the onset of the war. This bias is bad in a number of ways. First, it shortchanges the role of the military in crisis management, or the avoidance of war. Second, it short-circuits planning on what comes after the war—a lesson we learned yet again in post-Saddam Iraq. But most important, it absurdly isolates the warfighting scenarios, leading to war planning that focuses on the war and little else.

But don't walk away with the impression that only the Pentagon is to blame for this state of affairs. In many ways, the ultimate fault lies with Congress and their insistence on having their say—every year—on almost every single program within the defense budget. So if Congress says yes to a five-year program in year one, only to change its mind later, you can hardly fault the Pentagon's lack of strategic planning. In some ways, you could say the Pentagon does its level best to plan horizontally in a vertically challenged budgetary environment imposed on it by the Hill.

Perhaps the best way to describe the limiting effect that vertical thinking has on strategic planning is to show how it prevented the Pentagon from both recognizing and embracing the strategic security environment that has emerged in the globalization era. I like to tell this story in terms of my early training as a political-military analyst on how to think about strategic surprise.

When I came to CNA at the beginning of the 1990s, I was taught how to think about strategic surprise in terms of what I like to call the classic Cold War vertical scenario. This scenario had several distinct characteristics. First, it always unfolded with lightning speed, meaning there was almost no effective warning time about this "bolt from the blue." Second, in a balance-of-power world like the Cold War, we knew beforehand both who our enemies were and who our allies were, which was quite convenient. Third, because we war-gamed this scenario countless times, we were able to preprogram our operational response, meaning little adaptive planning was required. Fourth, the scenario unfolded like a single hand of poker, meaning you placed your bet and then laid down your cards, allowing for no evolution in strategy and no switching sides during the conflict. Finally, the world stood still until the war was over, and then the winners got to divide the spoils.

What you should recognize in this scenario is basically a highly idealized rendering of World War I and World War II, and by that I mean all the complicating factors have been removed to make the modeling of the conflict more "robust"—which is Pentagon code for "more detached from reality." The two classic scenarios of this genre were the Soviets streaming through the Fulda Gap in Germany and triggering World War III, and the "Mini-Me" version, where North Korea pours across the demilitarized zone into Seoul.

Now, my problem with this education was that it did not seem to prepare me at all for the post–Cold War era—go figure! That is because I never actually experienced this sort of scenario, not even in Iraq's invasion of Kuwait, which triggered our "rapid response" called *Desert Storm* a leisurely six months later. What I did experience across the 1990s was cognitive dissonance, meaning I was taught to expect one thing and kept encountering something completely different. In short, the post–Cold War era did not compute.

Instead of that classic vertical scenario, what the 1990s looked like was more a collection of messy situations that, once they had lured the United States into some sort of military response, seemed to drag on endlessly. Most seemed like the sort of situation where you discover some rotted wood along the trim of your house, and so, thinking you can handle it yourself, you tear off the damaged piece and get to work. Six months later when the contractor finally hands you that staggering bill, you are the proud owner of an entirely new roof. Of course, as you describe the situation later to friends and family, the entire cost came as a complete shock to you— out of nowhere! When in reality, your vertical scenario had been in the works for years. You simply were not paying any attention.

The Pentagon is a lot like that, primarily because it did the right thing across the Cold War and worried obsessively about a vertical scenario that would have marked The End of the World As We Know It (TEOTWAWKI, for the uninitiated). Speaking as one small part of humanity that survived the Cold War, I have no argument with that approach. But the legacy of that focus on strategic surprise is pretty much what guarantees America will suffer a 9/11-like shock to the system now and then, unless we start thinking more horizontally and—by doing so—listen better to what the strategic security environment is trying to tell us.

Hank Gaffney taught me how to put my natural inclination for horizontal thinking to good use in diagnosing security situations in the world around me. Hank used to present these wildly complex vugraphs in the 1990s that displayed a number of bad security situations around the world as horizontal scenarios, meaning he would measure the "pain" or "instability" in any situation and plot it out over time as it rose and fell—"peaks and valleys," he would call them. His argument was that the Pentagon tended to ignore these situations until they reached some critical point where they magically tripped our "national interest" alarm, and then the White House would call over to the Pentagon and say, "*Do something about that now!*" Of course, the Pentagon would respond with complete shock: How could anyone have predicted this? Then the military would rapidly muster an interventionary force and respond to the "crisis," afterward bragging that it handled the situation with virtually no warning time.

It was those vugraphs that eventually pushed me to defining what I call the Post–Cold War Horizontal Scenario, which I describe as follows: First, there is no clear beginning or end to the conflict, meaning it feels as if it has been around forever and that it will continue well past our lifetimes. Think about the Middle East. When exactly did the hostilities start there? Was it the late 1980s or the early 1970s? Or was it when Israel was created in 1948? Or how about the Crusades eight centuries ago? And exactly how much longer will we be hearing about a "forthcoming" Middle East peace plan? Expect one anytime soon?

A second characteristic of these horizontal scenarios is that the definition of the enemy changes over time. When the United States went into Somalia in late 1992, at first the enemy was the chaos that prevented relief workers from dealing with the famine. Then it became the lack of a functioning central state. Then it became all those warlords running around the place. Then we decided it was one warlord who was the real problem. Then we suffered more casualties in a single day since Vietnam and—presto!—we decided the United Nations was the problem and we got the hell out of that Wild West shooting gallery.

Another annoying feature of these scenarios is the revolving cast of allies, who seem to enter and exit our military coalitions like it's festival seating or something. I am not just referring to the French here, either. Countries seem to switch sides these days at the drop of a hat—or perhaps just a hint. Think about our secretaries of state jetting around the world trying to get all sorts of small powers to subscribe to our latest public offering, promising this or that aid package in return. What kind of "imperialist power" has to go around begging every little country sitting on the UN Security Council to let it—*pretty please*—invade some country and topple its horrible leader that nobody likes? Does that seem a dignified way to run a world empire?

Unlike the classic vertical scenario, these horizontal ones feature loads of adaptive planning for the military. Rather than one giant battle, it is strike after skirmish after ambush after . . . Planning is done on the fly. It is not chess but something closer to soccer. The ball is always moving, and substitutions are constantly changing the composition of both your team and your enemy's. But worse still, your political leadership's definition of the "problem" you are trying to solve keeps changing, making your attempts to keep score almost meaningless. You want to know what today's definition of the problem is? Try reading the op-ed pages; you will have plenty to choose from.

Probably the most unpleasant aspect of these post–Cold War horizontal scenarios was the sense of irrelevance they bestowed on the U.S. military. In many ways, the 1990s seemed like one unending string of babysitting jobs that always placed the military on the margins of what for the rest of the world seemed like a decade of momentous positive change. So what did the Pentagon do during the go-go nineties? It periodically tussled with *Monty Python*'s Black Knight, Slobodan Milosevic, systematically dismembering his body politic as he idiotically taunted us to fight on. We also spent a dozen years keeping Saddam in the box defined by his northern and southern no-fly zones.

Did we respond to the mini-holocaust raging in Central Africa? Not really. That one was simply too far away from friends that mattered, like Saudi Arabia and Israel in the Middle East or our NATO allies in Europe.

Actually, it was the spread of globalization itself that was the dominant horizontal scenario of the 1990s. Where it extended and connectivity grew between any national economy and the global economy, security rule sets seemed to likewise expand. But where globalization did not effectively take root, there the security rule sets seemed thinner and—in some sad cases like Central Africa—completely absent. But if you were handicapped by the typical Pentagon mind-set of focusing strictly on downstream, potentially juicy vertical scenarios, globalization's growth across the nineties slipped under your strategic radar, quietly reshaping the international security landscape America faces today.

Hank Gaffney's biggest gift to me was helping me recognize and understand such horizontal scenarios and—by doing so—providing me a crucial tool to map out the strategic landscape that slowly came into focus across the 1990s. I stopped scanning the strategic horizon looking for "near-peer competitors" capable of delivering the "bolt from the blue" that would trigger the Big One. Instead, I began to see the global security environment for what it really was, a complex web of almost unlimited horizontal scenarios that all required some level of understanding if I was ever going to fashion a comprehensive vision of America's role in securing global peace.

MAPPING GLOBALIZATION'S FRONTIER

If we think of globalization as the ultimate horizontal scenario, then we immediately move beyond the simplistic notion that globalization is a binary outcome—*first it was not there, and then it was*. Globalization is not a *yes* or *no*, despite the all-encompassing outcome suggested by its name (by definition, globalization must be everywhere, right?). Rather, globalization is a process, a pathway, a *what* combined with a *where*. Understanding where globalization has taken root and where it has not is the first step toward mapping the international security environment of the twenty-first century. For the military, the importance of this demarcation cannot be overstated. It is like the difference between land and water, jungle and desert, mountains and grasslands. Knowing where globalization begins and ends essentially defines the U.S. military's expeditionary theater. It tells us where we will go and why. It tells us what we will find when we get there, and what we must do to achieve victory in warfare.

I will propose a new map of the world that captures this challenge and the threats it poses. It will not be an East-West map. It will not be a North-South map. It will be a map that shows you which regions are *functioning* within globalization's expanding web of connectivity and which remain fundamentally *disconnected* from that process. It will show you that where globalization has spread, there you will find stable governments that neither require our periodic military interventions nor warrant our consideration as threats.

But look beyond globalization's frontier, and there you will find the failed states that command our attention, the rogue states that demand our vigilance, and the endemic conflicts that fuel the terror we now recognize as the dominant threat not just to America's future security but to globalization's continued advance.

Before I can draw this map in full, though, I need to define what I mean by globalization's spread. To do that, I must describe more fully what I mean by globalization's Functioning Core, or those regions that are progressively integrating their national economies into the world economy.

Globalization is a condition defined by mutually assured dependence. To globalize your economy and your society, you must accept that the world will reshape your future far more than you can possibly hope to influence the world in return. The continuity of the past, where son followed father in occupation for generations, will in most cases end with callous disregard for tradition. Moreover, if you globalize you will import from that world outside far more than you can possibly offer in return. While your culture will be added to globalization's ever-evolving mosaic, your society will—in return—be challenged to adapt to an amazing array of content flows (e.g., ideas about the role of women, free speech, "proper" education) that come with globalization's connectivity. The same will hold true for the goods and services you can offer the world, which will pale in comparison with all the products that will flood your markets, challenging your producers and firms to adapt to a new competitive landscape or die. Most important, while your influence regarding global rule sets will be small, globalization's influence regarding your internal rule sets will be enormous. In fact, your importation and adoption of these global rule sets will be the main price you pay for leaving your disconnectedness behind.

Sound incredibly difficult? It is. Americans tend to forget how difficult this is because most of the hardest compromises we made in building this country now seem far behind us—the Civil War, universal suffrage, civil rights. The reason Americans are so unconsciously comfortable with the emerging global rule sets is that they so intimately reflect what we have become—a multicultural free-market economy whose minimal rule sets (telling us what we cannot do, not what we must do) allow for maximum individual freedom to go where we want, live where we want, and conduct our lives how we want. Of course, when you extend that rule set to the entire planet, you are going to find yourself dealing with a lot of issues you thought you would never encounter—again. So the temptation is great to simply throw up our hands and exclaim, "We will never understand those people!" When in reality, understanding them requires us—in most instances—simply to look into our past and remember ourselves.

For example, America's greatest outbursts of nationalism have typically occurred during periods of increased interaction with the outside world (think of World War II and the early Cold War years). When global events have drawn us out of our natural inclination toward isolationism, we don't just engage the world, we *embrace* it with a messianic fervor that other states often find quite disturbing. But such nationalism is, in many ways, a natural response on the part of individuals to any society's growing connectivity with the outside world. That is why globalization's progressive advance will trigger more nationalism around the world, not less. This may seem counterintuitive, but as nations join the Core, expect their societies (especially their youth) to demand preservation of cultural identity. This is only natural and right, but we need to understand such nationalism for what it truly represents: not anti-Americanism per se, but a fear of lost identity. Globalization empowers the individual at the expense of the collective, and that very American transformation of culture is quite scary for traditional societies.

Americans often seem flabbergasted when those who oppose globalization around the world protest that it is "forced Americanization." We shouldn't be. Because we are furthest along in this grand experiment called the United States, and because that model of mutually assured dependence characterized by minimal rule sets greatly predates globalization's advance, we may well enjoy a lead in this historical process. But with that lead comes responsibility, for either we use our tremendous power as a nation to make globalization truly global, or we condemn some portion of humanity to an outsider status that will naturally morph—through pain and time—into a definition of the enemy. And once we have named our enemies, we will invariably wage war, unleashing the death and destruction that come with it.

Remembering that disconnectedness itself is the ultimate enemy, America can, by extending globalization in a fair and just manner, not only defeat the threats it faces today but eliminate in advance entire generations of threat that our children and grandchildren would otherwise face. In short, there is simply no possibility of keeping the threat "outside, over there" anymore. If we as a nation accept the logic of globalization's advance, our definition of *us* must include all of *them* who now feel left out of globalization's benefits, as well as the *them* who would employ all manner of violence to deny its advance. This historical process is neither forced assimilation nor the extension of empire, but the expansion of freedom first and foremost.

But expanding that freedom requires that we understand both its presence and its absence, and how globalization's frontier defines this age. Real freedom exists within defined rule sets that reduce life's uncertainties to the point where individuals can *efficiently* run their own lives, avoiding the tyrannies of extreme poverty, endemic violence, and talent-stifling political repression. A China, no longer trapped by the impoverishing inefficiencies of sustenance agriculture, *joins* globalization's growing Core. A South Korea, spared the inefficiency of having to be an armed camp thanks to American might, *joins* globalization's growing Core. An India, no longer defined by the mindless inefficiencies of a caste system, *joins* globalization's growing Core. In each instance, as entire populations are liberated from the debilitating inefficiencies that kept them largely disconnected from the integrating whole, not only does their freedom increase but ours does as well. For each time we expand globalization's Functioning Core, we expand for all those living within it the freedom of choice, movement, and expression.

So how do I define this Functioning Core?

First and foremost, a country or region is functioning within globalization if it accepts the connectivity and can handle the content flows associated with integrating one's national economy to the global economy. Most societies welcome globalization's connectivity, when they are able to attract it. But not every society can handle the content flows that come with all that connectivity, meaning all the ideas, products, services, mass media, and so forth that flow into the country as a result. How a society handles that content flow, and the behavior it engenders (both good and bad), depends largely on the nature of its legal rule sets. A country like the United States lets its people have virtually unlimited access to global content flows. If you behave badly on the basis of that access, we have a downstream legal system that will punish you—but only after the fact. Most traditional societies around the world prefer to maintain upstream controls over access to content. Such traditional societies emphasize censorship, or the denial of access to what is officially considered "bad" content. In a wide-open democracy like the United States, extremely little content is preemptively declared off-limits—child pornography and certain drugs being good examples. But in more traditional societies, the list can be quite long, and herein lies the destabilizing effect that globalization's connectivity can bring. If you are a young woman living in Iran and want to discuss sex, dating, and marriage, guess where you go? If you are one of the two million regular Internet users in that country, you probably log on to a Yahoo chat network at your local café and escape the mullahs' censorship.

My favorite example of this effect is what happened to Barbie, the toy doll for young girls, when she decided to launch her one-woman invasion of Iran. Barbie apparently infiltrated Iranian toy stores at some point in the 1990s, exploiting the retail networks of the global economy. Soon after, a government-backed children's agency labeled Barbie a "Trojan horse" for Western influence, complete with her revealing attire. Despite—or perhaps because of—this official warning, Barbie apparently proved too popular with young Iranian girls. Eventually, concerned local officials engineered a counterattack—the moon-faced Sara doll clad head to toe in an Islamic chador. But this officially approved anti-Barbie was not enough to stem Barbie's negative influence, and so orders went out to local police to detain Barbie wherever she was found. Barbie has become a doll on the run.

Another good example of how a country's fear of content often trumps its desire for connectivity was Nigeria's attempt to host the 2002 Miss World competition. This effort came about because Miss Nigeria was awarded the title in 2001, and national leaders wanted to capitalize on that achievement to showcase Nigeria's growing connectivity to the outside world. The outcome was a complete disaster, in large part because a major portion of Nigerian society simply could not handle the content flow associated with that event. In Nigeria's predominantly Muslim north, having a baby out of wedlock is enough to get a young woman sentenced to death by stoning, according to the strict Islamic law practiced there. Not surprisingly, many of the Miss World participants threatened to boycott the competition if it was held in Nigeria. But that was nothing compared with the rioting triggered in the north following a newspaper column that appeared in a Lagos-based daily. In it, the author made light of Muslim protests against the upcoming competition, and suggested that if the prophet Muhammad were alive today, he might well have taken one of the young beauties as a wife. By the time the wave of violence abated in the north, several dozen Christian churches had been burned to the ground and several hundred people lay dead in the streets. Soon after, the Miss World competition was moved to London, and Nigeria became just a bit more disconnected from the Functioning Core of globalization.

But most modernizing societies fall into the same category as China, which is wiring up its population so rapidly that it has sparked an Internet boomlet among international investors. China is of two minds regarding the Internet: it craves the connectivity, but it would also like to keep its billion-plus people under "mouse arrest." By that I mean deny them access to certain "bad" Web sites like "Playboy.com" or the search engine Google, where apparently it is quite easy to locate sites that criticize the Communist leadership. Who wins out in the end? I say, track the money. If China continues to attract foreign direct investment for its telecommunications infrastructure, then it will inevitably be a case of "build it and they will surf" wherever they damn well please.

A second way to describe a country or region as *functioning* is when it seeks to harmonize its internal rule sets with the emerging global rule of democracy, rule of law, and free markets. Naturally, we would like to see all three occurring at once, but significant movement on any front is more important than the lack of progress in the other two. That is because there is more than one way to skin this cat, and America should not be in the business of mandating any one approach above the other. The best approach is simply to let the locals decide where to start, because they will know best what is likely to succeed first.

Mikhail Gorbachev set in motion Russia's trajectory toward functioning status when he decided, as the last leader of the Soviet Union, to launch the political reform process known as glasnost, or "openness." He also launched an economic reform process called perestroika, or "restructuring," but this proved to have far less impact. In fact, his dream of saving the Soviet economy through perestroika was killed by glasnost, because the latter so undermined the Soviet political order that the country disbanded within half a decade. At that point, the economic reform of Russia began in earnest, but because the political "openness" preceded—and in some sense, precluded—the necessary reform of the legal system, the subsequent privatization of the vast Soviet-era economy unfolded under conditions of rule-set anarchy, where the powerful took what they wanted and the masses were effectively shut out. By the mid-1990s Russia was consistently described by Western observers as suffering from a "mafia-style" or "robber baron" capitalism, and capital flight out of the country proceeded apace. Then came President Vladimir Putin's push to create a "dictatorship of the law," and within a few years, Russia experienced its first net inflow of capital— in effect, Russian money coming home because it was now safe for it to do so.

Of course, that flow can and will reverse the minute investors lose confidence in the Kremlin's commitment to rule of law, as they did immediately following the Russian government's decision to investigate the giant oil firm Yukos and imprison its then-CEO, Mikhail Khodorkovsky, in 2003. Thus, the second-quarter capital inflow of almost $4 billion became a third-quarter outflow of almost $8 billion. But the Khodorkovsky affair is—in and of itself— an amazing expression of just how far Russia has come in a single generation. History may well judge it to constitute the biggest political crisis of Putin's presidency, and it has already turned "Russia's richest man" into a political figure in his own right. But this controversy likewise presages the inevitable rise of political power based on private wealth, and that development alone speaks volumes about the new rule sets that have already transformed Russia.

Thus, within an amazingly short time span of less than two decades, Russia effectively synchronized the bulk of its internal rule sets with that of globalization's emerging rule set. By doing so, Russia was transformed from America's number-one threat to a country deemed worthy of limited membership in NATO. Think about that for a minute. If I had come to you in 1985, the year of Gorbachev's ascendancy, and asked you what would have to happen for Russia to be able to join NATO twenty years hence, you probably would have replied, "World War III." Yet it has happened, not because we started building Star Wars and not because Ronald Reagan demanded that Moscow "tear down that wall." It happened because the Soviet Union's first great technocratic generation of leaders, exemplified by Gorbachev, saw a system that was being left behind by history—not just by its archrival the United States but increasingly by a united Europe, Japan, and even its erstwhile comrade China. Gorbachev began this process hoping to save the Soviet Union, only to bury it and the Cold War in the process. But what he gave the world was a Russia reborn. Russia, while embedded within the Soviet Union, was one of the most isolated, disconnected countries in the world. Not surprisingly, it was a huge source of danger and threat to the United States. When Russia ended its disconnectedness, it ceased being a military threat.

Russia decided to reconnect itself to the world first through political reform, then economic reform, and finally ongoing legal reform, but China has taken close to an opposite route. Under the reformist leadership of Deng Xiaoping in the early 1980s, China focused first on economic reform, especially in the agricultural sector. When that unleashed a decade of impressive growth, popular pressures for political reform naturally ensued, culminating in the Tiananmen Square protests of 1989. Following the bloody crackdown, China focused more on reforming its legal rule sets regarding business versus those involving political freedom. This choice set in motion a huge influx of foreign capital across the 1990s, transforming China from an emerging market to a global manufacturing superpower and a key pillar of globalization's Functioning Core.

A Chinese friend of mine who had been active in the democracy movement explained how this rule-set shift changed his outlook: "Before Tiananmen, we believed that freedom is 90 percent political and 10 percent economic. A few years later, we came to realize that real freedom is 90 percent economic and 10 percent political." You may find my friend's change of heart troublesome, but think about your own daily life and then try to tell me that second formula isn't a better description of how things really work for the vast majority of Americans. Anyway, my friend's rebalanced equation makes perfect sense to me when I think about China's sequencing of rule-set reform.

Is China a democracy yet? No. In terms of economic freedom, though, it has synchronized its internal rule sets with those of globalization to a great degree, and as we witness the birth of a litigious society there, I become increasingly confident that China will accomplish the same in terms of its legal rule sets. Nowhere is this seen more clearly than in China's joining the World Trade Organization, from which, in effect, Beijing's leadership is importing legal and economic rule sets they could not otherwise generate effectively on their own—a sure sign of their weakening authoritarian grip over the political system as a whole. China will be a democratic society within a generation, because by synchronizing their internal economic and legal rule sets with those of globalization's Functioning Core, China will end up accepting far more internal change than its Communist leadership ever bargained for.

So if Russia's path was political-to-economic-to-legal rule-set change, and China's is economic-to-legal-to-political rule-set change, can a country begin with legal rule-set changes first? It can, and frankly most do, although most observers would be hard-pressed to describe the initial rule-set shift as constituting what we like to call rule of law. Basically, this third way is the single-party-rule method, in which the country is administered by a single dominant party that—in a fairly technocratic style—engineers a systematic, state-directed economic development strategy, typically described as export-driven growth. While this dominant leadership holds elections that are open to competing parties, the political system is so rigged that no serious challenges are allowed. Often, the dominant party is ruled over by a single long-term leader, such as Singapore's Lee Kuan Yew, or Malaysia's Mahathir Mohamad, but this is not always the case. Both Japan's dominant Liberal Democratic Party and South Korea's Democratic Liberal Party ruled their respective states for decades while rotating top leaders in an otherwise noncompetitive political environment.

In this third model, then, strong legal rule sets form the first piece of the puzzle, followed by strong economic rule sets. Over time, as the country's economy grows and a middle class appears, invariably we see popular demands for more political openness, as we have witnessed in recent years in South Korea, Mexico, and Japan.

As we go, it is important to keep the definition of *functioning* fairly loose, in large part because the global rule set itself is undergoing constant revision—especially in the realm of free trade. The so-called Washington Consensus of the mid-1990s, derided by critics as a sort of free-trade-at-all-costs philosophy, does not hold sway today. In the current round of negotiations within the World

Trade Organization, known as the Doha Development Round, developing economies seek relief from the Old Core's protectionism in agricultural trade. In return, advanced economies are pushing harder for more protection of technology patents and copyright of intellectual property. Simply put, the process of defining global rule sets is as important as the ultimate results, because it is through the adjustment of existing rule sets that the Functioning Core accommodates new and aspiring members.

This is why the mere act of gaining admittance to the World Trade Organization is a crucial step forward for emerging markets. Show me a country moving in this direction, like Russia, and I will show you a member of the Functioning Core—or a country I do not worry about much as a potential security threat or danger. But show me a country not even considering such a step, like North Korea, and I know one of two things must be true: either that state is not providing for its people and thus failing them on multiple levels, or that state seeks to make its way in the world by working around existing global rule sets or ignoring them completely.

Of course, always trying to play by globalization's evolving rule sets does not guarantee success, it just makes success more likely—on average. But when states do follow the rule sets adequately and their economies still end up being abused in the global marketplace, as in Argentina or Brazil in recent years, then it is incumbent upon those international organizations and the largest economic powers that dominate them to adjust the rule sets accordingly. That is simply the squeaky wheel asking for grease, and that has to be allowed. As Dani Rodrik points out, China managed to integrate with the global economy while breaking plenty of the rule sets along the way, remaining one of the world's more protectionist economies until quite recently. So clearly, how we define what's good behavior will depend a lot on *when* we choose to judge. China's path looks a lot more forgivable now than it did ten years ago.

So if these are my fundamental definitions of what constitutes *functioning* within globalization's Core, which countries can be considered in? My list of the Functioning Core of globalization consists of North America, Europe both "old" and "new," Russia, Japan, China (although the interior is less so), India (in a pock-marked sense), Australia and New Zealand, South Africa, and the ABCs of South America—Argentina, Brazil, and Chile. That is roughly four billion out of a global population of six-plus billion.

I am leaving some smaller states off the list for now, and I will explain why once we get to the issue of where U.S. military crisis-response activity occurred across the 1990s. But before I do that, I need to offer some explanation of how I define the opposite of *functioning* within globalization—or what I call *disconnectedness*.

While I will hold off throwing statistics at you for now, let me say that disconnectedness from the global economy can be described in a variety of ways. First, there is the problem of simply losing out on connectivity because you fail to attract the kind of foreign investment that fuels it. Maybe your country is simply so impoverished that foreign investors shy away from it out of habit. But frankly, since multinational corporations are always on the lookout for cheap labor, poverty alone is not a significant impediment. Usually, foreign investors simply do not see enough rule sets in place to give them a sense of confidence for placing long-term bets. Good evidence of a lack of sufficient rule sets would include regular financial crises or a recent state bankruptcy.

So what keeps these rule sets from appearing? Wars are one obvious problem. War zones typically signal the absolute absence of rule sets. Frequent leadership changes are another bad sign, since the routine rotation of leaders through something approaching a free election is a basic political rule set that most investors want to see. So if leaders are coming and going willy-nilly, that means extralegal means are probably being employed—coups d'état, political assassinations, and the like. Every time something like that happens, a country's internal rule sets tend to flux, creating the sort of uncertainty that investors hate.

On the other side of that ledger are the leaders who simply stay too long. Almost any leader is reasonably good for the first four to six years, which is why many countries limit leadership terms. The problem is when the "great leader" decides he needs to stay longer than the prescribed limit—"for the sake of the people." As soon as a leader declares himself "president for life," disconnectedness becomes a near certainty. That is because as soon as a leader makes his rule absolute, he starts treating the national economy as his household economy. In Africa, this is known as the Big Man problem, Liberia's Charles Taylor being just the latest in a very long line. If all economic activity with the outside world has to go through the Big Man's pockets (Taylor, for example, looted the government for $100 million), then the country's connectivity will be minimized over time because only those foreign firms willing to put up with such corruption will pay that price. Then there is simply the logjam of having every economic deal go through a single door. Imagine how little trade the United States would enjoy if the President himself had to sign off on every single deal—after exacting a substantial bribe, of course.

One of the worst problems with Big Men, of course, is that they tend to beget Little Big Men, or their sons as successors. Typically, this leads to even greater disconnectedness, because the Little Big Man, having grown up as the anointed prince, tends to treat the nation less as his money box and even more as his plaything. North Korea's Kim Jong Il is the prototype of this category, although we are beginning to see a new variant in Central Asia, where it looks like both Kazakhstan and Azerbaijan are heading down the path toward hereditary succession.

Countries ruled by royal families (here I am referring to nonconstitutional monarchies) would also fall into this general category, because all the problems that cause connectivity to be limited in the case of the Big Man are found here as well—simply multiplied. Typically, the Big Family holds hereditary right to the natural resources within the country—otherwise what would be the point of being king?

A country blessed with raw materials is likewise susceptible to disconnectedness, especially if those raw materials are its primary export. Historically speaking, countries whose economic well-being relies extensively on the exportation of raw materials are some of the least connected states in the world. One reason that is true is that typically some Big Man will rise up, grab political power by force, and then quite naturally put himself in complete charge of overseeing the exploitation of those natural resources "on behalf of the people." A worse variant is when the country is routinely racked by internal conflict among those groups competing for control over the raw materials. In several sub-Saharan African nations in recent years, precious-metals mines and oil fields have become the primary prizes for long-running battles between various rebel factions.

Theocracies also have a dampening effect on connectivity with the outside world, because—of course—the whole point of having religious leaders in power is to ensure the purity of the faith within one's borders. Achieving that typically requires strict control over what content enters the country, and what kind of linkages exist between the faithful and the unbelievers outside.

Sometimes disconnectedness is simply beyond a nation's choice. For example, lacking good transportation connectivity with the outside world is sometimes enough to retard integration into the global economy. In general, some of the most disconnected states in the global economy lack access to ports and are located deep within vast continents. Paraguay is a good example of such a state. One of the ways Paraguay overcomes this deficit is to specialize in cross-border trafficking of illegal goods, like contraband cigarettes. It is estimated that as much as one-fifth of Paraguay's GDP is derived by smuggling goods across its porous borders with Argentina, Brazil, and Bolivia.

Disconnectedness is often self-imposed by the pursuit of illicit gain. Criminals, for example, must maintain as much practical disconnectedness from normal life as possible, in order to stay "off the net" and avoid prosecution. States that garner a significant portion of their GDP through illegal activities are naturally some of the least-connected states, because—in effect—a low profile is good for business. Bolivia, a landlocked South American nation, is home to one of the world's largest commercial fleets. Under normal circumstances, you might expect Bolivia to be a highly connected player in the global economy, except that all those vessels fly under a "flag of convenience," meaning they are ships of foreign origin taking advantage of Bolivia's exceedingly loose rule set regarding shipping registries. As such, Bolivia is not really connected to the global economy; it is more like a back door used by smugglers. States that engage in smuggling of any sort typically fall into this category, which is why most of the so-called rogues are routinely accused of engaging in drug-smuggling activities. North Korea, for example, conducts extensive heroin smuggling around Asia, in addition to selling counterfeit currencies.

Another example of why disconnectedness occurs can be found in how a society treats its women. States that tend to view women primarily as birthing machines are invariably more disconnected than those that let women enter the workplace, in large part because the economy is denied access to more than half its labor pool, thus limiting its ability for exports of either goods or services. In general, any society that keeps its women isolated from everyday life tends to be more disconnected. Examples of this isolation include the practice of female circumcision, "honor killings" of women who engage in out-of-wedlock sex, and restricted access to education or everyday privileges like driving a car. Some academics have gone so far as to argue that the real fault line between civilizations lies not in how they view politics differently but in how they view gender equality differently. A recent World Values Survey by the University of Michigan found that Muslim and Western populations differ very little in their approval of democratic ideals, but that a large gulf exists between the two over such gender-driven issues as sexual equality, divorce, abortion, and homosexuality. What most states try to isolate their populations from is not the West's political values but its social values, because the latter content flow is far more challenging to traditional societies.

Because the connectivity associated with globalization tends to empower women relative to men, it will be opposed on that basis by most men in traditional societies. Connectivity is essentially gender-neutral, meaning it offers the same economic advantages to women as to men, but that is a huge problem in societies where the males have traditionally conducted economic transactions and have thus controlled family incomes. A great story along these lines was reported in the *New York Times* a few years back. From a remote village in Guyana, a collection of village women began selling their hand-woven hammocks over the Internet, reaping relatively large profits. It was a wonderfully heartwarming tale, which included Guyana's state phone company installing a special satellite system to connect this isolated village to the global communications grid. But this sliver of connectivity deeply threatened the all-male regional leadership, which immediately feared the women making that much money without male oversight. The result? The men took over the enterprise, the woman who ran the Web site quit in protest, and within weeks the village women were struggling to find customers.

Sometimes the very government agencies you would assume would encourage connectivity fight it themselves, preferring absolute control over a smaller pie to risking loss of control if that pie were to grow. A good example of this phenomenon is how the rising use of Internet telephony across Africa is meeting with fierce resistance from government-owned telecoms. Africans have long suffered limited telecommunications connectivity with the outside world thanks to the strict control over such services by state-run phone companies. These companies, known for being rife with corruption, are now counterattacking subscribers they suspect of Internet telephony, shutting down their service in retaliation. Ghana's national phone company was so expert at depressing popular demand for telecommunication services that when a new wireless service was introduced in 1996, the company's executives predicted a customer base of probably 3,000 subscribers, only to end up with 100 times that amount in less than seven years. Based on that sort of success and numerous others, some Western high-tech executives are predicting that Ghana could become for West Africa what Bangalore is to India—a global high-tech hub. Ghana, of course, is the single most peaceful state in West Africa and one of the few on the entire continent to be rated as "free" by Freedom House in its annual survey of democracy. The global forces of telecom connectivity apparently like what they see in Ghana, and want to lift it out of its relative disconnectedness as a result.

Iraq under Saddam Hussein was so disconnected from the global telecommunications grid that in the immediate aftermath of the 2003 war, the global satellite phone industry experienced a miniboom as a result. Since Iraq had simply been passed over by the Information Revolution, it completely lacked a cell phone infrastructure and its wireline industry was antiquated. So when Saddam's statues were falling all over Iraq, ordinary citizens had no other way to reach loved ones overseas than to beg the international media pool for calls on their satellite telephones. Once the fighting stopped, Kuwaiti entrepreneurs rushed in armed with portable cell phone towers and a plan to provide the country with complete cell phone coverage within six months. Based on cell phone penetration rates in other Middle Eastern countries, experts are predicting an Iraqi subscriber base of at least six million out of a total population of twenty million.

What these examples of disconnectedness being overcome say is that globalization's frontiers are far from fixed. They also say that peace and stability are essential for such connectivity to flow from the Core to the Gap. That means the fundamental measure of effectiveness for any U.S. military intervention inside the Gap must be: Did we end up improving local security sufficiently to trigger an influx of global connectivity? Not whether we created an instant democracy or a loyal military ally—or even defeated an enemy in record time. Increasingly, our military interventions will be judged by the connectivity they leave behind, not the smoking holes.

MINDING THE GAP

Around the same time in the early 1990s that I was working on what became . . . *From the Sea,* the Center for Naval Analyses received an urgent request from the rear admiral in charge of the Navy's Office of Legislative Affairs (OLA). This flag, named William "Bud" Flanagan, was known by all as a hard-charging ship driver blessed with a velvet touch, which made him perfect for OLA, because that post involved the care and feeding of senators and congressmen of particular importance to the department's annual budget push. Since everyone knew Bud was going places (he eventually rose to the rank of full admiral, or four-star, in almost record time), CNA told me to drop everything for a couple of weeks and assist Flanagan.

The request was unusual: I was to put together a package of PowerPoint slides that would drive home the point that the Navy-Marine team was the premier crisis-response force in the U.S. military. Now, making the Navy look good was hardly an unusual task for a CNA analyst, but the focus on crisis response right when the Navy was putting together this new vision of "influencing events ashore" was striking. The Navy had spent decades defining itself in terms of countering and defeating the Soviet Navy, and in all that time it spent precious little effort collecting, much less interpreting, its crisis-response activities around the world. After all, these were just the lesser includeds.

A colleague of mine at CNA, Adam Siegel, had just concluded a huge study of all naval crisis responses since World War II, and my job was to expand his historical database to include the Army and the Air Force, focusing on the last four presidential administrations (1977–1991). The typical way these data are collected is by counting the individual operations, meaning if the Marines performed a noncombatant evacuation operation in Liberia (e.g., rescuing American nationals from a dangerous environment), that was considered a single crisis response. But since not all responses are alike, counting each as one data point can hide a lot of context. If the Air Force flies one cargo plane of relief goods into an earthquake zone, it's called a single crisis response. And when the Marines send hundreds of soldiers into Lebanon and end up with 200-plus dead after a car-bomb attack, that would count as one crisis response as well. In short, it can quickly become a game of comparing apples and oranges, with some services stressing numbers of responses and others emphasizing magnitude of response.

This is exactly what happened, as Siegel's original report triggered a "research war" among the services. Competing think tanks working for the Army and Air Force quickly cranked out their own historical databases of service-specific crisis responses. By doing so, they sought to correct the "false impression" that the Navy and Marines were the premier crisis-response force. Why such an effort? In the early 1990s, all four services were already going out of their way to show how little their role in U.S. national security would change *simply* because the Soviets went away. If, five years earlier, they justified their budget primarily on the Soviet threat, now they went to great lengths to "prove" that most of their past operations had little to do with the Soviets, but instead involved managing the "chaotic world," which—of course—was growing more chaotic by the moment. So each service tried to make the case that it alone performed the great majority of the "truly important" crisis responses. That "lesser included" sales pitch was used to buttress the far more important argument over which service actually "won" *Desert Storm.* Because the Navy and Marine Corps felt they had the weaker case regarding the Persian Gulf War, they naturally pressed harder in their arguments about crisis response. All of this interservice jousting revolved around the budget's bottom line: each service wanted desperately to convince Congress to cut the other guy instead.

When I began building this all-service database with the help of a Navy lieutenant commander, I could not help feeling that the numerology of counting up the individual responses was the wrong way to go, in large part because the time lag between the start dates and end dates for these nonroutine operations seemed to grow longer the closer you got to the end of the Cold War. It was not just that the Pentagon seemed to be conducting more crisis responses as the Soviet empire faded away during the 1980s, but also that those responses grew significantly longer in length. Hit-and-run operations that were typically measured in days were gradually being displaced by serious babysitting jobs that dragged on for months, and those longer jobs seemed to be concentrating in and around the Middle East.

As someone who worked for a defense contractor and kept strict records of my billable hours, I was intrigued by the notion of—in effect—calculating the Pentagon's billable days in terms of crisis response around the planet. In many ways, the U.S. military is the world's largest security consulting firm and service provider. Like any good consultant, they go wherever the client lives, so if the market for U.S. security services was shifting from Europe to the Middle East, or from East Asia to Southwest Asia, then the Pentagon simply needed to adjust to the new demand pattern.

So I added up all the response days, and the results were rather striking: the Middle East was already accounting for more than half of all the four services' cumulative response days in the 1980s, with the percentage rising to 75 percent for the Navy and Marine Corps. More important, the cumulative number of response days for all four services was rising over time. There were not that many more individual operations in the 1980s than in the 1970s (an increase of only 20 percent). It was just that the responses in the 1980s were getting a lot longer, so the total number of response days increased by roughly 70 percent. This trend, as we would later learn, accelerated even more across the 1990s, as some crisis responses dragged on for year after year, a few encompassing almost the entire decade. In retrospect, those never-ending crisis responses should have been seen as a sign of the shift in the strategic environment: at some point you stop calling it a crisis and begin defining it as a permanent reality.

But back in the early 1990s, the services were less interested in arguing about shifts in the strategic environment than in demonstrating their worldwide utility, such were their fears that Congress was set on "bringing the boys back home." The Defense Department was desperately searching for a way to describe the military's role in securing the post–Cold War security environment, or something that emphasized how our forces deployed around the world provided the glue for global stability while deterring the Big One. To that end, Pentagon strategists preferred arguments and data that made it seem like we needed to maintain our "presence" just about *everywhere* in the world.

Well, that is not exactly true. The Pentagon was deeply concerned that because the Soviet threat was disappearing, we would lose our long-term bases in both Europe and Northeast Asia. They were afraid that if that happened, NATO would lose focus, and if the Russians ever became dangerous again, we would be in the position of having to reinvent that wheel. In Asia, the "resurgent Russia" concern was less prominent than our fear that if we pulled out— or were brought home by Congress—Japan might go nuclear to defend itself against a rising China and we would feel like the odd man out militarily just as the vaunted "Pacific Century" dawned.

That was the problem, in many ways, with the data I generated. Here we go back to Defense Budget 101: preparing for a distant war against Russia or China meant more money for ships and aircraft. To vote against preparing for that fundamental sort of threat left a member of Congress open to charges of being "soft on U.S. defense." But spending money on all these lesser includeds? That is a vote a member could say no to with far less risk. No one is ever accused of being "soft on international security"; rather, they are typically lauded for "putting America first" and "taking care of things back home." If underequipped troops are sent overseas for crisis response, Congress does not catch the blame, the White House does—for sending American troops into harm's way in the first place. So while my analysis was greatly welcomed by Admiral Flanagan for how it showcased the Navy's strong role in the Middle East, the Pentagon as a whole was not at all interested in building a strategic vision around crisis responses—these lesser includeds.

Yet, a mere decade later, this is *exactly* what I am proposing we must do if America ever hopes to win this global war on terrorism. The Pentagon must first and foremost reshape the U.S. military to facilitate its crisis-response capabilities, and all the Military Operations Other Than War skill sets and resources that go with it, while simultaneously downgrading the Defense Department's long-term preparation for the Big One with some future near peer. This involves nothing less than turning upside down more than half a century of Pentagon practice—in effect, reversing the priorities that have defined America's long-range strategic planning since the Defense Act of 1947. I am not talking just about a new defense "contract" between the U.S. Government and the American people but also about a new security "contract" between America and the rest of the world. Such a reordering is crucial for two reasons: First, America cannot afford to fund both the respond-all-over-the-Gap force and the hedge-against-the-Big-One force in equal measure; the former's share of the budget must grow dramatically as the latter's decreases dramatically. Second, by deemphasizing the Big One force, America sends strong signals to fellow Core powers, but especially to China, that our sense of common cause in this global war on terrorism extends far beyond overlapping hit lists. If America tries to have it both ways, it will not only fiscally bankrupt the government, it will end up destroying the Core's long-term unity, and possibly even globalization itself.

In short, this country needs to start equating "national defense"— even "homeland defense"—with "Core security." If joining the Core and acknowledging its security rule sets does not even get a country off the Pentagon's long-range list of potential enemies, then America has little hope of shrinking the Gap through the war on terrorism. Instead, it will probably fracture the Core into competing security rule sets: one dominated by the United States, another dominated by the European Union plus Russia, and a third dominated by China plus Japan. "Realists" might describe this as nothing more than the inevitable return of multipolarity in international security, but I would call it nothing less than a historical tragedy.

In the aftermath of 9/11, America faced a unique historical opportunity to recast the strategic environment in such a way as to dramatically expand the insiders' security community known up to now as the "West." If, over the years, we fail in this task, the blame will fall primarily on the Bush Administration, less in terms of motives than of execution. For example, I see America's best motives in the Bush Administration's ongoing push to shift our overseas military basing out of its Cold War concentrations in Western Europe and Northeast Asia and closer in toward those regions where our crisis responses have since been concentrated—in other words, out of the Core and into the Gap. This is America stepping up to a task that only it can fulfill. But the diplomatic execution of this historic shift is crucial. If America seems to be acting in a zero-sum manner, as in "my gain is your loss," then we are likely to damage security relations in "old Europe" while simultaneously setting in motion long-term confrontations with both Russia and China over our expanding long-term presence in Central and Southwest Asia.

History is not just judging the actions of the Bush Administration. In many ways, it is waiting upon them. To date, the administration's sins of omission far outweigh its sins of commission. It has ably responded to the terrorist attacks of 9/11, but it has not gone nearly far enough in explaining those actions to the world, much less compromising enough on the international means once it has become clear that our national ends would be achieved—the slow internationalization of the postwar Iraq occupation being the prime example.

To say that perceptions matter is a gross understatement. What actions the Bush Administration takes in this global war on terrorism and the nature of its explanations regarding those choices may well determine which alternative global futures are still possible in the near term and which are postponed for several generations. Perceptions are damn near everything when it comes to proposing radical redefinitions in the security rule set that has defined the West for more than half a century, and a strategy of preemptive war inside the Gap is exactly that—a radical redefinition that can easily be misinterpreted to suggest that America reserves the right for unilateral military actions inside the Core as well. Following World War I, the world "lost" Russia to the forces of disconnectedness and spent most of the century dealing with the consequences. To assume that today the world cannot possibly lose some country or region of equal magnitude to a similarly exclusionary ideology is to forget that history often repeats itself, albeit always in subtly different ways.

I have told you which parts of the world I consider to be *functioning* within globalization and why. I have also explained what I mean when I say the rest of the planet, or roughly two billion people out of six billion, seems to be largely *disconnected* from this globalization process—lying beyond globalization's frontier. Now let me show you why those definitions matter, because the map of U.S. crisis-response activity since 1990 corresponds almost perfectly with these definitions of who lies within, and who is stuck outside of, globalization's Functioning Core.

If you turn to the maps in this the book, you will see displayed the roughly 140 separate military responses, or named operations, the U.S. military has engaged in over the time period of 1990 through the end of 2003, excluding purely humanitarian responses. The icons on the map correspond to five different categories of response: evacuation operations, peacekeeping and humanitarian relief operations, contingency positioning, show of force, and combat operations. Let me explain each briefly in turn:

+ Evacuation operations typically involve U.S. troops entering into dangerous, but not necessarily hostile, situations to rescue U.S. nationals. These deployments usually do not involve actual shooting.

+ Peacekeeping and relief operations are just that: going into desperate situations, either after conflict has ceased or following a disaster, and trying to restore order so recovery can begin. While these situations are dangerous, they are usually nonhostile. Of course, that can change quickly, as we found in Somalia in the mid-1990s, when we lost eighteen personnel in a raid designed to capture the lieutenants of the warlord Mohamed Farrah Aideed—the *Black Hawk Down* story.

+ "Contingency positioning" is an activity that we engaged in a lot more during the Cold War than during the 1990s. It essentially involved moving our forces around the world like chess pieces to influence the actions of some potential foe. Since we mostly deal with small fry these days, these potential foes do not pay a whole lot of attention to how many carriers we have offshore, because, frankly, there is not a whole lot they could do about that anyway.

+ "Show of force" is a more muscular version of contingency positioning, which is mostly a naval effort. When America is "showing force," it is typically putting boots on the ground, moving weapons systems and combat platforms into the field, or moving lots of supplies into a theater of operations. So if contingency positioning is like a dad yelling, "Don't make me come in there!" to his kids in the next room, then show of force is Dad actually getting off the couch and going in there, but stopping short of corporal punishment.

+ The final category, combat, is obviously the one we care most about. That involves shooting, killing, and lots of smoking holes. In the 1990s, combat constituted about one-fifth of our cumulative crisis-response days for the four services.

Now, at first glance, this display of crisis responses does not exactly reveal any compelling pattern. It looks like a whole bunch of dots spread all over the planet. Your eyes are drawn to four clusters, and when you check the country names, those groupings seem to make sense. After all, our four biggest interventions in the 1990s were—going from left to right on the map—Haiti, Yugoslavia, Iraq, and Somalia. When you add up the cumulative crisis-response days for those four clusters, you pretty much capture 80 percent of the Pentagon's business in the 1990s. As is the case with a lot of businesses, about 20 percent of your customers give you about 80 percent of your sales. These are your big customers, so you pay a lot of attention to them.

So you might be tempted to simply draw four circles around those four intense clusters of responses and say, "Those four bad situations are basically the story of the 1990s. There is no unusual pattern, no larger meaning—just a couple of basket cases (Haiti, Somalia) and two bad boys that needed to be slapped around now and then (Milosevic in Serbia, Saddam in Iraq)." And that is exactly what I thought in the summer of 2001, when I first analyzed this database while working as a consultant for my old mentor Hank Gaffney at the Center for Naval Analyses.

In reuniting with Hank, I was moonlighting from my job at the Naval War College. This was the period when my war college work saw me deeply involved in my "new rules sets" research partnership with the Wall Street firm Cantor Fitzgerald, the endeavor that reunited me with now-retired Admiral Bud Flanagan, who, upon leaving the Navy, joined Cantor as an executive vice president in charge of developing new market opportunities for the firm outside of its traditional focus on sovereign debt or bonds. I was also reunited in this effort with Bradd Hayes, my old NFCPE buddy, who, having retired from the Navy, was working as a research professor at the Naval War College.

I picked up the outside work with Hank because the New Rule Sets Project was so focused on economics and globalization that I wanted to keep up my skills in analyzing more bread-and-butter military topics like crisis response. But it was more than that. I was searching for something to connect the two lines of work.

The New Rule Sets workshops, which brought together Wall Street and the Pentagon to discuss the future of the world, were designed to help the defense community better understand how globalization was altering America's definitions of national security, as well as the world's definitions of international stability. The workshops themselves were fabulous affairs, conducted on the 107th floor of World Trade Center One, just above Cantor Fitzgerald's offices, in one of the world's most amazing restaurants, Windows on the World. Better still, the material they generated about the future of global energy and investment patterns was being warmly received throughout the Pentagon and the intelligence community. I was getting invitation after invitation to give my slick PowerPoint show around the Beltway, so everything seemed to be working as far as the project was concerned.

But deep down I felt as if I were stuck in a rut, analytically speaking. I wasn't closing the deal, so to speak. I wasn't producing strategic concepts that sold senior Pentagon leaders on what I knew was the profound connectivity between—as I called it—America's "exporting of security" and globalization's progressive advance. The briefs I gave did not end with the kind of discussion I was looking for; there was no "So what are we going to do about this?" Instead, the principals I briefed generously declared the work fascinating and brilliant and patted me on the head, and as they walked me to their office doors, I got the usual kiss-off of "Thank you for your contribution to national security."

But that was just it: I didn't feel that I was contributing anything. Here I was going on and on in this presentation about—in effect— what a wonderful world it is. Heck, I even used a sound clip of Louis Armstrong's version of "What a Wonderful World" in the brief's title slide sequence because it reflected my genuine belief that globalization is the defining historical process of our age, with security playing a supporting role in this great planetary drama. But the upshot of my brief seemed to be: Globalization is sweeping the planet, the military is babysitting some bad boys on the margin, and never the twain shall meet. I simply was not connecting these two dots with reproducible strategic concepts. I lacked a bottom line—that phrase that lingered on everyone's lips long after I left the room.

A big part of the problem was that antiglobalization lacked a real villain. I mean, at that point, all I could reference was "Seattle Man," or the protesters who shut down the World Trade Organization meeting in that city a couple of years earlier. In terms of conflict, the best billing I could come up with was "Seattle Man versus Davos Man," the latter representing the global financiers who met every year in Davos, Switzerland, at the World Economic Forum. You can imagine how that matchup excited Pentagon strategists:

middle-aged guys in business suits harangued by young grungy protesters hoisting signs and massive puppets. Not exactly the crowd
scene you need to send out a carrier to disperse. So these protesters
smashed a few windows and defaced a few Web sites—big deal! If
that was all my "grand historical struggle" was generating in terms
of violence, then I should be briefing metropolitan police departments, not the Pentagon.

So the work I was doing for Gaffney on crisis response wasn't
just my keeping my finger in the pie of "real" security analysis; I
was actively looking for something I could import to my research
with Cantor Fitzgerald that would better connect the worlds of international security and economic globalization. I was getting tired
of always being the flaky futurist talking about some fabulous tomorrow where everyone got along; I was looking for some real-
world operational data that grounded my theories of globalization
in the here and now. Simply put, I wanted my work to matter inside
the Pentagon. I knew I was sneaking into offices primarily because
my PowerPoint presentation was state-of-the-art, but I wanted the
ideas to impress as much as the animation.

It was just before 9/11 that these two seemingly very disparate research pursuits started jelling together in my mind. In the crisis-
response work I was doing for Hank, I was not happy with just
pointing out the four clusters of responses and saying that's all
there was to the 1990s. Hank, always the great skeptic, kept rejecting my attempts to describe America's crisis-response activity according to some grand strategic logic. He knew as well as I that
there was no such logic inside either the Pentagon, which did as it
was told, or the White House, which responded as it was prompted
to by world events. He complained that I was trying to impose order where there was none, but I was certain there was a logic to all
these responses, even if the U.S. Government remained blissfully
unaware of it. To me, it felt as if the currents of history were sweeping us along to something; it was just a matter of clearing the right
bend in the river and we'd see it finally.

As I stared at the display of U.S. responses across the summer of

2001, I kept searching my mind and everything I knew about the world to come up with some larger strategic analysis of what that pattern meant. I knew those four clusters all resulted because America *chose* to pursue those situations. No one made us do it; we decided to do those and not others—such as going into the Congo or getting more involved with Colombia. So I knew I was not staring at a map of global instabilities per se, just an illustration of our choices. I figured the overlap was fairly strong between the two data sets, because—frankly—the U.S. military is the only force in the world capable of traveling long distances and actually doing something significant once it gets there. When I checked out lots of maps detailing significant conflicts around the world, sure enough I found that virtually all of them fell within the rough pattern of U.S. responses.

So just for the heck of it one day, I drew a simple line around virtually all of the icons to see what sort of shape I would end up with. The extreme outliers I ignored (e.g., Northern Ireland, North Korea), to keep the figure from looking too weird. Anyway, I was trying for something like a 95th-percentile sort of capture—leaving out the truly extreme data points.

The result was a shape that stretches across the world map, encompassing the Caribbean Rim, the Andes portion of South America, virtually all of Africa, the Balkans, the Caucasus, Central Asia, the Middle East, and most of Southeast Asia. That basically defines the market into which the U.S. tried to export security since 1990, responding to situations and trying to increase regional security.

What do I see in this shape? What I do not see are any of the countries we have ever thought about as potential near-peer competitors (e.g., united Europe, Russia, China, Japan, India). What I also do not see is anything close to a Big One or even a classic, "bolt-from-the-blue" vertical scenario. I feel as if I am looking at a host of horizontal scenarios, with the little icons representing the peaks of the usual "bad stuff" that we chose to address.

I start thinking to myself, what this shape captures is where the bad stuff usually happens, or—with apologies to Maurice Sendak—*where the wild things are.* So in the post–Cold War era the United

States tends to send its military to where the wild things are, to the places and situations where the normal rules about not resorting to violence and warfare simply do not seem to hold. These are the world's bad neighborhoods, where the gangs live by their own cruel rule sets, where life somehow seems cheaper. These are the enter-at-your-own-risk regions—you know, the *early* Oliver Stone movies like *Midnight Express* and *Salvador.* These are the places where people still go medieval on one another, and the rest of the world simply does not care because it's just so offline from the *wonderful world,* where the "good stuff" and the "good life" are to be found.

But just saying "here are the good parts and there are the bad parts" doesn't really provide any linkage between globalization and international security. In fact, it seems to suggest that these two worlds are essentially disconnected: the rich get richer, the poor get poorer, and never the twain shall meet. Surrendering to that logic means giving many Pentagon strategists exactly what they want: a rationale for ignoring these lesser includeds because—after all—intervening in these situations never does any good anyway. That's why so many of them are drawn to Samuel Huntington's *Clash of Civilizations* argument: it tells them that these conflicts among *those people* are intractable—a code word for quagmire.

That sort of historical pessimism simply drives me nuts, in large part because I believe America needs to stand for so much more than simply abiding by the status quo around the world. Our entire society was built by people who refused to accept the old ways, the old divisions, and the stifling cultural pessimism that says, "This is how it has always been, so get used to it." I didn't join the field of national security simply to stand watch for a generation of preventable bloodshed, I joined to solve problems, intractable conflicts— the whole shebang. If ending the Cold War meant we "solved" the threat of World War III, then I wanted my career to be about drilling down to those lesser includeds to see what the solution set there would ultimately turn out to be. Chalking it all up to a "clash of civilizations" just seemed like a recipe for sitting on my hands for the rest of my career, ginning out academic tomes that sorrowfully chronicle the plight of the Gap's failed states and feral cities ("Oh, the humanity!").

Like my buddy, the fictional captain of the USS *Enterprise,* James T. Kirk, I don't believe in the no-win scenario. That makes me sort of a freak in my business, because futurists in general tend to be awfully pessimistic sorts who love to point out how everything is going to hell in a handbasket, "so here's my advice on how to survive the coming crash!" These gloom-and-doomers are always going on about how all the "chaos" is increasing while all the good life is slipping away. But that just isn't the world history I've been fortunate enough to witness over my life. Thanks to the work I've done on the New Rule Sets Project, I know that the rise of globalization has had an awful lot to do not just with expanding that wonderful world I readily recognize, but also in shrinking those horrible neighborhoods where war was once an immutable force, an intractable problem, a fact of life.

My research partnership with Cantor Fitzgerald during the summer of 2001 serves as a sort of strategic vision life preserver. It keeps me afloat in the sea of pessimism that defines my field of national security studies. The long discussions I have with Bud Flanagan and his partner at Cantor, Phil Ginsberg, are like manna from heaven for this starving futurist. These guys are all about futures worth creating. Unlike the military types who always go on and on about "intractable problems" leading to "inevitable conflicts," these guys always talk in terms of solutions waiting for markets to enable them. For an inveterate optimist like myself, Bud and Phil are like breathing pure oxygen after working all day in the mines. They can tell you about which new drugs get approved and why, what it takes to lay a transregional natural gas pipeline, and how much pollution a city like Beijing can stomach until it finally gets serious and does something about it. They simply do not believe in no-win scenarios, and I love them for it.

When I listen to Pentagon strategists talk about the future of Asia, it's always about why we'll eventually end up fighting wars there. But listening to Bud and Phil, I get a completely different image: Asia is where all the big deals are being made. As far as they're concerned, Asia is the next great piece of the globalization puzzle. China isn't the problem, it's the prize. That's why none of the Pentagon's vertical scenarios about China make any sense. China wants the good life too much to succumb to its worst impulses.

Back to the slide.

Thanks to my interactions with Wall Street, I decided that my great big blob stretching along the planet's middle signifies not just where U.S. military forces intervened in the 1990s but those parts of the global economy that just don't seem to work. Some may seem rich, like the Persian Gulf oil states, but none are really developed, and most are going downhill over time.

This portion of the world simply does not function well. While the "real world" seems to be coming together, this chunk of humanity seems to be growing more isolated over time—isolated by disease, poverty, violence, and the amazingly bad ways in which women and children seem to be treated. Frankly, these people don't even seem to live on the same planet as we do. And it's because their world is largely disconnected from the one we enjoy.

But it is more than that. In my world, women aren't raped *en masse* as a tool of political terror. In my world, people don't rise up *en masse* and hack to death with machetes and axes everyone they can find from some other ethnic group. These aren't "real world" images I recognize. These are nightmares we only get a glimpse of now and then on the evening news: a gang of teenagers rapes a woman jogger in Central Park, white supremacists in Texas drag an African-American behind their truck, or a clean-cut teenager is beaten to death in Wyoming because he's gay.

The difference in magnitude between my world and *that* world is huge. In my world, we get all upset as a society when just one person *has to die that way*. But in *that* world, people seem to die *that way* all the time—in huge clusters. And nobody seems to care.

But why should we care? Except for the Persian Gulf, the violence that periodically erupts across the rest of this combat zone doesn't seem to matter one whit to *our* global economy. The good life we enjoy seems only dimly connected to that pain, and when we try to step in and do something, it always seems to blow up in our faces.

Then it's a quagmire and we don't know how to break it off. Then it's blindfolded American hostages paraded on videotape and we'd give anything to see *those bastards* dead. Then it's *Black Hawk Down* and we can't wait to get out of that hellhole. . . .

But then one crisp September morning it's both towers of the World Trade Center collapsing after being struck by bolts out of the blue.

Then it's my workplace suddenly transformed from a sleepy college campus into an armed camp.

Then it's my boss telling me that the Office of the Secretary of Defense has just bought out my salary and now I'm working directly for the Pentagon.

Suddenly it doesn't feel like two disconnected worlds anymore. Suddenly the shape on my slide jumps out at me as something else—a dividing line between a *real world* whose functioning we take for granted and an *unreal world* whose disconnectedness we'd better learn to understand. Suddenly I'm no longer just looking at a map that plots out past operations, but one that outlines future strategies. Suddenly I don't need the bogeyman of a near-peer competitor to motivate my "defense transformation," because I realize we simply don't have the military that we need to deal with all this disconnectedness, all this pain, all these lesser includeds. Suddenly I understand the danger isn't a *who* but a *where.*

Suddenly my eyes light up . . . because I know I've finally found that one slide.

Fast-forward to March 2002 and I'm walking into the Secretary of Defense's briefing room. It's four o'clock in the afternoon and around the table sit all the senior aides to Secretary Donald Rumsfeld and Deputy Secretary Paul Wolfowitz, both of whom are currently overseas, which is why these guys are free to take my brief. At this level, someone like me is lucky to get a fifteen-minute slot to pitch three or four slides. My immediate boss in the Pentagon, Vice Admiral Art Cebrowski, the Secretary's senior adviser on the future of warfare, has arranged a ninety-minute window.

I dive in with my presentation, firing off my arguments in rapid succession. When I get to the slide that displays U.S. crisis responses over the 1990s, I offer my definitions of globalization's Functioning Core and Non-Integrating Gap. I have their attention, all right, but I can see them searching the slide for the answer to the "So what?" question. Then I click my remote and that big red blob dissolves into view, encompassing all the regions they intuitively realize are now in play for the Defense Department in this global war on terrorism. I say, "What you are looking at are the battle lines in this war. This is the expeditionary theater for the U.S. military in the twenty-first century."

Suddenly their eyes light up . . . and the Pentagon has a new map.

To Live and Die in the Gap

In the March 2003 issue of *Esquire,* I published a piece on the Core-Gap thesis entitled "The Pentagon's New Map." The text was passed around the Pentagon like crazy. One of my colleagues at the War College had it forwarded to him by e-mail roughly a dozen times from friends inside the building, each declaring, "You have got to read this!" I knew immediately what all the e-mails and reprints signified: I had finally created a reproducible strategic concept.

The moment and the map had met.

Outside the defense community, the article generated even more heat, and I must admit I was completely unprepared for both the volume and the harshness of the response by readers. My e-mail in-box was overflowing with hate mail, and *Esquire* itself received a huge flood of letters, the majority of which were harshly negative, mostly because I came out clearly for the war against Iraq. Many of the people who wrote in thought I had generated this grand theory simply to justify the war, when in reality I had developed the Core-Gap thesis long before the Bush Administration started their full-court press to depose Saddam Hussein.

The reason I so easily fit an argument for the war within my "shrink the Gap" strategy wasn't that I thought Saddam had to go right then, but that I knew he had to go sometime, and the spring of 2003 was as good a time as any.

Hussein's regime was a textbook example of everything we need to eliminate in the Gap: a bad leader who stuck around way past his expiration date, a regime that terrorized its population for decades, and a society so decimated from violence that it could take years to find and dig up all the mass graves—much less identify the remains. Of course, there are plenty of people in our political system eager to debate for months on end whether or not Saddam really had weapons of mass destruction, and that is right and proper, but for me, that was never the point. Taking down Saddam forced the United States to take responsibility for the security environment in the Gap, and that's why I supported the war. By reconnecting Iraq to the world, we are not just rehabilitating a longtime pariah, we are stepping up to the role of Gap Leviathan in a way no other nation in the Core could even dream about.

Of course, that's pretty scary business.

It's scary to Americans who wonder what that role will entail in blood and treasure. It's scary to other great powers who wonder if the United States plans to extend its influence purposely and permanently at their expense. It's scary to all the other nasty regimes inside the Gap, who will be wondering who's next. Frankly, it's scary to just about everyone, because no one in the U.S. Government has really made the long-term case about where exactly we intend to go with all these new strategies, new bases, and new willingness to topple regimes preemptively.

Probably the scariest notion is that *no one* in the U.S. Government has really thought this whole thing out beyond Iraq, meaning the Bush Administration always had Saddam in its crosshairs and took advantage of events to nail him when it could. If that were the case, then a lot of the arguments I offer in this book might seem easily dismissed. But that would be shortsighted in the extreme. Saddam was always going down, because confrontation with the outside world was just about the only shred of legitimacy his regime had left following its disastrous invasion of Kuwait. Having to play that card for all it was worth meant his rule was always just a step or two away from the inevitable endgame.

I think the simplest explanation of how this global war on terrorism has come to define the Bush Administration's foreign policy is that these policymakers are essentially Cold War types who came into power determined to tie up what they felt were the loose ends of that bygone era, or America's relationships with fellow great powers. By doing so, they hoped to clamp down on the "chaos" of the post–Cold War era. Their biggest mistake was assuming that if they got Europe, Russia, China, Japan, and India in line, then all the "smaller bits" would likewise fall into place, when in reality the rogues of the world aren't taking advice, much less orders, from anyone nowadays. China does not control Pakistan or North Korea, and Russia's ability to steer former client states is virtually nonexistent.

The terrorist attacks of 9/11 woke this administration—and this country—to the new realities of the international security environment, where the lesser includeds of the Cold War have risen to the top of the threat pile. This unprecedented development is less the result of all those rogues and transnational actors getting their hands on dangerous technologies than the great powers simply moving beyond the military competitions of the past and into the shared reality of membership in globalization's Core. That Core represents, in many ways, the promise of great-power unity many experts identified in the immediate aftermath of the Cold War's collapse, or what George H. W. Bush dubbed the "new world order." That order did not jell across the 1990s, primarily because the United States refused to step up and define the essential security rule sets that would cement that unity and direct it toward common purpose. America failed that historical moment primarily out of fear for what it might entail in terms of our management of the global security environment.

As the go-go nineties unfolded, that choice not to act seemed quite reasonable, because it appeared as though globalization itself would play Leviathan to the security system, forcing strict adherence to basic economic rule sets. If a country misbehaved, then the international marketplace would punish its economy far faster and with greater vehemence than any sanction or diplomatic response could. Meanwhile, all the United States had to do militarily was simply babysit the chronic rogues sitting on the outskirts of the global economy, making sure they did not rock the Core's boat, as it were.

What 9/11 proved was that the Core continues to ignore the Gap at its own peril. The Bush Administration decided, quite rightly, that new security rules were in order. But for now, these rules stand simply as America's new formulation of its inherent right to self-defense. Since we are, by far, the world's largest military power, those assertions come off as quite frightening to the rest of the world, because it remains unclear to what lengths this nation will go in order to secure that defense. The rest of the Core's great powers are equally interested in achieving the same sort of security for the global economy, but they remain, quite reasonably, skeptical that the Bush Administration's definition of "victory" in this global war on terrorism will not involve sacrificing the Core's security for America's defense.

Where the Bush Administration's senior policymakers have

failed most egregiously to date is in their inability to move beyond their own, antiquated balance-of-power mentality, which twists both their language and the logic. A *global* war on terrorism has to promise a happy ending for the planet as a whole, not just for America, or the "West," or even all the Core's great powers. The win-win solution here involves both the Core and the Gap, but instead of articulating and advancing such a global agenda, the Bush Administration has consistently lapsed into political gamesmanship of the most venal sort in its interactions with fellow great powers—to wit, the "punish France, ignore Germany, forgive Russia" formulation following those nations' resistance to the United States–led war in Iraq. That sort of boneheaded diplomacy has undercut what has otherwise been a bold, even visionary effort by this Administration to forge a new international security rule set, generating fear when genuine respect was clearly in the offing.

I recognize that fear, because it's jumped out at me in all the letters and e-mails I continued to receive about my *Esquire* article even *after* the war in Iraq concluded. Once the debate simmered down about whether we should go to war, people started asking questions not just about where America is heading with these new rule sets, but what we hope the world might look like when we finally get there. Taken in that light, "shrink the Gap" strikes many readers less like a battle cry and more like an exit strategy. A task once begun feels half done.

It continues to amaze me how much that simple map outlining the Gap is so provocative to so many different readers. Don't get me wrong, most of the letters I still get are negative, but for a different reason than before. Instead of just being labeled a warmonger, now I'm often accused of "writing off" a large chunk of the world as "hopeless," when I intend just the opposite. All the map really does to people is challenge them to explain how they would propose we "shrink the gap," and that is what makes most readers so uncomfortable with my thesis—it suggests we have some moral responsibility to do better by the Gap. It's not about revenge and it's not about making ourselves feel good. It's about doing the right thing because we can.

From the voluminous flow of messages I received from around the world, I would surmise that there are three basic responses most people advocate when confronted with the Core-Gap thesis. The first basic response I would locate on the left, or liberal, end of the political spectrum. What these people are most upset about is the notion that the U.S. military is clearly headed toward "perpetual war" all over the Gap, which in their minds will only make things worse there. They advocate a sort of Hippocratic, "do no harm" approach that readily admits that the Core is largely to blame for the Gap's continuing misery and therefore should rescue those in pain, but do so primarily through state-based foreign aid and private charities. The "do no harm" aspect refers to their strong desire to see America bring its military forces back home and stop all these military interventions overseas, the underlying assumption being that fewer military interventions on our part would actually improve the international security situation by not scaring our allies so.

The second basic approach is simply to say, "That's the way things are" and to blame the Gap for its own problems. These responses came more from the right or conservative end of the political spectrum. These writers' basic point is that the Gap is not America's problem and that if we make it so, we will eventually end up running some "empire" that will corrupt both our souls and our political system. If the left wants to pray for my soul, the heartiest right-wingers are more interested in kicking my ass. To them, I am clearly a key player in the latest conspiracy of the one-world government that wants to enslave the American people under the tyrannical rule of the United Nations, the Jewish cabal that runs Wall Street, or the *Seven Days in May* crowd waiting deep in the Pentagon's basement for the signal to launch their military *coup d'état!*

The more mainstream response from the right focuses on the notion that shrinking the Gap is simply too big a problem for the United States to take on—militarily or otherwise. Instead, they bluntly advocate a sort of civilizational apartheid that strikes me as a mirror image of what I believe many violent antiglobalization forces would also prefer—including Osama bin Laden. Rather than fix the Gap, these respondents prefer segregation. The most common way this gets expressed is the idea that if America would only end its dependence on foreign oil, illegal narcotics, and cheap immigrant labor, we could just build a big fence around this nasty neighborhood called the Gap and not have to deal with it anymore. People who advocate this twenty-first-century form of isolationism do not argue so much for pulling our military forces home as positioning them around the Gap as a sort of global border patrol, making sure the bad stuff stays in the Gap so we can continue our good life in the Core—you know, *Buy American!*

Then there are those who have written in agreement. These respondents see both a moral culpability on the part of the Core and a moral responsibility on the part of the sole surviving superpower, the United States, to shrink the Gap by all means possible—including the use of force in the worst situations. This moderate middle views the Gap's plight more pragmatically, citing the history of past colonialism by Core states in terms of both the good and bad legacies, the right and wrong lessons to be drawn, and their underlying optimism that America—always the reluctant imperialist—would do better than those European powers had in centuries past. The only morality these moderates touched upon was the immorality of *doing nothing.*

I obviously prefer the middle way too, because the whole utility of defining the Gap lies primarily in its use as a framework to guide our strategic sense of progress or failure. Like the Cold War containment theorists, I believe it is essential that we be honest with ourselves about the world we live in, and to me, that means—first and foremost—that we identify the sources of mass violence in the system and work to progressively shrink those sources. What I like about the Gap is that it reflects an undeniable historical record: when America finally broke free from the Cold War and let the resulting international security environment tell us where we as a nation needed to redirect our "security export," the Gap was the demand pattern that emerged. There is no denying that problems in the Gap reflect a tremendous legacy of past abuse and unfairness on the part of the Core in general, but "shrinking the Gap" as a strategic vision is not about making amends for the past. Instead, it is a practical strategy for dealing with the present danger that will—on regular occasion, I believe—reach into our good life and cause us much pain if we continue to ignore it. But more than just looking out for ourselves, shrinking the Gap is a strategy that also speaks to a better future for that roughly one-third of humanity that continues to live and die in the Gap.

To that strategic end, it is important for Americans to understand how life is so dramatically skewed within the Gap. When the philosopher Thomas Hobbes described what living in a world without a Leviathan was like, he said a man's life would be "solitary, poor, nasty, brutish, and short." That description captures the relative differences between life in the Core and the Gap. In the Core, we have our all-encompassing Leviathan that prevents mass conflict from breaking out either between states or within them—known respectively as the principles of collective security and the rule of law. In essence, the Core does not need an external Leviathan because we have internalized the principles. As such, the United States truly plays no significant Leviathan-like role across the Core, nor does it need to, given the fact that all the great powers that desire the deterrence capability of nuclear weapons already possess them—with the possible exception of Japan.

But no such Leviathan exists throughout the Gap, except for those times when the United States—with or without the United Nations in tow—musters the necessary will to extend our security rule sets there. So if the Core seems to be living the dream of Immanuel Kant's perpetual peace, then the Gap remains trapped in Hobbes's far crueler reality.

Life in the Gap is poor.

To live in the Gap is to be surrounded by significantly higher rates of poverty. First, there is the generally low level of income. Of the 118 countries listed by the World Bank as "low-income" or "low-middle-income" (below $2,936 per capita annual), 109 are located inside the Gap. Then there are the truly impoverished, or those living on less than $1 per day. According to World Bank statistical surveys over the past two decades, about two-thirds of Core states feature poverty rates of less than 10 percent, while two-thirds of Gap states suffer rates above 10 percent, and one-third feature rates above 30 percent. In numerous African states, the poverty rates rise as high as 60 to 70 percent. Americans simply have no understanding of how crushing that kind of poverty can be. Simply put, we have never been that poor in this country—not even in the Great Depression.

Life in the Gap is nasty.

To live in the Gap is to be less free, on average. According to Freedom House's 2003 survey of states around the world, 48 countries out of a global total of 192 surveyed were rated as "not free." Of those 48 states, 45 are located within the Gap. The three that are not inside the Gap are the Cold War leftovers China, Belarus, and North Korea. Of the other 60 or so other states located within the Gap, half are considered "free" and half "partly free." In contrast, of the almost 90 countries considered "free" in the world, close to two-thirds are located within the Core.

To live in the Gap is also to suffer bad political leadership, which comes in two categories: leaders who cannot last long enough in power and those who insist on sticking around for too long. The first type of leadership engenders political instability, while the second tends to result in authoritarianism.

Using the *CIA Factbook* and looking back over the past thirty years, I can find almost a hundred countries that change their leaders either too frequently or not frequently enough. Of those 94 countries falling outside that happy medium, 87 are located within the Gap—or over 90 percent. When we look at the Gap as a whole, 30 percent of the countries there experience turnover less than every four years (on average), while almost 60 percent suffer leaders who tend to overstay their welcome (defined as staying longer than six years, on average). Only one out of every ten states in the Gap appears to feature a stable rotation of leaders. In contrast, nine out of every ten states in the Core fall within the happy medium of peaceful leadership rotation every four to six years. What does that tell us about the Gap? It tells us that the Gap simply lacks the robust political rule sets that define the Core's overall stability.

Life in the Gap is short.

Of the 50 states with the highest life expectancy rates (76 to 83 years), four-fifths lie within the Core. However, if we are to look at the 50 states with the lowest expectancy rates (37 to 57 years), all but one (South Africa) lie within the Gap. On average, the Gap enjoys a life expectancy that is more than a dozen years shorter than in the Core. Imagine what gets lost in that shorter life span—the experience, the wisdom, the time to build and sustain institutions, the time spent raising the next generation. Then imagine the implications of having a population so skewed toward youth.

To live in the Gap is to be surrounded by a younger population. All of the countries in the world featuring a median age of less than twenty years old fall within the Gap (spread across Africa, Southwest Asia, and Southeast Asia), while all of the countries featuring a median age above thirty-five years old are located in the Core. What does having a younger population get you? On average, younger populations are more violent and prone to crime. It is a general rule of societies that the vast majority of crime is committed by young males under the age of thirty. Societies with "youth bulges," defined simply as one generation's proportion of youth significantly surpassing that of the preceding generation's, are also more prone to political instability. Right now the Middle East as a whole is experiencing a youth bulge, while Africa will remain in the throes of one for another couple of decades, because of continued high birth rates combined with deaths from AIDS. The problems associated with youth bulges ensue as that "bulge" grows up, because the political system is stressed in terms of increased crime rates, greater demands for education and training, and finally requiring more jobs from the economy. If the economy cannot grow to meet such demands or if the political system cannot similarly adjust, then you have a problem, because—after all—revolutionaries and terrorists tend to be young men angry at the system, not the middle-aged wondering what happened to their youth.

Life in the Gap is brutal.

Hobbes said the worst thing about life absent the Leviathan was "continual fear, and danger of violent death," both of which occur in spades inside the Gap. No matter what list of "current conflicts" you want to work from (e.g., University of Maryland, Federation of American Scientists, Global Security.org), you'll come up with a number somewhere short of three dozen, with 80 to 90 percent of them falling squarely inside the Gap. These wars will generate refugees, most of whom simply move into the next country over to escape the violence. That means most of the people fleeing these wars in the Gap never actually leave the Gap. Based on data from the U.S. Refugee Committee's 2002 global survey, Gap countries currently account for 96 percent of the people forced to leave their country to escape warfare or similar deprivations, and 93 percent of all people similarly displaced internally within their home countries. According to the United Nations High Commissioner for Refugees, an average of twelve million refugees seek formal asylum in another country each year. Virtually all originate in the Gap, but only one out of every four actually makes it into the Core.

Those who typically have a harder time escaping conflict zones are children, especially those orphaned by war or lured into combat units. Their lives are by far the most Hobbesian. Imagine a guerrilla war like the one America faced in Vietnam, but instead of sending nineteen-year-olds, we drafted kids as young as twelve. In the recent long-running war in the Congo, at least ten separate armed groups operating across the country were actively recruiting child soldiers. This phenomenon is not restricted to Africa but is seen throughout the Gap, as entire generations of a nation's youth are forever brutalized by a host of long-running rebellions or civil wars.

Naturally, the worst conflicts eventually draw in some sort of international response in the form of peacekeeping operations. Of the sixteen current United Nations peacekeeping missions, all fall inside the Gap. Even when such long-running wars finally end, the shadow of conflict can extend for decades in the form of unexploded land mines. Of the eighteen countries identified by the U.S. State Department as suffering "severe impact" from unexploded bombs, all lie within the Gap.

Of course, not all the violence found inside the Gap stems from war. Of the three dozen groups officially designated by the U.S. State Department as "terrorist groups," 31 operate primarily inside the Gap. Likewise, 19 of the 23 states certified by the State Department as "major drug producers" are found inside the Gap. When all these main sources of Gap violence (rebels, smugglers, terrorists) begin to network with one another, therein lie some of the most difficult challenges in America's global war on terrorism.

Life in the Gap is solitary.

Not surprisingly, given all these difficulties, states in the Gap tend to be far less connected, in a simple communications sense, than states in the Core. A good measure of communications connectivity today is the number of Internet hosts found in a country. No surprise here: the more developed your economy becomes, the more connected your people become. So the most connected societies tend to be found in North America and Europe, while the least connected societies are found in the Middle East and Africa. But that rule of thumb hides some irregularities that better define the challenges ahead in shrinking the Gap. As technology expert John R. Harris notes, there are a host of "reluctantly connected economies" around the world. By "reluctantly connected," Harris means that these societies are less connected than they should be in comparison with other states with equal levels of development (measured as per capita income). In effect, this category is made up of those more traditional Gap societies that are wary of having to deal with all the content flow associated with Internet connectivity. Not surprisingly, 20 of Harris's 21 "reluctantly connected" states are found within the Gap—China being the exception. As I noted earlier, China's strategy here is one of selective censorship, although most indications are that the Chinese Communist Party's attempts to filter out the "bad" are failing.

I could go on and on with similar data, but I can almost hear some readers exclaim, "Enough, already, you had me at Leviathan!"

The point of that bombardment was merely to draw a clear line between the Gap's Hobbesian reality and the Core's Kantian peace. So how do we get the Gap to move from Hobbes to Kant? More Locke, as in John Locke, considered the philosophical father of the legal rule sets that define modern democracy. If you want to move the Gap from Hobbes to Kant, you need to focus on extending rule sets from the Core to the Gap. Remember the old Chicago Cubs double play of Tinker to Evers to Chance? Just think of the Gap's progression as Hobbes to Locke to Kant, or from conflict to rule sets to peace—understanding, as I said earlier, that the sequence of rule-set adoption comes in a variety of flavors.

In my mind, the only way America and its close allies will ever come to grips with the challenges of shrinking the Gap is to admit to one another that globalization's Core-Gap division severs the international security environment into two distinctly different rule sets. Once we accept that underlying reality, we can help states trapped in the Gap begin their rule-driven migration into the Core.

DIFFERENT WORLDS, DIFFERENT RULE SETS

Experts say that the mark of true intelligence is the ability to hold two opposing concepts in your head at the same time, to understand the truth of each while realizing their differences. I think the Core-Gap thesis challenges most people in the same way, forcing them to move beyond the usual pigeonholing arguments that define the foreign policy debates in this country today. Recognizing the Core-Gap divide does not automatically place you in one political camp or the other, and since the strategies required to move states from the Gap to the Core will invariably be multifaceted (e.g., military interventions, foreign aid, private-sector investments), arguments over how to shrink the Gap are equally difficult to classify.

My wife worries that I am secretly becoming a Republican, and judging by all the names I got called thanks to the *Esquire* piece, it seems like a legitimate concern. I guess what I find most amusing about all the labeling and epithets is the assumption that only a "hard-hearted conservative" would advocate war, when the country just experienced eight years of Democratic rule only to see our forces deployed around the world like never before. In many ways, the Bush Administration is doing the very same thing the Clinton Administration did: waiting until America gets bonked on the head and then bonking back commensurately. Clinton suffers through the embassy bombings in Kenya and Tanzania in 1998 and strikes back with cruise missile attacks against al Qaeda training sites in Afghanistan and Sudan. Bush suffers through the far greater 9/11 attack and strikes back—commensurately—with invasions of Afghanistan and Iraq. Clinton did not call his strikes "preemptive," but they were. Bush calls his wars "preemptive," and the world worries about America creating an entirely new—seemingly unilateral—rule set for global security. That fear is understandable but overblown, in my judgment.

It is neither a Republican nor a Democrat approach when America strikes back at the Gap, because when the Gap strikes out at America, it has little to do with the policies of one administration or another. It has to do with America being intimately identified with a historical process that some within the Gap fear will destroy the world they know and love—and they are right to fear it. Globalization will eventually remake the entire Gap into an image we in the Core recognize far more than those currently trapped there. America has supported the advance of globalization for decades, through Republican and Democratic administrations, whether we realized it or not. Up until recently, we had a Cold War to occupy our strategic attention span, and so we paid no mind to that globalization process, but now we are finally—thanks to 9/11—seeing the world for what it truly is: divided between the connected Core and the Non-Integrating Gap.

Dealing with that strategic environment will not be a Republican task or a Democrat task, but an American task that stretches across decades. The Clinton Administration skillfully pushed the U.S. political system to realize our system-administrator role when it comes to economic globalization. By that I mean America took the lead in enunciating the overarching economic rule sets that guided globalization's advance across the 1990s, otherwise known as the Washington Consensus. Did that consensus last forever? Hardly, but that just points out that "system administration" is a nonstop job. Fine-tuning the rule sets never ends.

As I've said earlier, I believe the Bush Administration has, by and large, come to the conclusion that America needs to step up and play a similar system-administrator role in the realm of international security. In other words, it has come to realize that globalization's security rule sets need to catch up with its economic rule sets. Where the Bush Administration has failed to date is (1) in not correctly identifying the Gap in all its splendid disconnectedness, and instead letting the problem set be narrowly—and wrongly—described by the Pentagon as an "arc of instability" that many of the Administration's critics rightfully interpret as code for Middle Eastern oil producers; (2) in not being explicit with both the American people and our allies about the need for different security rule sets for the Core and the Gap; and (3) in not providing the public and our allies with a vision—or a story with a happy ending—that puts all these security rule-set changes into a larger context.

In short, the Bush Administration needs to level with the American public as to where this whole thing—this global war on terrorism and the preemption strategy—is really going. And if these policymakers themselves are unclear as to these strategies' ultimate course heading, then they'd better let the rest of the citizenry in on the inside debates that apparently continue to rage between Colin Powell's State Department and Donald Rumsfeld's Defense Department. Because until the Bush Administration describes that future worth creating in terms ordinary people and the rest of the world can understand, we will continue to lose support at home and abroad for the great task that lies ahead. That would be a real shame, because—in many ways—the Bush Administration has made all the right moves security-wise, it just does not seem to know how to explain those moves in a way that does not scare the hell out of everyone.

I have a little trick I like to use when I give my grand-strategy brief on the future of globalization: when I get to this point in my talk, and start discussing what I think are the different security rule sets operating in the Core versus the Gap, I will ask the audience to yell out their worst fears about the Bush Administration's foreign policy so far. Someone yells out, "We're a global cop!" And I reply, "... in the Gap!" Another blurts, "We're always so unilateral!" And I retort, "... in the Gap!" A third offers grimly, "We start wars preemptively!" And I follow with, "... in the Gap!" I know it sounds like an infomercial gimmick, but frankly, it works.

All the new security rule sets that the Bush Administration seems to be pushing do appear to many observers as reversals of long-held and cherished principles of U.S. foreign policy across the Cold War. These policies constituted a "winning hand" that led the West through some very dangerous and dark days. Many Americans and many allies are simply flabbergasted that now, with the Cold War in the bag, our government would ever consider going back on these bedrock principles of collective security, deterrence, and multilateralism.

The answer is, America is not going back on any of these ideals. They all still apply in spades—inside the Core. Inside the Core we have achieved something awfully close to Kant's perpetual peace—not just inside the Old Core but likewise inside the New Core of Russia, India, and China. If we simply have the vision and the courage to understand that amazing historical achievement, and not resort to fear-driven needs to locate some near-peer competitor to guide our strategic planning, then we will likewise realize that this rock-solid security rule set simply does not extend into the Gap—for now. Understanding that the Gap remains a largely Hobbesian world should induce neither dismay at globalization's limits nor panic over the security tasks that lie ahead. Rather, we simply need to roll up our sleeves, much as we did following the Second World War, and set about building the security rule sets that will guide the historical process of shrinking the Gap.

Harry Truman set in motion an enunciation of security rule sets that guided our Cold War strategy for decades, but those rules had no discernible political pedigree other than that singular American ability to be both pragmatic and optimistic at the same time. George W. Bush is making a similar push today, and if his can-do spirit strikes many critics as cockeyed and simplistic, all I will say in response is that morale matters when the road ahead is both long and challenging. We will need many presidents—Democrat and Republican—over the coming decades who will keep our political system, our public, and the rest of the Core focused on the prize we seek: making globalization truly global by shrinking the Gap.

I vividly remember when President Bush enunciated this "new" preemption strategy in a televised speech. Soon after the broadcast I was talking to my mom on the phone. She's taught college courses on the U.S. political system, so I'm always trying out my new theories on her. My first reaction was, "Man, this guy is really serious about shrinking the Gap!" That's an occupational hazard in this line of work: you're constantly deluding yourself that everything is falling into place "according to my master plan!" My mother's first reaction was less kind. Brushing past my usual megalomania, she exclaimed, "Don't those idiots in the White House realize they're destroying the concept of deterrence? For heaven's sake, does this mean we're supposed to attack China tomorrow because they have nukes and might use them against us?"

That's when it clicked for me: I realized why so many Americans might be freaked by Bush's "new" policy, when in reality, the strategy of preemption is not new, nor will it be universally applied. Mutually Assured Destruction, deterrence, and collective security inside the Core are not altered one whit by the Bush Administration's new strategy of preemption, because it simply does not apply to the Core—only to the Gap. Inside the Core we have a host of official mechanisms, both bilateral and multilateral, to deal with any security issues that arise. September 11 did not change any of that rule set, nor does the global war on terrorism. When the Bush Administration talks preemption, it is talking about actors and regimes in the Gap that we must prudently assume might be undeterrable, simply because they do not live in the same world or adhere to the same security rule sets that we do. Our goal in using the preemption strategy is not to destroy the Core's security rule set but to extend it.

Now, that might sound scarier than it really is. Think about how police are permitted to use deadly force within our society: much of the time they do so preemptively. Frankly, that's the ideal. We want the bad guys stopped—if necessary, dead in their tracks—before they can do someone great harm. That is an amazingly difficult responsibility we impart to our police, and our confidence in doing so is driven primarily by our faith in the legal system—or internal-security rule set—that we have erected around this preemptive use of deadly force. We assume that whenever a cop steps over the line and ends up killing someone preemptively without probable or just cause, that officer will be taken off the streets and if need be severely punished for the mistake. But the fact remains, Americans have no problem with the preemptive use of deadly force to uphold the internal-security rule set we call "the law."

America has spent the last half century trying to extend that internal-security rule set around the planet. Throughout this process we have consistently displayed the willingness to act preemptively. During the Cold War, all those preemptive actions were cloaked within the larger anti-Communist strategy of "hold that line!" So we tended to lose sight of the underlying reality whereby we put an amazing amount of faith in our military establishment not to go overboard and end up destroying the planet. Of course, we maintained the polite fiction that the president was the man with his finger on the "button," but in reality, our hair-trigger standoff with the Soviets was so preprogrammed in all its complexity that he was no more in complete control of the nuclear standoff than the man in the moon. What controlled that standoff was both sides understanding that *no one* controlled the standoff, therefore the nuclear option was not a line to be crossed. But we should never kid ourselves about the true nature of that bargain: we were always set to preemptively wage war—that was the primary rule set. It worked so well over the Cold War because both sides had—believe it or not—incredibly professional military leaders and suitably careful political leaders who constantly validated that rule set.

And you know what? Our political and military leaders still understand the validity of that particular rule set—as it applies across the Core. Of course, the Pentagon is still populated by far too many strategists who want to tinker with that rule set regarding China, and these people need to be pushed off the historical stage as quickly as possible. But I am completely confident—based not just on my regular exposure to senior personnel (both political appointees and career bureaucrats) in the U.S. government, but more so in terms of my continual interactions with the next generation of military leaders (the commanders and lieutenant colonels of today)—that this distinction between where deterrence still works and where preemption becomes necessary is not only completely understood, it is already largely internalized by most security decision makers.

Where we fail as a defense community is in making this distinction clear and understandable to both the American public and the world. What holds us back are those outdated strategic concepts that we simply have a hard time giving up, like the need to focus on the Big One instead of the strategic environment as a whole. So when we employ this preemptive option against a Saddam, for example, more than a few critics—not to mention the seriously overpsyched advocates—think the correct follow-on question is "Who's next?" Naturally, when we preemptively strike a Saddam, we hope to create a certain demonstration effect, meaning we extend the desired rule set. But the rule set we seek to extend is not some half-baked notion of *"You'd better watch it, world, 'cause you never know what might set America off!"* Rather, at a moment like this, we need to explain very carefully the sum of the rule-set violations that triggered our preemptive response. Like a cop explaining to a review board why he drew his pistol and shot the suspect dead, we need to make our case very calmly and completely and truthfully.

I believe the Bush Administration has made that case against Saddam, and nothing we have found in Iraq since—such as the dozens of mass graves and killing fields—convinces me that we did not do the right thing. But instead of debating the larger meaning of what America has just done, not just to the Middle East but frankly to the world as a whole, we waste a lot of strategic debate going back over, *ad nauseam,* the decision to go to war.

I know, I know. This is America, and in America there are no time limits on debates as important as those involving war. But in my mind, what really needs to be debated now is how we as a nation define the size of the task ahead. Was the problem just Saddam? Is it just al Qaeda? Is it Israel and Palestine too? Do we finish it off when there are no members left in the Axis of Evil? Is it all about the "arc of instability"? Or do we include the rest of Africa? Or most of Southeast Asia? How about Colombia? Where does this "present danger" end?

With regard to this strategy of preemption, I think four things need to be spelled out clearly to both our citizens and the rest of the Core: (1) that arms control as we have known it for decades is now dead and buried; (2) that is it not a question of "when" unilateralism makes sense, but "where"; (3) that while it is okay for America to—in most instances—get the ball rolling on specific security threats inside the Gap, eventually all jobs there are multilateral efforts; and (4) since there is no exiting the Gap militarily, there is no such thing as an exit strategy. Let me deal with each of these points in turn.

One of the ways I came around to this strategic vision, which I believe is less a theory than an objective reality that has been staring all of us in the face for more than a decade, was in understanding how the Core-Gap division effectively kills arms control as a useful tool of American foreign policy.

We do not need any arms control whatsoever inside the Core. Everyone who really needs nukes already has them, but if the Japanese ever decide they truly want them, I don't think even that development triggers the need for any arms control. Since Mutually Assured Destruction and deterrence still hold throughout the Core, all the advanced states there readily understand the "crystal ball effect" of nukes—as in, we all know where we end up collectively if anybody decides to use them, so nobody is going to use them. Now, don't get me wrong, I have nothing against doing whatever is possible in terms of military-to-military ties between, say, the United States and China to increase awareness on both sides regarding strategic postures, especially as we develop limited missile defense capabilities. But that is not arms control. That is simply maintaining good intra-Core security transparency.

If we do not need any arms control within the Core because it is superfluous, we also do not need it between the Core and Gap, because it is completely futile. Here I am talking about most of the efforts to limit technology transfer, which usually involve America throwing sanctions at the problem and, in the process, pissing off the rest of the Core while stopping nothing in the process. In almost every instance of initial technology transfer, we are talking about private firms from fellow Core powers seeking to make a buck by selling the same sort of military-related technology that we routinely share among ourselves in the Core, and which America often sells to its own particular allies within the Gap. We will never stop this technology transfer, we will simply drive it underground. Having it out in the open beats guessing about who is smuggling what. Moreover, I always think it is bad when America is put in the position of wagging its finger at the Gap for wanting to get its hands on the same technology we develop at will and employ with regularity. I want lots of technology transfer from the Core to the Gap as a rule, because I think giving them access to such technology is an important part of shrinking the Gap.

You might counter with "But all we really want to stop being transferred is the technology associated with weapons of mass destruction." Here I am in agreement, but since I don't think sanctions or treaties are really going to stop that transfer from Core to Gap, I shift my response on that point to why I believe arms control inside the Gap is likewise a complete waste of time. Assume the transfer is going to occur despite our best efforts. Now, we have people inside the Gap we simply do not trust with weapons of mass destruction. They do not adhere to our security rule sets and, frankly, would like to see them torn down. So why do we think there is any utility in pursuing arms control or sanctions of any form?

At this point, if you have a bad actor, whether he is a superempowered terrorist like Osama bin Laden or a rogue leader like Kim Jong Il, who has checked a long list of boxes that says he is not to be trusted and the world would be a better place without him, then I say you move on to preemption. There is no negotiation at this point in the process, because you have given *them* plenty of warnings and requests to cease and desist. In the case of a regime, you simply keep ratcheting up your demands for compliance, and when the regime cannot comply and cannot be provoked into a precipitating action by your constantly growing military pressure, you preempt. In the case of a terrorist group, you skip even those preliminaries and preempt the moment you have any of them in your crosshairs.

Now, that may sound pretty harsh, but again, in many ways this is simply America taking the same sort of security rule sets that keep us safe within our borders and working to extend them to that Gap that lies in the great beyond. You may ask, What gives America the right to make such decisions? The simplest answer is that "might makes right" when we are talking about America playing Gap Leviathan. On some level, if other Core powers want a greater say in how we exercise that power, they simply need to dedicate enough defense spending to develop similar capabilities. Absent that, America earns a certain right for unilateralism in the Gap. If, over time, the rest of the Core disapproves of the "service" America is providing on their behalf, they have ways of making their displeasure known to us (a subject I intend to cover later).

What we have to make clear to both Americans and the rest of the world is that it is not a matter of the U.S. Government acting unilaterally *whenever* it pleases, just *wherever* it needs to inside the Gap. It's a lot like talking to cops in Los Angeles about how they behave during their workday. You ask, "Do you act the same way in Brentwood as you do in South Central?" And they say, "No." You ask, "Why?" And they reply simply, "Because I like to make it home for dinner every night in one piece." Simply put, the same security rule sets that define upper-class Brentwood do not extend to the harsh, inner-city reality that is South Central. Denying that reality is unfair to the personnel whose lives are put at risk in extending the security rule sets we all take for granted in *our* neighborhood.

In many ways, that is the essential beef the United States has had with the International Criminal Court, going all the way back to the Clinton Administration. It's not that America wants one rule set for itself and another for the rest of the world, just that America needs special consideration for the security roles it undertakes inside the Gap. In effect, we don't want fellow Core members applying their Kantian rule sets to our behavior inside the Hobbesian Gap. So what has the Bush Administration done to deal with this bifurcated world? America is pressuring nations around the world to sign a special bilateral agreement in which they pledge not to take us to court over any military interventions we may undertake within their borders. It's sort of a "pre-nup" in this global war on terrorism. Over seventy countries have already signed these treaties, and virtually all of them are Gap states. But who is lodging the biggest protests about these accords? The Europeans, naturally.

America will need to act unilaterally inside the Gap on a regular basis not just because we need a free hand whenever American lives are put at risk, but also because—quite frankly—no other military power on the planet comes even close to matching our capabilities. In effect, our unilateralism inside the Gap is functionally defined. So yes, we may get the U.N. Security Council to "bless" us with a resolution and "dress" us with coalition partners that, to be blunt, we simply do not need in the initial warfighting phase of any intervention, but in the end we'll be kicking down the door largely on our own whenever the scenario is significant in size—as in Iraq. Yes, there will always be a few key allies we can count on, all of whom are likewise distinguished by some lesser ability to project their own military force around the planet (and all of whom resemble our melting-pot profiles—being either the Brits or any one of a number of their former colonies, such as Australia, Canada, India . . .). But have no delusions: the United States owns the only "fist" in the business.

Of course, it's one thing for America to act unilaterally in "kicking down the door" and toppling some bad guy, and quite another thing to actually follow through on the peace that also needs to be won. In this follow-on effort, we not only need friends, we need a lot of friends. But it is not a bad thing for America to, in effect, write checks with its military strategy of preemption that it cannot possibly cash using the defense budget alone. By that I mean, sometimes somebody needs to take that nasty first step in dispatching the bad guy—you know, the Clint Eastwood character who rallies the settlers into defending the homestead. In the end, if the high plains drifter tries to do it all alone, he's gonna get nailed, but if he waits for the crowd to muster its courage, then everyone's more likely to take some bullets. Sometimes *leaders gotta lead.*

In my mind, the difference between unilateralism and multilateralism in this situation is very subtle. America is being multilateralist when it says, "Hey, Core, everybody follow me in!" And then the rest of the Core follows us in. America is being unilateralist when it says, "Hey, Core, everybody follow me in!" And then nobody except the Brits and Aussies tag along. But either way, American soldiers will end up being the tip of the spear. Getting everyone else along for the follow-through effort simply brings us back to the point about America needing to be more explicit with its allies about the better world we seek to create whenever we undertake these necessarily difficult tasks.

What if our allies do not like our definition of that "better world"? Obviously, it cannot be a matter of America declaring, "Follow me or get out of the way!" So the discussion of security rule sets is a never-ending process, just as it is inside our country, where the Supreme Court is constantly revising definitions of our most basic legal principles. But that discussion is not a substitute for action, so let's not confuse the United Nations with the executive branch of some hoped-for future world government. The UN is closer to a congress, or a combination debating society and rule-setting body. For the foreseeable future, America comes closest to the Core's executive branch function, primarily because we own the world's preeminent military force. But that structural reality only highlights the great importance of how America explains itself whenever it employs its military might around the planet. So far, we have explained the need for war, but not the promise of peace.

The Bush Administration has not yet pitched that larger vision of a future worth creating. Instead, with no "happy ending" attached to this pretty scary tale we seem to be spinning out, most people around the world are more than nervous about our intentions. That's not just bad, it's tragic, because we are wasting a precious moment in history here—a moment when the world is looking to us quite naturally to spell out the new rule sets. But what do we give them instead? Just preemption, nothing more. Or worse, instead of the Bush Administration offering more, we leave it to the political pundits to toss out phrases like "empire," "World War IV," and "crusade."

All those foolishly hyperbolic descriptions prevent us from having the debates we as a nation truly need to work our way through if we are ever going to come to grips with the long-term security challenge of shrinking the Gap. And here's where I get to my final point about this Administration—and every one that follows—getting level with the American public: we are never leaving the Gap and we are never "bringing our boys home." There is no exiting the

Gap, only shrinking the Gap, and if there is no exiting the Gap, then we'd better stop kidding ourselves about "exit strategies." *No exit means no exit strategy.*

Why I Hate the "Arc of Instability"

In the summer of 2002 I gave a speech at a Washington, D.C., conference of defense contractors that got me quickly called on the carpet in the policy shop of the Office of Secretary of Defense (OSD). I had always worried about this happening with one of my talks, because when you speak bluntly about the future, what you say can often collide with the polite truths of the present. My sin was this: I said that America's new military bases in Central Asia would become a permanent feature of the landscape there. The exact quote was, "I believe fifty years from now, they will be as familiar to us as Ramstein Air Force Base." Ramstein is a huge, permanent hub for American military operations located in Germany. By comparing our new bases in the former Soviet republics of Kyrgyzstan and Uzbekistan with Ramstein, I was suggesting that our recent moves into Central Asia signaled the sort of long-term export of security that we ended up pursuing in Europe following the Second World War.

I believe America will end up exporting security on that scale not just to Central Asia, but also to the Middle East, Africa, the Caribbean Rim, and—yes—even Southeast Asia, a place we swore we'd never return to after losing Vietnam. The bases we create throughout the Gap will, by and large, never reach the scope of Ramstein, because we will want lots of small, Spartan-style facilities dotting the Gap, not the sort of giant, Mall of America bases we built in Europe and Northeast Asia for World War III. But yes, over the decades, these bases will become, in aggregate, as familiar to U.S. servicemen and -women, and the American public as Ramstein became to the generations who lived through the Cold War. That's how big our security commitment to the Gap will end up being. That's how long the road ahead truly is.

Now, the reporter who wrote up my "startling prediction" pulled the usual trick and counterposed my quote with one from Secretary Rumsfeld himself, in which he proclaimed, "We don't have any particular plans for permanent bases." When I read the article, I joked to a colleague that it was like I had predicted Rumsfeld would be dead in fifty years, only to have my "startling prediction" contradicted by an immediate statement from him that he "didn't have any particular plans for the great beyond." Simply put, we can both be right on this point.

Well, the day the article appeared in the Pentagon's *Early Bird* news service, I got a call from OSD's policy shop, asking, in effect, who was I and why was I saying these things. That gives a sense of how vast the "office" of the Secretary of Defense truly is. When you tell people you're working in OSD, a lot of them think you have a cubbyhole down the hall from the secretary himself. In reality, OSD is a huge management organization of several thousand employees. I had been briefing my material for months throughout the Pentagon and intelligence community, including basically all of Secretary Rumsfeld's senior personal aides earlier that spring, but there were entire divisions full of hundreds of policymakers who had no idea who I was or what my ideas were.

A couple of weeks later I gave my brief to a collection of relevant DASDs (pronounced *daz-dees*). The Deputy Assistant Secretaries of Defense are fifth-tier policymakers (after the Secretary, Deputy Secretary, Under Secretaries, and Assistant Secretaries) with direct oversight of the career worker-bee bureaucrats who really make the Pentagon trains run on time. DASDs are politicals, meaning appointed by the current administration. So they come and go over the years (most stay in positions for a mere 18 to 24 months), while the worker bees are permanent. In many ways, the DASDs enforce the administration's vision throughout the rank-and-file civil servants, a category I belonged to at that time (as a Naval War College professor), despite my second "hat" as Assistant for Strategic Futures in the Office of Force Transformation.

I wasn't brought in to have my hands slapped for the press story.

The DASDs were perfectly friendly during the brief. They listened politely and then followed up with a host of questions. When we were finished, all the DASDs in the room basically turned to the special representative sent down from the office of the Under Secretary of Defense for Policy to check me out, waiting for this guy's final judgment. He simply shrugged and said, "Nothing I see here goes against the stuff we're trying to do in our shop." So, in effect, I was given a clean bill of health and sent on my way with no restrictions on my daily activity. Because I wasn't saying anything publicly that worked against their emerging long-term plans, there was no need to clamp down on what I was saying in the brief.

I was relieved and more than a little bit surprised. I didn't kid myself that I converted anyone in the room that day about the Core-Gap theory in its full glory, because clearly that vision goes beyond the pure security issues that fill up the DASDs' in-boxes on a daily basis. But what was amazing was how no one in the room challenged any of my judgments concerning the Pentagon's need for a "new ordering principle" that would ditch the decades-long focus on great-power war and deemphasize China as a threat. You have to understand, the Bush Administration came into power with a serious focus on Asia as the future arena of global conflict—not Southwest Asia and sure as heck not Central Asia. The whole "defense transformation" they were pushing back then was driven by a fear of a rising near-peer in the East, not a collection of lesser includeds in the Middle East. Africa didn't even appear on their strategic map. So I left OSD that day convinced they were getting ready to make some big decisions about the future of U.S. military basing around the world. I knew such a review process had begun in the policy shop. Now I understood just how profound it was going to be.

Ten months later Greg Jaffe, the Pulitzer Prize–winning defense reporter of the *Wall Street Journal,* rang me up about the "Pentagon's New Map" article in *Esquire.* Like a lot of people, he had read it during the run-up to the war in Iraq and had found it interesting, but after the war, he came back to the piece, believing it to be sort of a Rosetta stone for decoding the stream of big policy changes he was seeing coming out of OSD. So we talked for several hours, by phone and in person, about the Core-Gap thesis. Then Greg did a round of interviews throughout OSD and even traveled to Kyrgyzstan to—in his words—"check out the Gap in person."

What Jaffe ended up writing for the *Journal* in a front-page story was really quite stunning in terms of the huge change it captured. In the piece, Jaffe described a "radical shift in strategy" that "puts less emphasis on China" and more on fighting terrorism throughout an "'arc of instability' that runs through the Caribbean Rim, Africa, the Middle East, South Asia, and North Korea," as it was described by OSD officials. Jaffe went on to say, "Worries about this arc of countries, largely cut off from economic globalization, increasingly are influencing how the military trains, what it buys, and where it puts forces."

Now, the story caused its own little media buzz, and since I was quoted in it as saying, "Disconnectedness defines danger," I got to go on National Public Radio with Greg Jaffe to discuss the strategy changes described in the article. I love going on NPR, because it's such an intelligent audience as a rule, and this time was no different. But what I heard in the questions we were fielding from our interviewer and call-ins made me realize what a great conceptual and real-world distance there is between my definition of the Gap and the Pentagon's definition of the Arc of Instability. By that I don't mean *"Argh! Those idiots understand nothing of my work!"* All these policymakers are incredibly smart, dedicated, and caring people who are doing their best to deal with the real world they find themselves managing today.

But what NPR's callers made me realize was that most Americans—and frankly, most of the world—are going to view the definition of an Arc of Instability as equating to "unstable Muslim countries that America cares about primarily because of oil." Remember back to the Iraq War debate: a lot of people belittling the Bush Administration's case for toppling Saddam, saying it had nothing to do with the global war on terror but rather represented the onset of American "empire" in the region to protect our oil interests there. In effect, what I heard on NPR that night was that American tendency to cut to the chase and get right to the punch line: "Sure, you can talk about the 'gap' and making globalization global, but in the end, all the Pentagon really wants to do is kill bad guys and protect oil fields."

After the Jaffe story appeared, I received dozens of e-mails from around the world, mostly from graduate students in security affairs, asking me to confirm that the Gap and the Arc of Instability were really one and the same. In effect, many of these suitably impertinent young scholars were demanding that I fess up and admit that my grand Core-Gap thesis was nothing more than window dressing for a smash-and-grab thrusting of U.S. military power into the oil-rich regions of the Middle East and Central Asia. Now, I realize that all grand strategy is ultimately reductionist: you take this gigantically complex world and reduce it down to a few key concepts and principles to guide your foreign policy. My "shrink the Gap" certainly qualifies. But seeing the concept get further reduced to just the Arc of Instability and all these negative connotations that phrase conjures around the world . . . well, that just drives me nuts.

You might think I am just being picky or sensitive about the phrase. After all, it probably doesn't appear anywhere outside of the Pentagon, right? Wrong. In October of 2003, *U.S. News & World Report* ran a cover story called "Global Cops: Inside the Pentagon's New Plan to Police the World's Most Dangerous Places." Inside was a two-page map that reproduced my Non-Integrating Gap exactly as it was drawn for the *Esquire* article. I was listed in the credits—good for my ego. But the phrase arching across the familiar shape read "Arc of Instability."

Let me try to make the case here that something vital is lost in this bureaucratic translation.

First, the arc concept is old, dating back to the Carter Administration, which used it to describe an "arc of crisis" that ran from the Horn of Africa up into Afghanistan. The whole point of describing that arc was to suggest that the Soviets were behind all of these crises in one way or another (sort of true), which meant America needed to start getting tougher in the region militarily, hence the Carter Doctrine that said we would limit Soviet influence in the Persian Gulf region. So besides carrying the baggage of being so centered on the Gulf and oil, it also carries a whiff of "We'd better step in there before somebody else does." That is absolutely the wrong signal to send right now to other great powers, but especially to a China concerned about future access to oil as its energy requirements double in the next two decades. In the late 1970s, the Soviets were right to look at the Arc concept as suggesting America was closing the loophole that had previously existed in our containment strategy. So it's no surprise today that the Chinese get nervous whenever they see a staunchly Sinophobic Pentagon describe an Arc of Instability that looks suspiciously like an encircling strategy.

Second, the Arc concept smacks of treating symptoms, not the disease. No amount of U.S. military presence in the Gap is ever going to make it stable in any lasting sense. Our presence can boost security, and security will allow for growing connectivity between the country in question and the outside world. Ultimately, any Gap country is made stable by being economically integrated into the Core and having the resulting economic development find expression in increased liberty over time, because liberty plus economic development will get you a stable democracy in the end. So all we do when we export security into any region is get the ball rolling, nothing more.

But that is not how the Arc gets interpreted either by our friends or our critics around the world. Instead, it gets interpreted as a babysitting job for the U.S. military, as we care for rigid authoritarian governments in the region in exchange for stable access to their energy. When the Germany daily *Die Zeit* lambasted the "Pentagon's New Map," they captured this image perfectly in the phrase *"Der Babysitter kommt im Kampfanzug,"* or "The babysitter comes wearing a military outfit."

Such suspicions make perfect sense to people on the outside of the Pentagon looking in. You can parody the Pentagon's logic as follows: *We're focusing on this arc of countries.* Why? *Because they're unstable!* How so? *They're full of bad guys!* So how do you make them stable? *Easy, kill the bad guys.* How do you know when you're finished? *No more bad guys to kill.* That will leave the region stable? *It'll sure as hell keep the oil flowing! Next question?*

Worse still will be the episodic nature of our activity in this approach: We'll go up-tempo as the "instability" flares up, but what will our role be in the times between spikes in hostile activity? Will our forces pull back into the shadows to reduce our "footprint" and our overt presence as occupiers, only to bulk back up again in response to a schedule *they* get to determine? Do we switch back and forth between friendly community police officer and killer SWAT? Can we expect the locals to buy both roles from the same people? Can we expect the same soldiers to play both roles?

My point is this: Using the Arc of Stability as an operating theory makes it seem as if America is only interested in getting what it wants, not what the Gap as a whole really needs. As usual, the Pentagon focuses just on the bad to be prevented or eliminated, not the good to be generated in its place. That's what you get when you think of war strictly within the context of war, instead of considering it within the context of everything else. America ends up looking like Assassination Inc., picking off bad guys so corrupt rulers throughout the Middle East can maintain *their* failing regimes and *our* access to oil. Tell me how this undercuts bin Laden's case against the House of Saud? The Middle East's connectivity to the outside world is stunted, plain and simple. For years that connectivity has been almost completely defined by oil and little else. To the extent we are viewed by the world as protecting only that slim connectivity and nothing else, our effort will seem completely self-serving. In other words, we will be viewed as protecting our good life and doing nothing to make life better in the Middle East.

Of course, you can say I'm being unfairly reductionist here, and unreasonable in demanding that the Pentagon consider all these issues that clearly lie outside its normal prerogatives. But the Pentagon put itself in charge of both this global war on terrorism and "transforming" the Middle East through the "big bang" of toppling Saddam's regime. To back away now from the full consequences of these actions looks disingenuous, to say the least. What America has started in that part of the world thanks to our invasions of Afghanistan and Iraq is definitely something beyond the Defense Department's purview, but that only makes the words we choose to describe and explain our security strategy all the more crucial.

A third reason I hate the Arc of Instability is that it suggests America is only interested in providing order, not justice. What I like about the Gap concept is that it provides a larger context that forces the conversation to move beyond just picking off the bad guys and toward a definition of what will make countries more than just "not unstable." As soon as the dialogue shifts beyond those symptoms to root causes, the challenge of how we generate greater connectivity throughout the Gap elevates our conversation from mere national security strategy to truly grand strategy. Once you do that, the Pentagon can't hog all the seats at the table— better still, neither can the U.S. Government. America cannot connect an Afghanistan or an Iraq—much less an entire Middle East—to the larger world all by itself. Only the Core as a whole can do that, led primarily by the private sector. When that economic connectivity ensues, then you start talking about not just a more orderly world but a more just world.

I also hate the Arc concept because it suggests sort of a barrier defense between the Core and the Gap, as in "We'd better hold the line here or we'll be swamped by all their terror and chaos!" Besides making it seem like we're holding back the Muslim hordes, there is a similarly distasteful sense that the Middle East is about as far as we're planning to move into the Gap. Now, I know the Bush Administration and the Pentagon have made serious noises about having future bases inside Africa as well, but when you look at the difference between how our government begged the world to let us take down Saddam and how the world ended up having to beg us to do something about Liberia, you can't escape this sense of Africa being a "bridge too far." After all, it's on the other side of the Arc. If we hold the line at the Arc, do we really have to do anything about Africa?

In addition, "holding the line" at the Arc also gets interpreted as anti-Islamic. You can't help picking up this vibe—that sense of *these people are crazy*. Whenever I go on talk radio I always field the question, "Isn't your Gap really just the same thing as saying Islam is the problem?" My answer is, The Gap contains all religions, and all religions inside the Gap are more fundamentalist than their counterparts in the Core. Catholics in the Gap are a whole lot more fundamentalist than those in the Core, as are Christians in general. Jews in the Gap, or basically Israel, tend to be far more fundamentalist than Jews in the Core. The same thing is true for Muslims.

All religions in the Gap are more fundamentalist because they play a different role from the one here in the Core. In the Core, religion is mostly about inner peace, whereas in the Gap it is still mostly about external networking—the goal being survival in hard economic times. Religion used to be more like that in America, say, a hundred years ago or right up to the point when we created a social welfare system. Until that point, religion in the Core served the same survival-network function that Islam so readily—and deftly—plays throughout the Gap. That a small percentage of believers seek to use that network for evil purposes should not taint the efforts of the whole, nor should it put us in the position of treating Islam in general as the problem or the enemy. As Daniel Pipes repeats endlessly, "If militant Islam is the problem, moderate Islam is the solution." But again, the phrase "the Arc of Instability" conspires to pigeonhole our approach to just the Muslim countries, because in most geographic descriptions of the Arc, the predominantly Muslim regions are emphasized.

On a more practical level, it is also important for us to realize that in this global war on terrorism, while many of the political grievances associated with the most prominent transnational terrorist networks are now centered in the Middle East, the operating environments of such groups span the Gap as a whole. The real seam we need to be working lies not just along that Muslim arc, but around the entirety of the Gap. In reality, one of the least-told stories of our global war on terrorism involves just that—the significant increase of bilateral security relations between the United States and a host of countries, or Seam States, that ring the Gap.

What are the Seam States? Classic examples include Mexico, Brazil, South Africa, Morocco, Algeria, Greece, Turkey, Pakistan, Thailand, Malaysia, the Philippines, and Indonesia. Why are they important? Whenever you look at global maps of where terrorist networks are centered, invariably all the ones we care most about are located inside the Gap. Moreover, as we track their movements, or what the military would describe as their "interior lines of communication," these too lie overwhelmingly inside the Gap. How those terrorists access the Core is through the Seam States. This is sort of like the September 11 terrorists who hijacked the planes flying out of Boston boarding those planes previously at a regional airport in Maine. In that instance, Maine, with its looser security rule set, was the "seam state" that was exploited. Since security tends to be higher in the "deep" Core states, terrorists invariably seek access through the Seam States, or gain access to the United States by transiting through Mexico or some Caribbean island nation, as opposed to walking through security at JFK Airport in New York City.

The U.S. security strategy vis-à-vis these Seam States is simple: get them to increase their security practices as much as possible and—by doing so—close whatever loopholes exist. This is what gets the U.S. government involved in helping Brazil achieve better transparency throughout the Amazon Forest, South Africa get a better grip over its banking networks, and Indonesia clamp down on rebels across its far-flung archipelago. Other countries where the Pentagon has increased security assistance since 9/11 include the Philippines, Algeria, Djibouti, Pakistan, and India. All these efforts would have made sense—and in some instances did make sense—on some level prior to 9/11, but thanks to the global war on terrorism all such bilateral security assistance expands with far greater speed and urgency.

This assistance is not so much purposefully focused on these Seam States as it is simply drawn to them by the circumstances of how terrorists seek to avoid our efforts at prosecution. A transnational terrorist organization like al Qaeda will exploit the Gap's disconnectedness to do things like disperse its gold throughout Africa, shift training activities to Asia, obtain guns from Latin American arms smugglers, and tap sympathetic financial networks embedded across the Middle East and—increasingly—Southeast Asia. But in the end, if al Qaeda really wants to bring its war home to America, it will need to exploit globalization's seams, like the Internet, commercial airline networks, and banking networks—plus the Seam States that mark the geographic dividing line between the Gap and the Core. So if America is truly going to wage a global war on terrorism, it needs to work the Gap as a whole and the host of Seam States that surround it.

For all these reasons, then, I worry that the Pentagon's focus on the Arc of Instability not only sends the wrong messages to the rest of the world but also does not fully address the security issues associated with this global war on terrorism. Don't get me wrong, I do not want to expand the barrier mentality of the "arc" approach to the Gap as a whole, nor do I wish to see America's security assistance to Seam States take on the air of some twenty-first-century Maginot Line. Shrinking the Gap can never be allowed to devolve into a static us-versus-them strategy.

That brings me to probably the biggest reason why I hate the Arc of Instability: using this term just seems like a historical cop-out. In effect, it becomes just the latest excuse advanced economies use to explain why the least-developed regions are being left behind—yet again. Throughout the Cold War, neither the capitalist West nor the socialist East went out of its way to integrate the less-developed countries of the Third World into their privileged economic communities. In effect, there were two "mini-global" economies, and memberships in both were effectively closed to those countries I now identify as belonging to the Gap. Instead of offering genuine economic integration, both sides spent far too much time and resources recruiting and maintaining client states, or political allies in the superpower rivalry. In the most egregious cases, these states became the superpowers' proxies in futile "hot" wars that had no effective bearing on the ultimate "correlation of forces" between the two camps. In short, both sides largely used and abused the Third World.

All through the years, these disconnected states begged for a better deal, typically using the United Nations as their platform. Remember the New International Economic Order of 1974? Neither does anyone else. That's because what the less-developed countries heard from both economic blocs essentially amounted to this: "We'd love to help out more, but frankly we're so tied up in this Cold War that you'll just have to wait." With East and West now combined in globalization's Functioning Core, there are no good excuses for why the nations of the Gap must remain on the outside of the global economy, noses pressed to the glass. Simply put, the bill has finally come due, and the "Arc of Instability" suggests nothing more than a meager down payment. "Stabilization" addresses the collective sins of the past but does not speak to future integration. Connectivity does, and that's why I believe the Non-Integrating Gap beats the Arc of Instability hands down.

The Core's political case for integrating the Gap's regions cannot be defined by fear but must reflect a system-level understanding of the increasingly symbiotic economic relationship that evolves between the two. Over time, the Core will need the Gap as much as the Gap needs the Core. Our security strategies and the language we use to enunciate them must reflect this larger understanding of how the Core and Gap inevitably come together out of enlightened self-interest.

Chapter 4

THE CORE
AND THE GAP

IN THE PENTAGON, they love to use the expression "drinking at the fire hose" in the context of briefs that deliver an overwhelming amount of new information in a rapid flow. Since military officers typically change billets (or jobs) every two to three years, they are constantly finding themselves in the position of having to catch up on a load of detailed information that everyone else at their new posting already knows. So the phrase is part lament and part plea, as in, "I'm drinking as fast as I can here!" In the roughly thousand briefs I've delivered over the past decade and a half, I must have heard that expression from audience members about 90 percent of the time. In terms of strategic vision, I am the fire hose!

Being a fire hose on strategy is both good and bad: People either love you or they hate you. Either you're the most profound thinker they've ever come across, or the glibbest piece of nonsense they've ever heard. I've given talks to large audiences where half the personnel leave the room within ten minutes of my opening my mouth, only to have the remainder sit absorbed for two-plus hours and then give me a standing ovation. And, yes, those who leave tend to be older and those who stay tend to be younger, so there's that sense of "my day will come." But then there's that old joke about Brazil, "Country of tomorrow, and it always will be!" You worry about that too.

If you think all this nervous chatter is leading to some wild tour of the future, you're right. I've spent three chapters spelling out the past and the present, telling you repeatedly that the Pentagon's biggest sin in strategic planning since the end of the Cold War has been its inability to think beyond war as it has traditionally defined it. I've told you that this narrow strategic approach has blinded the Pentagon to the new security rule sets that have emerged with this current, expansive phase of globalization. I've even gone so far as to charge the U.S. Government with possibly derailing globalization's future advance as they continue to pursue this global war on terrorism in too myopic a fashion. I have preached repeatedly the necessity of understanding war within the context of everything else, and this chapter is going to be about that *everything else*.

I aim to do nothing less than explain how the world works in terms of the Core-Gap divide. The model of globalization I present here follows the KISS principle, as in, *Keep it simple, stupid!* It will reduce all of globalization's grand complexity down to four essential elements, or flows, that I believe define its basic functioning from the perspective of international stability. These four flows are (1) the movement of people from the Gap to the Core; (2) the movement of energy from the Gap to the New Core; (3) the movement of money from the Old Core to the New Core; and (4) the exporting of security that only America can provide to the Gap.

In this chapter, I will try to convince you that America's exporting of security around the world is crucial to globalization's continued functioning and future expansion. But it's not simply a matter of "send the troops, and globalization will follow." This is not some "globalization at the barrel of a gun" dogma. This is about keeping these four basic elements in balance, or avoiding the sort of pathway that I believe the Core is currently stuck in thanks to a combination of our collective responses to 9/11 (including the war in Iraq), the always contentious arguments we have about trade, and the growing realization among the world's populations that this globalization thing is going to require a lot more work than we had anticipated back in the 1990s.

In short, this chapter is about relating security to the *everything else* I believe is essential to protect if this war on terrorism is to be truly won, if globalization is to be made truly global, and if the Gap is to be truly shrunk. So pucker up, because I'm about to turn the hose on full blast.

THE MILITARY-MARKET LINK

Eliminating the disconnectedness that defines the Gap goes far beyond simply defeating those forces willing to use violence to achieve or maintain it, because these terrorists are nothing more than parasites feeding off this political and economic isolation. Once that isolation is ended, and broadband connectivity is achieved for the masses, the forces of terror and repression can no longer hold sway. Will they ever disappear completely? Absolutely not. But they will have to take their acts truly underground, off the net, and into the world of illegitimacy. That is how you turn a "heroic" terrorist into a common criminal: you surround him with a society deeply connected to the larger world of rules, opportunity, and hope. You render him an outcast among his own. You shame him out of existence. What you cannot do is simply catch him and kill him, because there will always be more. Over time, your violence will be delegitimized and his honored, unless yours is employed on behalf of a society growing in connectivity. Your effort must be intimately identified with that growing connectivity; your war must be in the context of *everything else*.

By the mid-1990s, my fear that the Pentagon simply wasn't "getting" that *everything else*—or globalization—became so profound that I seriously considered going back to school for an MBA. I figured I just could not acquire the necessary knowledge about how the world really worked in this era of globalization if I remained trapped in the Pentagon's insular mind-set. I was convinced that a rising near-peer simply wasn't in the works, meaning the role of Leviathan in the global security system was ours for the taking. But instead of moving in the direction of increased understanding of globalization, the Pentagon seemed more determined than ever to withdraw from the world.

The debacle in Somalia seemed to kill the "new world order" rhetoric once and for all, and the Pentagon was relieved to get out of the nation-building business. Around the same time, the military began realizing it was stuck keeping Saddam in the box for the long run, and felt itself being pushed toward interventions in the Balkans, two assignments that looked to be quagmires in the making. Meanwhile, the glide path of force-structure reductions engineered by Joint Chiefs Chairman General Colin Powell in the early 1990s was proceeding apace, shrinking the military year by year. So with the Pentagon being pulled into real-world operations that ate up resources, it was getting harder and harder to pursue the "revolution in military affairs," or RMA, that many Pentagon strategists believed was possible because of the emergence of the Information Revolution.

In effect, there was a tug-of-war between the Pentagon and the Clinton White House over the role of the U.S. military in managing international security. Strategists in the Pentagon saw a globalization-fueled strategic environment that was unmanageable at best and chaotic at worst. The Clinton Administration was strongly focused on recasting the international financial architecture to promote free trade, and therefore relegated the Pentagon to babysitting the chronically disconnected states on the margin. Neither side saw the Gap as a threat environment of any note—just a bad neighborhood to be monitored while the real world moved ahead with economic globalization. While the Clinton Administration truly believed in the notion that the rising economic tide would lift all boats, the Pentagon did not, believing globalization would only increase global instability by exacerbating the divide between the "haves" and "have-nots" and propagating dangerous military technologies throughout the system.

The U.S. military harbored its own definition of a "future worth creating," and it had nothing to do with globalization. It dreamed of missile defense and going *mano a mano* with a high-tech Chinese military in the Taiwan Straits somewhere around 2025. Their globalization scenarios envisioned trade-bloc wars and future security environments that alternated between *Mad Max* moonscapes and *Blade Runner* shooting galleries.

At the time, a lot of foreign policy specialists were arguing that if America was too forceful (read, *unilateral*) in its security leadership, it would inevitably trigger the rise of competing "poles" in the system—like a united Europe or an emboldened Japan. I just felt that the strategic default position of waiting around for a rising near peer seemed inadequate and dangerous. Did we win the Cold War just to hang back and let the world run itself? Wasn't that the same bold choice we made after World War I?

More to the point, I had a growing sense that even though our allies constantly spoke in public about the need for American military restraint, what they would say privately was radically different. I got a taste of this in 1993, when I participated in a two-week government-sponsored seminar in Salzburg that brought together "future leaders" from around the world to discuss the post–Cold War security order. As part of my participation, I gave a seminar presentation that outlined what I thought were the major camps of thought in the U.S. foreign policy establishment regarding America's role in international security. The details of the discussion were less impressive to me than the confessions many participants made to me regarding their own governments' complete inability to think about global security in a comprehensive fashion. As one senior-level official in the Greek defense ministry confided, "Only an American can even think like this, because only America has the military capabilities necessary to deal with global security issues in any real way." As much as my foreign colleagues derided America's penchant for believing only we can run the world safely, most expressed relief that at least someone was worrying about globalization's larger security issues. The challenge was to figure out how the

U.S. military mattered with regard to globalization. That's why I figured getting an MBA might help me in my quest. I just wasn't seeing the military-market nexus whatsoever, even though I knew intrinsically that it was there. After all, America's biggest trade and investment partners were also our biggest military allies. Surely that wasn't merely an accident of history. If globalization was really going to sweep the planet, wouldn't America—as the world's biggest economy—necessarily build new security relationships around the world as a part of this process?

One of the main reasons I left Washington in 1998 was my realization that I needed new conversation partners in my quest to discover globalization's military-market link. At first glance, leaving the Navy's premier private-sector think tank to join the Naval War College seemed like a move in the wrong direction. Now I would be joining the Defense Department for real, losing my status as a skeptical outsider paid to voice my objective criticisms. But the War College had something CNA did not: an open conduit for serious conversations with Wall Street regarding the security issues arising from globalization.

I came to the War College for the express purpose of utilizing the Center for Naval Warfare Studies' ongoing research partnership with Cantor Fitzgerald to explore the military-market nexus that my limited understanding of globalization simply lacked. If I was going to be present at the creation of some new world order, I needed to understand how that world worked in an economic sense. The real peace dividend of the Cold War was a world that essentially worked economically, or one that was no longer divided between competing economic models. If during the Cold War our military power defended capitalism from Communism's threat, then certainly some protective role still remained in this complex, messy world. History hadn't ended. If anything, it had merely resumed, and I was there—in the words of one popular song— "watching the world wake up from history." The question was, Wake up to what?

That is what Cantor Fitzgerald was worried about. Having survived the 1993 bombing of the World Trade Center by Islamist extremists who advocated America's military withdrawal from the Middle East, this ambitious company tried to break away from the "masters of the universe" confidence infecting much of Wall Street in the nineties to ask some difficult questions about what rejecting the new rule set might look and feel like in the era of globalization. The key figure in this conversation was Bud Flanagan, a retired four-star admiral and a character of rare vision, who, upon joining the firm in 1996, quickly established an unprecedented research partnership between Cantor and the Naval War College. A series of historic "economic security workshops" ensued, exploring such real-world scenarios as a terrorist strike on Wall Street, war in the Persian Gulf, and a financial crisis in Asia—all of which proved amazingly prescient. More important, though, the workshop series led to new channels of dialogue between the Pentagon and Wall Street, conversations that, in Flanagan's view, were essential to expanding the American military establishment's nascent understanding of how globalization was altering our definitions of national security.

Flanagan was just the sort of mentor I was looking for when I arrived at the Naval War College in the summer of 1998. Fortunately for me, Bud was looking for someone to expand the seminar series beyond its original focus on specific scenarios to a broader exploration of globalization itself. In effect, Cantor was interested in "mapping" globalization's emerging Core rule set and, by doing so, engaging the national security community in a discussion of the major security threats that might disrupt or even disable globalization's continued advance. Bud was concerned that the 1990s might be a replay of the 1920s, so the question was, What would it take for the 2000s to turn as sour as the 1930s? Or, *What could kill globalization?*

The main finding of the New Rule Sets Project workshops was a simple but compelling model of globalization as a series of key resource flows that needed to be kept in relative balance to one another. Those four flows were: the movement of people (migrations), energy (primarily oil and natural gas), long-term investments (foreign direct investment), and security (the "export" of U.S. security "services" to regional "markets"). The notion of keeping these four flows in balance really just meant that nothing in the global system should be allowed to prevent the flow of any of the resources from regions of surplus to regions of deficit. In effect, labor, energy, money, and security all need to flow as freely as possible from those places in the world where they are plentiful to those regions where they are scarce.

Cantor's interest in seeing financial rule sets expand around the world led me to the military-market nexus: Where security enables the steady rise of connectivity between any national economy and the outside world, markets logically emerge to manage the marginal risks that remain, and where markets can effectively manage risk, investments invariably flow toward desired resources, such as relatively inexpensive but dependable labor. Over time, these essential transactions engender further connectivity among nations and regions, reflected in the rise of more complex and suitably entangling rule sets that moderate the behavior of not just nation-states but likewise firms and individuals. The desired security end state of this integration process is a community of states within which rule-set transgressions find certain—if not immediate—resolution through universally agreed-upon legal means. In other words, the military never has to get involved.

When you look at the military-market nexus in this manner, then the successful application of U.S. military power around the world must be defined in the same self-negating manner as foreign aid: ultimate success means you stop doing it in a particular country or region. Or to put it more specifically, wherever a market maker like Cantor Fitzgerald plays the role of a rule-set enforcer, there you should expect to find a marginal role for the U.S. military, and vice versa.

Admittedly, I am an economic determinist, but I'm darned proud to be one. My credentials are nearly impeccable: I once taught Marxism at Harvard. From those nefarious beginnings, though, I found rehabilitation at the hands of my Wall Street mentors, Bud Flanagan and his longtime collaborator Philip Ginsberg, a true Renaissance man who probably would have had a brilliant teaching career if he hadn't been so focused on the practical applications of his degrees in economics. What these guys taught me over the years and through the several workshops we codesigned and conducted was that security and economics were two sides of the same coin, both built around the principles of connectivity and rule sets. With security, you mostly deal with the disconnected and the rule breakers, but conquering that challenge is what yields the economic opportunities associated with growing connectivity and adherence to rule sets.

To Bud and Phil, it was all about knowing what the rules were and either playing by them or accepting the consequences of nonadherence. Phil once explained to me why Cantor didn't dive into Russia in the early 1990s, when plenty of other firms were rushing in with their investments. "Those guys simply weren't playing by the rules we believe are essential to making markets work. So if we give them money, and then at some point we want that money back, maybe they'll just tell us, 'Too bad.' So then what do we do? Hire some Russian mafia to get our money back? We don't need money that badly. If they don't want to play nicely, we simply stay home. No rules, no money." So when Russia went bankrupt in 1998, Cantor did not get burned as other firms did. Russia in turn lost out on the connectivity that would have accompanied that resource flow.

After several of these economic security workshops, I sat down one afternoon and tried to capture them in a string that I was certain would describe the military-market link I had so long been hunting. Being so Catholic, I arranged them in a Decalogue, sort of a Ten Commandments for globalization:

1. Look for resources, and ye shall find
For decades, both futurists and environmentalists have gone on and on about how the world is running out of resources, especially in fossil fuels. But it simply isn't true. The historical record is in-

controvertible: the more we look for "nonrenewable" energy, the more we find. Confirmed oil reserves have jumped almost 60 percent over the past twenty years, according to the Department of Energy, while natural gas reserves have more than doubled. Our best estimates on coal say we have enough for the next two centuries. So supply is not the issue, and neither is demand, leaving only the question of moving the energy from those who have it to those who need it—and therein lies the rub.

2. No stability, no markets

To get from producers to consumers, energy needs markets, and markets don't grow in a vacuum. I could have saved Karl Marx the effort of writing his very long *Das Kapital*. The *Popeye* cartoon character "Wimpy" summed up everything you need to know about capitalism when he promised, "I will gladly pay you Tuesday for a hamburger today." Capitalism is built on trust, and markets simply organize that trust into complex mechanisms of credit, which is what Wimpy was all about. Credit is extended to participants in markets based on a collective faith in the future, or the sense that your operating environment won't just allow a return *on* your investment, but a return *of* your investment as well. That's what Phil was worried about with Russia in the 1990s: not enough political and economic stability to allow markets there to operate freely, thus generating the unacceptable risk of losing it all.

3. No growth, no stability

Growing economies generally beget happy societies, despite the inevitable disparity in individual wealth that ensues. Richer societies are, on average, much happier than poorer ones. But the most consistently contented countries are those with rising per capita incomes, meaning money really does buy happiness, up to a point. Big increases in income within developing economies lead to big increases in happiness, but once you reach about $20,000 per capita, other, less material factors kick in.

How growth buys stability is even easier to prove, because the richer the country, the more likely it is that it will become a stable democracy. There are no authoritarian states featuring widespread development, although there are a few rich countries, notably in the Middle East, that are fairly authoritarian, and that's because both the power and the money are concentrated in the same hands. But when broadband economic development does occur, the longevity of any resulting democracy becomes virtually infinite. As Fareed Zakaria has noted, when a democratic regime achieves a level of per capita GDP above $9,000, it essentially becomes "immortal," meaning no such state has ever collapsed.

4. No resources, no growth

Developing economies use energy less efficiently than advanced ones, and truly poor societies are the most wasteful. An advanced economy like the United States can achieve one percent of growth in GDP while increasing its energy use less than one percent. An emerging economy, like China, will—on average—grow its economy and energy use at roughly a one-to-one rate. But most poor economies require more than a percent increase in energy consumption for every percent of economic growth (or an "energy elasticity" above 1.0). Obviously, we want Gap economies to grow and—by doing so—demand less energy over the long run. Moving countries from the Gap to the Core will be energy-intensive in the near- and mid-term, and most Gap countries are highly dependent on energy imports—Developing Asia being a case in point. Without stable access to reasonably priced energy, these countries will find it difficult to grow without severely damaging their environments.

5. No infrastructure, no resources

Infrastructure is the essence of economic connectivity, and nowhere are the demands greater than in the energy trade. As the planet progressively decarbonizes its energy usage (e.g., moving from coal to natural gas for generating electricity), the world economy will need a whole lot more long-distance pipelines connecting cities, states, and regions. The same will be true due to burgeoning fleets of automobiles in emerging markets like China, which will drive up the global demand for oil in coming years quite dramatically. That is why dependency relationships that would have seemed impossible during the Cold War are now becoming commonplace: Russia is supplying natural gas to Europe, for example, and there are plans to build oil pipelines from Siberia to both China and Japan. Add on top of all that the networks required to generate and move all that electricity, not to mention all the oil and liquid natural gas that currently move through major ports, and you quickly realize that developing an economy is first and foremost about moving energy.

6. No money, no infrastructure

According to Department of Energy (DOE) projections, "Many developing nations have ambitious goals to expand their electricity infrastructure over the coming decades." As DOE warns, "Some plans may prove feasible and others not." The biggest concern—naturally—is the availability of capital. Most developing economies cannot self-finance, so it comes down to a combination of loans (both commercial and public), foreign aid, the listing of companies on stock exchanges, and foreign direct investment (FDI) by firms willing to acquire equity in networks. Of that group, foreign investors represent the greatest potential flow. For example, while official developmental aid (ODA) from the advanced countries was almost twice as large as the private sector's FDI flow to emerging markets at the end of the Cold War, by the end of the nineties FDI had outpaced ODA roughly four to one. While foreign aid administrators are notoriously picky about how they dole out money, they come nowhere near the kind of scrutiny demanded by foreign investors using their own money.

7. No rules, no money

Back to Phil Ginsberg's basic point: foreign investors need to see rule of law, transparency, and good corporate governance before they will put their money at risk overseas. So the countries with the strongest economic rule sets inevitably attract the greatest amount of FDI. In 2001, the *Economist* ranked Asian economies by the strength of their rule sets, and Singapore came out consistently on top. Not surprisingly, Singapore is a magnet for foreign direct investment, enjoying one of the highest flows as a percentage of GDP in the world. As one Chinese securities regulator told the *Economist,* "Until two years ago, no one here had heard of 'conflict of interest' or 'fiduciary duty.'" His answer for the problem? "Right now we're just pushing concepts into rules." Last year China attracted the largest single share of FDI flowing to emerging markets.

8. No security, no rules

Forget Clausewitz and his notion of war as politics "by other means." Conflict is at best the temporary suppression of normal rule sets, and, at worst, the obliteration of rules. Madagascar is one of my favorite examples of rule-set loss. This island off the eastern coast of Africa became a magnet for FDI in the textiles industry across the 1990s, only to suffer the most incredible outcome any stable democracy could imagine following a presidential election: both contestants remained convinced they had won. Can you imagine such a thing happening in the United States? (Okay, almost never.) Well, because Madagascar does not enjoy the same robust legal rule set that the United States possesses, these two candidates began squaring off amid significant incidents of violence. The result? The country came to a standstill overnight and investors caught the chill, leaving the economy substantially less well off in the process. The potential downside from even larger security lapses is not hard to imagine: think of how Silicon Valley might view India's back-office potential following a nuclear exchange with Pakistan, or what would happen to FDI flows into China if its Communist leadership finally decided to invade Taiwan.

9. No Leviathan, no security

Security rule sets will always need to be backed up by someone willing to use force on their behalf. Historically, states did this for themselves, creating an every-man-for-himself environment described as the "security dilemma" (basically summarized as, "Maybe I should attack you before you decide to attack me"). During the Cold War, much of the world's population deferred to the super-powers, or the dual Leviathans East and West. Now only the United States stands as potential global security Leviathan. The toothless United Nations is not up to the task, nor is feeble Russia or a barely united Europe. As for the rising Chinese, they were recently excited about sending a whopping 800 peacekeepers for temporary duty in the Congo, so don't expect them to rush a quarter-million troops to the Persian Gulf anytime soon. Only the Pentagon can truly as-sume the Leviathan role, along with a handful of potential help-ers like the Brits and their former colonies (e.g., Canada, Australia, India).

10. No will, no Leviathan

Spending American treasure on securing global peace is one thing (because we're rich), but spending American blood is some-thing altogether different. A big part of the so-called Vietnam Syn-drome was the notion that the American public is casualty-averse, something many strategists believe was reinforced by the terrible experience in Somalia, when the bodies of American soldiers were dragged through the streets of Mogadishu. But in reality, Ameri-cans are not risk-averse, even with their sons and daughters, *if* two basic conditions are met: (1) the goals are well defined; and (2) the cost seems worth the potential gain. According to polling expert Steven Kull of the University of Maryland, "The critical question in the American public's mind is not whether there are body bags, but whether the military operation makes sense to them and whether they think it's succeeding." Poll after poll has demonstrated this American will to act as Leviathan under the right conditions. On the eve of the war with Iraq, an overwhelming majority of Ameri-cans declared that invasion was a reasonable course of action pri-marily to remove Saddam Hussein as a continuing threat to his own people. In my opinion, such a war can be filed under "Do unto others as you would have them do unto you," and it is that sort of moral compass that makes for a just global Leviathan.

Understanding the military-market link is not just good business, it is good national security strategy. Osama bin Laden understood this connection when he selected the World Trade Center and the Pentagon for his targets. We ignore his logic at our peril. In many ways, the wars that will define this era of globalization will be quite symmetrical: we will seek to extend globalization's connectivity, and those who oppose us will seek to derail globalization by disrupting that connectivity. A bin Laden engineers a 9/11 with the expressed goal of forcing the Core to clamp down on its borders, seek its energy elsewhere, take its investments elsewhere, and "bring the boys back home." He wants all of that connectivity gone, because its absence will afford him the chance for power over those left disconnected.

Understanding globalization's most crucial strands of connectivity (the flows of people, energy, money, security) helps us understand the nature of the grand historical struggle we now face. It puts this war on terrorism within the context of everything else. It helps us understand why our loved ones won't be coming home anytime soon. It helps us realize the balance of life all around us and why America's continued role as security Leviathan across the Gap is necessary not only for keeping the violence *over there,* but for making sure that globalization makes it *over there.*

If you want a happy ending to this story, you will find it here. These flows speak to how we make globalization truly global. They form the outline of the future worth creating.

THE FLOW OF PEOPLE, OR HOW I
LEARNED TO STOP WORRYING
AND LOVE THE POPULATION BOMB

When I turn fifty, I will worry about my PSA, or my prostate specific antigen. But at forty-one, I worry about my PSR, or what the United Nations calls my potential support ratio. My personal PSR is currently projecting out at 1.5, meaning my wife and I have three kids we hope will be willing to support us in our old age. So if Vonne and I split Emily, Kevin, and Jerome between us, we'll each end up with 1.5 persons working on our behalf after we reach sixty-five. That's how you calculate a PSR: it's the number of people between the ages of fifteen and sixty-four for every person above sixty-five.

The UN calculates PSRs by national populations. Right now, America's collective PSR is somewhere in the range of five to one, meaning there are five people between the ages of fifteen and sixty-four for everybody over sixty-five. That's not bad, but it's a lot lower than it used to be. Worse, as our population ages over the coming decades, our PSR is going to decline dramatically. The PSR for the planet has slid somewhat over the last half century, but nothing like it will over the next. In 1950, the world PSR was twelve to one, which reflected the fact that most of the world remained rural and agrarian. When you're still on the farm, having lots of kids makes sense, because you can use all the help you can get. By the time our planet reached the third millennium, our PSR dropped to nine to one. That's not too bad, primarily because Globalization II (1950–1980) involved only a fraction of the global population (America, Western Europe, Developed Asia). But the decline is accelerating.

My wife, Vonne, and I are in the process of adopting a baby girl from one of the poorer, interior provinces of China. We're not doing this to raise our personal PSR, but it will incidentally have that effect, and in so doing we are—in a tiny way—setting in motion the migration that will have to be repeated millions of times in the decades to come as the Core's population grows older *much faster* than the Gap's: the movement of people from there to here. This great shift defines the first of the four massive flows I believe are essential to protect if Globalization III is going to advance.

China currently has a surplus of baby girls, thanks in large part to its one-child policy of the last couple of decades. Much as India has done, China has been working hard (and often brutally) to control its population growth as part of its push for economic development and integration into the global economy. As both nations topped one billion souls recently, signs abounded that each was rather successful in limiting births, setting the stage for a momentous and unprecedented turning point in human history that will occur sometime in the middle of the twenty-first century.

Sometime around 2050, humanity will begin to depopulate as a species. That's right. In about five decades the world will reach a turning point that, in past ages, would have frightened us if we were able to understand its significance. But in the middle of the twenty-first century, the fact that we'll begin depopulating as a species won't seem scary (though it's never a bad idea to keep a close watch on those *damn, dirty apes!*), and we should welcome this turning point, even as it presents us and the globalizing world with a task of immense proportions.

What's so amazing about this upcoming reality is how, for decades, all we've heard about from the experts is that overpopulation is the real threat, and how we'd all eventually be eating soylent green or at least some indigestible tofu. I don't know how many frightening educational films I was forced to sit through in grade school, all of which suggested the world was simply going to suffocate under the crushing weight of all these people! Instead, I'll probably live to witness this amazing turn of events, a culmination of tens of thousands of years of effort on the part of humanity to grow its numbers and—by doing so—come to dominate the planet Earth.

The experts who still want to scare you on a regular basis are absolutely right when they note that global population, which currently sits at over six billion people, will rise roughly 50 percent over the next half century. That part's pretty much a given, absent some giant meteor striking the planet or the Klingons attacking. Right now, the best "medium" projections point to a planetary population of approximately nine billion by the year 2050. At that point, our birth rates and death rates will equal out, and our population will cease growing—give or take a few hundred million. But here's the amazing part: because people will keep living longer and fewer babies will be born on average, at the same time we top out as a global population, the old (sixty years and older) will begin outnumbering the young (under fifteen).

That is completely against nature as we have come to understand it across our short reign on this planet. Frankly, we shouldn't be able to do this as a species—the predators out there should hunt us down in sufficient numbers to deny us this amazing achievement. Yet it will happen, thanks in large part to China's and India's efforts, but primarily because economic development in general leads to lower birth rates. Over the past half century, fertility rates (babies per female) in developed economies dropped from six to three. I can see this in my own family. My parents had nine kids, but those nine kids have only begotten eleven kids so far, and except for the international adoptions, my siblings and I are pretty much done. That reduction-by-generation effect is spreading across the Core right now, but the trend will not reach much of the Gap until late in the twenty-first century. At 2050, the UN predicts, the forty-nine least-developed economies will still feature fertility rates above the replacement value of 2.1, meaning much of the Gap will still be growing even as the global population peaks.

So it's a fairly reasonable prediction to say that by 2050, there will be nine billion people on the planet, and that will pretty much be the high-water mark for our species. Of that nine billion, roughly two billion will be over age sixty (more than a tripling of our current global total of just over 600 million), and roughly two billion will be fourteen and under, leaving approximately five billion in between. The problem with this picture is how all these billions will end up being arranged around the planet. Too many of the two billion young will be in the Gap, while too many of the two billion old will be in the Core. Someone will have to turn us over in our beds when we're old, and our population trends simply aren't providing that someone. By 2050, the global PSR will drop to only four to one. That means we'll have less than half as many workers for every person sixty-five and older as we have today.

Now what does that trend assume? Globalization will continue to expand around the planet, triggering increased rates of urbanization and industrialization, so there will be significant increases in productivity. That will help make that four-to-one PSR more bearable. People will live a lot longer too, as life expectancy for the planet moves from the mid-sixties to the mid-seventies by 2050. So it's reasonable to expect that people will work longer as well, which should help slow down our PSR slide a bit.

Even if we stipulate the rise in both productivity and retirement ages, there will be no escaping the reality that unless people get on the move in large numbers in coming decades, globalization's workers and retirees will not be sufficiently co-located to prevent a devastating drop in the Core's PSR.

By 2050, the Old Core will have a collective PSR in the range of just two to one, or half the global average. Meanwhile, the New Core contingent dominated by India and China will have a PSR of roughly five to one. The least-developed economies in the Gap will still have a PSR in the double digits, or roughly ten to one. So there's no mystery about what will have to happen. Young people will need to move from the Gap to the Core—or more specifically, the Old Core. This is what the UN calls "replacement migration." The Census Bureau predicts that almost two-thirds of America's population growth by 2050 will be accounted for by Latinos immigrating here from Central and South America. This Latinization of American culture is already showing itself in the youngest age ranges of zero to five, so if you want to see the future of America, keep an eye on Nickelodeon and the Cartoon Network, because there you'll see shows progressively geared toward a rising Latino viewing share.

Another place to see that future is in Texas, Florida, and Southern California, where Latinos now are the dominant minority population. Bill Clinton and George W. Bush are no accidents. Expect to see a lot of future presidents coming from southern states, armed with more than just a smattering of Spanish phrases in their stump speeches.

The good news for America is that this influx of Latinos is business as usual for a nation built largely through immigrant flows over our blended history. Latinos are nothing more than the latest wave, along with, to a lesser extent, Asians. According to the UN's calculations, America is letting in sufficient numbers of immigrants on an annual basis to shore up our PSR in a reasonable fashion. The UN predicts that we'll need to let in just over half a million per year through 2050 to keep our fifteen-to-sixty-four cohort size at roughly its peak absolute value, or 200 million. Because we're a relatively young nation, we won't hit that peak value until around 2015, whereas aging Europe and Japan hit their peaks almost a decade ago.

Happily, the UN projects that we'll hit that total easily, since we average somewhere between 750,000 to one million immigrants each year—and that doesn't include those who enter the country illegally. Even with that influx, America's PSR will decline from roughly five to one down to three to one by 2050 (beating far worse ratios in Europe and Japan), but a certain amount of decline is only natural as productivity grows. Anyway, we'd need to let in about ten million immigrants a year to keep our PSR fixed at five to one, and that is simply impossible, politically and otherwise. Instead, most Americans should expect to retire in their mid-seventies, not their mid-sixties or—God forbid—their mid-fifties.

The news, unfortunately, looks a lot worse for insular Japan and xenophobic Europe. If America has its problems with immigrants, what with bilingual education and all, our issues pale when compared with those of the rest of the Old Core. Europe already has its share of right-wing, anti-immigration politicians exploiting people's worst impulses, and Japan has such a dismal record of accepting immigrants that the Land of the Rising Sun is heading toward its sunset at warp speed. According to the UN, Europe is likely to let in about 300,000 immigrants per year between now and 2050, when it really needs to let in something in the range of 1.5 million each year if there's any hope its PSR won't drop below two to one by mid-century. Japan's situation is even worse. It is difficult to project any immigrant flows for the country between now and 2050 because there's nothing in its history that would indicate any willingness to let immigrants in at all, but the UN estimates that Japan will need to average roughly 600,000 immigrants a year over the next half century.

How big of a change would these larger flow numbers be for Europe and Japan? If Europe were to let in 1.5 million immigrants each year, by 2050 a quarter of its population would be foreign-born. That I can imagine happening. As for Japan, as much as one-third of its 2050 population would be foreign-born if they pursued the immigration rate required to stabilize their absolute number of working-age citizens. Simply put, that wouldn't be Japan anymore; that would be an entirely new country. I personally believe that would be a better Japan, because I think that insular society has so much to offer the world that letting more of that world in will let the Japanese achieve the "normal" nationhood they have sought ever since their brush with the apocalypse in 1945—such are the tides of history.

Given that a lot of people will have to move from the Gap to the Core to keep globalization on track, the question becomes, How can this massive shift be achieved? Immigration is the obvious—and most socially challenging—route, but there are two promising trends that we'll need to promote in addition to permanent immigration: the "virtual migration" of jobs from the Core to the Gap, exemplified by India becoming a "back office" for the U.S. economy; and a "global commute," best displayed by the Philippines' amazingly mobile workforce.

Virtual migration has been around for a while, we just hadn't noticed it. When my wife, Vonne, was working as a unit secretary in a major Virginia hospital in the mid-1990s, she helped send the doctors' audiotaped medical chart logs to India via the Internet for overnight transcription. Instead of paying more to have it done in the United States by non-medical experts, the hospital ended up paying half as much for Indian medical professionals to perform the service outside of their day jobs. It's not just the back office–type jobs that have migrated to India and elsewhere, but virtual face-to-face service jobs like customer call centers, where the "Susan" who ends up taking your complaint is really Nishara working in Bangalore. Then there is the huge role Indian software companies have played in the rise of Silicon Valley over time. In effect, India has become the overnight software patch that keeps our information technology industry humming on a daily basis: tasks that would have sat overnight in America are now beamed to India for resolution by the next business day. It is often said that Indian information technology workers, the largest single pool on the planet, write half the world's software. Most will never see America, and yet they are an integral part of our nation's computer-fueled productivity gains.

The other positive trend is the emergence of the global commute, and no country exemplifies this development better than the Philippines. The government there has systematically facilitated two-year deployments around the world by a major portion of its labor force (roughly 10 percent of its total population of 76 million). These global commuters are specifically recruited by the government for this program, which mobilizes the OFWs, or Overseas Filipino Workers, in significant numbers for temporary labor duty all over the planet. In 2001, these workers sent back in remittances $6.2 billion, constituting almost a tenth of the national GDP. Factor in the multiplier effect on the national economy (every dollar sent home generates three to four dollars of growth), and you're looking at a flow that shapes a significant portion of their domestic market demand.

Not surprisingly, of the top twenty nations frequented by Filipinos in their global commute, fifteen are Core states (U.S., Japan, Hong Kong–China, U.K., Taiwan, Italy, Canada, Germany, South Korea, Greece, Guam, Switzerland, Netherlands, Austria, and Australia). The rest are rich Gulf states plus Malaysia and Singapore—

two of the most Core-like states in the Gap. The difference in wage-earning potential is huge: nurses in the Philippines average $15,000 a year, but close to $50,000 in the United States, which has accepted so many of these global commuters as to trigger a nursing shortage in the Philippines.

Making this global commute possible are low airfares and new telecommunications advances, like inexpensive text-messaging, which acts as a cheap but essential lifeline between parents working overseas (two-thirds of OFWs are women) and their families back home, where the government goes out of its way to support OFWs with special events promoting free medical care and celebrating their role as *bagong bayani,* or "new heroes," of the Filipino economy. Filipinos were prominently represented among the first foreign workers rushed into Iraq as part of the postwar rebuilding process. Why? Ninety percent of Filipinos can read, compared with just two-thirds of Iraqis, and most Filipinos learn English in school as a legacy of a long American occupation in the first half of the twentieth century. As the Philippines' secretary of labor and employment declared in the weeks leading up to the war, "If they're looking for skilled workers, they'll come to us." *Wired* magazine has described the program as "an example of socioeconomic engineering on an unprecedented scale," arguing that the Philippines is doing nothing less than "creating the world's most distributed economy, where the sources of production are so far-flung it boggles the mind."

The aging Core will need to accept the Gap's desperate ambition for a better life, because in doing so, we shrink the Gap one motivated worker at a time. The importance of this flow of remittances to the Gap is hard to overstate. Latin American workers toiling overseas send home roughly $15 billion a year, or more than five times what the region receives in foreign aid from the Core. Any connectivity that facilitates this flow, whether on a permanent or temporary basis, expands globalization's reach. Conversely, any restrictions placed on such movement in the name of a global war on terrorism will end up doing more damage to America's long-term interest in seeing globalization succeed than any number of suicide bombers can ever hope to achieve.

In effect, this flow of labor from the Gap to the Core is globalization's release valve. With it, the prosperity of the Core can be maintained and more of the world's people can participate. Without it, overpopulation and underperforming economies in the Gap will lead to explosive situations that spill over to the Core. Either way, *they* are coming. Our only choice is how we welcome them.

THE FLOW OF ENERGY, OR WHOSE BLOOD FOR WHOSE OIL?

When I'm giving a brief or speech to nonmilitary audiences, I often encounter a lot of cynicism regarding America's security interests in the Middle East. In short, it's moral outrage over all that violence in the name of cheap gas. Whenever I'm confronted by this anger, I don't try to deny the essential truth of the matter, I just argue the larger context. Americans tend to forget that cheap gas doesn't work just for us but for people all over the planet—people who can't just "kick the habit" as easily as many might assume a rich country like ours could. So when we're talking about a crisis in the Middle East possibly sending oil prices skyrocketing, it won't be Americans who suffer most in that scenario, it will be the truly poor, located overwhelmingly in the Gap. I don't pretend that our "good life" isn't protected each and every time we use military force to stabilize things in the Persian Gulf; I just think it's important to realize that countless others around the planet benefit far more whenever America performs those military deeds that only it can possibly manage.

Occasionally, when you encounter that harsh, blood-for-oil rhetoric, what you really find hiding behind the words are anti-Semites whose arguments that America should "get off oil" are really just another way of saying we should abandon Israel to its just deserts—

you know, a "live by the sword, die by the sword" sort of realism. But mostly when people play this card, it's about the immorality of spilling American blood to protect unworthy people. When "those people" are identified as "greedy" oil companies, my gut reaction is to advise people to get off their high horse (whatever model they drive) and take an economics class, because the notion that only a few executives at big oil companies reap the lion's share of the value flowing out of those wells is simply preposterous. Simply put, everyone in this country benefits from cheap petroleum because it flows throughout our economy and not just into our gas-guzzling cars.

But when that righteous anger is directed at the House of Saud or the Emir of Kuwait, I don't disagree with that innate sense of distaste or injustice, I just believe it's misdirected in terms of goals. America shouldn't be about protecting royal mafias who have largely kept themselves rich and their people disconnected. We need to be about the revolutionary goal of liberating these societies from repressive leaderships and letting individuals pick and choose on their own how they wish to be connected with the larger world.

Does that mean regime change in most instances? Hardly. That option only makes sense when the leadership on top not only treats its own people badly but also seeks to export danger or violence elsewhere, either by seeking weapons inappropriate to its defense needs or supporting terrorism and other criminal activities abroad. No, connecting the Middle East to the outside world is not about replacing leadership, by and large, but about expanding connectivity—in any form possible. We will need to accept that many Muslims will, for a variety of cultural and religious reasons, continue to prefer disconnectedness even when connectivity is offered. America just needs to establish an image as the provider of connectivity, not the protector of those elites who prefer to keep their societies largely cut off from the outside world. We need to stand for the *ability to choose.*

I sincerely believe that the real reason that plenty of Arabs hate America is not the oil trade, but because our political and military relationships with the region seem to focus on *nothing but the oil trade*. America needs to represent so much more, and perhaps we can demonstrate that capacity in postwar Iraq. The realist in me says oil is what brought us to the Middle East, but the optimist in me says "that's fine" as long as we leverage that slim connectivity into a larger effort to integrate the region into the global economy in such a way that the masses find real opportunity in the economic interactions that ensue.

But the oil is also the region's salvation on one crucial level: at least the Middle East has our attention. Whenever I field that "blood-for-oil" question from audiences, I typically respond, "Hell, yes, it's all about oil. Thank God it's all about the oil. Because I can show you parts of the world where there isn't any oil, and there's plenty of people dying, and no one seems to care whatsoever." There's no denying that oil has been the curse of Arab economic development, as it has been for numerous other countries around the world, but without it, the Middle East's pain would be as distant to most Americans as that half-a-holocaust that's already unfolded in Central Africa over the last decade. As Nicholas Kristof of the *New York Times* warns, we all had better be prepared to explain to our kids and grandchildren when they inevitably ask, "What did you do during the African Holocaust?" You want to know why you haven't attended any peace rallies or war protest marches on that one? Because there's no oil there, so American troops aren't sent, so millions die with no one paying any serious attention. That's what "no oil" plus "no American blood" equals. Doesn't exactly feel like the moral high ground, does it?

The Middle East has commanded our security attention over the last three decades, and America has done almost nothing to help the situation there. What makes suicide bombers possible? It's not the poverty, because most of these terrorists are middle class and educated. It's that they have no realistic expectations of a better life—either for themselves or their children. According to Scott Atran, a terrorism expert at the University of Michigan, "The factor is diminishing expectations. No matter how rich or poor, if you have not achieved what you expected, you are more likely to back a radical policy." That's what drives a father of two small kids to strap on sticks of dynamite and step onto a crowded Jerusalem bus for his instant of courage—he's simply got nowhere else to go in his life. What kills expectations of a better life faster and more completely than anything else? Disconnectedness. A person with connectivity always has options: to move, to change careers, to get more education, to do whatever it takes to make something better happen for his or her kids. The disconnected have no options. They have educations they can't use, conversations they can't repeat, plans they'll never fulfill. When you deny people their hope in a better future, you leave them with nothing but the will to deny your desired future. That's what makes suicide bombers.

You may counter, "Isn't it really hatred of the Israelis that drives most of this terrorism?" In the immediate sense, yes, but ultimately, no. When individuals cannot find opportunity in life, they are reduced to fighting over what's left over: the land and the cultural identity they attach to its history. But define a society by connectivity and the individual opportunities it provides, and you will see that primordial attachment to the land disappear—generation by generation—as mobility trumps tradition. In the meantime, Israel remains the whipping boy, the excuse, the symbol of everything Arab populations want but do not have—in large part—because if Arab leaders provided them that level of connectivity and individual freedom, it would eventually eliminate the ability of elites there to maintain their political standing. So the kings and the mullahs and the presidents-for-life blame it all on Israel and—by extension—the United States. Does anyone really believe that the Middle East would not still have developed all the same problems if Israel had never come into being? Don't kid yourself, the ruling elites there would have had to invent an "Israel" if none existed.

The Middle East remains the region most disconnected from the global economy by many measures—and it's getting worse with time. The world has doled out a handful of Nobel Peace Prizes over the past three decades, all celebrating breakthrough achievements in Middle Eastern peace. What do we have to show for our efforts? Are Arabs any better off now than in the early 1970s?

In 1980, the Middle East accounted for 13 percent of global exports. Today that share is 3 percent, with the overwhelming bulk being oil and natural gas. A generation ago, the Middle East attracted 5 percent of the global flow of foreign direct investment. Today that number is a mere 1.5 percent. Worse still, eight of the largest eleven economies in the region do not currently belong to the World Trade Organization, meaning the progressive synchronization of economic rule sets is not occurring.

So while Latin America and Developing Asia have moved off their dependency on raw materials and into manufacturing as their main source of exports, the Middle East remains trapped in a colonial-era economic relationship with the outside world. Simply put, the Middle East exports oil and terrorism and virtually nothing else of significance to the global economy. The value of U.S. imports of manufactured goods from Hong Kong alone is twice that of imports from the entire Arab League. That's one city versus an entire civilization.

Saddest of all is perhaps the lack of any Middle Eastern stake in the financial future of the planet. Yes, these states depend on the outside world to buy their oil, but they do not use the money they receive in return to invest in any sort of future. It is estimated that Muslim countries currently hold somewhere in the range of one-fifth of a trillion dollars in personal savings. Where is this money invested around the world? Basically nowhere. It sits in bank accounts, doing nothing whatsoever, in large part because of Islamic strictures against earning interest. International financial firms are trying to figure out a way to unleash all that potential investment power, and some are optimistic it can be done while respecting Islamic religious practice. After all, Muslims long ago figured out ways to buy houses using special "Islamic mortgages" that reclassify interest payments as "rent."

Malaysia is now promoting itself as a global hub for Islamic finance, utilizing a special "standards board" that consults with international Islamic experts. Who has proven most resistant to Malaysia's efforts to market these instruments throughout the Muslim world? Strict Muslim scholars in the Middle East have raised the strongest objections, but by working with them directly, international banking firms have been able recently to issue "Islamic bonds," or instruments of sovereign debt acceptable to Islamic religious law. Compare this sort of connectivity with the underground banking of the *hawala* networks, the informal international funds-transfer system prevalent in many Muslim societies and exploited by terrorist groups because they leave no paper trail. To offer Muslim countries the legitimate connectivity of international finance, the West needs to adjust its rule sets to accommodate Islamic sensitivities.

The Middle East's plight is that of basically all countries that have depended on raw materials for export throughout history: it's just about the slowest way to grow an economy and often leads to economic failure over the long term because prices of raw commodities tend to fall with advances in the technology of extraction and processing. When competing against countries that aggressively educate their populations, countries with large natural endowments will lose every time. Think about it. What is the most developed—not to mention the most globalized—economy in the Middle East? That would be Israel, a country without a shred of energy self-sufficiency, despite being located in the middle of all that oil and natural gas. Yes, U.S. military aid assures Israel's security, but their own, self-financed intellectual capital drives their economic success. As Fareed Zakaria puts it, "trust fund" states like Saudi Arabia simply have it too easy with all that wealth buried underground. Living off the fat of the land, they never "tackle the far more difficult task of creating a framework of laws and institutions that generate national wealth." Simply put, they do not create the rule sets that lead to connectivity.

But of course, the Middle East's slender connection to the global economy is an important one. In 2001 the planet burned just over 400 quadrillion (Quad) Btu of energy (e.g., oil, gas, coal, renewables), and almost 40 percent of that total was supplied by oil. Of the oil used last year by the world, just over 70 percent of it was imported from a foreign source. The Persian Gulf itself accounted for only about a quarter of that global trade, or 17 million barrels per day (mbd) out of a total of 56 mbd. But the Middle East accounts for just over half the known global reserves of oil. So as the world proceeds into the future and continues to increase its consumption of oil, the Persian Gulf will account for roughly half of that increase. Naturally, growth in oil consumption around the world will vary in the next couple of decades, and this is where things get interesting.

North America has been the global demand center of energy markets for so long we cannot imagine a future that does not place America at the head of that line. But that future is coming. North America burned 116 Quad Btu in 2001, with Asia right on our heels at 113 Quad. But while we'll burn only about 50 percent more energy by 2025, Asia's demand will come close to doubling, meaning those nations will be looking for a lot more energy from the planet than we will—roughly 40 quadrillion Btu more. A good rule of thumb for calculating Quad Btu is to divide that number by 2, with the result representing how many millions of barrels of oil you would need to burn each day to achieve that energy. So 40 Quad would equal about 20 million barrels of oil per day—roughly what the U.S. consumed in oil last year, importing more than half.

By 2025, Asia will burn 211 Quad Btu, according to the latest Department of Energy projection. Right now, DOE estimates that that need will be met with 39 percent coal, 37 percent oil, 13 percent natural gas, and 11 percent renewables (e.g., wind, solar, hydro, nuclear). The 37 percent oil share (38 mbd) will be devoted largely to transportation needs, which are expected to grow dramatically by 2025—basically a fivefold increase in the number of cars. Of course, if all those cars are gas-guzzling SUVs, then the millions of barrels of oil per day that Asia would need to burn would be pushed up quite a bit. On the other hand, if hybrids and/or fuel-cell cars capture a large share of that growing market, then the barrel number could be lightened quite a bit. (There is a lot of give in these projections, or what the Pentagon likes to call "swag.")

Either way, Asia produces very little oil for itself today, and by 2025 the region as a whole will import more than 90 percent of its oil requirements, or 35 out of 38 mbd. That is roughly twice as much as Asia imports today (18 mbd).

Six OPEC members located in the Persian Gulf—Iran, Iraq, Kuwait, Qatar, Saudi Arabia, and United Arab Emirates—control two-thirds of the proven, "conventional" oil reserves and over 90 percent of the excess productive capacity in the system.

Of the 18 mbd Asia imports today, just over half comes from the Persian Gulf, but of the 35 mbd Asia will import in 2025, 22 mbd—60 percent—will come from the Gulf. Meanwhile, the Persian Gulf's share of North America's oil imports will decline slightly from 22 percent today to 20 percent then. The Gulf will boost production for export from 17 mbd today to 36 mbd by 2025, and 11 of those extra 19 mbd will go to Asia, while just under 3 will go to North America. That means the Persian Gulf will be the main source of oil to accommodate Asia's rising economic prominence within the global economy.

So let's say that in 2025 some evil mastermind decides to cripple the Gulf's exporting of oil. In that scenario, North America would have to go find 6 mbd somewhere else in a global marketplace with a capacity of roughly 60 mbd, while Asia would be shopping around for three and a half times that amount. North America would be facing the loss of roughly 7 percent of its total energy requirement, whereas Asia would be trying to replace almost 20 percent of its Quad Btu.

So when America sends its military into the Gulf to protect all that oil, it's clearly our blood, but is it really our oil? Would we be better off just ignoring the 80 percent that goes elsewhere? Of course, since most of that oil goes to fuel some of our largest trading partners in Asia (e.g., China, Japan, South Korea, Singapore), perhaps we shouldn't get too picky about saying whose oil it really is. As one DOE security expert once told me at a War College workshop, "If you come to my backyard and take 1,000 gallons of water out of one end of my pool, guess what? The water's going to go down on the other end, too." So not only would we eventually feel Asia's economic pain, but our financial markets are so good at quickly processing international risk that we'd feel it first on Wall Street, long before the prices of all those Asian imports shot up.

Globalization means never having to say you're autarkic, so here's how I would array the codependent relationships: we are codependent with Asia because we depend on their willingness to buy our sovereign debt and they depend on our willingness to buy all their exports; but Asia is codependent on the Middle East because Asia depends on the Middle East's energy exports and the Middle East depends on Asia's economic growth. So when instability in the Middle East threatens to upset this apple cart (or the similar daisy chain that exists among the United States, Europe, and the Middle East), then it is our obligation to step in to stop the Core's economy from being damaged.

When we fight, then, we are not simply fighting for a level of affluence back home in the States. Such assertions are shortsighted in the extreme. When globalization gets sidetracked by skyrocketing oil prices, it won't be America, or Europe, or even Asia that gets left out in the cold. It will be the Gap, the poorest of the poor, that suffers the most. If we were to allow the Persian Gulf to break down as global oil supplier, not only would that ravage economies there that depend desperately on the oil revenue, but most of the Gap would immediately be priced right out of the market. I'm not just talking inflation here. I'm talking about millions upon millions of lives ending prematurely due to economic deprivation, most of whom will be the youngest children and the oldest adults—just the way it was in Iraq during all those years of UN sanctions. We won't call these deaths "casualties," because there won't be any smoking holes. In fact, we won't call them anything at all because we won't even notice them. They will just be dark-skinned people dying somewhere far away.

So I guess I'm not too sure what Jesus would drive, I'm just certain he'd want us to care more about the rest of the world beyond our borders.

But wait a minute! All this stuff about oil is just so passé! I mean, we're right on the verge of the hydrogen age! Plus we're moving rapidly from coal to natural gas to generate electricity! To hell with the Gulf and all the suicide bombers there! I'm telling you, Jesus would definitely drive a fuel cell! And you know why? Because it would lead to peace and stability in the Middle East! Just like that.

Right?

Wrong.

First, I dislike the notion that our main goal in moving from combustion engines to fuel cells is so we can write off the Middle East as soon as possible. It is not in anyone's interest to turn the Gulf into Central Africa, where people kill each other nonstop and nobody seems to care because they have no resources that we need. I want fuel cells because they're neat technology, because it'll make a better world for my kids, and because it'll give General Motors a chance to sell us an entire new fleet of cars—and that's got to be good for America!

The second reason I distrust this scenario is that Asia's skyrocketing demand for natural gas will keep it interested in the Middle East and Central Asia over the long run anyway. Same dependencies, just different energy type. Asia will roughly triple its use of natural gas between now and 2025, from 11 trillion cubic feet (Tcf) today to 27 Tcf then. Asia went outside of the region to acquire only a fraction of that 11 Tcf last year, but it will either have to triple domestic production over the next two decades (fat chance) or it will have to go out of region for the rest. I know many energy experts say natural gas is a lot more plentiful around the planet than just that gas associated with oil fields, but again, is my goal in Globalization III simply to help Asia gain energy self-sufficiency so both they and we can consign the Middle East to future oblivion? We must imagine a future worth creating where the Muslim Middle East gets to come along too. Otherwise, perhaps Osama bin Laden is essentially correct, and we should accept his offer of civilizational apartheid.

The third reason I dislike the "let's move right on to hydrogen" scenario is that I don't think cutting off what slender connectivity the Middle East currently has with globalization will lead to lasting peace in the region. I simply don't see that pathway unfolding unless we replace that slim connectivity with broadband, individual-level economic connectivity between the masses of the Muslim world and the Core as a whole. The clock is running on the Middle East and on any hope we may have of someday integrating it into the Core. The bin Ladens of the Muslim world know they're in a race. They know they have only so much time to successfully turn back the clock on most Middle Eastern societies, and they will fight more desperately with each passing year.

That will only make our race with destiny all the more difficult to sustain, because as these forces of disconnectedness strain to kill us in new and more diabolical ways, we'll need to push ahead with efforts to ensure just the opposite outcome of greater connectivity. How hard will it be to spare a billion-plus Muslims from a future of diminishing expectations? I'm guessing more agony than ecstasy, but it is indisputably the right thing to do. And it simply cannot happen on its own.

It will be a cross we will bear for years. And, yes, we will need to turn the other cheek time and time again. But there will never be peace in the Middle East until the region joins the world. If we surrender the region to the bin Ladens of disconnectedness, we will end up losing far more than access to cheap oil. We will be surrendering globalization's promise of eternal peace.

THE FLOW OF MONEY, OR WHY WE WON'T BE GOING TO WAR WITH CHINA

I knew my workshop series with Cantor Fitzgerald was in trouble when the spies started showing up. Not a lot of spies, mind you, just three. They weren't going to participate in the event whatsoever—not even the meals. I was not to introduce them or refer to them in any manner as I facilitated the session. They would sit in the back in the room, interacting with no one, just . . . being there. When my department chairman told me in advance about this trio, he said he couldn't say who they were, and when a eighteen-year veteran of the CIA tells you someone has no identity as far as you're concerned, well, you just sort of have to go with it. "They just want to observe," he said with a finality that told me my super Top Secret clearance wasn't going to get me any insider dope on this one whatsoever. But I didn't need any. The workshop we were putting on involved the future of foreign direct investment in Asia. These guys were "observing" because both the Pentagon and the intelligence community had developed a laserlike focus on China as the "rising near-peer competitor." Our workshop was just giving *whomever* another chance to line up China's future in their sights.

Of course, the purpose of the workshop as far as Cantor and I were concerned was to explore the inescapable reality that Developing Asia was going to need a lot of money to finance a doubling of its energy demand in a mere generation's time. This was the second workshop in the New Rule Sets Project. The first was on energy, and we billed that one as the "motive," as in, "Asia's gotta have it!" This second workshop would be about "opportunity," as in, "Who's gonna pony up the money?" The third event would be about the "crime" of all the environmental damage that might result. Motive, opportunity, and crime all coming together in a neat little package. We made no assumptions about China's bad intentions one way or the other, but we knew, to borrow a phrase from *West Side Story*, that if China ended up acting "depraved" it would be "on account of being deprived." So nothing personal, strictly business. China had needs, and we wanted to see those needs met, because we knew how hard it might be for them—and by extension us—if those efforts fell short.

Naturally, not everyone felt the same way about China in my business as the new century dawned. In fact, the entire Pentagon strategic planning community was refocusing most of its vast energy to contemplating and preparing for war with China in some distant future scenario. We were hiring China experts by the barrelful. All our war games pretty much had to involve some unnamed large Asian land power with an unhealthy interest in a small island nation off its coast, otherwise they wouldn't get approved. Hard thought was being given to reconfiguring our military presence in Asia to counter rising China's influence. The Defense Department may have been very circumspect in its official documents about that unidentified "peer competitor," but inside the Pentagon they were deep into planning the next Cold War.

Every Pentagon review was saying the same thing: the future of war would be Asia, and America would need a new generation of long-range weapons to counter China's military power. This push started under the Clinton Administration and picked up speed only when the transformation advocates of the Bush Administration took control of the Pentagon. The new Defense Secretary, Donald Rumsfeld, had participated in recent blue-ribbon panels on the future of space warfare and missile threats, and he knew exactly where America needed to refocus its strategic military planning: Asia. You want to know about the "intelligence failure" of 9/11? There was none. We simply were focused on the wrong part of the world, on the wrong type of conflict, and the wrong enemy. The intelligence community was doing exactly what the political leadership in both the White House and Congress wanted—find us a familiar enemy. So the Company sent three spies to watch our workshop on the future of investment in Asia.

These guys probably weren't spies in any real sense, just analysts who obviously worked some very hush-hush subjects. But their "I was never here" shtick posed some problems for my little gathering atop World Trade Center One. Bud Flanagan and Phil Ginsberg of Cantor Fitzgerald always had a hard time convincing Wall Street executives to show up for these events, because these guys are more secretive than the CIA about their future plans, and most were more than a bit uncomfortable having Pentagon strategists and Langley intelligence officers in the room while they discussed strategy. As one CEO put it to me over drinks after the workshop, "I'm not looking to provide these guys with future targets, because that's an awful lot of my money going into that facility in China."

Of course, the whole point of the workshop wasn't to generate target lists but to get two very different cultures in the same room, discussing the same subject. Both the Pentagon and Wall Street had China in their sights in the year 2000, they were just thinking about projecting different sorts of power into the region. While the Pentagon dreamed of long-distance push-button missile wars with China, Wall Street fretted over long-term foreign direct investment triggering rule-set wars with China. Both, quite logically, were concerned about the same downstream outcome: China on the outside of the emerging global system, looking in. The Pentagon assumed that China would never be able to adjust its rule sets enough to truly integrate with the Core, and even if it did, that Beijing's Communist leaders would only pursue that outcome to grow their military capabilities for the seemingly inevitable clash of civilizations. Wall Street, however, viewed China as running a juggernaut of rapid economic development that either would pull them dramatically into globalization's Core or spin them out of that rule set into some universe of their own, like "capitalism with Chinese characteristics," or "the Asian way." Wall Street was, in its own way, just as concerned as the Pentagon about China pursuing a separate path, because they feared an opportunity for expanding globalization immensely might be lost in the process. The Pentagon, not surprisingly, saw its opportunity materializing just as Wall Street's would disappear.

Cantor Fitzgerald, in particular, was concerned that Asia hadn't cleaned up its act following the Asian Flu of 1997–98, when the region's penchant for cronyism and cozy banking relationships between the government and private sector was revealed as a major weakness in the financial order there. In this regard, fellow Old Core member Japan was more part of the problem than of the solution. Bud and Phil's point going into the workshop was that Asia tended to self-supply its foreign direct investment to a high degree, meaning Asian investments mostly stayed home in the global economy. Because the Asian nations mostly invested in one another, no outside rule set challenged the crony capitalism rife there.

Investment flows from the United States and Europe, as best as could be estimated, represented no more than a quarter of the money behind the Asian miracle of the last twenty years—crucial, but not decisive in changing rule sets. If Asia was going to double its energy consumption in the next twenty years, it would need a ton of Western money to pull it off. That necessary flow would dramatically increase the influence of European and American financial houses in encouraging better economic rule sets throughout the region. In our workshop, participants estimated that the combined U.S.-European share of FDI going into Asia in coming years should logically double from its current level of 20 to 25 percent to at least 40 to 45 percent. So the opportunity, in Bud and Phil's vision, was to cement China's membership in the Core by satisfying its insatiable demand for energy over the coming years. Naturally, that sort of vision appealed less to Pentagon strategists, because if China was truly integrated, they would lose their much-hyped near-peer competitor.

Why is foreign direct investment so important in this regard? Unlike commercial bank loans or financial flows in or out of stock markets, FDI is real ownership signaling long-term commitment. It involves foreign ownership coming into a national economy and, by assuming equity control over firms they either buy or generate from scratch, importing new rules that basically say, "This is how we conduct business." By its very nature, FDI involves a clash of cultures, but instead of the massive strategic exchange of arms envisioned by some Pentagon strategists, this clash is played out over countless business deals, planning meetings, and regulations issued.

Foreign direct investment is Wall Street's way of saying "China belongs on *our* map, not the Pentagon's." In return, all the Pentagon needs to do is focus on deterring any near- or mid-term scenario that could destroy the investment climate, so, yes, we do need to pay attention to India and Pakistan, China and Taiwan, and the Koreas.

Let's talk some numbers. The cumulative flow of foreign direct investment around the world over the course of Globalization II (1950–1980) and Globalization III (1980 and counting) has been on the order of $7 trillion. But rather than talk actual dollar amounts by region, it is more revealing to speak about the percentage spread, as in "Who's attracted the most money over time?" and "Who's sent the most money over time?"

When we talk about where the money has gone over the decades, it has flowed primarily to the regions lying outside the Gap, as North America (24 percent), Europe (39 percent), and South and East Asia (21 percent) have attracted over four-fifths of the long-term investment. In contrast, the long-disconnected Soviet bloc has attracted a mere 3 percent (almost all since 1990), but even that small amount puts it ahead of the Middle East and Africa (2 percent for each). Latin America has attracted the rest (9 percent), with the vast bulk going to Core members Argentina, Brazil, and Chile. Put in Core-Gap terms, around one-third of the population (the Gap) has had to get by on barely one-twentieth of the money made available by the global economy for long-term investment.

When you examine the flip side of that flow, or who has money available for investment outside its borders, the Core-Gap distinction gets even more profound. Three key pillars control the vast bulk of long-term investments. Not surprisingly, these three constitute the Old Core of Globalization II: the United States, the (now) European Union, and Japan. This relatively small slice of the global population (approximately one-eighth) controls over four-fifths of the money. If you want to join the Core, you must be able to access that money—plain and simple.

That fundamental reality of the global economy explains why we won't be going to war with China. The Pentagon can plan for it all it wants, but it does so purely within the sterile logic of war, and not with any logical reference to the larger flows of globalization. Simply put, those flows continue to reshape the international security environment that the Defense Department often imagines it manages all by its lonesome.

Let me paint you the same basic picture I love to draw each time I give my brief to Pentagon strategists and, by doing so, give you a realistic sense of what China would be up against if it chose to challenge the United States–led globalization process using military means.

China has to double its energy consumption in a generation if all the growth it is planning is actually going to occur. We know where the Chinese have to go for the energy: Russia, Central Asia, and the Gulf. That's a lot of new friends to make and one significant past enemy to romance (Moscow). But Beijing will pull it off, because they have no choice. To make all that energy happen, China has to build an amazing amount of infrastructure to import it, process it, generate the needed energy products, and deliver it to buildings and vehicles all over the country (though mostly along the coast). That infrastructure will cost a lot, and it's common when talking to development experts to hear the "T" word—as in "trillions"— casually tossed around. Where is China going to go for all that money? Certainly, it will do what it can on its own, thanks to its booming exports. Certainly, it will tap its biggest trade partner, Japan, for all it can. But when it really wants to tap the big sources of money, there are only two financial communities that can handle that sort of request: Wall Street and the European Union. So when you add it all up, for China to get its way on development, it needs to be friends with the Americans, the Europeans, the Muslims, and the Slavs. Doesn't exactly leave a lot of civilizations to clash with, does it?

The importance of this momentous but ongoing historical achievement cannot be overstated: the shift from Globalization II to Globalization III is a shift from a small minority of the world (basically one-tenth) enjoying globalization's benefits to roughly two-thirds of the planet joining the party.

So tell me, if you are a George Kennan, or any one of the other wise men from that time long ago, and you were smart enough back in the late 1940s to target Europe and Japan for integration into a revived global economy, whom would you target today? Half the world's population in Developing Asia, where economies are growing rapidly and energy demands are skyrocketing? Or would you work to keep such potential "peer competitors" at arm's length?

And that, my friends, is how you make a roomful of Cold Warriors cry.

THE FLOW OF SECURITY, OR HOW AMERICA MUST KEEP GLOBALIZATION IN BALANCE

There are many different ways a superpower like the United States goes about making other states feel more secure. Sometimes exporting security means training their future military leaders at our schools, like the Naval War College. Other times it means having our ships visit their ports, to let them know—like a cop walking the beat—that we are there when they need us. Still other times, it means setting up shop in their neighborhood, stockpiling some of our equipment and supplies, telling them we are ready to help out if anything really bad happens. Sometimes those really bad things do happen, and then we use all of our influence with the involved countries to deal with the situation as best we can. In this way we stop wars from happening.

That is exporting security. It consists of America giving the world something we have in abundance: a belief in the future. It is a wonderful gift, and frankly, only the United States has either the wherewithal or the generosity to actually provide it. It is one of the best things we provide the planet, and it has changed the course of human history for the better.

This exporting of security is, in large part, nothing more than a by-product of the U.S. military's continuous worldwide operations. We are the only military in the history of the world to possess a planet-spanning command scheme. But exporting security is also done on a person-to-person basis, across countless exchanges, meetings, and conversations. In short, it's a people business as much as a platform business—as much face-to-face as aircraft fly-overs and carrier port calls. I know this, because I have personally engaged in this sort of business myself over the course of my career, and once that activity took me all the way to the historic port city of Bombay, known today as Mumbai.

I visited Mumbai in spring 2001 to represent the United States along with a vice admiral (Commander, U.S. Seventh Fleet) at the first-ever International Fleet Review held by the Indian Navy. The Indian Navy was fifty years old, and this was basically its coming-out party, because, in the Indian way of looking at time, five decades as a navy was only about halfway to adulthood (i.e., they believed a navy took a good century to mature). The five-day mega-event involved eighty ships from twenty different nations and more parties and concerts than I can remember. It was like being in Washington, D.C., for the bicentennial, because the entire city of Mumbai, which is bigger than New York City, was completely turned on for the celebration.

Before leaving for India, I asked several of my fellow professors to "murder board" my PowerPoint brief, meaning I rehearsed the brief in front of them and they critiqued my performance and content. The advice I got was quite sound, but nonetheless wrong.

My colleagues warned me that my usual briefing style of speaking rapidly and using lots of jargon would go over the heads of the hundred or so admirals in attendance. Virtually all would know English, but my delivery style would confound them. So I prepared to speak more slowly and simplify the brief. But when I ascended the stage weeks later in Mumbai, I got so excited standing there in front of several hundred naval officers from around the world (including twenty chiefs of navies), that I forgot all that advice and gave my usual brief.

It seemed to go well, and my Indian hosts declared it the high-light of the symposium. What they especially liked, of course, was that it highlighted India as a crucial military partner of the United States.

I then spent the rest of the five-day event receiving compliments from the heads of all the navies, and here is where I was taught a real lesson. Contrary to my colleagues' fears, all these foreign naval leaders understood my talk completely, judging by the detailed nature of their praise for the material and their extremely intelligent counterpoints. I was both pleased and quite stunned by the response. How could all these admirals follow my inside-the-Beltway material so well? The answer was simple: Most had studied in the United States, with almost half of them being graduates of the Naval War College. I wasn't talking to a bunch of foreigners; it was more like a college reunion.

Even more amazing than that were all the conversations I had with those admirals about naval history, or—more specifically— the role of carriers in naval power projection. None of these Gap navies *has ever owned any carriers,* and yet all these admirals just loved going on and on about the "age of the carriers" as though it were a shared history. Of course, in a way it was a shared history, because the U.S. Navy and its carriers have interacted with friendly and not-so-friendly navies around the world for decades. That's exporting security: when *your* military history and *their* military history are so blended that it is like you are part of the family. You are a known commodity, a trusted friend.

Why is this shared history so important? Most Americans just do not understand what a huge disparity exists between our military capabilities and those of the rest of the world. We really own the only global military, whereas everybody else pretty much has just national or, at best, regional militaries. If we are not out there using our military to export that security, these bonds will simply never be created.

This fundamental reality was made greatly apparent to me when the President and Prime Minister of India conducted their "review of the fleet" in Mumbai harbor, zigzagging past all eighty ships in rapid order on their "presidential yacht," which was really an Indian Navy frigate gussied up for the event. The bigwigs sat up front on the bow, I sat in the cheap seats at the stern. In such a review, it is impossible not to notice that, compared with the United States, the rest of the world's navies are simply the equivalent of our Coast

Guard. The United States owns the only blue-water navy in the world. The size disparity in ships was so great that when we finally passed by the sole U.S. Navy ship in the review, a mere guided-missile cruiser (one of our smaller surface combatants), I almost fell off my chair. It was substantially more impressive—not to mention simply bigger—than every other ship in the review. It was as if we had been reviewing a line of Coast Guard cutters and then all of a sudden this gleaming bruiser loomed over us. Everyone on board took out cameras at that moment and snapped pictures.

Several hundred thousand citizens of Mumbai lined the harbor to witness the review, but in a typical Indian mob scene, tens of thousands more were kept out of the harbor district by police barricades, so as to avoid complete gridlock. So those who could not get to the harbor came *en masse* to the area around the naval base where the presidential yacht debarked, lining the street along which the official cars would pass as we exited the naval compound. My car, adorned with American flags on the hood, along with a sign on the side describing me in my entire titular splendor, followed that of a British naval expert in the exiting parade of limos. When the crowd saw the British flag flapping smartly in the breeze, a nice cheer rose. But when they spotted the American flag, the cheer turned into a frenzy as people jumped up and waved their arms ecstatically, shouting at the top of their lungs.

At first, I was simply too stunned to do anything but stare out the window. Of course, it had nothing to do with me. A trained monkey in the backseat would have gotten the same response. This was the biggest party in Mumbai's history, and average citizens were simply thrilled that America decided to show up. So after about a minute of watching the rolling wave of cheering Indians, my handler, a young Indian Navy commander, leaned over in the backseat and showed me how to wave my hand like I was the Queen of England. There I was with this asinine smile frozen on my face, rotating my right arm at the elbow to achieve that wonderfully robotic wave of my hand. This went on for several more minutes as we picked up speed along the avenue. When we were finally past the crowds, my cheeks actually ached.

That was fun, but later that night I got to do something a bit more serious. At a cocktail party, the conversation became heated as the subject of Kashmir arose. Kashmir is the disputed region lying between India and Pakistan, and the two states have been fighting sporadically along this border for decades, the last true war occurring in 1971. More than a few separatist groups operating out of the Pakistani side of the border have been waging a very bloody terrorist campaign against Indian control over the territory, and Pakistan's tendency to grant these groups free rein within its borders—in some instances supporting them tacitly—is a subject of great controversy and potential war between the two governments. America cares greatly about this situation, because both sides possess nuclear weapons in enough abundance to kill millions on each side if it ever really came to war again.

Before I went to India I received some advice from my local intelligence unit: stuff I might look out for, questions I might ask, and good answers I might provide to tough questions from foreign officials. A basic primer on how to behave in conversation.

So when Pakistan was raised as a security issue for South Asia, a lot of pointing fingers came flying out from my Indian hosts and most of them found their way to my chest. The basic message was loud and clear: "You Americans have no real sense of how dangerous the Pakis are. But someday, when the right trolley car comes rolling down the track, we're going to jump on that car and show you truly how bad these people are! We only hope you have the sense to support the right side when it finally happens."

My reply was the same one I've been giving for years to both Pakistanis and Indians: "No one on our side wants to see this war, and if you think America is automatically going to jump in on your side and back your military, then you're wrong. All we're going to do is try our best to shut down the conflict as quickly as possible, then we're going to send in the relief workers, diplomats, and radiation experts to sort it all out." In my opinion, any nuclear exchange would be a horrific outcome for both sides, but worse for India because it would kill much of its connectivity to the global economy, whereas Pakistan—a truly disconnected state—would lose far less in the end.

My message was my own personal variant of what the U.S. Government has been telling India quietly for years. Those sorts of messages are an important component of both diplomacy and what I call the exporting of security; they just make clear to our friends what we believe are the essential security rule sets. By making those rule sets clear, in countless exchanges between our nation and India, we draw a little closer to them and they draw a little closer to us.

Does that export stream actually work? In the aftermath of 9/11, Pakistan was in a world of trouble with the United States, because we knew al Qaeda was operating all over Pakistan's northern sections bordering Afghanistan.

America had no choice but to get back in bed militarily with Pakistan following 9/11 and our invasion of Afghanistan, but we also escalated our military-to-military cooperation with India, so both sides were feeling they had a big friend in the United States. Then Kashmiri separatists bombed the Indian Parliament in New Delhi on December 13 of that same year, and that's when things got very scary, very fast. India massed about a million troops on the border with Pakistan, both sides feinting that maybe—just maybe—this time they would light it up for good.

Why didn't it happen? Thomas Friedman of the *New York Times* argues that India's great connectivity with the global economy made them think twice about the economic fallout of such a disastrous event, and I think he's absolutely right. But it was also clear that both sides did have someone in their corner who had immediate access to all the key security players and was able to mediate a peaceful outcome, working largely behind the scenes. That someone was the U.S. Government in the form of Deputy Secretary of State Richard Armitage, with an assist from Secretary of Defense

Donald Rumsfeld. These two officials conducted important exchanges with leaders on both sides, emphasizing the continuing
commitment of U.S. security assistance to each, and—by doing so—
helping both governments move beyond the moment of insecurity.

That's what exporting security allows America to do: we can
step into virtually any tense security situation around the world
and act as an honest broker, even when circumstances force us into
the role of rule-set enforcer. The key thing that provides the United
States access in any crisis situation is that our security product is a
known commodity. Whenever you're watching the TV news and the
journalist is interviewing some ordinary citizen trapped in some
Gap war zone, you will hear this again and again: "Why doesn't
America come in and do something about this?" We heard it from
the Bosnians, the Kosovars, and the Macedonians in disintegrating
Yugoslavia over the nineties. Today you hear it from Palestinians,
West Africans, Colombians, and Indonesians—to name just a few.
If you listen closely enough, you'll hear it at some point from basi-
cally everyone in the Gap.

Again, let's look at some historical numbers to get a better sense
of what I am describing here. As noted earlier, U.S. crisis-response activity has increased dramatically since the end of the Cold War, suggesting that the global demand for our security exports has likewise
risen significantly. If we count up the number of days each of the four
services logged in responding to these security situations, we basically tally the "billable days" for the Army, Air Force, Navy, and
Marine Corps (but not the supersecret Special Operations Forces)
in their exporting of security. I generated this data as a consultant
to CNA, and I believe it accurately captures the stress factor many
military leaders cite regarding the increased tempo of U.S. crisis-
response activities in the 1990s. Simply put, many in the Pentagon
have long—and rightfully—complained that the U.S. military was
being stretched too hard by the rise in overseas activity across the
decade, and these data capture that complaint better than any others I have come across.

When we add up the crisis-response days (meaning all nonroutine operational days) for the four services in the 1970s, we come up with 10,415 total days—not including the ongoing war in Vietnam that effectively ended in 1973. In the 1980s, that total rises to 17,382 days, or an increase of 66 percent. That plus-up was hard, but not impossible, to accommodate. But look what happens when the Soviets go away in 1989: the total jumps fourfold, to 66,930 days. What was the real global demand for our services? I think it is fair to say far above 100,000, but 66,000 was what we chose to provide.

How did that grand total break down across the nineties? About 10,000 of those days refer to the usual "cats and dogs" we deal with across the world: a *coup d'état* here and a show of force there. But almost all of the increase we track from that baseline total of the 1970s represented America choosing to export security specifically to situations we deemed most important, either because they involved the global economy (Iraq in the Persian Gulf) or key allies (Israel in the Middle East, NATO with regard to the Balkans), or because the suffering displayed simply moved us to do something about it (Haiti, Somalia, and—to a certain extent—Bosnia). Were there other places we could have exported security across the nineties? Central Africa certainly comes to mind, as does Colombia. But like any global consulting force, the U.S. military can handle only so many clients at a time. The question is, Did we choose wisely?

That question is worth asking because U.S. security is the only public-sector export from the Core to the Gap that matters in the age of globalization.

When I speak of exporting security, I am not talking about arms transfers or the number of cruise missiles fired. I am talking about the time and attention the United States spends on any region's ongoing or potential security problems. Does that export of security make a difference? I believe it does. America has spent the last quarter-century quietly exporting security throughout East Asia, and we have better bilateral security relationships with states in that region than states there have with one another. That is an amazing accomplishment that has allowed governments there to focus less on a military hedge against the dangerous outside world and more on economic development. Japan was our first great success story in this regard, then South Korea. Once we got past the "domino theory" and Vietnam, you can thank the U.S. military—in no small measure—for giving the other Asian Tigers the confidence to focus on their economic development as China focused on its own. That's the fundamental goal of U.S. security exports: filling both a physical and fiscal space in the region. We are the cop on the beat, making sure nobody feels too threatened by anyone else, and so their government budgets are put to better use than arms races.

What did we get in return? The Asian miracle and China's rise as a manufacturing superpower are not a bad return on our investment. Let's not forget that Asia played a significant role in our economic expansion of the past decade. In the Core, nobody does anything by themselves. Increasingly, we rise and fall in tandem.

But where America's security exports have been hesitant, intermittent, or nonexistent, there you will find most of the violence in the world today: the Gap.

Does this mean we need to invade a country to integrate it into the Core? In many ways, just the opposite is true. Of the thirty-seven major conflicts spread around the world in the 1990s, thirty-four occurred in countries with annual per capita GDP totals of less than $2,936. So it is basically the case that when a country rises above that $3,000 mark, they seem to get out of the mass violence business. How do you get them above that line? Official developmental aid is a nice start, but it is mostly a Band-Aid to help stop the worst hemorrhaging, which invariably involves ongoing internal conflicts. Foreign direct investment is what moves you above that line, but FDI does not flow into war zones, because it is essentially a coward—all money is. So if you want to get those Gap countries above that line, you focus on those bad actors that account for the bulk of the insecurity in any country or region. Once that source of insecurity is removed and stable connectivity is achieved, corporations are always looking to move in and take advantage of cheap labor. But by and large, they will not enter states in which rebels are trying to break off a big chunk of the country—unless we are talking oil or precious metals.

Are U.S. security exports necessary to shrink the Gap? *Absolutely.* Are they sufficient? *Absolutely not.* To employ a medical analogy, we must never confuse emergency response with long-term rehabilitation.

As we wage this war on global terrorism, we really wage a war on disconnectedness, because it is the limited connectivity between Core and Gap that must be preserved and expanded for the latter to be progressively integrated into the former. Globalization must be kept in balance throughout this process, meaning certain crucial flows must be maintained. This chapter has outlined what I believe are four essential flows. Let me review each in turn.

First, people will have to flow from the Gap to the Core. As the Core ages and youth bulges across the Gap, we must let that high water move naturally to the lower ground. The temptation to fire-wall off the Core from many Gap flows will be intense in coming years, and especially in the realm of human migrations. The Core will toy with immigration restrictions to keep *them* out. We will tinker with student and worker visa programs, fingerprinting some but not others, and—in doing so—send none-too-subtle signals that America is no longer the friendly place it once was. A certain amount of this rule-set tightening is both inevitable and good, but it is also very dangerous, because it will suggest a wall is rising between the Core and Gap, and nothing will diminish expectations of a better life faster throughout the Gap than this harmful perception.

Second, energy will have to flow from the Gap to the Core, but especially to the New Core in Developing Asia, where energy growth will be most dramatic. The integration of that half of the world's humanity into the Core is the greatest *ongoing* achievement of Globalization III. To surrender that achievement is to erase most of the connectivity developed since the end of the Cold War; it is to give away our peace dividend.

Third, for that energy to flow, security must be achieved in the

Middle East and Central Asia, and that means security must flow from the Core to the Gap, but most specifically from the United States—the world's sole military superpower. For that flow to be effective over the long run, the Core as a whole must become deeply invested in the process. Here is where our collective—and not just the Pentagon's—visioneering has failed us: we have yet to enunciate both the future worth creating and the realistic pathways toward achievement. I have little doubt that pathway begins in the Persian Gulf, but it must travel elsewhere—not just along the "Arc of Instability" but throughout the Gap—before globalization will achieve any lasting sense of balance.

Finally, investment has to keep flowing from the Old Core to the New Core. Europe, the United States, and Japan need to keep financing the progressive integration of South Korea, China, India, Russia, South Africa, Brazil, Argentina, and Chile—to name the most crucial economies. Historically, the global economy has expanded when there was excess money in the system, meaning investors were desperate for good returns and willing to take more risks to achieve them. The Old Core puts money on the table in direct correlation to how positively it feels about the future. If Wall Street, for example, sees a future worth creating, they will finance it. But if they see dangers ahead, even if they be of America's own doing, the money will come off the table and globalization's advance will be starved for funds.

Of that New Core group, China is the most worrisome, while India is the most promising.

China is most worrisome because the hardest rule set still needs to be changed—the authoritarian rule of the Chinese Communist Party. The Party is leveraging its authority to the hilt, promising the emerging middle class all manner of new legal rule sets if only they will resist challenging that rule. The Party is also bribing the military with enough funds and—more important—just enough rhetoric about Taiwan's "return" to keep the People's Liberation Army (PLA) happily dreaming up its own war games of future conflict with the United States, in turn, emboldening strategists on our end to continue their desperate search for an enemy worth creating. The final card the Party can play in this dangerous balancing act is, of course, nationalism. It redirects the energy of the emerging middle class outward, away from needed political change and toward an external enemy, while simultaneously securing the PLA's obedient submission. But the rule-set fallout from a United States–China conflict over Taiwan would be enormous for globalization, effectively barring Beijing from stable Core membership for the foreseeable future.

India, as UN diplomat Shashi Tharoor argues, is probably "the most important country for the future of the world." If globalization succeeds in the United States or the European Union, no one will be too surprised. After all, globalization demands less change of these countries than it does of the world around them. And if globalization fails in China or Russia, few will be surprised, for it requires much change from both societies—perhaps too much too quickly. But whether globalization succeeds in India should interest just about everyone, for if it succeeds in a democratic society where half the population is impoverished and one-quarter is Muslim, then it can succeed just about anywhere. Conversely, if it cannot succeed in a free-market economy featuring the world's largest pool of information technology workers, then there is little hope for the Gap.

These four flows (people, energy, investments, security) are all crucial not merely to preserving the Core but to shrinking the Gap. Right now we are living through a period of intense rule-set change—a catch-up period. We are backfilling political rule sets to realign them with economic rule sets that had leaped ahead. The same is true for security rule sets in relation to the growing role of information technology in defining the connectivity associated with globalization's advance. In the United States, this rule-set reset has already been framed by two very controversial but compelling new packages: Congress's USA Patriot Act of 2002, and the White House's National Security Strategy of that same year. In the former, sweeping new antiterrorism laws were put in place, and in the latter President Bush formalized the previously announced option of "preemption" as the preeminent military strategy in conducting the global war on terrorism.

Clearly, both of these new rule sets put these four crucial flows at risk. The Patriot Act could have a Core-wide demonstration effect, influencing how nations not only deal with potential terrorists in their midst but also how they manage permanent immigration, temporary visas for educational and work purposes, and tourism in general. So far, human connectivity between the Core and Gap seems to have suffered quite a bit, as traffic on all levels has slowed or been redirected since 9/11. Some of this flow reduction is expected, as new rule sets are put in place and adjusted, but to the extent that these flows become permanently depressed or diverted, globalization will remain out of balance.

The new U.S. strategy of preemption puts at risk the flows of energy, security, and investments. In the eyes of many around the world, America may already be guilty of attempting to export too much security to the Gap too fast in the course of toppling Iraq's Saddam Hussein and undertaking the long-term occupation of what can accurately be described as the "Yugoslavia of the Middle East"—a crossroads of civilizations. Clearly, few informed observers around the world—not to mention here at home—bought into the extreme optimism expressed by some Bush Administration officials about a one-year-to-eighteen-month rebuilding/occupation process. In cancer terms, this was not going to be a mere lumpectomy and then send the patient on her way. This is a full-body transformation of Iraqi society, which cannot occur in a regional vacuum, hence the Bush Administration's honest embrace of the goal of transforming the Middle East as a whole. We may have gone in for a penny, but we have assumed the full pound, and that is only right, because how we transform the Middle East will reshape the world's energy market in coming years and decades.

How America's too vigorous export of security puts investment flows at risk is a far more complex tale, logically stretched out over a far longer time frame. In essence, Core states prefer to invest in other Core economies, because they see a shared vision of a future in that process. Foreign states have bought U.S. debt over the years—both public- and private-sector—not merely because America is a good financial risk, but because they preferred to be associated with both America's future and the world that future portends. So America enjoyed all the privileges of owning the world's preferred reserve currency, meaning it has never been hard to sell our debt around the world because other countries love holding dollars, which has become Globalization III's equivalent of Globalization II's gold standard.

But the dollar will not remain "as good as gold" forever, if only because the European Union's euro will invariably rise up as a reserve currency "near-peer competitor." Over the longer run, an East Asian equivalent of the euro must inevitably arise, probably a combination of China's yuan, Japan's yen, and South Korea's won. In short, each pillar of the Core will market its own reserve currency and, by doing so, sell its own vision of a global future worth creating. While the United States will clearly remain the world's sole military superpower, economically speaking, the playing field will be multipolar, giving the system as a whole the opportunity to "vote" with their reserve currency choices on competing future images of globalization's advance and the rule sets (political, economic, social, and security) that define that advance. America can certainly go it alone militarily, but it cannot go it alone financially. The share of total investment in the U.S. economy that is financed by foreign sources now reaches close to 20 percent, while in the 1970s that share rarely rose above 5 percent. In the end, that money will do most of the talking, because shrinking the Gap will largely be a private-sector affair, driven by foreign direct investment flows—not U.S. tanks.

The rule-set reset triggered by the system perturbation known as 9/11 has unleashed profound forces of change that continue to reshape the strategic security environment. In that regard, 9/11 serves as a historical template for a new definition of international crisis: that which temporarily destabilizes but permanently alters the functioning of the global economy. This new definition of war-versus-peace speaks not to megatonnage, or Armageddon-like casualty totals, or even the conquest of one state by another. It does not measure destruction but disruption, and its ultimate impact is described not by body counts but by rule counts—as in the new rule sets that emerge in its wake.

When America dropped nuclear bombs on Japan in the summer of 1945, it ushered in a new era of warfare. At the time, and for a long time after, we believed this new form of war constituted a real threat to global stability, when, as we later discovered, its emergence ultimately resulted in nothing less than the end of great-power war. From the vantage point of 1945, however, it was clear to America's "wise men" that an entirely new set of rules was needed to guide U.S. national security planning in the decades ahead. These rules were built around a new definition of international crisis, one most closely realized in the Cuban missile crisis of 1962. But that definition of international crisis has outlived its usefulness, as has the ordering principle it was founded upon—the model of great-power war.

Today, America and the world stand at a crossroads similar to the one we faced following World War II. The terrorist attacks of 9/11 have provided us all a glimpse of the new form of international crisis that will define our age. As such, I believe it is absolutely essential that this country lead the global war on terrorism, because I fear what will happen to our world if the forces of disconnectedness are allowed to prevail—to perturb the system at will. But as we wage this war, we must keep in mind that not all compromises are worth making, not all risks are worth taking, and not all futures are worth creating. Globalization will remain out of balance so long as America herself remains out of balance, and America will remain out of balance until we achieve new understanding of what constitutes real crisis in our age.

Chapter 5

THE NEW
ORDERING
PRINCIPLE

IN 1982, A FLEDGLING movie director named Godfrey Reggio released an art film that explored humanity's increasingly complex and lasting impact on the planet through the extensive use of time-lapse photography. Its title was *Koyaanisqatsi,* a Hopi Indian word meaning "life out of balance." The trick of time-lapse photography has always greatly intrigued this futurist, because I like the notion of being able to fast-forward history's unfolding. Globalization as a world-historical process often strikes a lot of people—and societies—as a sort of fast-forward, or time-lapse, experience: that which *was* is so rapidly replaced by that which *will be*. The concept of "life out of balance" is a natural response to that sense of life sped up—rule sets out of whack or missing altogether. We tend to associate that feeling with disruptions in our personal lives, or whenever fate has pulled us out of *normal time* into crisis.

My wife and I had our own *koyaanisqatsi* moment back in the summer of 1994, when I discovered a lump protruding through the abdominal wall of our two-year-old firstborn, Emily. I distinctly remember the sensation of first touching this lump, which swam around her lower abdomen whenever she shifted position, like the fin of a shark circling for a kill: we had unwittingly stumbled into a war zone.

A mere four hours after I received the shocking call from Emily's pediatrician telling us her ultrasound had revealed something very serious, Vonne and I were sitting in a Georgetown University Hospital conference room with the chief of pediatric oncology and the head pediatric surgeon. It was a beautiful, cloudless summer day— July 8, 1994. The doctors and the attending social worker were amazingly blunt in their assessment: the cancer, known as Wilms' tumor, had apparently spread from her kidney to both lungs. We were told that Emily had a decent chance of surviving, "But you will all pay a steep price."

Two weeks later we arrived home after two major surgeries, five days of chemo, and Emily's first radiation session. As we went to bed that night, I received the final kicker to our fortnight of surprises: Vonne told me she was pregnant. She had waited until we got out of the hospital to dare take the test. *Koyaanisqatsi.*

The steep price the medical professionals had predicted included bankruptcy and divorce. The historical odds said this medical war would destroy our finances and send Vonne and me down such different pathways that we would inevitably find each other unrecognizable. The only way we could survive, according to our kindly social worker, was to forge a new balance in our lives. We needed to decide what was essential, and what was superfluous. We needed a new definition of both normalcy and crisis. We needed nothing less than a new ordering principle for our marriage as a whole, one that would guide our planning for a family worth preserving.

As I later wrote of Emily, "she is the girl that lived." She tangled with her *Voldemort* while just a toddler and, like Harry Potter, she walked away with a nasty scar. Kevin, our second-born, kept us centered throughout the year-and-a-half struggle. He was our little Buddha, the serene center of our otherwise tumultuous universe.

We never did go bankrupt, although we came close, and Vonne and I did not divorce, although those were some of the worst years of our marriage. By the time things had settled down four years postdiagnosis, we had changed friends, cars, hairstyles, religions, towns, jobs, and our entire outlook on life. Some of these changes were permanent, others not, but all occurred for a reason—our life needed a new balance. We had babies to keep, bathwater to toss. We had new rules to enforce, others to revamp. We had met a parent's worst nightmare, and embraced it for all it was worth.

To me, Emily's cancer was an amazing gift—as twisted and cruel as that sounds. It taught us many valuable lessons and reordered our lives for the better. It showed us what it means to want a future so badly that you will do whatever is necessary to achieve it, even as that effort kills many past dreams of a life well led. Most important, it gave us a confidence to make difficult decisions regarding which connections in our lives must be maintained at all costs, and which could be severed with acceptable loss.

When the terrorists struck on 9/11, the world achieved *koyaanisqatsi,* and many things were thrown out of balance: our citizens' sense of individual security, our nation's definition of acceptable risk, and our world's acceptance of American military power. All must be reordered, rebalanced, and redefined, because— in many ways—our country now faces the same threats Vonne and I once embraced. We can bankrupt our nation fiscally and morally if we are not careful in the battles we choose and the connectivity we sacrifice. Amid the avalanche of new rules we rush to apply, we can easily leave globalization permanently divided—Core against Gap, Old Core against New Core, America against the world. We need a new ordering principle for U.S. national security, one that reassures our friends as much as it deters our collective enemies.

Osama bin Laden's message on 9/11 was essentially this: You will never be able to live with us in your midst. We will attack you from within. We will never give you peace. Your only choice is to remove us from your world by removing yourself from ours. The only alternative to this outcome is that one of us must die.

That is absolutely right—one of us must die. Either the Core assimilates the Gap, or the Gap divides the Core. Either the forces of connectivity prevail or the dictators of disconnectedness thrive.

This cancer either spreads or we exterminate it. There is no exiting the Gap; there is only shrinking the Gap. Achieving the latter means all the bin Ladens must be defeated, no matter their ideologies, their hatreds, or their threats. For if we fail in this struggle, globalization will never become truly global, and thus will remain painfully out of balance—*koyaanisqatsi*.

OVERTAKEN BY EVENTS

Before September 11, 2001, I spent as much time as anyone in the Pentagon describing the likely aftermath of a 9/11-like event, although I spent virtually no time wondering what might actually serve as a trigger, because I do not believe such "vertical scenarios" can be predicted with any accuracy. Frankly, that is the best anyone can do in this business, and those who tell you otherwise are either trying to sell you something or they are just plain lying.

As I watched the two towers of the World Trade Center fall, I, like the rest of the world, was gripped by shock and horror. But as the days passed and the aftermath became clearer, I became excited in the perverse way that only a security scenario planner can—I realized I had covered this ground before.

When I arrived at the Naval War College in the summer of 1998, my timing was just about perfect, because that same month Vice Admiral Arthur K. Cebrowski took over as president of the college. Admiral Cebrowski was well on his way to becoming a legendary figure within the military—the widely acknowledged "father of network-centric warfare." In many ways, Cebrowski stands as the General Curtis LeMay of his age, the flag officer whose vision of future warfare remade not only his own service but the entire defense establishment. Needless to say, I was looking forward to both meeting this great man and working for him.

Then, to my severe disappointment, I was handed my first assignment. The task came directly from Cebrowski: a study of the security issues surrounding the upcoming Year 2000 computer problem, eventually known to all as Y2K. I was flabbergasted. It seemed like the dumbest idea I had ever come across. It was just a software glitch, for crying out loud! It wasn't going to have anything to do with international security! I complained about the assignment to my dean, but I was told unceremoniously that as the professor with the least seniority, I was perfect for the job. I knew no one else on the faculty who wanted to lead the study, because it just seemed so "out there," and Cebrowski was both famous and infamous for being "out there."

What Art was really trying to do with this study was push the military to think seriously about what constituted a system crisis in the age of globalization. He saw Y2K as a heuristic device, or a teaching tool, that would allow us to educate the Pentagon about the changing definitions of crisis and instability in the Information Age. Whether Y2K turned out to be nothing or a complete disaster was less important, research-wise, than the thinking we pursued as we tried to imagine—in advance—what a terrible shock to the system would do to the United States and the world in this day and age. What was so neat about the study, which I directed, was that it soon became an exploration of so much more than just Y2K-the-software-glitch. In fact, we spent almost no time discussing that aspect of it with all the experts we convened for a series of workshops in the study, which was called "The Year 2000 International Security Dimension Project."

Instead of focusing on the trigger of the software failures, we assumed those failures would happen and instead asked, If Y2K turns out to be a global disaster, what will this process of disruption and associated responses (economic, political, social, and security) look and feel like? Remember that a lot of people were generating Y2K scenarios during the countdown, and most of these tended to the extreme, primarily because they were written by techies who know the vulnerabilities of all that connectivity and who, by the nature of their personalities, tend to have a very dim view of humans in general. In short, you had a lot of Web heads predicting a worldwide panic quickly becoming The End of the World As We Know It.

Most of these people were fun to talk to, some even to meet in person, but I never liked any of them getting too close to me physically, and giving out any personal information was strictly *verboten!*

Anyway, what we did in the workshop series was first bring together a host of network experts from as many sectors of the economy as possible to discuss the range of possible disruptions. I also added to this first group a number of social-behavioral experts who could help us understand popular perceptions and reactions. From their inputs, I generated a six-phase scenario that explored the buildup toward January 1, 2000, then the onset of the crisis, and then its unfolding aftermath to the point where it effectively ended or was superseded by some follow-on crisis. Then we had a second workshop to bring together an international group of experts to discuss how the world would react to the worst-case scenario as framed, which was followed by a third workshop with U.S. national security officials in Washington, D.C., where we ran them through the scenario and had them brainstorm likely U.S. military responses around the planet. The last workshop with Cantor Fitzgerald involved getting input from financial players about the likely reactions of global markets to the scenario as laid out. Our goal in these workshops was simple: On New Year's Day 2000, there would be no reason for anyone in the U.S. Government to say, "I had no idea it could be like this!"

Now, I knew there was a lot of paranoia among certain segments of the population regarding Y2K, the end of the Second Millennium, and so on, so I sought permission from the Naval War College to post all my workshops' materials on a publicly accessible Web site. I could see some journalist writing a shocking exposé about how the Pentagon was using these War College workshops to secretly plan martial law in response to the social chaos that would erupt on New Year's Day when all the lights went out and the computers crashed, so I was hoping to be as transparent as possible to allay any such fears. I was told no. Being a good Catholic, I decided to circumvent that rule set and seek forgiveness later, and posted the entire project's analysis on my own personal Web site at Geocities.

Many thousands of hits later, I had achieved fairly high visibility in the online Y2K debate, but because all this Naval War College material was being posted at Geocities and not on the college's official server, wild rumors began circulating on the Internet that the site was really just a front for a CIA-supplied cover story designed to lull the public into believing that the Pentagon was really sharing information with them when in fact the secret plans for martial law were well under way! Naturally, I was considered to be nothing more than a figment of the CIA's imagination.

Then an article was posted on the *Deseret News* site by the famous muckraking journalist Jack Anderson. In "The Government's Secret Y2K Plans," Anderson and his fellow author identified me as the leader of the government's "security project" that had been secretly "coaching every branch of the military" as they quietly planned "a sophisticated social-response network in case civil unrest should erupt." My standing in the world of the *X-Files* aficionados shot up astronomically thanks to the article, and after a few close encounters with some of them following speeches at various conferences, I decided to buy a home security system.

Now, most ordinary people who visited my Web site came away relieved that at least someone in the U.S. Government was thinking about Y2K in a systematic fashion and being open about the security implications of the worst-case scenarios. In general, our scenario material, as scary as it might have seemed to some, was incredibly well received around the world. The U.S. Agency for International Development taped my PowerPoint presentation and made it available to all their missions around the world, and the U.S. Information Agency did something similar for select foreign audiences. I ended up giving the brief around a hundred times throughout the U.S. Government and to various industry conferences, and I consulted with Y2K officials of numerous foreign governments. By the time I was done traveling the world, I had briefed the President's Special Adviser on Y2K, the Deputy Secretary of Defense, and the Commander in Chief of the U.S. Special Operations Command.

Did this kind of scenario planning have any positive effect? One thing I did end up advocating widely as a result of many early conversations with Middle East experts such as Daniel Pipes was that the United States should expect terrorist strikes against symbolic targets in major cities during the millennium celebrations. The notion was that terrorist groups in general could be expected to take advantage of the whole-world-is-watching effect to shock the United States into realizing that the new millennium would feature a new world order not to our liking—a concept I labeled the "first-strike" dynamic. When I first started pushing this issue in late 1998, a lot of the defense community initially resisted the notion that preparations for Y2K should include a significant antiterrorism aspect, because after all, this was just a software issue, right? The Pentagon's tendency was to worry first and foremost about some disastrous miscalculation occurring between the United States and Russia over strategic nuclear weapons.

Where this message was far better received was within the intelligence community, where senior leaders were already leaning in the direction of an aggressively offensive strategy vis-à-vis terrorist threats in the months leading up to Y2K. Was anything ever prevented from happening? In late 1999, the United States captured an al Qaeda operative coming across the border from Canada with the goal of bombing Los Angeles International Airport in the last few days of the millennium. At his trial, Ahmed Ressam detailed al Qaeda's plot to strike against high-profile targets in the United States, Europe, and the Middle East as the new millennium dawned. In the end, plots to attack a U.S. warship in Yemen and Western tourists in Jordan were likewise discovered and derailed.

What was important about all Y2K preparations in general was that both the public and private sectors began moving toward a larger understanding of globalization's connectivity and how it altered our definitions of crisis and instability. Outside of the U.S. Government, my material found a lot of receptivity from the banking, information technology, energy, and insurance industries. Inside the U.S. military, the biggest fans of the project were—by far—Special Operations Command in Tampa, through which I had the privilege of briefing every major "spec ops" command world-wide via video teleconference. At first glance, that is a strange collection of bedfellows, but looking back now through the lens of the global war on terrorism, I feel my project's largely self-selected audience mix was perfectly logical.

Besides terrorist strikes timed for maximum value, I wrote about opportunists taking advantage of any chaos ensuing from Y2K to sow additional fear through acts of malicious mischief. The historical classic of this genre is to put poison down the well and then blame some ethnic group for doing it, thus misdirecting responsibility while inciting violence. Did we get this with Y2K? Nothing big. Did we get this with 9/11? In spades, through the subsequent anthrax attacks. In that "fellow traveler" situation, someone sought to generate follow-on panic and did so quite effectively. What accompanied the envelopes in several instances? Crudely written threat letters purported to be from Muslim terrorists.

In my worst-case scenario I posited the seemingly unbelievable notion that a major stock market could be disabled for days on end, triggering additional "market quakes" around the world and eventually pushing the global economy toward recession. The report described government efforts at "keeping up appearances," even as extraordinary measures were taken to protect key leaders. I predicted a surge in people buying guns and private security services, and a rise in social stress. The scenario envisioned hate crimes against ethnic groups blamed for the problem, and warned that certain authoritarian states might take advantage of the tumult to crack down on political subversives or separatists within their countries. My briefing warned about an "islanding" phenomenon within certain industries where business "backstabbing" would occur, such as insurance companies refusing customers certain basic coverage. This breakdown in business connectivity would also be expressed in supply-chain delays due to monstrous delays at critical network nodes, such as borders, ports, and airports.

None of this happened as the millennium dawned. In fact, my

worst-case scenario (dubbed *Y2 KO!*) was off as far as Y2K and "millennium mania" were concerned. But all these predictions did come true in the days and weeks following 9/11. Stock markets did quake around the world. It was not just Vice President Dick Cheney but an entire "shadow government" that was sent away to "undisclosed locations." Americans did buy more guns. Many people could not sleep, were afraid to open their mail, and sought psychiatric medication at significantly higher rates. Civil rights groups reported a surge in hate crimes against Arabs and Muslims in both America and Europe. Governments all over the world passed new laws to fight terrorists, and some used the global war on terrorism as an excuse to crack down on internal groups (e.g., China and its Uighur separatists) or cast old conflicts in a new light (Russia's struggle with Chechnya's rebels). Insurance companies suddenly refused terrorism coverage, and many industries saw the return of warehouse inventories to guard against disruptions in supply chains—from just in time to just in case. In all, an amazingly complex story that no one could have foreseen, unless they had spent some time seriously examining how globalization's connectivity redefines the concept of a national security crisis.

One of the most interesting scenario lines presented in the report was the notion of a political backlash against the current political leadership for letting the disaster happen in the first place. The response of the leadership in return? They would appoint an "answer man," preferably someone with a strong military background, to serve as a new source of authority within the government. This person would be armed with extraordinary legal powers, which might strike many citizens as threatening their basic civil rights. Here I think the report predicted the sorts of response America has seen in the creation of the Department of Homeland Security and the immediate appointment to that position of Pennsylvania Governor Tom Ridge, a decorated Vietnam War hero. But the real "answer man" is clearly Attorney General John Ashcroft, with his USA Patriot Act of 2002. All that remains now in that scenario line is the "legal deconstruction" by the judicial system, leading to the permanent enunciation of new political "rule sets" regarding what constitutes un-American activities in the age of global terrorism.

My point in citing all this is not to celebrate my foresight, because every time I feel that temptation I check my calendar to remind myself of my scheduled meeting for late September 2001, at Cantor Fitzgerald, on the 105th floor of World Trade Center One. Rather, it is to point out the need for a new ordering principle for U.S. national security. Our now-old ordering principle—great-power war—has simply been overtaken by events. To truly transform the U.S. military, we will need a system-level definition of crisis and instability in the age of globalization. My phrase for such a new ordering principle is System Perturbations.

I worked this definition throughout the multiyear study I led on Y2K, then buried the concept while I plotted globalization's great "flows" with Cantor Fitzgerald for two years. But when the Twin Towers fell on 9/11, I realized I had not found some new strategic concept: it had found me. Soon, I hope, it will find the Pentagon. But understanding that large organizations typically change only in response to significant repeated failures, I am confident that if the Pentagon cannot muster the institutional movement in this direction today, eventually it will have to. The terrorist attacks of 9/11 may have served as the first great "existence proof" for this concept, but there will be others. I guarantee it.

There will be other 9/11s until the entire U.S. Government—not just the Pentagon—adopts a new and broader definition of national security crisis and reorders our entire national defense establishment around it. The Department of Homeland Security is not enough. The new Northern Command is not enough. The frightening USA Patriot Act is not enough.

The National Security Act of 1947 created the Defense Department we know today. Unfortunately, that national security establishment was built for a world long since passed, to wage a type of war no longer fought, and to manage crises one great power at a time.

Simply put, we need a new Pentagon to go along with this new map.

THE RISE OF SYSTEM PERTURBATIONS

There was a time during the buildup toward Y2K when I caught my-self actually wishing something bad would happen, and I hated myself for doing that. One of the occupational hazards of working in this business is that you are constantly thinking about the worst possibilities, so you tend to discount any good outcomes as mere "luck" while citing all the negative projections as the "way things really work." Of course, I generated a variety of scenarios for Y2K, ranging from that bad one I just described to a very positive one in which the world came together in new ways and learned all sorts of wonderful things about robustness and resiliency in the Information Age, and everything worked out just fine in the end. Naturally, no one in my audiences—either military or civilian—wanted to hear anything about that scenario, even though that was the one I pre-dicted for the Core in general. Still, when that scenario did unfold, I could not help but feel a tinge of disappointment, I guess because when bad things really do happen, people in this business not only feel more validated, they simply feel more important and useful.

If predicting positive events in general is hard for most Pentagon strategists, then predicting positive downstream outcomes from negative events is even harder. In general, the rule is: Only bad out-comes follow bad events. Of course, life is not like that—ever. Any big event, good or bad, triggers all sorts of positive and negative downstream outcomes, because crisis always equals opportunity for someone. In the Y2K scenarios, I called this the "dinosaur ef-fect." In the land before time, the dinosaurs ruled all. Then the meteor hit and the dinosaurs could not adapt to the weather change—it got colder. But mammals came through the resulting cold period quite well. So the meteor was a very bad event for di-nosaurs, but just fine for mammals, because they could handle the rule-set change in weather while the dinosaurs could not. So one of the questions I liked to ask in all the Y2K scenarios was, Who are the dinosaurs and who are the mammals?

In the end, Y2K was not a good test for the concept of System Perturbations, because history was kind enough to schedule the event in advance, giving us loads of preparation time. That means we settled on a host of new rule sets in advance, working things laboriously by committee effort, and we were prepared.

But 9/11 was a real shock—one that separated dinosaurs from mammals. One of the most amazing stories about Cantor Fitzgerald following 9/11 is that the firm was able to get its electronic global bond markets back up and running within forty-eight hours of the terrorist strikes. How so? They had backup facilities and plans in place, so the London office took over by start of business Thursday morning, September 13. As Cantor CEO Howard Lutnick told me as the company was preparing for Y2K, he realized that life had already changed dramatically from when the World Trade Center was bombed in 1993 by al Qaeda. At that point, when all the computers went down, Cantor had people around who could "still do it with pencil and paper." But by 1999, those people were all gone, meaning electronic backups were their only route.

But here is the most amazing part about Cantor's resurrection following 9/11: they actually turned a profit in the fourth quarter of 2001. Amid all that human loss and suffering, Lutnick, Flanagan, Ginsberg, and a host of others kept that company alive and functioning. How, you ask? Cantor created its own worst nightmare competitor in 1999, and they called it eSpeed. It was set up as an electronic clone of the traditional Cantor firm, meaning if a competitor was going to create the perfect online version of Cantor in order to steal its market away, it would have looked an awful lot like eSpeed. It was—in effect—a "cannibalizing agent" within the company, designed to steal business from the traditional company and migrate employees along with that business to the new version of the company.

When Cantor lost 685 employees in one fell swoop, the company as a whole could survive, in large part, because eSpeed and other entities like it within Cantor's family of companies were able to shoulder more load. In short, Cantor had both mammals and dinosaurs in its stable of companies. The "meteor" that struck on 9/11 might have come close to wiping out many of the humans who worked in both companies at their New York headquarters, but eSpeed could weather the storm in a way that the traditional company could not have. Moreover, eSpeed's innate distributedness, or connectedness, could be put to immediate use, bringing the electronic bond markets run by Cantor back up within two days of the attacks. Absolutely no luck was involved in Cantor's survival. Those guys simply thought ahead like any good strategic planners.

When the strikes unfolded on 9/11, I can remember thinking, This is it. This is what we've been thinking about all these years: a huge warlike event occurring in peacetime, something so big that it forces us to rethink *everything*. It's the meteor that will separate dinosaurs from mammals in defense. It will tell us what we need to know about *war within the context of everything else*. The impact on our community will unfold over years, but eventually this will change *everything*.

But it is in the security realm where the adjustment will be the hardest and take the longest, because it takes years—even decades—to raise new generations of military leaders and construct new force structures that match the perceived changes in the security environment. Unless, of course, you have a cannibalizing agent already in place, like a Special Operations Command. But cannibalizing agents do not become ascendant unless dramatically new rule sets are recognized as coming to the fore. When those new rule sets are recognized and given credence, we begin to understand the utility of defining system-level crises like 9/11 as something more than just as a gang of terrorists attacking three buildings in the United States. That "something more" is what I seek to organize in the strategic concept I call System Perturbations.

When the United States took down the Taliban in Afghanistan, we got some sense of the new rules of military engagement, if only because the Special Operations Forces were afforded unprecedented prominence. But these changes did not stem from 9/11 per se, and reflected more the operational and tactical requirements of the situation in Afghanistan, not the world at large. It was not until President George W. Bush unveiled the strategy of preemption in June 2002 that our first serious understanding emerged of the changes in store for national security as a result of not just 9/11 the attack, but 9/11 the new definition of a national security crisis.

This country did not have an avowed strategy of preemption prior to 9/11. That we have one now is not because almost 3,000 Americans died that day, or because important buildings were destroyed. We have a new strategy of preemption because 9/11 told us that we are living in a new world, a new international strategic environment. September 11 told us that although deterrence still holds in the Core's Kantian peace, the reality of the Gap still being a Hobbesian world means deterrence is not enough. Deterrence is simply not enough in a world where the ability to wield weapons of mass destruction is becoming as globalized as everything else, because there are forces whose desire to achieve disconnectedness is so profound that they will ignore our security rule sets like Mutually Assured Destruction and will use WMD quite wantonly if given the chance. September 11, the System Perturbation, placed the world's security rule set in flux and that development—at least in the mind of the world's true military Leviathan—created a demand for new rules. Preemption is the big new rule. It was created by 9/11. By creating that new rule, 9/11 changed America forever and through that process altered global history. That is a System Perturbation, set in motion by one man with a vision—Osama bin Laden.

For a System Perturbation to be triggered, people's worlds need to seem turned upside down, but that can be achieved in a variety of ways, not merely by blowing things up. When the Arab world saw Marines walking through the streets of Baghdad in the spring of 2003, their world was turned upside down. Their sense of what is right and what is possible—their rules for how things change in the Arab world—was completely rearranged in one morning's time. The same was true for the Western world watching the World Trade Center towers collapse in real time on TV. People were simply shocked by this image. It *was* perverse: the first live-broadcast mass snuff film in history. And we all experienced it together—by design.

So the *medium* through which the vertical shock is translated into horizontal scenarios is important, with the basic rule being, the denser the medium, the more rapid and profound the *transmission*. Think about how sound travels through air as opposed to through a liquid or a solid. I have to yell pretty loud to have you hear me 100 yards away, but a whale song can be heard for miles across the ocean. Then think about being a kid and putting your ear down to the railroad track and being able to hear the train coming from an incredibly great distance. Again, the denser the medium, the stronger the transmission. The fact that virtually everyone in America could visually experience the two towers' collapse in unison made our collective sense of the world being turned upside down far more profound than if the news of that event had taken hours, days, or even weeks to sweep the countryside. So all the connectivity of the Information Age and globalization is crucial in defining the extent of the system that can be perturbed. Except for the most disconnected parts of the Gap, most of the planet knew about 9/11 *on* 9/11. That is what made it such a profound vertical shock.

So the definition of System Perturbation is driven by the connectivity of globalization. Prior to globalization, there were such earth-shattering triggers as Jesus Christ's death and resurrection, the American Revolution, and the invention of the steam engine, but all these triggers took years, decades, even centuries to play out. We really do not see a System Perturbation in the way I like to define it—with all apologies to the complexity theorists—until we see globalization. So for me, the first true System Perturbations were events like the Great Depression or World War II. In effect, it took system-level shocks to kill a system-level economic process like Globalization I.

This vertical shock generates an outflow of horizontal waves whose cascading effects can cross sectoral boundaries, actually growing with time. This is what Thomas Homer-Dixon calls "complex terrorism." When someone takes down a World Trade Center, they do more than kill people and destroy a building, they stop the New York Stock Exchange, they kill cell phone traffic in the New York area, they trigger a loss of electrical power that lasts in downtown Manhattan for days, and so on and so on. A good example of horizontal waves actually growing in strength comes in the form of the SARS "superspreaders," or the Typhoid Marys of that epidemic. One baby in China, for example, was dubbed the "poison emperor" because of all the follow-on cases he generated. It took merely one sick person traveling on a plane from Hong Kong to Toronto to trigger the World Health Organization's decision to warn against traveling to Toronto, effectively sending that city's and region's economy into a tailspin. Thomas Friedman of the *New York Times* likes to talk about "super-empowered individuals" like Osama bin Laden, but SARS superspreaders would clearly fit his description as well. It is quite possible that just one of them did enough damage to take a percentage point off China's sizzling GDP growth for the year. That, my friends, is serious power, in my mind signaling the ascendancy of the lesser includeds as the most consistent source of international instability and major crises.

Rule-set clashes need not be defined purely by security situations. China's political leadership and the World Health Organization clearly experienced a rule-set clash over Beijing's initial stonewalling on data concerning SARS' spread in China. China tried its usual we'll-tell-you-what's-politically-convenient approach, and the WHO said in effect, "That isn't nearly good enough if you want to avoid even more bans on travel!" When Beijing realized that bans on travel included business travelers cutting major investment deals, they found religion on SARS transparency big time and *voilà!* Political leaders in China declared that anyone covering up SARS cases would be punished most severely. Talk about a rule-set reset!

Rule-set clashes can occur during the run-up to a System Perturbation as well. When the Bush Administration openly declared that it was going to topple Saddam Hussein's regime not simply to remove him from power but to "transform" the Middle East, that declaration—almost a vertical shock in itself—set off a clash of rule sets between Europe and the United States that has extended far beyond either the subject of Saddam's removal or the time frame of the occupation. If Europe ends up moving toward a more united defense policy vis-à-vis the world, the System Perturbation known as *Operation Iraqi Freedom* is likely to be defined historically as the trigger for that lasting horizontal scenario. Another profound horizontal scenario stemming from that "big bang" might be a different sort of NATO or a new sort of UN Security Council—again, serious rule sets sent into significant flux.

But not all rule sets will change following a System Perturbation. A Chinese news media outlet may run a SARS exposé today, but do not expect one on senior party corruption anytime soon. France will still be France in the UN Security Council, because France is still a veto-wielding permanent member, and that is not going to change anytime soon. Russia may be a *de facto* member of NATO, but Russia can still be counted upon to be Russia as far as, say, its relationship with Iran is concerned. So any System Perturbation will result in a combination of new rules, the persistence of certain old rules (no matter how dysfunctional they may seem), and the mixing of both old and new rules.

How these rule-set changes unfold may well seem quite haphazard at first glance, and the connectivity among them may be very hard to trace if you view "national security crises" through very narrow lenses. Osama bin Laden declared a new sort of war on the United States on 9/11. Thanks to that act, there will probably be better access to cheaper AIDS drugs throughout the world. Thanks to bin Laden? *Hardly.* Because the war on terrorism involves pharmaceutical manufacturers? *Now you're getting warmer.* Because System Perturbations like 9/11 can set in motion seemingly unconnected downstream rule-set changes?

Here I believe we stumble upon a story worth telling.

The terrorist attacks occur on September 11, 2001. Then "anthrax man" (or woman) strikes to take advantage of the resulting situation. Within a short time, there are five dead and eighteen sick in the United States. Soon after, Canada, normally a wonderful rule-set follower, tells Bayer, the giant German pharmaceutical company, that it is going to crank out a generic form of Bayer's patent-protected drug, Cipro, as part of its national security response to the anthrax crisis. Does the United States take a similar step? Doesn't need to, thanks to Bayer suddenly finding it in its heart to flood the U.S. market with Cipro, turning on factories across Europe like crazy.

At that point, a bunch of sub-Saharan African nations sitting—figuratively—in the back of the room raise their hands and say, "Wow, that is one neat trick. We've been asking for patent relief for the AIDS 'cocktail' drugs so Indian and Brazilian pharmaceuticals could crank out generic versions for use here in Africa at a mere fraction of the usual cost, but when we asked for that sort of rule-set relaxation, you guys said, 'No way. What you're asking is too hard and too unfair.' We've got millions dying in Africa, but you said, 'No . . . shareholders . . . research and development costs . . . *very* complex.' But now you have less than a dozen dead and all of a sudden you seem to change the rules as you need to. What gives?"

Well, as the United States tried to think of a good answer, these nations set about threatening to derail the launching of the so-called Doha Development Round of trade negotiations that were scheduled to begin at the Doha meeting of the World Trade Organization in Qatar, November 2001. The advanced economies were determined to launch this round, which they had planned to launch back in Seattle in 1999—until Seattle Man the *über*-protester appeared on the scene, smashing up all those Starbucks and ingesting all that tear gas instead. The Core's major economies were determined that the debacle of Seattle would not be repeated, hence the choice of isolated Doha as site for the meeting, and after 9/11, their determination for success was all the stronger. No one wanted to be seen as giving Osama bin Laden the right of veto over the Doha Round simply because he had pulled off 9/11. But because 9/11 begat anthrax mania and anthrax mania begat the hypocrisy of the Core telling the Gap to "do as I say and not as I do," this much-hyped Development Round was being set up for another failed launching, until . . . the Core relented in the personage of U.S. Trade Representative Robert Zoellick, who skillfully engineered the compromise on AIDS-drugs patent relief that proved a crucial milestone in launching the Doha Round.

Of course, the rest of the story is not as uplifting. Soon after, the major American drug companies, who supported Republican candidates with three out of every four dollars they donated toward the 2000 election, immediately began placing phone calls, begging for relief. Guess what happened? America started backtracking, at one point being the only member of the World Trade Organization to oppose the agreement it helped launch. But U.S. opposition was not completely cynical, because as soon as the Core indicated it would relent on patent relief regarding certain life-threatening epidemics such as AIDS, Gap states started proposing similar relief from baldness and sexual dysfunction. At that point, the Core's giant pharmaceutical companies stood up in unison and said in effect, "Over our dead bodies!" So, needless to say, contentious negotiations will long continue on this issue, although great progress has been made, such as a WTO deal, with U.S. blessing, to let Indian and Brazilian pharmaceutical companies disregard international patents as they crank out AIDS cocktail drugs cut-rate. More progress on many such fronts is inevitable simply because governments all over the world can eventually be expected to lean on big drug companies to force them to invest more time and effort in antidotes and vaccines, two drug categories long ignored for being—quite frankly—too Gap-oriented. So in the end, whether he wanted to or not, bin Laden probably has saved countless lives across the Gap by launching the terrorist strikes of 9/11.

That is also what I mean by System Perturbation.

And, yes, I know it's a clumsy phrase, but let me tell you why I seek to reinvent this wheel: I think 9/11 proved a new type of national security crisis exists in this age. I think that new type of crisis is intimately linked to the process of globalization, which is itself a vaguely bland term that still will get you as many definitions as the number of people you ask to describe it. I purposely chose to create not just a new buzz phrase but frankly a whole new national security lexicon. My goal is nothing less than a revolution in how the Pentagon thinks about war and peace in the twenty-first century.

THE GREATER INCLUSIVE

During my twenty-month stint as the Assistant for Strategic Futures in the Office of Force Transformation, Office of the Secretary of Defense, I gave my brief on the Core-Gap divide and System Perturbations to a wide variety of federal agencies involved in national security. At the end of virtually every presentation, I was asked, "How much does this brief reflect the thinking going on in OSD?" Until Art Cebrowski and I—between us—actually briefed all the senior leadership in OSD, I would interpret that question as a *So what?* You know, someone asking whether or not he should take you seriously, in a fairly direct fashion. Later, after the *Esquire* article came out, I became more confident that the material reflected the thinking "on the third deck," where senior OSD leadership has its offices inside the Pentagon, because of the way the article was passed around the Defense Department as an authoritative source. The Chief of Naval Operations, for example, e-mailed a copy to all the admirals in the Navy.

These other federal agencies were really interested in knowing how committed the senior leadership of the Pentagon was to defining a new ordering principle for U.S. national security, because *they were already there.* I finally realized that what they were saying was, "Tell OSD they're not alone." I heard this from officials in the State Department, Homeland Security, the Agency for International Development, the intelligence community, the Coast Guard, the Joint Staff, several combat commands, the Army, the Navy, the Air Force, the Marines, and the Special Ops. And I heard it from the private sector, especially banking and finance. I heard it from governors and mayors. I heard it from foreign militaries, such as those of Singapore, Australia, and Brazil. I heard it in question after question, phone call after phone call, e-mail after e-mail. After a while I felt like that elephant in the Dr. Seuss book *Horton Hears a Who*. I mean, just about everyone was yelling out, "We are HERE! We are HERE! We are HERE!"

What they were all telling me is that we need to expand our definition of national security crises in the age of globalization—beyond commanders in the field, beyond the Pentagon, beyond the Defense Department as a whole. After more than half a century of almost complete segregation thanks to the terror of nuclear war, the Pentagon needs to reconnect to the world—to war within the context of everything else. We need to break up the old hierarchies between the Big One and all those lesser includeds. We need something that covers the whole enchilada—that makes us one with everything. We need a greater inclusive.

The signs are all around us: CIA operatives steering their own unmanned aerial vehicles now have the okay to conduct assassinations of terrorist targets upon sighting. They do not have to ask the Pentagon or the FBI for permission. That is a new rule set. The Justice Department had one list of priorities before 9/11, and a new one afterward. That changes not just the department's rule set but the rule sets of basically every other law enforcement agency throughout the country, because when the FBI focuses on terrorism and cybercrime, local cops get left holding the bag on everything else. That is a new rule set that affects every single citizen in this country. When the Attorney General says he wants to double the number of Neighborhood Watches around the country as part of the global war on terrorism, that is a new rule set. When three out of every four mayors in the United States say they have neither the money nor the manpower to handle any significant terrorist strike, they are screaming out for a new rule set. When the FBI Director opens a new office in Beijing, that is a new rule set. When the Coast Guard revamps its worldwide operations to stress port security at home, that is a new rule set. When Washington, D.C., gets sensors to detect radiological releases, when airports are told to start accounting for shoulder-fired missile threats, when the President proposes the biggest increase in U.S. foreign aid in several decades, when the White House considers a domestic spy agency and the CIA expands domestic operations—all these indicators scream out "WE ARE HERE!"

Officials in OSD, if they had their way, would pursue a serious revamping of the laws that define our national security establishment. They know the Defense Department was fundamentally built for another era, another threat, another world. They are working toward a new ordering principle. The question is, How far are they willing to go?

The Defense Department's ordering principle can be defined as the core conflict model around which everything is planned, procured, organized, trained, operated, and—most important—incentivized. If you change the rule set on how to become a flag—an admiral or general—then you will find yourself with a new military in less than a decade. That is really how quickly you can change the entire outlook of the organization, because in the up-or-out world of the military, we have an entirely new military leadership every ten years.

After I give a brief in the Pentagon or, really, in front of any crowd of security professionals, I find myself surrounded by a small crowd who cannot shake off the challenge I have tossed at their feet. I have had this conversation with so many people in so many venues, I can recite it verbatim: I say, "9/11 is a new form of crisis," and some say, "No, it is only a supercrime. Catch the criminals responsible and life goes on. We may have to change the way our commanders do business around the world, but that won't take much. Just load their staffs with liaison officers from other federal agencies. Play the terror war like the drug war. That's all the transformation that's required. Don't *confuse* this military."

But plenty of others do agree with the notion that 9/11 represents a new form of national security crisis, so with them, I take the conversation one step further. Next I say, "New rules of war come with this new form of crisis, so we need a new ordering principle." And among those still talking with me, some will say, "No, the rules remain the same. We still only do nation-states. If you need a Taliban or a Saddam taken down, fine. But we can't be in the business of nation building, or serial assassinations around the planet. Our product line should remain the same, even if perhaps we need to reposition our suppliers—the services—in terms of the people they crank out. Don't *ruin* this military."

But there are some who have answered yes to those first two questions, and with these few I posit the last and hardest question, "Do newcomers define the rules? Are superempowered individuals like bin Laden and transnational terror networks like al Qaeda fundamentally altering the nature of war in the twenty-first century?" And among those still in the conversation, some will persist, "No, the rules are still defined by states, so that is where our focus must lie. So, yes, we must transform Defense as a whole, but we need to maintain a firewall between us and homeland security. We've given them Northern Command and that's enough. We took down Saddam and that's enough. At the end of the day, we still need to concentrate on defeating other militaries, not running some damn empire. Don't *crucify* this military."

At the end, only the younger officers, the ones who will run this world in a decade, are left in the conversation. They know it will take something more than tinkering to *transform* this military. These future flags are looking for a new ordering principle. They want a *definition of war that goes beyond warfare. And they want it now.*

Let me remind you how we got to this point, because it is crucial to understand that the Pentagon is a victim of its own incredible success to date in managing the global security environment. I know I go on and on about the Pentagon's bad habits and all those "strategists" I refuse to name but lambaste at will, but deep down I truly believe that not only is the United States Government the greatest force for good the world has ever known, but the U.S. military is the single greatest instrument of that good as well. Show me a part of the world that is secure in its peace and I will show you strong or growing ties between local militaries and the U.S. military. Show me regions where major war is inconceivable and I will show you permanent U.S. military bases and long-term security alliances. Show me the two strongest investment relationships in the global economy and I will show you the two postwar military occupations that remade Europe and Japan following World War II. Show me globalization made truly global and I will show you a U.S. military playing Leviathan throughout the Gap. Show me a future worth creating and I will show you a price worth paying—even at the cost of some of our loved ones.

In the Cold War, we faced a system-level threat: the Soviets. We optimized for that threat. We made it our ordering principle. On the level of the nation-state, we waged careful proxy wars, because we could not risk taking on the Soviets directly. Way down within nations, we worried now and then about the least of the lesser includeds—the terrorists, drug traffickers, and so on. But those were left completely to law enforcement, because we had bigger fish to fry.

Now what do we have? Some will say the Pentagon should be solely in the business of keeping Americans alive, but that seems absurd. We cannot pull back our forces into fortress America and hope to keep the world at bay. Others say we should admit we are already fighting World War IV, country by country, so let us order ourselves around that goal, "just as we did back in the big one—you know, Dubya Dubya Too!" But that is simply fearmongering. Ann Coulter may want to kill all *their* leaders and turn *them* all into Christians, but that just will not do for those of us interested in leaving something better behind for our kids than the do-it-yourself instructions for *Götterdämmerung*.

America is a system-level power, really the *only* system-level power. If we do not possess a system-level definition of crisis and instability, then exactly who will? We solved global nuclear war by inventing Mutually Assured Destruction and selling it to the world. We have effectively ended interstate aggression by inventing a New World Order and—that's right—we successfully sold it to the world. Only the worrywarts still sending me daily e-mails fret anymore about global nuclear Armageddon. Meanwhile, state-on-state war has gone the way of the dinosaur, thanks to America's willingness to remind everyone on a regular basis that we are the last superpower standing. Reaching down past the near-peer competitor, down past the regional bullies, we are now waging wars on individual bad actors throughout the Gap. That transformation of U.S. military power over the last generation is nothing less than amazing.

WE ARE HERE!

The same U.S. military that specialized in deterring the Soviets twenty years ago now increasingly specializes in stopping bad people from doing bad things. Twenty years ago our standard of warfare was being able to respond within eight to nine minutes of a Soviet launch of intercontinental missiles—all at the push of a button. Within a short time, we will close in on a standard of warfare where an unmanned aerial vehicle operating on the other side of the world can locate, identify, and kill a terrorist within eight to nine minutes—all at the push of a button.

WE ARE HERE!

America has basically arrived at a point in world history where— if we really want to—we can render organized mass violence of all sorts essentially obsolete. We have helped move the Core toward that standard over the past half century. We could do the same for the Gap, if we can muster a similar, long-term effort. But we need a new ordering principle for national security, or something bigger than just great-power war. In the Cold War, great-power war basically covered all the lesser includeds, but not anymore. Now building a force primarily for that sort of war leaves us desperately short for the *everything else* we find ourselves doing so often in this global war on terrorism. You want a good example? We have a military that can take down a bunch of Saddams every year—easy. What we do not have is a military that can effectively occupy an Iraq—not one. Plus we need a force able to do that and still perform a host of other tasks around the world at the same time.

Here is another example, relayed to me by a friend of mine, a Navy captain whom I will call Phil. Phil told me the following story about his efforts leading a group of U.S. Navy ships operating in the Arabian Sea south of the Persian Gulf following 9/11.

Phil's basically out there operating with ships that—he'll tell you straight off—are really designed first and foremost to engage and destroy other ships. His problem is, he's trying to track and capture al Qaeda operatives we think might be using high-speed boats to escape from Southwest Asia into the Horn of Africa and thereupon disappear deep inside the Gap. This is the classic interdiction problem, or what the drug-ops guys call a go-fast event. That term really has a double meaning: not only are the targets going fast, but you have to decide awfully fast whether that target needs to be checked out or, if need be, targeted for destruction.

Our military has had this problem for a while, like when civilian airliners wander into war zones. Think back to when a Navy ship shot down an Iranian Airbus during the Persian Gulf "tanker war" of the late 1980s. Phil's problem was similar, in that he was conducting "warfare" in the middle of peace. He was waging a global war on terrorism, but everybody else in the neighborhood was just going about their business. So in effect Phil was operating under a serious handicap: his ships were really built to fight other nations' navies, but here he was tracking individuals across a system; plus he was conducting *war within the context of everything else* and did not have the operational mind-set he felt he needed to do the job right.

You can say, "Come on, it's just a matter of stopping boats, and the Navy knows how to do that." But it was harder than that. He couldn't stop every boat, or even check out all the go-fast events. It was like he was a cop training in one of those pretend shooting galleries where the life-size cutout figures come popping out at you and you have to think on your feet: Is that a bad guy or not? Do I shoot or not? Will I get shot or not? Of course, the military trains for that sort of rapid decision making all the time. Phil just felt as if he wasn't operating in his usual shooting gallery.

So, as Phil tells the story, he sets up his own "neural network." He just starts stopping any old boat in order to talk up the local fishermen, figuring they knew the *everything else* part. He gets local knowledge. He makes himself a known commodity. He shifts from warrior to the cop walking the beat. He learns to separate the real data from the background noise.

One day Phil was tracking high-speed vessels roaring out of the Gulf and heading toward the East African coastline. He consults his neural network, checking out the particulars of this go-fast event, asking his local sources, "What do you know about this and how long has it been going on?" They reply blandly, "Oh, about a couple thousand years." It turns out this particular go-fast event is nothing more than the annual pilgrimage by a certain class of fishing boats to the coast of Africa in search of some delicacy that's available in big numbers only that time of year. Phil shoulders his firearm, so to speak, and walks away from the situation that much smarter about how to spot the bad guys in this neck of the woods.

That is waging *war within the context of everything else.*

But it is also an officer trying to shift back and forth between warrior and beat cop at the drop of a hat. It is also the U.S. military trying to wage a new type of war with a force built for another type of war. Finally, it is also the Pentagon letting itself be painted into corners, thanks to an outdated rule set.

The legacy of our focus on great-power war is a military whose structure is best described as "the few and the expensive." The problem is, our future enemies prefer to wage war using "the many and the cheap." We field a huge carrier or a B-52 bomber that can waste an entire city on the fly, but *he* fields a suicide bomber who can infiltrate a defended zone, like an embassy compound or a crowded port, and be more politically effective—pound for pound. *He* is built for the *everything else* environment, we are not. But that can and will change. We will build smaller, faster ships in larger numbers, not to replace carriers but to complement them. We will build smaller, better unmanned aerial vehicles, not to replace fighter pilots but to complement them. We will field more nonlethal technologies, not to replace guns but to complement them. We will build a stabilization force that puts the right boots on the ground, not to replace our Leviathan force but to complement it. Our shrink-the-Gap military will feature both SWAT and cop-on-the-beat capabilities, not to replace the UN but to complement it. We will define future war as something bigger than just preparing to fight another great power's army. Over time, we will master the *everything else.*

You may be thinking, "Oh, that's great for running our empire overseas, but tell me how all this *war within the context of everything else* makes Americans safer at home. You tell me you're going to remake our military, but it still sounds like some force running around out there, while our security is still largely over here. Your ordering principle needs to make me feel safer at home, not just feel better about our troops fighting overseas."

It is when we look at the interrelationship between those "home" and "away" games that we really come to understand how completely things have changed. In short, the Pentagon's ordering principle of great-power war has already taken a backseat to something larger, or what I describe as a System Perturbation. I like to use a medical analogy to explain what I mean here.

When our daughter Emily had to go through fifteen months of chemotherapy, Vonne and I had to come up with a larger definition of "the threat" than the one to which we were accustomed. It was not that Emily was now subject to a wider array of threats, because they were all there all along. It was just that, given her significantly depressed immune system, we needed to protect her more deeply.

Most parents, when they think about bad things happening to their kids, concentrate on what can happen to them when they step out the front door and enter that bad, scary world outside. Sure, you also worry about something hitting home or some problem starting with your child, but most of the time, it is that outside world you fear the most, because, you figure, your kids are safe at home.

Well, when Emily was fighting her cancer through all those long months of chemo, we faced threats from all angles. Of course the cancer could kill her, but it looked like the chemo would do the trick. Then there was the chemo itself, but Emily was handling the poison pretty well. That left the last big problem, which is actually the one that kills most pediatric oncology patients: catching some illness when the immune system is down for the count. Simply put, Emily could catch a cold and die because her body could not adequately defend itself. She was like this perfectly open system, into which any bad thing could easily enter and wreak deadly havoc.

So we designed a defense-in-depth strategy to keep Emily alive all those months. First, we worked on her insides. We stuffed her full of protein every chance we got, trying to build up her weakened immune system by pushing the best building blocks for blood production. Second, we kept the defensive barrier between her and the outside world—her skin—as strong as possible. Here we had a big problem: a permanent chest catheter that was like a huge hole in Emily's defensive perimeter—a drawbridge we could not raise. Since it lacked the normal defenses associated with an orifice (like a mouth or nose), we needed to keep the catheter entry site especially clean, in addition to the rest of her surface. Finally, we worked to keep her operating environment, or our town house in northern Virginia, as antiseptic as possible. That meant we ran our home like a hospital—actually a lot cleaner. Moreover, we severely restricted access by outsiders. If you had the slightest sniffle, we barred you at the door. If you did not like that, too damn bad.

In many ways, what we were trying to do with Emily is similar to what we now refer to as homeland security: trying to keep this incredibly open society from being harmed by bad things vectoring in at us from that nasty world outside. We had to put up with Emily's depressed immune system because that was the price we paid to beat the cancer. Likewise, America needs an open society because that is the price we pay for linking up so effectively with the rest of the global economy.

So how do we keep America-as-we-know-it alive? Same basic routine: we bolster our immune system, we man our perimeter defenses effectively, and we try to root out those nasty sources of terrorism out there in the global environment. Some examples of who does what: America's immune system is basically its first responders, or the police, fire, emergency medical, and so on. You cannot stop every bad thing from entering the system, so you need to keep that immune-system response capability strong. The protective membrane force? That is more like your FBI, Customs, Coast Guard, and so on. Much of our Department of Homeland Security is found here. Who works to keep the outside environment clean? Here we are talking about the Defense Department, by and large, in what used to be a pure "away game."

But of course there is no such thing as a pure away game anymore. We cannot restrict our worries to bad things happening to Americans only when they head out the door and travel overseas, which is the most practical way the Pentagon thought about the safety of Americans prior to 9/11—what we call noncombatant evacuation operations.

Today, our definition of national security is not just a matter of being able to play "over there" versus "back here," but being able to play in all arenas simultaneously: over there, back here, *and* along the perimeter. Welcome to the three-front war, where nothing is sacred and no one is ever absolutely safe.

When the United States invaded Iraq in the spring of 2003, we fought a three-front war, whether most Americans were aware of that or not. We massed a huge security force to protect Americans all across the nation. We increased our border security operations to levels not witnessed since the Second World War, or the days immediately following 9/11. This combined internal/perimeter defense operation was named *Operation Liberty Shield*. It was done solely in conjunction with our invasion of Iraq. This is the first time we have ever taken such dramatic steps *preemptively* to secure our nation as part of a planned overseas intervention. That is because our toppling of Saddam Hussein's regime was no simple intervention; it was no mere major-theater war. *Operation Iraqi Freedom* was an overt attempt to create a System Perturbation centered in the Persian Gulf: to throw rule sets there in flux, to shake things up, to trigger a Big Bang that would transform the region's security system and, we hoped, so much more. It was *war within the context of everything else.*

America is attempting to do things today in global security affairs that people everywhere—in this country and around the world—are struggling to describe. The world desperately needs a new lexicon for this new security environment, otherwise America will never be able to make itself understood. Our problem right now is not our motive or our means, but our inability to describe the enemies worth killing, the battles worth winning, and the future worth creating.

THE BIG BANG AS STRATEGY

At this point, I should probably tell you that I am the real Agent Mulder of *X-Files* fame. What I mean to say is, a lot of people *out there* are certain I am the real Fox Mulder, and if they are that certain, then at least some of the rumors must be true. I could deny it, as I have many times before, but even I have to admit the evidence is getting to be overwhelming. So I figure I might as well come clean and confess everything. That way I can tell you the *real* story behind the war in Iraq and the so-called Big Bang theory. By doing so, I can pull back the curtain and show you the Bush Administration for what it really is—a bunch of crazy idealists hell-bent on *transforming the Middle East!*

The story of my Mulder-like career of nonstop conspiracy really needs to be told by a man smoking a cigarette, but here I go anyway: First off, I never worked at the Center for Naval Analyses, that was strictly my cover while I received eight years of training at the Agency—you know, *somewhere in northern Virginia.* But to make it look good, the Company sends me to Rhode Island when I'm ready to be put into play. That way, it's not so obvious what I'm up to. So they get me this gig at the War College, where I, like, *never* seem to teach a class! Come on! That's a dead giveaway. Why the college? Those guys had those supersecret workshops going on with Cantor Fitzgerald. Yes! *That* Cantor Fitzgerald. Run by a bunch of Jews. Those guys control almost all the government bond trading in the universe. You remember the '93 bombing, right? That was the pretext for the workshops—all part of the big plan to be revealed at a later date.

So what's my first assignment there? Planning the Pentagon's *coup d'état* for Y2K! Jack Anderson broke that story, but the signs were there all along. I mean, that phony Web site at Geocities, the fake bio on his Web site, right down to the kid-with-cancer story— so humanizing! But Y2K fails to provide the pretext for the ZOG takeover—you know, the Zionist Occupation Government. I mean, after Anderson broke the story, many of us were too afraid to go through with the plan, so the whole thing fell apart: the Marines never took over Washington, Cantor never engineered a financial panic, and the Agency never got around to assassinating all those American leaders to clear the way for the ZOG. So the Clintonistas had to go. If they couldn't pull it off with all those Jews running Treasury, then we'd have to try again using Defense. So the ZOG masterminds, working with the Agency, fix the 2000 election and Bush beats Gore. I vote for Gore, by the way, just to cover my tracks.

Now the ZOG conspirators basically have control of the Pentagon, with the Jews Paul Wolfowitz and Doug Feith running the show as Deputy Secretary of Defense and Under Secretary of Defense for Policy, respectively. Rumsfeld? Strictly a front man, because he seems so . . . non-Jewish, I guess. Anyway, this is when I really go into action. After the Y2K plot falls apart, I get into bed big-time with Cantor Fitzgerald, and we hold even more secret workshops atop the World Trade Center, planning the 9/11 terrorist strikes. Here I got obvious, what with all the WTC images on my project's logo. Duh! Like I wasn't trying to leave a clue here or there!

So I spend all of the new millennium shuttling back and forth between the World Trade Center and the Pentagon, working out the details of the strikes, which, to totally throw everybody off our trail, would involve blowing up those two very same buildings! Brilliant! So boom! On 9/11 it all goes down real scary-like, but as we know (because it's all over the Internet), all the Jews running Wall Street conveniently weren't in the towers that morning. Anyway, at this point, the next stage of the plot goes into effect and I start my new job working for the Secretary of Defense, but not too close, mind you, so they make me an Assistant for Strategic Futures in this obscure "transformation" office (remember that word!). Now it all really comes together: Ashcroft is putting together his personal Gestapo, the White House is rewriting the Constitution. All we have yet to do in the Pentagon is get ready to take over the Middle East's oil fields.

Here is where all my workshops with Cantor about investments, energy, and so on start to be revealed for what they really were: Star Chamber summits of key heavyweights in the conspiracy, ginning up blueprints for an American empire in the Middle East, with the Jews running everything both here and there. With America so stoked about 9/11, the Pentagon now has a free hand to start eliminating obstacles in the way of an Israel *über alles* in the Middle East. First, we have to take down the Taliban and erase all our loose ends with bin Laden, because that guy would have spilled the beans if the wrong people captured him alive. But that's what those bunker-busting bombs are for. Then it's Saddam's turn so we can get our hands on all that oil. At that point, we want to leave the world guessing for a while, plus Bush has another election to steal before launching the ZOG for real. The key indicator? Watch for Colin Powell to be pushed out of State right after the election, clearing the way for Wolfowitz. At that point, we start taking down regime after regime across the Middle East (Condi Rice calls it "transformation," get it?), and by the time 2008 rolls around, it's all a *fait accompli*. Then we stick another Clinton back in the White House (Hillary, from the great state of New York, of course!), and our work continues.

My job in all of this? Same as always: seemingly innocuous academic explaining the world from Newport, covering tracks like crazy. You need an explanation for 9/11? I've got one. You need a rationale for Iraq? I've got one. You need a map for decoding all the rest of the wars to come? Hell, I published a beauty for you in *Esquire*. I mean, we're not even trying to hide things anymore! Powell may say there's no list. Rumsfeld may say there's no list. But Barnett, finally out of the closet, has got a list! It's right there with the map, for crying out loud!

Notice, how, right after the war, I quit my job in the Pentagon and went back to being just a lowly college professor? That was all part of the cover-up, including my teaching for the first time in my career. What's up with that? Merely to divert attention from my writing the book that will sanitize the conspiracy for public consumption, coming out in the spring of 2004 in order to help get Bush reelected (though you can count on me to vote Democrat again, just to be sneaky).

Whew! It was good to get that all off my chest. I had been fighting to hide my true identity my whole career, but all those e-mails I have received over the past two years finally convinced me that the jig was up. It just feels so right to finally admit it all in public. Then again, maybe I signed my own death warrant, not that that wouldn't be a clever way to divert attention from. . . .

Either the suspense is killing me or I am having a midlife crisis. But you have to admit, it all lines up neatly to a twisted mind, and one of the great joys of the Internet is, these people can send you e-mails pretty much around the clock, demanding you finally come clean, threatening to rat you out, or simply begging you to *stop this war, Agent Mulder!*

Of course, there are always plenty of conspiracy theorists who come out of the woodwork every time there's a 9/11, and it's tempting to ascribe such nutty views to only the fringe types. But then you get the Prime Minister of Malaysia speaking at an international forum of Muslim countries, decrying how "the Jews rule the world by proxy," and you realize that this sort of nonsense is being used by some very powerful people for very cynical purposes.

Now let me begin the serious apology, or the story I think really does explain why we went to war in Iraq.

The Bush Administration came into power committed to defense transformation, which it defined primarily in terms of technology, as in, "We need to 'skip a generation' of technology and move toward the military we know we really can build in this information age." Their preferred rationale for that transformation was a near-peer competitor, or the "rising" Chinese security threat. Were they largely cynical in this? I believe so, but no more than anyone else talking up a "revolution in military affairs," or "network-centric warfare." Simply put, all these transformation advocates saw a future military there for the taking, and worried that if America did not grab that future first, someone else would. In reality, no country out there is making any serious effort at that "transformational military"—not the Chinese, not the Europeans, no one. Our lead on the rest of the world is getting bigger, not smaller, and so the stories the transformation gurus resorted to telling were getting all the more fantastic with time. They needed an enemy worth fighting and did not have one, so they made one up.

Did the Bush Administration come into power with a chip on its shoulder about Iraq? You bet. Were they on a line toward making something happen? Not really. Their commitment to transformation kept their focus firmly on China—witness the P-3 spy plane brouhaha with Beijing in the spring of 2001. This Administration had no stomach for nation building, no interest whatsoever in the Gap, and particularly no desire to start building peace in the Middle East. They said all these things quite openly; they were going to focus on the big pieces. They were going to focus on security issues across the Core: targeting China, Russia, and India for their undesirable behavior and whipping NATO and the Europeans into shape. Absent 9/11, this Administration would have done nothing for Africa, nothing for the Middle East, nothing for the Gap as a whole. They simply did not care. Their future worth creating was limited to the Core; they were virtual know-nothings about the Gap. Plus they really wanted to pull back from overseas military commitments in order to finance the fabulous technological transformation of the military they wanted more than anything else. This group had absolutely no interest in "empire"—just the opposite. If they had had their druthers, America would have let the Gap burn unceasingly while they plotted brilliant future wars with China. That "plot" was not facilitated by 9/11, it was *destroyed* by

9/11. Nonetheless, conspiracy theories abound that the U.S. Government actually staged the 9/11 terrorist attacks.

The terrorist attacks spared us a pointless and dangerous pathway of confrontation with the Chinese, and to a lesser extent with Russia and India. It put the Middle East back on the map, along with Central/South Asia and Africa, although Southeast Asia and Latin America still seem largely forgotten. September 11 killed the search for a near-peer competitor by elevating al Qaeda and the Axis of Evil to that function for the time being, thanks to the global war on terror. But most important, 9/11 gave this Administration a genuine rationale for defense transformation, although it is going to end up shaping that transformation in ways they never could have imagined.

In the end, 9/11 is going to consummate a split that has been building within the U.S. military since the end of the Cold War: between the "big stick" warrior force and the "baton stick" constabulary force. Both will end up being transformed, meaning the Defense Department as we now know it will cease to exist, and it is the war against Saddam Hussein that set all this in motion.

Where I take my hat off to this Administration is its willingness to finally see the strategic security environment for what it really is: one world that works just fine (the Core) and one that does not work much at all (the Gap). In a heartbeat, they effectively abandoned their previous effort to recast the Core's security order and now have largely embraced the goal of reducing the Gap's security disorder. I say "largely" because it is unclear what sort of real follow-through on security this Administration will pursue anywhere in the Gap besides the Middle East, but since I believe that region is the logical place to start, I think patience is in order.

Anyway, the mess America will find itself managing in the Middle East alone will effectively transform our military into what it needs to become to play Leviathan to the Gap as a whole. I do not cite this as a possibility; I mean it as a virtual certainty. The only question is how long it will take our leadership to discern the coming changes, embrace them fully, and describe them completely to the American public and our allies so we can debate their meaning openly. Until then, the conspiracy types will rule the grand strategy roost, which is pathetic in the extreme.

Let me tell you how 9/11 begat the Iraq War, how that war constitutes the strategic pursuit of a System Perturbation, and how I see this Big Bang unfolding across the Middle East in coming years. This, I believe, is the real backstory of the coming transformation of U.S. national security.

September 11 was a vertical shock of immense proportions, setting off a vast array of horizontal scenarios that continue to this day to recast our society, national security, and America's relationship with the outside world. Most of these changes have been long needed and—by and large—are much appreciated by the American public, but they have raised serious questions not just about "who's next?" but "where is this all leading?" Where this all leads to is extending our security rule sets around the planet, shrinking the Gap by integrating it with the Core, thus making globalization truly global. The main struggle of our age is over how best to achieve connectivity that is just and ordered, and the main threat we face are those forces determined to pursue disconnectedness as a means for power and control.

Until 9/11 awoke us to the reality that globalization, the greatest horizontal scenario of them all, was not going to proceed uninterrupted or unchallenged by war, national security strategists were fundamentally oblivious to the connections between the world of security and the world of economic integration, other than their myopic focus on the proliferation of dangerous military technologies. Now we know that to solve the major security questions of our age, we must extend globalization's reach in a deeply connected, broadband manner. This is not a task we face in China, where connectivity is growing by leaps and bounds each year. It is a task we face throughout the Gap, but first and foremost in the Middle East, because of the clustering of endemic deficits there: a deficit of freedom, a deficit of economic development, and a deficit of security. The security deficit is what drives the lack of connectivity between that region and the rest of the world, which, frankly, would prefer no connectivity to the region absent the energy ties—other than U.S. support for Israel.

As a 2002 UN report noted, "The Arab region has the lowest level of access to Information and Communication Technologies (ICT) of all regions of the world, even lower than Sub-Saharan Africa." Thanks to that stunted connectivity with the outside world, the Middle East's deficits of freedom and economic development have only gotten worse in recent decades. They come together to diminish expectations of entire generations. Recent opinion polls in the region suggest that roughly half the young people wish to emigrate to other countries—half! How can you build a future when half of your young people would prefer living elsewhere? This is a region desperate to connect to the rest of the world.

Those diminished expectations generated the hatred that expressed itself on 9/11. Strip away the religion and the rhetoric, and 9/11 was nothing more than an act of desperation: the Middle East simply does not work for the vast bulk of the people who live there. The bin Ladens of that region blame the ruling elites there and the West for this sad state of affairs, and are convinced that greater disconnectedness is the answer, allowing these societies to go their own way, which they define as moving away from all that Westoxification.

These seemingly disparate realities all come together in the following simple conclusion: The only way America can truly achieve strategic security in the age of globalization is to destroy disconnectedness. We fight fire with fire. Al Qaeda, whose true grievances lie wholly within the Persian Gulf, tries to destroy the Core's connectedness on 9/11 by triggering a System Perturbation that throws our rule sets into flux. Their hope is to shock America and the West into abandoning their region first militarily, then politically, and finally economically. They hope to detoxify through disconnectedness. America decides correctly to fight back by trying to destroy disconnectedness in the Gulf region. We seek to do unto al Qaeda what they did unto us: trigger a System Perturbation that will send all the region's rule sets into flux. Saddam Hussein's outlaw regime was dangerously disconnected from the globalizing world—from our rule sets, our norms, and all the ties that bind the Core together in mutually assured dependence. He was the Demon of Disconnectedness, and he deserves death for all his sins against humanity over the years.

But disconnecting the Great Disconnector from the Gulf's security scene is only the beginning of our effort, because now Iraq becomes the great battlefield for the soul of the whole region. If America can enable Iraq's reconnection to the world, then we will have won a real victory in the globalization struggle, and the transformation of the Middle East will begin in earnest. Winning the war brought no security to the United States. In fact, by committing ourselves to Iraq's eventual integration into the Core, we temporarily reduced our security. But winning the war was the necessary first step to winning the peace we wage now, and that follow-on victory will increase U.S. security in the long run quite dramatically. By that I do not simply mean regime change in other countries seeking WMD or supporting terrorist networks, I mean really "draining the swamp" of all the hatreds that fuel the violence we suffered on 9/11. I mean destroying disconnectedness across the region as a whole.

That second victory will be very difficult to achieve. Our efforts to integrate Iraq into a wider world will pit all the forces of disconnectedness in the region against us. Therefore we must enlist the aid of all the forces of connectedness across the Core—not just their troops, but their investment flows and their commercial networks. We need to demonstrate to the Middle East that there is such a thing as a future worth creating there, not just a past worth re-creating. That is all the current bin Ladens offer the population—a retreat from today's diminished expectations. They do not promise any future whatsoever; they merely offer a return to the past. If America cannot muster the will, not to mention the Core's aid, to win this struggle in Iraq, we will send a clear signal to the region that there is no future in the Core for any of these states, save Israel. Moreover, once an Iraq is "liberated" from American "tyranny," Israel will go back to being the region's full-time whipping boy, standing in for the Core as a whole.

That will constitute a tragedy not only for Israel but for the world as a whole. A Middle East that seeks to survive in the future solely on the slim connectivity offered by its energy exports to the Core will have no future whatsoever in globalization's advance. As the Core progressively decarbonizes its energy profile, moving off oil and into hydrogen to power vehicles, the Middle East's security deficit becomes a cross not even the United States will long be willing to bear. That clock is ticking right now. Once that tipping point is reached, it will be a slippery slope ride to the same sort of depths we have witnessed in Central Africa over the past decade. If we are lucky, we will end up with nothing more than a giant Taliban-like "paradise" that keeps the West out, the women down, and our narcotics flowing.

What is so amazingly courageous about what the Bush Administration has done in trying to generate a Big Bang throughout the Middle East is that it has committed our nation to shrinking a major portion of the Gap in one fell swoop. By doing so, I believe this Administration has forced America to finally come through on promises repeatedly offered during the Cold War but never delivered. In effect, America has been telling the Gap for decades that we would really love to come in there and help straighten things out security-wise, but we always seemed to have some bigger fish to fry: the Soviets, the fabled near-peer, our own self-improvement as the world's sole military superpower . . . whatever. But by taking down Saddam Hussein and turning Iraq into a magnet for every jihadist with a one-way ticket to paradise, America has really thrown down the gauntlet in the Middle East—it has finally begun exporting security for real. In the past, we always had ulterior motives: to keep the Soviets out, to keep the oil flowing, to keep Israel safe. But reconnecting Iraq to the world is so much bigger than any of those goals. It is about creating a future worth living for a billion Muslims we could just as easily consign to the past.

That is the U.S. Government I have loved and admired. That is the America I am thrilled to call my home. That is the world I want to live in someday.

Political commentators who prattle on about how George W. Bush has "staked his entire presidency" on Iraq cannot see the forest for the trees. Bush has staked a whole lot more than his political career on Iraq: he has set a showdown between the forces of connectedness and disconnectedness in our world. I know my Core-Gap division often makes the world seem too neat, because, in reality, there are plenty of forces within the Core who favor disconnectedness over connectedness, and we will face as many battles with them in coming years as we will face with the bin Ladens of the Gap. That is because many governments in the Core still view the world system as a balance of powers, and so any rise in U.S. influence or presence in the Middle East is seen as a loss of their influence or presence there. Too many of these "great powers" are led by small minds who prefer America's failures to the Core's expansion, because they see their national interests enhanced by the former and diminished by the latter. They prefer the Gap's continued suffering to their own loss of prestige, and they should be ashamed for their selfishness.

That is not to say that America's motives in the Gap, or more specifically in the Middle East, are selfless, because they are not. In the end, it took the System Perturbation of 9/11 and all the pain it inflicted to motivate America to finally do something significant to address the region's long-standing security issues, and by "significant" I mean something more than just keeping rogue regimes in the box. But the Big Bang as grand strategy has plenty of arguments going for it, even if these advantages seem illusory to Old Europe.

First, when the United States acts as System Perturber, we set the timing of the rule-set creation. Osama bin Laden got to pick the date of 9/11. But America was able to select—long in advance—the spring of 2003 to launch the Big Bang, which gave us maximum time to make our case to the rest of the Core regarding our motives and goals. If we did poorly in this regard, we have only ourselves to blame. The bigger point is that we made time to argue our case; we were not rash in our strategic tempo.

Second, when the United States perturbs the system, we set the conditions under which the new rules emerge. We can decide to fight the war in such a way as to signal to the rest of the world, "This is what happens when the rule set is transgressed as badly as this regime has done." But rather than just signaling threat, the way in which we wage war can show the promise of a better future as well. We showed Iraqis and the world that this was not a state-on-state war between the United States and Iraq, but between a multinational coalition and a collection of bad actors who had hijacked a society's freedom for a couple of generations. We also waged war with an eye to the economy's recovery, putting us in the strange position of actually caring about Iraq's future far more than did the enemies we fought.

Third, when America orchestrated a Big Bang in the Middle East, we targeted a specific audience for rule-set export. *Operation Iraqi Freedom* was a message to the region as a whole, not just Iraq, which, in many ways, serves more as trigger than target. The Big Bang targets Iran's "sullen majority" that has already given up trying to create any future in that country. It targets Bashir Assad's regime in Syria, letting him know that our patience with his slow pace of reform is finite, and that we do hold Damascus responsible for what goes on in Lebanon vis-à-vis Israel. It targets the House of Saud, telling the royal family that we will no longer turn a blind eye to their "export dumping" of terrorism around the region, much less to our society. It tells the region as a whole, America will stand beside you as you seek greater connectivity with the world outside, because we are never leaving the Middle East until the Middle East joins the Core.

Finally, the Big Bang shifts the dialogue in the Middle East from "why" to "why not?" Think of the three biggest voices there over the past decade: Yasir Arafat, Saddam Hussein, and Osama bin Laden. What did any of these voices have to say about a better future for the region? About a more connected future? About a more peaceful future? Basically nothing, Arafat's Nobel Peace Prize notwithstanding. But we have heard many new voices since: a Jordanian king, a Qatari emir, and a Nobel Peace Prize–winning female Iranian lawyer and human rights activist. All with something different to say, but all speaking in the future tense about a Middle East that belongs in the world, not separate from it.

What are the likely pathways for this Big Bang? The application of System Perturbation as grand strategy is a risky affair, by anyone's measure, because two dynamics are set in motion, only one of which the United States can exert much control over. First, there is the question of Iraq itself. Let me posit a spectrum of outcomes, ranging from a successful *makeover* of Iraq to the frightening notion that Iraq will become America's *West Bank*. A second spectrum describes the impact of Iraq's transformation—for good or bad—on the rest of the region. On the negative side we could describe Iraq as the Muslim world's new *chosen trauma,* and on the positive side we could imagine the hoped-for *Big Bang* spreading throughout the region as a whole.

The worst-case scenario is a combination of *America's West Bank* and *Islam's chosen trauma* that I call *Black Hawk Down—the Series.* In this pathway, America remains trapped in the "mother of all intifadas" that never seems to end, counting up close to 1,000 annual combat deaths in what is supposed to be a peacetime occupation. But our military presence never quite achieves that status, because jihadists from all over the world flock to Iraq looking to kill Americans in a big shooting gallery. So American soldiers die unceasingly, but in dribs and drabs that are covered extensively by the evening news back home. Instead of the one tragic big-screen tale, it is more like a reality-TV series played weekly, to numbing and/or enraging effect on American viewers. The only upside to this scenario is that America is essentially trading soldiers for civilians, in effect using the former as bait overseas to deflect attacks on the latter back home. The downside is clear: The more the occupation becomes an international tar baby, the more likely it is that America and America alone will be left holding the bag.

The best-case scenario is just the opposite: the *makeover* of Iraq proceeds apace and triggers a *Big Bang* effect elsewhere in the region. Here we would be talking about significant political reforms in Saudi Arabia, Iran, and Syria, along with the region as a whole opening up significantly in economic terms. Likewise, the Israeli-Palestinian situation would settle into a peaceful coexistence. In this scenario, which I dub *Persia Engulfed,* U.S. military presence in the region would remain prevalent, but behind the scenes. It would simply become accepted as a fact of life, as it was in Europe during the Cold War. The biggest force-protection issue for such bases would be protests by peace groups, not suicide bombers. But the main measure of progress in this scenario would be a significant decline in public defense expenditures and a commensurate rise in broadband economic connectivity between the masses and the global economy. A good signpost would be a sharp decrease in the so-called wallers in major cities, or underemployed young men who spend their days leaning against walls waiting for their adult lives to some-day begin. These disenfranchised urban youth are prime recruits for terrorist groups. If the Middle East truly joined the world, either these young men would have jobs come to them or they would em-igrate to jobs abroad.

Clearly, where we started in this process following the war was in the worst-case scenario, in which U.S. soldiers were dying in twos and threes on a regular basis. The longer America remains stuck in this scenario, the harder it becomes to leave it, because the harder it becomes to attract other Core militaries to this hardship duty and the easier it becomes for our enemies to draw in new recruits from abroad. As Paul Wolfowitz has said, Iraq becomes the "super bowl" for terrorism, and the longer that continues, the harder it becomes for America to remember why 9/11 convinced us that this effort once made so much sense.

How does America move the pile from the worst-case outcome to the best-case? Three routes seem most likely. First, the most di-rect route from worst to best cases happens when America interna-tionalizes the occupation force in Iraq and successfully "indigenizes" the apparatus of political control, meaning we put Iraqis in charge of Iraq and the world becomes its bodyguard. Then you work to attract foreign direct investment like crazy and let Iraq's more than adequately educated masses do the rest. I believe this scenario will be largely set in motion within eighteen months of Saddam's removal, possibly paving the way for a second Bush Administration in the November 2004 elections, assuming the economy recovers enough and the public forgives the President for all the debt rung up on his watch.

Say that scenario falls apart, or takes a lot longer to materialize. Then the most roundabout route from worst to best cases describes the third scenario, or what I call the *Arab Yugoslavia* pathway. Here, any successful or unsuccessful development in Iraq may be followed by the United States being pulled into some new neighboring instability (e.g., Iran, Turkey, Syria, Jordan, Saudi Arabia, Egypt). If success in Iraq triggers sequential "baby bangs," then clearly this is an exhausting route, but it's one worth taking. But if a "bleeding Iraq" simply spills across borders, then it will feel like America is buying one big babysitting job on the installment plan. So the key distinction here would be: Do the responsibilities incurred seem additive or merely one damn thing after another? If it is the former, then "imperial fatigue" sets in, but if it is the latter, then America is far more likely to be able to internationalize the Core's continuous response, much like in the former Yugoslavia scenarios across the nineties. There is a thin line between "peace breaking out all over" and "chaos breaking out all over," so calm American leadership would be at a premium, because international perceptions would matter.

The harder route from worst to best cases is captured in the last of the four scenarios, which I name *The New Berlin Wall*. In this pathway, change comes slowly to the Middle East no matter what happens in Iraq, primarily because nothing can really change until the Arab-Israeli conflict is resolved. I call it the *The New Berlin Wall* because I believe a physical divorce between Israel and the West Bank (plus Gaza) is the most likely route toward a lasting peace. Israel is currently constructing a "security fence" to divide itself from the West Bank, in large part because the fence already separating Israel from the Gaza Strip has largely prevented any suicide bombers emerging from there. Plenty in the West are upset about Israel's construction of the wall, but this anger is both misguided and shortsighted. The barrier is not Israel's creation, but that of Islamic Jihad, Hamas, and the al-Aqsa Martyrs Brigade. Israel's population agrees to this wall because it keeps suicide bombers out while creating a de facto border between the two states, separating a demographically moribund Israel from a youth-bulging Palestine. Simply put, this wall makes sense today and it will make even more sense tomorrow.

The way America solves this situation is exporting security not to Israel but to the wall and the border it marks—basically that left by the 1967 war. The United States should spearhead a long-term peacekeeping mission along this barrier, effectively walling off Israel from Palestine. Israel, its security intact, will do just fine without Palestine. Meanwhile, the Core will need to pour aid into the West Bank and Gaza for two to three decades, or long enough to wait out all the hatred that currently suffocates peace there. By that time, the extremists in the West Bank will be gone or buried, and Palestinians will finally raise a generation untouched by war. It will not be too much money, nor will it take too long. The West has successfully sat on walls elsewhere around the world (Berlin, Korea, Cyprus), and we can do it here too.

In my mind, the road from the worst to best cases lies more logically through the West Bank than through Baghdad or Teheran. Any dream of transforming the Middle East without first dampening this conflict remains just that—a dream.

The biggest threat to the Big Bang lies not in jihadists drawn to Iraq but in our own inability to fully comprehend the sacrifices involved in the outcomes we seek. When al Qaeda sought to wage war on the West through the System Perturbation of 9/11, their goals were negative, or simply the promotion of disconnectedness. But what America seeks in the Middle East is far harder. The Big Bang as grand strategy seeks Iraq's eventual integration into globalization's Functioning Core. That integration is simply impossible without the world's help in integrating Iraq, as well as the region as a whole moving toward global connectivity. These goals extend so far beyond the war as to make our military victory in Iraq almost inconsequential—just a slight perturbation of the system. It is only the *everything else* part that makes the war in Iraq worth winning, otherwise we are guilty of waging war simply for war's sake. In this interconnected world, war fought only within the context of war is a complete waste of blood and treasure. It is the equivalent of waging war according to the Gap's twisted rule set, not extending the Core's security rule set.

Until we as a nation come to understand the nature of system-level crisis in this globalized world, not only will we remain unable to discuss security issues intelligently among ourselves and with our allies, but we will learn little from our own attempts at fostering positive system-wide change through the demonstrative use of American military power. A myopic focus on "direct threats" to U.S. national security is what gets us shocks like 9/11, or bolts seemingly from the blue.

We live in a world system. We enjoy that world system more than any other country. We also pay more—militarily—for that system than any other country in the world, and yet we debate wars as though each were somehow a transaction between ourselves and merely the country in question, as in, "What did America really get in exchange for the war in Iraq?" We are the world's Leviathan. Every war we wage perturbs the world system on a multitude of levels. Until the way we plan war in the twenty-first century matches the complexity of the peace we live in the twenty-first century, America will remain more feared than admired for our global war on terrorism. But once that complex understanding is first achieved and then wielded through the grand strategy we pursue, America will resume its historical role as the most revolutionary force on the planet.

Chapter 6

THE GLOBAL
TRANSACTION
STRATEGY

LAST SUMMER I TOOK my kids to New York City for a weekend of sightseeing. Naturally, one of the attractions we took in was the Statue of Liberty and Ellis Island. You cannot tour either without being deeply impressed by the symbolism both convey of the immigrant experience that defines our nation's history: America has long stood as the beacon of liberty to the rest of the world. It has served as the escape hatch for millions upon millions of dreams over the last two-plus centuries: religious freedom, political expression, the right to own property. It has been the place where individuals can connect talent to ambition in ways unthinkable around much of the rest of the planet. But the American dream remains fundamentally linked to a place as much as a concept: to join this party is to live within our borders, to join our citizenry, to become one of us.

Americans have long debated whether our good fortune imparts to us special obligations to share this dream with others beyond our shores. Since so many of us came to this land as a means of escaping freedom's absence elsewhere, we typically content ourselves with the notion that America's living example is gift enough to history—we show the way. In this manner, I will argue that America has served quite ably as globalization's ideological wellspring: each and every day we put on display—for all to see—the almost unlimited utility of broadband economic connectivity, freedom of action within minimal rule sets, and the unbridled ambition afforded by the apparent certainty of long-term peace. Thus, the American experience speaks to globalization's advance because we have come closest to perfecting its historical equation: the individual pursuit of happiness within free markets protected from destabilizing strife by the rule of law.

But the question remains: Does America owe the world anything more than its example? Over the Cold War we stood up to Communism and all the threats to our good life it represented, and by doing so we successfully encouraged the spread of that good life in the form of a global economy resurrected from the ashes of two world wars and expanded far beyond any previous high-water mark. This effort took several decades, roughly a hundred thousand lives, and trillions in treasure, but it has culminated in half the world's population being invited to the same good life we have long enjoyed—the same fundamental freedoms, the same sense of security, the same belief in a future full of potential. And yet roughly one-third of humanity—more than two billion souls—remains on the outside, noses pressed to the glass. What more do we owe them?

I believe America owes them nothing more and nothing less than the same basic peace that we have long enjoyed. Not a Pax Americana, because we seek not to extend our rule but merely our *rules*. We claim no power over others on this basis, because to extend these rule sets is to expand the Core's membership and enable globalization's continued advance. It is to issue a standing invitation to all nations currently trapped within the Gap: embrace these rules and join our community. What is so special about the globalization that America has nurtured and protected these seven decades is that it represents the active exportation of the same liberty we have so long enjoyed within *these united states*—a fundamental connectivity that empowers individual ambition through the provision of choice and thus opportunity. It is our liberty road show, or the promise of freedom made universal. What is sacred about America is not our land, but our union, and that union can and should be extended—first through collective security, then economic connectivity, and finally political community.

But many forces within the Gap are threatened by the rising connectivity engendered by globalization's creeping advance, because it imperils their ability to control the lives of others. Believing humanity's paths to happiness are single, and thus enforceable by all-knowing elites, these forces demand that their particular definition of the good life hold sway no matter how much violence is required, how much freedom is repressed, or how many lives are wasted. And they will constantly dangle before our weary eyes the same deceptively seductive bargain that all dictators offer: *Just grant me these for my own and I will trouble you no further.* It was all the Taliban in Afghanistan asked. It is all Osama bin Laden asks. It is all the forces of disconnectedness will forever ask. And to all such pacts America's answer should always be *no!*

We should not be in the business of building up firewalls between the Core's good life and the Gap's sorry existence, offering the latter merely our charity as a lifeline. To deny anyone in the Gap access to the same bright future we may presume as our birthright is to engage in the same sort of exclusionary ideology that dictators of all stripes have long employed to enslave their subjects. In the end, our sin of omitting the Gap from a future worth creating will be as reprehensible as any committed by the forces of disconnectedness we now engage in this global war on terrorism. Turning a cheek is one thing, but turning a blind eye is quite another.

The good news is that as globalization extends its reach, it forces us to engage distant threats not out of mindless aggression but out of an expanding definition of the *self* we seek to preserve. For much of our relatively isolated history, that *self* was merely these United States. After World War II, it expanded to a "free world" that was, in fact, nothing more than a closed-club West consisting of North America, Western Europe, Japan, and a few choice others. Now, years removed from that long Cold War, the *self* has grown to the

Core as a whole, if only we have the confidence and courage to define yesterday's achievements as tomorrow's building blocks and not retreat into the past's self-negating focus on the balance among powers *within* that shared community. To move beyond that myopic strategic vision, one that requires an enemy to be the mirror image of ourselves, is to realize that victory in this war on terrorism requires nothing less than shrinking the Gap out of existence—to make the *self* all-inclusive.

I no longer believe that America can be made safe at the expense of others. In this increasingly interconnected world, our vulnerability is not defined by the depth of our connectedness with the outside world but by the sheer existence of regions that remain off-grid, beyond the pale, and unconnected to our shared fate. For it is only within such disconnectedness that the "logic" of 9/11's destructiveness can be accessed: *If I cannot enjoy your good life, then neither will you.* To bring these regions online with globalization's expanding rule sets is to engage in the only strategic transaction worth pursuing in the twenty-first century—offering the Gap freedom in exchange for the Core's security.

America's task is not perpetual war, nor the extension of empire. It is merely to serve as globalization's bodyguard wherever and whenever needed throughout the Gap. This is a boundable problem with a foreseeable finish line. Moreover, if properly reconfigured, our military currently possesses all the skill sets needed to play both Leviathan across the Gap and "system administrator" to the Core's ever-deepening security community. It is not a question of "paying any price" but rather being far more explicit—both with ourselves and our allies—about what America seeks to achieve through the application of military force in this global war on terrorism. In short, we need to make clear to all—but especially to ourselves— that the *American way of war* serves a purpose far higher than merely assuring this country's security or imposing its justice upon others. To achieve this lofty aim requires nothing less than recasting the very structure of the U.S. military, a subject to which I now turn.

You're Ruining My Military!

My entire career, I have heard this complaint from Pentagon audiences: "What you are proposing will ruin this military!" I heard it when I contended we should mentor the Russian military. I heard it when I argued we should seek to manage the post–Cold War era, not just sit back and wait for the near-peer competitor. And now I hear it when I say the U.S. military should play "system administrator," or rule-set enforcer, for globalization's advance. What critics fear is that strategists like me will—if we have our way—drag the military away from its "warfighting" core values and into a larger, messier context where the commanders will lose control to outsiders, where funding for high-technology combat systems will lag, and where the warrior spirit will be lost. They are right to level this charge, and yet I will plead Not Guilty. Yes, I do wish to change this military dramatically, but I likewise believe the time has come to admit that we need two militaries: one to fight wars and one to wage peace.

Today, America basically outspends the rest of the world on defense. Add up the entire world's state spending on defense and America accounts for roughly half. Moreover, when you realize that America's military is built to go overseas while the rest of the world's armies are really built to stay at home, our advantage in what is known as "power projection," or the ability to send our forces a great distance to wage war, is simply overwhelming. You want a military that only goes in with overwhelming force? You got it, 24/7/365. It is not a guideline to which we must adhere. It is not a standard for which we must constantly strive. It simply defines the international security environment in which we live. No enemy can stop us, and frankly, none of our allies can really project power on their own—unless we help them. We are the world's Leviathan. We decide under what conditions wars will be fought between states— except when we can be trumped by nuclear weapons.

When that condition exists, then our Leviathan rule set defers to the larger rule set known as Mutually Assured Destruction, or MAD. Fortunately, the only countries able to launch such wars vis-à-vis the United States all belong to globalization's Functioning Core (United Kingdom, France, Russia, China, India), leaving only the "proliferators," otherwise known as Gap states that desire or actually possess nuclear weapons, as significant state sources of danger for the system. Not a direct threat to the United States, mind you, but only in the sense that any use of nuclear weapons on their part would represent a serious breach of that long-stable rule set.

The question this country has struggled with since the end of the Cold War has been, What should we do with all this unprecedented power? Some have argued we must refrain from using it, lest we incite other great powers to rise up against us. But we have used this power with great frequency, and no state or collection of states shows any sign of seeking to counter our advantage. The only signs of adjustment we see around the world are states simply accepting our overwhelming power by seeking to specialize in niche military capabilities that can be married with our own in coalitions (e.g., Norway, Poland). The rest is just smoke and mirrors, plus the Chinese obsessing over Taiwan. Simply put, we are the world's Leviathan, and that status will not change.

Others have argued that America should use its force overseas only when our national interests are directly challenged or put at risk. Of course, that argument is typically coded to mean that our "interests" should be narrowly defined, lest we find ourselves managing an empire not of our choosing. But drawing a firm line between what America cares about enough to wage war and what the rest of the world cares about enough to wage war is hard, because wars between states are disappearing, leaving only conflicts within states or bad behavior by regimes as the main criterion for waging war. These internal situations are simultaneously everyone's problem and no one's problem, which makes them perfect situations for the United Nations. But because the UN does not wage war but only keeps the peace, it too defers to the Leviathan America as initial rule-set enforcer for the planet as a whole.

So to declare the United States has no "interest" in some egregious rule-set transgression merely because it occurs within a state and not between them is to say that America's interest in extending the Core's security rule set is not universal—in effect, that globalization need not be made global. Such arguments typically come off as Scrooge-like: "We shall always have the poor, and if they must die by their own hand, then let them be speedy about it and reduce the surplus population!" America will never be that uncaring simply because we are a nation built on universal ideals of freedom and equality, not limited to definitions of ethnic identity or "sacred lands." As the world's first multinational union, we are globalization's wellspring, its inspiration. We can no more disown it than disown ourselves. Our interests are global because globalization must be global.

We all should ask, What gives America the right to render judgments of right and wrong, or good versus rogue? If America takes on the worst offenders in order to extend the Core's rule sets, then why not take on all offenders? Why not just admit we run an empire?

What gives America the right is the fact that we are globalization's godfather, its source code, it original model. We restarted globalization after World War II and we have made it largely in our image. After fighting in two world wars, this was our solution to great-power war, and it has worked amazingly well. But we cannot abandon our creation now that we have already picked all the low-hanging fruit and only the toughest cases, such as terrorism, remain. This gift of global connectivity generating peace is one we must keep on giving, because to let the process stall is to risk its demise, to possibly lose all for which we have sacrificed so much in the past. The Cold War's peace dividend is not a resource to be consumed by those lucky enough to sit currently at the Core's table, but a benefit that must be made universal.

Why do we do it? Because we can and because it is good, by any rational estimation. And because if we do not do it, nobody else can or will, and nothing good can follow from such inaction.

America stands at the cusp of a new age in warfare. Big wars are *out,* small wars are *in.* Focusing on the big threat in the environment is *out,* managing the threat environment as a whole is *in.* A do-it-all, go-it-alone force is *out,* and specialized niche forces provided by allies are *in.* Does this mean the Pentagon eventually gets out of the big war business and devolves into a military social worker for the Gap? Absolutely not, but it does mean that the U.S. military is logically headed toward a bifurcation into two different forces: one that specializes in high-tech, big-violence war, and one that specializes in relatively low-tech security generation and routine crisis response.

The need for such a splitting of the force is highlighted in the near term by our experiences in postwar Afghanistan and Iraq, but as the global war on terrorism unfolds, this institutional momentum toward bifurcating the U.S. military into a Leviathan force and a System Administrator force will only pick up speed. The System Administrator force will demonstrate our willingness to follow through on the interventions started by the Leviathan force, while simultaneously offering broader coalition opportunities to allied militaries that simply cannot keep pace with the transformation of our combat capabilities.

So in the end, it is not about "ruining" this military but returning it to its original roots. The Cold War military as we knew it no longer exists. From the early 1990s onward it has progressively bifurcated into two very different militaries—a process the Pentagon has had the devil of a time managing. All I am proposing is that we admit to ourselves that this splitting of the force into two militaries is no accident, but a logical response to the changing strategic environment of the past decade and a half.

The Pentagon needs to accept this growing bifurcation of the force, because we need both kinds of military if we are going to continue fulfilling America's essential transaction with the world— that of exporting security to the Gap while simultaneously maintaining the Core's collective security. We need both the capacity for deterrence and preemption provided by the Leviathan force, and the postwar security-generation capacity of the System Administrator force. In many ways, this unfolding bifurcation is nothing more than a back-to-the-future outcome: for the vast bulk of our national history we had a System Administrator force in the Department of the Navy and a Leviathan wannabe in the Department of War. We forced those two historically distinct roles into one department when we created the Department of Defense in 1947, primarily in anticipation of the hair-trigger nuclear standoff that subsequently developed between the United States and the Soviet Union. With that era now dead and buried, our military establishment naturally reverts to what it once was—a force able to wage both war and peace at the same time. Having and employing both types of force is how the Pentagon will do its part in shrinking the Gap across the twenty-first century.

THE ESSENTIAL TRANSACTION

For about a year after 9/11, the master PowerPoint brief that I delivered throughout Washington described the Core-Gap divide and the rise of System Perturbations, and then made the argument about crafting a new ordering principle for the Defense Department. I always thought it was a fairly optimistic brief. I mean, here I was telling people about the Gap being the problem, that the entire world was not full of chaos. But as it turned out, I was simply scaring the hell out of people, and I could tell so by the questions they asked afterward.

Finally, after one brief to a very large, mostly military crowd at the Naval War College, a retired admiral named Tom Weschler stood up and said, "You've explained this Gap and you explained this new form of crisis. I'm on board. I want to shrink your Gap and get better at dealing with your System Perturbations. My question is, What do we get in return for doing these difficult things?"

The admiral was asking for a happy ending, and my brief did not have one. It described suffering and crisis and asked for changes, but what I was not giving my audiences was something to be hopeful about in exchange for completing these grand historical tasks. Everybody needs that happy ending, that sense of hope in the future, otherwise you are simply trying to sell people *diminished expectations*—not a great motivator.

Let me tell you what we get when we do these difficult things. What America gets in return is the end of war as we know it. It gets a global economy with nobody left on the outside, noses pressed to the glass. Most important, it gets a definition of what constitutes the finish line in this global war on terrorism. In sum, shrinking the Gap gets us the final piece to the puzzle that is global peace. The end of the Cold War solved the threat of global conflict, and America's continued willingness to play Leviathan has effectively ended state-on-state war. What stands between us and the goal of making globalization truly global is the threats posed by the forces of disconnectedness—the bad *individual* actors that plague the Gap. Defeat them by denying them the Gap as their own and the Core wins this war on terrorism, plain and simple.

The admiral's question marked a turning point in my work, sending me back to the mapping of globalization's flows that I did in the New Rule Sets Project with Cantor Fitzgerald. Once I reacquainted myself with the material, the much-needed happy ending immediately revealed itself: if the Core gets better at dealing with this new form of system-level crisis, it should be able to keep the four great flows (people, energy, investments, and security) in reasonable balance. Keeping those flows in balance is what allows globalization to continue its advance.

But it is not a matter of keeping those spigots wide open. Besides strengthening its ability to deal with System Perturbations, the Core must engage in a certain amount of firewalling, or preventing the worst sort of flows into, out of, and throughout the Gap: terrorism, pandemics, and the illegal movement of drugs, people, small arms, money, and intellectual property. Because if we do not adequately preserve the Core, it is likely to seek too high barriers between itself and the Gap, and that will disrupt the flows that truly need to occur if the Gap is to be integrated over time. So it is a careful balancing act.

Beyond those two basic goals, which frankly speak more to the Core's happiness than the Gap's, there is the all-important and far more active task of shrinking the Gap. Globalization's frontier cannot be allowed to solidify into a permanent divide between the connected and the disconnected. It must be constantly advanced, with clear victories regularly registering in the popular imagination. How the United States facilitates that advance is primarily through its private sector, or direct investment that moves the means of production from Core to Gap.

But treasure alone is not enough to shrink the Gap; some blood will be involved too. The Core's investment funds will not flow into war zones, failed states, and terrorist havens, so the Pentagon's essential task is to export security into those national and regional deficit situations that currently hold up economic integration. Saddam Hussein's regime was such a black hole, as was Charles Taylor's in Liberia. North Korea's Kim Jong Il is probably the worst of the bunch. The drug lords in Colombia are a security sinkhole. So is basically any repressive leader inside the Gap who simply refuses to leave power, like Castro in Cuba, Chavez in Venezuela, Mugabe in Zimbabwe, and Qaddafi in Libya—to name just a few "big men." They should all go, and none of them should be succeeded by the idiot son, brother, nephew, or cousin. After four decades, isn't there anybody in all of Cuba worthy enough to rule besides Fidel and his brother Raul? These dictators should go not just so that their own nations can be liberated from their repressive grasp, but also so that neighboring states can escape from the negative investment climate their continued presence generates.

Historical data demonstrate that foreign direct investment correlates highly with trade flows, geographic proximity, and overall economic openness, so being stuck next to relatively closed countries suffering internal conflict and/or political repression is a sure way to reduce your attractiveness to foreign investors. Jordan will blossom as a target for foreign investment once Iraq is a connected, thriving society. The same will be true for Ghana in a calmer West Africa, or Uganda in a less violent Central Africa. Tunisia will certainly do better without Qaddafi next door, Botswana without Mugabe in Zimbabwe, Lebanon without Assad in Syria, and any of the Central Asian "stans" without all those leaders who seem to have trouble giving up their posts when their terms end. Even South Korea, an emerging market magnet for FDI, suffers from its proximity to its evil twin. The Gap does not lack for economies trying to globalize, but many suffer guilt by association with their region's security sinkholes.

These security situations will not get better on their own, because exploiting these situations is what helps keep the Muammar Qaddafis and the Kim Jong Ils in power. In short, where we let security deficits linger in the Gap, only bad actors will fill in the vacuum, and what they will provide is political intrigue, economic corruption, endemic violence, and a climate that facilitates the actions of the very same transnational actors we seek to defeat in this global war on terrorism. That is why taking down all the Saddams of the Gap is a good thing, because each regime change fixes a "broken window" and—by doing so—sends a signal to prospective bad actors regarding rule sets the Core is serious about enforcing.

Shrinking the Gap as a socioeconomic tragedy means first removing the security obstacles that survive like parasites in that chaotic political-military environment. It means understanding the military-market link, and trusting that connectivity will set the masses free much faster than economic sanctions, foreign aid, or UN Security Council resolutions. People in the Gap want the same freedoms we enjoy, either to say yes or no, but certainly to decide on their own. Rules enable that freedom to blossom, and security rule sets must always come first. You cannot build a future worth living if you are always running from fear, which is what consumes much of the creative energy now trapped in the Gap. America needs to release that energy not only because we will benefit from its application but also because it will leave a better world behind for subsequent generations.

But more to the point, there ain't no such thing as a free lunch. America has been living large in the global economy for so long that we simply forget we owe that world outside something in return. Americans constitute about one-twentieth of the world's population, but somehow we manage to produce one-quarter of the world's pollution and garbage while consuming one-quarter of the world's energy. That is living large, or having a disproportional environmental "footprint." But our economic "footprint" is just as huge. You could say America is expert at exporting sovereign debt and importing damn near everything else. How are we so able to live beyond our means? How do we consistently rack up federal deficits? We get the world to buy our Treasury bills because Uncle Sam is considered a great bet and the U.S. dollar is relatively cheap, considering it has long served as the world's *de facto* reserve currency—almost as good as gold. In sum, we live large because selling our debt—both public and private—around the world has always been easy.

Wall Street will say, "We deserve to live large like that. We generate more than a quarter of the world's wealth in GDP. And the deal on T-bills is simply too good to be true. Do you know what it costs to print those little pieces of paper? Almost nothing! And do you know what we get in return? VCRs, cars, computers. Stop complaining. If the world ever caught on to what a great deal we have going here, we could be in real trouble!"

Some economic experts will tell you that the reason America has yet to get into trouble on this seemingly unfair transaction is that, until recently, we have had no peer competitor in terms of reserve currencies. At the Cold War's end, some thought the Japanese yen might aspire to that role, but then Tokyo's bubble economy burst. A decade later, the European Union debuted the euro and now a real choice does exist. Eventually, a third choice will arise in the East, and it will probably center around a convertible Chinese yuan. Over time we will have serious competitors in the business of selling "futures worth creating." If America, through its foreign policy and national security policy, begins to resemble a future that the rest of the Core does not wish to emulate, then they will put their trust elsewhere, like in the euro. The rest of the world could stop buying our debt, which in turn would make our military spending untenable over the long run.

Why has this not happened before? It has not happened because America's essential transaction with the outside world is one of our exporting security in return for the world's financing a lifestyle we could far more readily afford without all that defense spending. Does this make us the world's mercenary? If it does, then we have lost little and gained much. Our cumulative combat losses since the end of the Vietnam War do not equal the price we paid in one day at Pearl Harbor in 1941 or on Normandy's beaches in 1944. Meanwhile, we have enjoyed an unprecedented string of economic booms since the early 1980s, corresponding to the expansion of globalization from the Old Core to the New Core. How many hundreds of millions of people were lifted out of poverty across that time? And is that huge total worth the lives of American soldiers we have paid in this exporting of security around the planet?

If these wars are judged solely within the context of war, then I say no, because, frankly, as a national security strategist I value American lives above all others. But if these wars are judged within the context of *everything else,* then I say yes. America pays the most for global stability because we enjoy it the most, and because our exporting of security has played a crucial role in generating the best quarter-century in human history, one in which the world has integrated politically as never before, grown economically as never before, and reduced global conflict as never before.

Remove America's export of security from that global equation and you will witness arms races cropping up all over the world, defense spending skyrocketing all over the Core, and mass violence erupting all over the Gap. That will not just depress our wonderful standard of living, it will cost the lives of millions upon millions. We can decide that America's "national security" is all about keeping Americans alive and to hell with the rest of the world, but that pathway will yield a hell across much of the world. Simply put, we can pay up front or get billed later, but globalization's advance will not wait for America to remuster a will once lost. By the time America were to reengage such a dysfunctional world, globalization would be lost. We made this mistake before in the "Roaring Twenties," a decade that now looks very similar to the decade we just lived through, and America can certainly abdicate responsibility in this decade just as we did in the 1930s, but this time we can't pretend we don't know what we are doing.

When America turned its back on the world following World War I, the globalization it inevitably helped destroy was largely of Europe's creation. But the globalization of today is largely of America's creation. We set it in motion following World War II, deliberately salvaging Western Europe and Japan when we could have just as easily walked away from these tasks. We protected these embryonic pillars of Globalization II through three and a half decades of Soviet military threat, and when that threat began to recede, we played bodyguard to Globalization III's inclusion of the emerging markets—more than half the world's population. We provided the security glue that let Developing Asia focus its resources on export-led growth despite remaining a powder keg of unresolved political-military disputes and rivalries. We stepped up to manage bad security situations in the Persian Gulf and the Balkans while Europe moved confidently toward economic union and simultaneously cut defense spending across the board. It was America that stood up as Gap Leviathan across the 1990s, after the Soviet bloc collapsed and ended its decades of malicious mischief there. So while the European Union and NATO progressively expanded to absorb former Soviet bloc states, it was the U.S. military that saw its crisis-response load increase fourfold around the planet. You want to know one very important reason the nineties were such a go-go decade? Because American G.I.'s were deployed all over the Gap, minding it while the Old and New Cores of globalization integrated unceasingly.

America provides the world a security product that is unrivaled, that has made globalization the immense success it is today for roughly two-thirds of the world's population, and that export will serve as the crucial first ingredient to extending globalization to the remaining third that currently does not enjoy its peace and prosperity. I see the Pentagon as both Leviathan to this world-historical process, and as System Administrator. By Leviathan, I mean America provides the *might* that will eventually outlaw all mass violence in the Gap, and by System Administrator, I mean America must make *right* every security deficit it seeks to fill throughout the Gap. For if we simply engage in drive-by regime change without waging the peace that must follow all such wars, then all our victories will remain forever hollow, and they will necessarily be repeated time and time again. *Desert Storm* was a hollow victory because all it did was beget *Operation Iraqi Freedom,* and that victory will likewise ring hollow until Iraq as a whole is integrated into the global economy and thus safely netted into the Core's collective security.

When America's exporting of security succeeds, integration follows, not just for the country previously isolated by conflict, but for neighbors likewise previously tainted in terms of investment climate as well. The Balkans are on a completely different track today from the one they were on just a decade ago, and America's military intervention was crucial to turning that tide. Central Asia will be a different place a generation from now because America is progressively guaranteeing its stability through the insertion of our military bases there. Without our exporting of security, that region expected nothing better than serving as playing board for a "great game" unfolding between a host of regional powers (e.g., Russia, China, India, Iran, Turkey), none of whom possesses the wherewithal to actually increase regional security; the best they could hope to do would be to partition it. The Persian Gulf of tomorrow will scarcely resemble today's if America successfully generates security and connectivity in an Iraq where, for an entire generation, there was nothing but isolation and war.

Of course, the rest of the Core must step into these improved security situations in order to enable political, social, and economic integration. Absent that follow-through, America's wars are nothing but wars, yielding neither economic gain nor political empire. They are just unwanted long-term babysitting jobs that benefit no one in particular. Thus America's essential transaction with the world is rendered null and void without the payoff associated with expanding globalization's frontier.

These transactions, therefore, are all highly connected. If you remove America as Gap Leviathan, you burden Europe with security spending right at a time when its population is aging dramatically. The same can be said for Japan, which after a decade of economic recession sports the world's largest bond market. As the recent Core-wide (excepting China) recession demonstrated, the world's biggest economies (U.S., EU, Japan) now rise and fall together. America can certainly push off its "defense burden" onto NATO and Japan, but in tough economic times, this is nothing more than rearranging deck chairs on the *Titanic*.

Meanwhile, any steps taken by America to reduce its exporting of security across Asia will threaten regional stability right at a time when every nation there is waking up to the reality of China's enormous economic power. But how stable is that economic engine of growth? One day China suffers SARS and its economic juggernaut virtually stops on a dime, because of plunging retail sales, a slump in export demand, and a collapse in tourism. The Chinese leadership, confident of its national security, pushes for selectively aggressive reforms as a result, instead of the usual stonewalling and repression, and FDI flows remain strong as a result despite all those canceled business trips.

But imagine the combination of a financial panic in China and a strategic standoff between Beijing and Washington over Taiwan, or perhaps just a downed spy plane. Would globalization suffer as a result? Only if you think China is easily removed from the Core's economic transactions. Paul Krugman likes to point out that China's central bank is one of the main purchasers of Treasury bills in the world, so—in effect—they finance our trade deficit. Who is the biggest source of that deficit right now? The Chinese economy, of course! What do they sell us most? Goods manufactured by Chinese labor working in U.S.-owned factories. But say, all of a sudden, China decides America's vision of a future worth creating through a war on terror is not their preferred pathway. As Krugman argues, "Nobody is quite sure what would happen if the Chinese suddenly switched to, say, euros—a two-point jump in mortgage rates?—but it's not an experiment anyone wants to try."

All the same arguments are easily applied to the Persian Gulf, home to 90 percent of the world's excess capacity for oil production. If America lets a Saddam run wild, or lets an Iraq-Iran "tanker war" stop oil flowing from the Gulf, or lets an al Qaeda hijack Saudi Arabia and yank it back to some seventh-century definition of the "good life," does anyone believe only a bunch of "crazy Arabs" and "Zionist Jews" will suffer in the end? What happens to Developing Asia's growing economies that will need twice as much energy in 2025 as they need today, when they are already quite dependent on the Gulf for oil? What happens to the rest of the Gap that suddenly finds itself priced out of the energy market unless it submits to crushing public debts, like those South America suffered in the 1980s, thanks in large part to the OPEC oil shocks of the 1970s? Does anyone doubt the generals will not return? Or that an America, too busy trying to put out fires in the Middle East, will forget sub-Saharan Africa's resulting plight in a heartbeat?

This is why I am amused by the notion that somehow the United States can act unilaterally in security affairs. Yes, we can wage war without asking anyone's permission or help, but the idea that we can somehow wage war isolated from the web of economic and political transactions we are continuously conducting with the outside world is simply ludicrous. In the era of globalization, there is only *war within the context of everything else,* and the idiots who sometimes wage war as though it were an end unto itself.

Is America guilty of that idiocy in the Persian Gulf? On some level, yes. There were Pentagon strategists who thought they could wage war in the Gulf as if it were some isolated venue, and not

smack dab in the middle of the Muslim world and global energy supplies. They dreamed of organizational charts, and seamless transi-
tions, and easily engineered milestones of success, only to be knocked
upside the head by the *everything else* and *everyone else* determined
to sabotage those desired outcomes. When the United States committed itself to rebuilding Iraq after the war, it committed itself to
integrating Iraq with the world at large, so our "unilateralism" in
war merely set in motion the inevitable multilateralism of peace. To
the extent that, before the war, the Pentagon bragged inappropri-
ately about being able to transition postwar Iraq to a stable domestic situation in eighteen months or less, strategists there inadvertently
raised the diplomatic price of the bargain the White House inevitably sought from the rest of the Core when that ambitious vision
proved false.

In exporting security around the planet, the United States is conducting a transaction essential to globalization's day-to-day health,
not to mention its long-term prospects for expansion. In effect, by
exporting security to the Gap, we trade our excess security for the
Gap's excess instability.

How does the Pentagon connect to this complex transaction?
Our humanitarian assistance works to mitigate suffering throughout the Gap, which can lead to unstable refugee flows if not properly addressed. Our crisis response helps to contain and isolate
explosions of social and political anger within the Gap, which pro-
tects investment climates in neighboring countries otherwise tainted
by spillover. Our projection of combat power deters state-based acts
of aggression throughout the Gap, which, because they are often motivated by desire to control natural resources, would otherwise disrupt what slim connectivity the Gap currently enjoys with the Core.
Finally, the day-to-day presence of our military forces throughout
the Gap, along with the military-to-military ties they promote, increases the political will of Gap countries to tackle internal and
transnational security issues, like terrorism and drug trafficking, in
addition to obviating regional arms races that might otherwise unfold. In short, America gets a lot for about 3 to 4 percent of its GDP

being devoted to the Defense Department, while the Core gains the greatest military contractor the world has yet seen—*and* interest on those T-bills to boot!

So it is not simply a matter of America deciding that it has the right to decide for the entire planet as to when, where, and why wars will be waged. By outsourcing the Leviathan function to the United States, the rest of the Core is essentially paying us to make those decisions wisely, albeit in consultation with them. Because our military has advanced so far beyond what the rest of the Core possesses, our allies have, by and large, lost their ability to fight alongside us unless we make special provisions for their participation, something we are becoming increasingly unwilling to do.

That leaves most of our allies able to join only in the postwar security generation or peacekeeping phases, which accounts for their great interest in our long-term commitment to such activities. Without such commitment, our allies essentially get left holding the bag, meaning the Pentagon could easily generate more postwar long-term babysitting jobs than the rest of the Core could readily handle. This is why America's story line regarding where this is all going is so absolutely crucial to gaining prewar and postwar coalition support. I am not just talking about Afghanistan and Iraq but all the other regime changes to come as well, because shrinking the Gap will involve the fall of many a "big man" there, in addition to all the terrorist networks we collapse. As this long-term effort unfolds, do the same allies need to cooperate with us in both war and peace? Absolutely not.

In fact, we do well to encourage specialization by individual countries in both realms—warfare and peacekeeping. Our mottoes for coalition partners, therefore, must be *come as you are* (meaning, bring what you can), and *come when you can* (meaning, we will take your help in either the warfare or peacekeeping segments of any major military intervention). As we have seen in postwar Iraq, soldiers die in the same numbers waging peace as they do waging war. It just takes longer. So there is no legitimate hierarchy of national sacrifice to cite here: if you as a nation are willing to put your people at risk in peacekeeping or in warfare, America must welcome you with open arms.

The key thing to remember in all of this is that the rest of the Core does not want to see America fail in its role as Gap Leviathan, they simply want to see us thinking about the system as a whole, and administering the system as a whole. This is why I propose that America truly needs two separate types of military force: one to serve as warfighting Gap Leviathan, and one to serve as peacekeeping System Administrator that organizes and facilitates the Core-wide exporting of security into the Gap. In short, we need a force for *might* and a force for *right*. When our Core allies see that America is serious about generating both types of military power, we will see the usual bandwagoning effect—meaning, friendly nations will join coalitions they know are certain to succeed. *Build it and they will come,* as they say, but they will come only if we decide to build *both* forces.

THE SYSTEM ADMINISTRATOR

Within a month of 9/11, I got a call from my old boss Art Cebrowski, former president of the Naval War College and now a senior adviser to Secretary of Defense Rumsfeld on defense transformation. He wanted a copy of an article I had written immediately following Y2K. In that piece, I posited what would happen to the Defense Department following a disastrous enemy attack against our networked economy. I described a scenario in which a Pearl Harbor–like catastrophe disabled some future, far more pervasive iteration of today's Internet, which I called the Evernet. As a result of that disastrous strike, I hypothesized that the big war–focused Pentagon would be "unmasked as almost completely irrelevant to the international security environment at hand," and therefore would subsequently be split into two forces: a big-war, highly lethal strike force that focused on "global deterrence" and a crisis-oriented, highly responsive protection force that focused on "network security."

The first force would serve as America's "killer application" for the twenty-first century, or the big stick we would pull out as needed to unilaterally crush enemies that rose up, while the second force would serve as America's cop on the beat, managing the world day to day in an integrated fashion with other U.S. federal agencies, the UN, and allied militaries. These two forces would operate under different rules, would pursue different missions and goals, and—by doing so—would reconstitute America's previously bifurcated national security structure of a Department of War and a Department of the Navy. Why did Cebrowski want the article? He said there was serious talk in the secretary's office about exactly these sorts of issues. Senior leaders there were beginning to realize that the Pentagon was not set up for the world it suddenly found itself trying to manage after 9/11.

To me, such a split was more than simply a back-to-the-future outcome, it was a return to normalcy for U.S. national security, which had been perverted into the Pentagon's current structure because of the decades-long hair-trigger strategic standoff with the Soviets. The military has long been too distant from American society, from the world as we know it, and increasingly from our own allies struggling to keep up with our technological advances. By "distant" I mean divorced from the everyday reality of why America employs military force around the world. Thanks to our endless theorizing about global nuclear war, all our reasoning regarding the use of force degenerated into vague abstractions—"national interest," "national will," and so on. In focusing on the Big One, the Pentagon became so fixated on the *how* that we forgot the *why*—much less how to explain it to the American public. Truth be told, the defense community is so out of practice in explaining the *why* that we prefer to avoid this conversation altogether.

Over time, the U.S. military evolved beyond the strategic environment to the point where it would never again face a genuine peer, but instead of asking the tough questions about how to deal with our *de facto* Leviathan status, we spent the post–Cold War era searching for a near-peer competitor and denying the split that emerged between our high-tech force and the low-tech missions we were constantly pursuing. Wars kept getting shorter and easier, but crisis responses kept getting longer and more complicated. The Pentagon was so unhappy with the situation by the end of the nineties that most transformation gurus wanted to "take our ball and go home" to plot endlessly for the distant war with near-peer China.

That fabulous Leviathan force was completely useless on 9/11. It could not stop the attack. There was no force to counterattack. Our fighter jets circled menacingly above New York and Washington for weeks, shutting the barn door long after the cows had escaped. In many ways, it was pathetic. America's unbeatable military force had let our homeland be sucker-punched and dropped to the canvas. Then the U.S. national security establishment did what it knew best, it retaliated against a nation-state, but even here it was an odd sort of war led by Special Operations Forces and CIA paramilitaries. The Pentagon was completely unprepared to fight in Afghanistan, but with its usual brilliance for adaptive planning, it nonetheless pulled it off using about one-fifth of its force to do four-fifths of the fighting. The warrior spirit was revalidated by our swift victory (*This is why we have this military!*), and when the Department of Homeland Security was proposed, it seemed as though the Pentagon had dodged a bullet of sorts—the splitting of U.S. national security would be between homeland and overseas, not within the Pentagon itself.

But the split I had long predicted was not obviated, merely delayed. The Pentagon had suffered serious losses in the creation of the Department of Homeland Security. The Coast Guard is essentially lost as a warfighting asset, returning home to the U.S. coastline, where it will focus on homeland security tasks the U.S. Navy is keen to avoid. The U.S. National Guard and reserves are likewise in many ways greatly diminished as a warfighting asset. *Operation Liberty Shield,* the domestic security alert that occurred in conjunction with *Operation Iraqi Freedom,* saw a great number of these troops called up, just as many in fact as were called up for *Operation Desert Storm.* But this time, many were used to guard key facilities and venues all over America, as well as military installations around the world.

Critics charged Secretary Rumsfeld with trying to wage war in Iraq "on the cheap," meaning he did not put enough troops in the field. The Pentagon was accused of fighting a "transformational war" merely to prove some pet theories, thus endangering American personnel. It would be a bloodbath, many "experts" predicted, with a block-by-block Stalingrad-like siege of Baghdad. The Pentagon, many retired flags opined (usually on network TV), was ill prepared to win this war. America's lack of allies, Central Command's lack of easy entry (thanks to Saudi Arabia and Turkey), and the Pentagon's stubbornness regarding the need for more heavy armor meant we would win, but quite probably at a terrible price.

True to its post-Vietnam form, the U.S. military came through the war with flying colors. Combat casualties were amazingly low, the enemy was unable to mount a stand, and the war passed quickly into occupation. Then came the hard part: dealing with a devastated economy, a brutalized society, and significant numbers of postconflict guerrillas and terrorists more than happy to wage asymmetrical war against a sitting force both ill prepared to manage the transition and eager as hell to leave. The warrior force was immediately transmuted—against its will, its ethos, and its skill set—into an occupation force. The Leviathan was transformed into System Administrator, the unilateral foreign policy was transformed into a multilateral *mea culpa,* and President Bush's upbeat May speech aboard a carrier steaming home in triumph was transformed into a sober September speech from the White House—the "end of hostilities" having quickly segued into the "long haul." Whether the Pentagon wanted to admit it or not, the split had finally arrived.

America now has, for all practical purposes, a Department of War and a Department of Everything Else. Both are housed, quite uncomfortably, in the Pentagon. Both are directed by a single leader, the Secretary of Defense. But these two "departments" remain fundamentally at odds with each other. One wants to remain greatly separated from society, from allies, and from the UN. The other realizes it needs to cut a new deal with society in terms of the National Guard and Reserves, with allies in terms of their willingness to provide peacekeepers, and with the UN in terms of internationalizing the nation building that will occupy our attention in Iraq for years to come. One force felt it did its job in Iraq brilliantly, and thus wanted to go home as soon as possible. The other force felt it was doing its job in Iraq the best it could, and it was desperate for new resources, new skill sets, and new partners. To this day, both forces continue to feel underappreciated, but both realize that no matter how well things went in postwar Iraq, this split will be replicated in every major intervention America undertakes in this global war on terrorism. "Military operations other than war" suddenly does not seem the lesser included it once was, triggering nervous debates about whether America needs a bigger military—not to mention emergency spending bills that are larger than *virtually any other country's entire defense budget*. The warfighting-obsessed Pentagon has long feared the rise of the near-peer competitor and it has finally arrived—from within.

Again, this is a problem of the Leviathan force's unprecedented success over the past generation. It can simply whip the world in any type of war imagined, but it is poorly constructed to deal with the peace that must invariably follow if permanent victory is to be secured. It is a first-half team playing in a league that keeps score through the end of the game. Outside of Vietnam, America is basically undefeated in war, but its historical record of postconflict nation building is way below .500, and that has to end. It has to end because shrinking the Gap is about growing connectivity and enabling economic integration, not just serial assassination and drive-by regime changes. Taking out bad guys is necessary in key instances, but it is never sufficient. America simply does not have a Pentagon able to win the peace, and winning wars is just not enough anymore. War must yield to peace, disconnectedness to connectivity, Gap to Core. If the Pentagon is not on board with this vision, then it will be forced to change. It does not have its own foreign policy and it never will. The Defense Department serves the larger purpose of U.S. foreign policy, or it does not serve at all.

The System Administrator force will be everything the Leviathan force is not. Where the Leviathan projects power menacingly, the Sys Admin will export security nonthreateningly. Where the Leviathan will be event-focused, the Sys Admin will be continuous—the former's vertical scenarios of war yielding seamlessly to the latter's horizontal scenarios of transition, integration, and peace. The Leviathan will destroy rogue regimes wielding immense lethality, but the Sys Admin will build nations wielding nonlethal technologies appropriate to the policing systems they will generate as legacies to the succeeding political order. The Leviathan will be punitive, bringing down enemy networks and blindsiding foes, but the Sys Admin will seek preventive cures that emphasize making networks more robust and crisis situations more transparent.

In operations, the Leviathan force will emphasize speed above all, preempting where possible and always staying on the offensive. Its high-tech capabilities will assure it access to any battle space a foe might prefer, and its relentless focus on disintegrating an enemy force and hunting down its remnants will keep our opponents desperately seeking more remote sanctuaries. The Leviathan's speed of command and maneuverability will allow it to get inside the enemy's decision loop (i.e., outpacing his speed of decision making), destroying his ability to mount coherent defenses. Its warfare will be Hobbesian in the extreme: very nasty, very brutal, very short. Most enemies will not choose to fight the Leviathan force whatsoever, meaning technical knockouts will become the norm.

In contrast, the Sys Admin force will emphasize deliberateness above all, because in occupying postconflict transition spaces it will necessarily stay on the defensive, guarding sites versus killing bad guys. The "access" this force will defend focuses on civilian partnerships to be maintained, allied forces to be integrated, and political victories to be won. It will serve as hub to the many spokes involved in postconflict security generation, humanitarian relief, and national reconstruction. Where the Leviathan force prefers unilateral freedom of action, the Sys Admin force will be thoroughly multilateral, bureaucratically multilingual, and able to coexist peacefully with any nongovernmental organization or private voluntary organization on the scene. These groups—like the International Red Cross, Save the Children, and Doctors Without Borders—will be made to feel not just welcome in any postwar or disaster environment but safe as well. The presence of these groups will not just be tolerated, but thoroughly accommodated with the zeal of a service-delivery company (think UPS or FedEx). The Sys Admin's decision loops will necessarily sync up with those of the relief agencies and the international development organizations, and both sides in this civil-military marriage will learn to live with each other over the long haul. The Sys Admin force will not be in a hurry to leave, and will remain until the locals are ready to assume control or the UN mission is up and running. All the broken windows will be fixed before this force departs, and the American public will come to understand that these are the troops that remain *after* we "bring the boys home."

These two forces will be organized quite differently. The Leviathan force will be young, overwhelmingly male, and preferably unmarried, while the Sys Admin force will be far older, more educated, gender-balanced, and often married with children. The Leviathan force will remain under military law, and will not submit to oversight from the International Criminal Court (ICC). It will remain a secret society, largely disconnected from Homeland Security and never transgressing Posse Comitatus restrictions against military operations within the homeland. Its entire ethos will revolve around killing bad guys *over there*. The Sys Admin force will be its complete opposite, moving progressively from military law toward civilian law. It will eventually submit to the ICC's oversight, and it will not be bound by Posse Comitatus restrictions on operating within the United States. It will be a far more police-like force, connected to society and always available for insertion into homeland security operations.

Unlike those in the Leviathan force, personnel in the Sys Admin force will alternate service in the ranks with periods of work outside in normal society. It will not be a case of up-or-out career paths but in-and-out career rotations. The Sys Admin force will revolve around protecting society from bad actors, and it will "serve and protect" both at home and overseas. To its detractors, this force will be a "mobile police state," pure and simple. But in truth it will represent not *American* justice, but *Core* justice, and as such it will be easily deployed for at-length duty across the Gap, enjoying as it will the financial support of the Core as a whole. Moreover, as the world's largest and most respected public-sector security consultancy, the Sys Admin force will attract foreign troops from the Gap as peacekeepers because—financially speaking—the provision of such troops is a moneymaker for developing nations. You may deride such a development as signaling nothing more than the resurrection of the French Foreign Legion (Gap supplies the soldiers, Core supplies the guns), but tell me, wouldn't you rather see Gap militaries being put to this sort of use rather than joining in the civil strife that currently plagues too many states there?

Where the Leviathan force defines the global war on terrorism, the Sys Admin force defines our long-term goal of shrinking the Gap. Done right, the Leviathan force is first-in, first-out, while the Sys Admin force is last-in, last-out. The Leviathan force does not wait on UN Security Council resolutions, although it will welcome them should they arrive in time. The Sys Admin force will not only welcome such resolutions but do everything possible to *attract* the UN missions that it is dedicated to supporting. Where the Leviathan force does not share information and is inwardly networked, the Sys Admin force will be purposely designed for outward connectivity. Its networks will emphasize not just "jointness" among the services, but interagency cooperation throughout the U.S. government and beyond. In essence, it will aspire to the role of universal translator, able to speak any bureaucratic tongue or private-sector language. Where the Leviathan force is shrouded in acronyms, coded language, and exclusionary terms, the Sys Admin force will employ plain English, transparent terminology, and a lexicon of inclusion. The Sys Admin force will not need to join the civilian world outside the Pentagon, it will largely live in that world.

These two forces will offer very different coalition opportunities to potential allies. The Leviathan force will be combat-oriented and Special Operations Forces–centric, so the ante for participation will be simple: Can your country provide SOF willing to kill on command and face death in combat? Because these individuals really are a breed apart, any number an ally can provide will gain that country entry into the posse of the moment, no questions asked. The Sys Admin force will be civil affairs–oriented and network-centric, so the criteria for participation will be more complex, but also more fungible, the question being: Can your country provide any niche capability that is self-supporting, modular, and easily networked according to international protocols? Where the Leviathan force distributes encrypted hit lists across hardened networks, the Sys Admin utilizes open-source code and hosts shared databases on the Internet. As far as the Sys Admin is concerned, so long as you can meet the basic interface standards, it will welcome as many units as your country can manage, assuming all your systems achieve log-in and maintain secure network connections.

These two forces will, by and large, not interact with each other, as the Leviathan will be activated only when certain thresholds are reached and certain tasks need performing. Like the SWAT team within any metropolitan police force, it will enter and exit crime scenes as dictated by circumstances, while the Sys Admin force will be an always-on, always-nearby, always-approachable resource for allies and friends in need. The Leviathan force will wage war with an eye toward leaving the situation as amenable as possible to follow-on management by the Sys Admin force, so precision of targeting and economy of force will be the watchwords. The Sys Admin will not be forced to deal with the Leviathan's unexploded bombs or unexplainable massacres. The Leviathan will focus on killing and removing bad actors while leaving behind societies otherwise unimpaired; it will surgically remove unwanted tissue, not riddle the body politic with smoking holes.

In terms of command, the current combatant commanders (Europe, Central, Pacific, Southern) will continue in their long-term evolution as the main purveyors of system administration. Not pro consuls so much as precinct captains, they will maintain the continuous presence of U.S. air, ground, and naval forces around the world, but increasingly focused around and throughout the Gap. Over time, the forces they field will feature smaller platforms (e.g., ships, aircraft) designed for greater loitering capacity (i.e., the ability to dwell and monitor), thus marking the Sys Admin's general trend toward "the many and the cheap."

In contrast, the Leviathan force will progressively withdraw from the world, maintaining a network of Spartan, launching-pad bases around the Gap, and leaving behind its signature Special Operations Forces as its early reconnaissance force. These SOF operators will work largely undercover throughout the Gap in their continuing prosecution of the global war on terrorism, drawing upon the larger Leviathan forces whenever larger-scale interventions are required. In terms of command function, the Leviathan force will rise from a progressive fusion of four current supporting commands (Special Operations Command, Strategic Command, Transportation Command, and Joint Forces Command). Compared with the always *out there* Sys Admin force, the Leviathan force will largely surge from bases within the continental United States to interventions overseas, and its force structure will reflect the philosophy of "the few and the expensive," spreading its platform capabilities over as many categories as fiscally feasible. Compared with the generalist, minimalist force structure of the Sys Admin, the Leviathan will favor the biggest possible tool kit of platforms, preferring to buy a few of many types versus many of a few types.

In terms of the current services, the Leviathan force tends to draw more from the Air Force than from the Army, and more from the Navy than the Marines. If we define the Air Force as logistics, combat, and strategic assets, then the latter two are drawn more to the Leviathan force, while logistics clearly plays in both. From the Navy, the Leviathan draws more on submarines, while the Sys Admin draws more on surface combatants in general. Naval air, or carriers, would serve as an effective swing asset, as would the Army's airborne troops. From the Army in general, the Leviathan force retains the heavy armor, while the Sys Admin absorbs the ground troops. The Marines are almost a pure "small wars" force, and therefore are better suited to the Sys Admin role. Each service's Reserves would be similarly dispersed, and a redefined National Guard will migrate overwhelmingly toward the Sys Admin ranks. In terms of who gets custody of the kids in this divorce, that is basically how it works out.

Over time, the defense budget's top line will remain relatively flat, growing only with inflation. Within a generation, the Sys Admin force will command the majority of the defense budget, taking advantage of the continuous transformation that the Leviathan force pursues, making this warfighting force ever smaller, more lethal, and more decisive in application. The strategic hedge maintained by the Pentagon as a whole will reside within the Leviathan force, matching its profound distance from society. Nuclear weapons will not be sanitized for the Leviathan's use but remain in their permanent status as sources of existential deterrence. In short, they remain for having, not using.

Likewise over time, the Sys Admin force will merge extensively with those assets of the Department of Homeland Security focused on border defense and internal disaster mitigation, as America's immune-system capabilities are progressively integrated with those of the rest of the Core. In many ways, the Leviathan's share of the Pentagon's budget will constitute the core defense spending associated with war, while the Sys Admin's share will reflect the nation's growing commitment to the Core's collective security. In essence, our success in shrinking the Gap will be reflected by the diminution of the Leviathan's budget and the expansion of the Sys Admin's funding.

Bureaucratically speaking, both the Leviathan and Sys Admin forces will remain within a single Department of Defense until the Core's continuing security integration eliminates all reasonable fears about the potential for a near-peer conflict. You might assume I am referring to some distant future, but this point will be reached before I retire in three decades' time. I have lived through much strategic change in my short career. I no longer think it logical to assume that war as we have known it is somehow immutable to the technological and economic forces that have transformed global-ization from merely a characteristic of the global security environ-ment to the primary force reshaping that environment. In sum, I see *the* future worth creating and I choose to embrace it.

This country spent most of the twentieth century running from fear in its planning for war, working not to create viable futures but to prevent unviable ones. That legacy of fear infects our world vi-sion still, causing our words to sound shrill and arrogant when they should ring with optimism and hope. Americans are reluctant war-riors, but at this point in human history, it is crucial that we have re-solve. With globalization achieving critical mass across the planet, our model of future peace prevails so long as our willingness to wage just wars does not falter. My definition of just wars is exceed-ingly simple: They must leave affected societies more connected than we found them, with the potential for self-driven connectivity either restored or left intact. We cannot demand democracy or free markets or adherence to some "imperial order" from vanquished foes, but merely transparency and the preservation of individual choice regarding connectivity with the outside world.

My vision of America's future military power will undoubtedly seem fantastic to many, living as they do in a world full of "chaos," "uncertainty," and "perpetual war." It is this purposeful distortion of reality that allows so many commentators today to seek to soothe the American psyche with warm words of praise for an emerging American "empire." But this is old fearmongering in new packages. America's gift to the world is not military empire but economic globalization and the collective security it both engenders and demands. Kant's world is expanding, while Hobbes's is ever shrinking. War and peace as we have known them across the twentieth century will not survive long into the twenty-first century. A new American Way of War emerges, remaking the world in its image much as the American Way of Peace provided the template for globalization's rebirth following World War II and its expansion ever since. Our side is not just winning, it is growing.

THE AMERICAN WAY OF WAR

In January 1998, Art Cebrowski and John Gartska published a seminal article heralding a new era of war entitled "Network-Centric Warfare: Its Origins and Future." It was a breathtaking piece that described a fundamentally new method of warfare based on using networks to defeat enemies with less mass—exchanging bombs for bits, so to speak. The article revolutionized a lot of thinking within the Pentagon, and within half a decade, this seemingly odd way of describing war (built around networks, not platforms like carriers or aircraft) had risen to the point of conventional wisdom across the military. While I was greatly impressed with the piece, and was very excited to meet Art when he came aboard as Naval War College president in the summer of 1998, I had a lot of problems with how this new concept of net-centric war was being applied. So much so that my first act upon joining the college was to send an article entitled "The Seven Deadly Sins of Network-Centric Warfare" to the U.S. Naval Institute's flagship journal, *Proceedings*, where Art's article had been published. Not everyone tries to impress their new boss in this manner (especially one so famously Catholic), but in my mind, I was just trying to start a conversation with the legend himself—without getting myself fired, I hoped.

My basic criticism of net-centric warfare was that its adherents were employing these concepts to describe fabulously large shooting wars with fabulously sexy great-power opponents (read, again, China), and I just did not see that world out there. Instead of disabling modern enemy information technology networks in war, I saw U.S. Marines struggling to resurrect archaic transportation networks in humanitarian response situations. Instead of facing enemies who were modernizing their forces in line with this information revolution, I saw even our own rich allies unable to keep up with our new purchases of technology, to the point where they simply had trouble communicating with us in coalitions. In short, I saw all this great technology being put to seemingly very old uses, and that struck me as tragic. What Art was describing in his vision was a fundamentally *American* way of war, one that promised not just better wars, and not just shorter wars, but perhaps the end of war itself. Art likes to say that "policy = power × moral principle." What I saw in net-centric warfare back then was lots of power in search of moral principle. I did not want to see it used simply to kill a lot more Chinese faster and more efficiently in war, I wanted to see it used to short-circuit wars and warfare in general. I want wars to be obsolete because America becomes so powerful that no one is willing to take it on, and thus America is willing to take on anyone—a self-reinforcing deterrence.

It was absolutely true that prior to 9/11, most net-centric war advocates were egging the Pentagon on in its misguided search for a near-peer competitor. They felt they needed a standard to work against as they transformed the U.S. military beyond its current capabilities, thrusting it into a new era of warfare. What was sad about this push was that it seemed like a solution in search of a problem, and I saw no moral principle in that. It seemed more like a mortal sin to this Catholic, and that's why my article disturbed Art so much. He felt I was accusing him of doing something very bad, when he felt he was trying to do something very good. What we both needed was a future worth creating, not just a bad one worth preventing. The American way of war needs that moral edge. We need to be liberators, not mere protectors of the status quo.

Our wars need to expand the good, not simply check the evil. We spent the Cold War trying to put so much fear out of our minds that we lost track of America's revolutionary story line, which sees us remaking the world in our own image of freedom, connectivity, and the rule of law.

When Art hired me after 9/11 to work in his new Office of Force Transformation at the Pentagon, we both laughed at the irony. Many in the business have long assumed we were enemies of sorts, because my article is often paired with his as the great counterpoint to his signature vision. In reality, we were both searching for the same happy ending, or a grand definition of why it would be a good thing for the world for America not only to possess such amazing military powers but to actually use them proactively to shape a better tomorrow. When Art pulled me aboard, he gave me one simple assignment: develop a strategic view of the world that would elevate transformation from a discussion of which weapons systems or platforms needed to be purchased or retired. His definition of transforming the Pentagon goes far beyond changing what it buys or how it buys it, or even how it wages war. In his mind, it is the very role of the Pentagon in U.S. national security that needs changing, and 9/11 plus the global war on terrorism provided us with just what the doctor ordered—a fluxing of the Cold War rule set that still dominated our thinking.

What is so crucial about the historical creation point at which America now stands is that we have the opportunity to redefine not just our way of war but that of the entire planet. Those commentators who warn about a "second nuclear age" simply do not get it. They argue that America has become so powerful in a conventional (or nonnuclear) sense that the only way any state will be able to counter our power in the future is to acquire and be willing to use nuclear weapons. This was allegedly the great lesson of *Desert Storm* ("Don't fight the Americans unless you have nukes!"), and many alarmists repeat that claim after *Operation Iraqi Freedom*. But the world and even the Gap is moving in another direction. What we saw across the 1990s was a host of emerging powers walk away from their nuclear potential, in large part because of what America did to Iraq in *Desert Storm*. Basically any Core member could be a nuclear power if it wanted to be, and yet no new ones have appeared beyond the five original nuclear powers—the United States, the U.K., France, Russia, and China, plus India, which is trapped in its own MAD situation with Pakistan. South Africa walked away from that capability. So did all the former Soviet republics that found themselves with nukes following the USSR's collapse but did not want them (e.g., Ukraine, Kazakhstan). Brazil could have developed them but chose not to. Germany has never reached for them, nor has Japan. South Korea never turned to this option, despite knowing that North Korea clearly has. We know Israel has them and we understand why, surrounded as it is by countries that, for decades, called for its destruction. But even as it has fought wars against all odds and suffered years upon years of terrorism, Israel has never made a serious move in the direction of employing them. All we really have to worry about right now is a handful of states (now just Iran, North Korea, Pakistan, and a few other possibilities) that clearly exist outside the security rule set to such a degree that contemplating such war with them is not idle speculation.

Meanwhile, America has elevated its particular brand of warfare to the point where we are able to fine-tune a defeated nation's ability to recover following the war that removes its ruling regime. We fight wars against individuals today, not countries, or societies, or even the government as a whole. We simply go after bad guys, using weapons with a real moral dimension, such as smart bombs and new nonlethal forms of warfare that target enemy systems without harming people. America has gotten so good at this that we no longer even need strategic surprise to defeat a well-armed enemy. A foe can know we are coming, even when we are coming, and there is nothing he can do to stop us. That kind of power, armed with moral principle, should equal a real grand strategy. America ultimately does not transform the Middle East to defeat terrorism, contain Islam, secure oil, or defend Israel. We seek to transform the region to end its disconnectedness, and if it is worth doing there, then it is worth doing everywhere it exists. What stands in our way is a collection of bad actors sprinkled across the Gap, some who have embedded themselves in corrupt, repressive regimes, and others who do not have regimes to protect but who desire to hijack societies and isolate them further.

This is an enemy worth fighting, because it is truly evil. This is a war worth waging, because not only can we defeat this enemy, we can eliminate it from the world's future and—by so doing—steer history down a far better path. This is a military worth building, because it signals everything good about this country: our connectedness, our faith in individual decision making, and the appeal of our ideals. When a Special Operations soldier laser-guides a bomb into a bad guy's house, killing all inside but sparing all around, we are saying that America owns the consequences of its wars. When we spare an enemy's infrastructure even as it puts our own soldiers' lives at greater risk, we demonstrate that Americans can love their enemies more than themselves. When the Pentagon invites dozens of reporters along with its fighting troops, it not only understands that the whole world is watching, it wants them to see the truth of this uniquely *American* way of war. These are new rules sets, and by exporting them around the world through our words and deeds, we make everyone safer by demonstrating how pointless war has become. So if you are a "big man" who believes you have the right to take some chunk of humanity offline to abuse them for your own purposes, you are wrong. If you believe you can get away with it forever, you are wrong. If you believe no one cares, you are wrong. And if you believe America cannot and will not stop you if you seek to acquire WMD, you are more than wrong—you do not belong in our future.

What is so important about seeing the international security environment for what it really is today is that America recovers its historical purpose in that knowledge: disconnectedness defines danger, so connectedness defines safety. When we wage war against the forces of disconnectedness, we generate safety for the planet as a whole. Is it hard to tell the good guys from the bad? Not at all.

Look for those who, if they had their way, would decrease connectivity for those they rule or seek to rule. Is Israel a bad state? Look
at its connectivity, and imagine how much more it would pursue
without its security problems. Is China a bad state? Does it seek
more connectivity over time or less? Is Iran a bad country? On top,
yes, but on the bottom, no. So target one, and not the other. Same
for North Korea, or any other country ruled by a bad regime. There
are no bad people save those who would deny others connectivity,
choice, and freedom. We will not always be welcomed as liberators,
because no one long enslaved is ready for freedom on Day One. We
know that freedom is sometimes a long process of awakening.

So the American way of war as we have come to define it is built
around the concepts of connectivity, networks, and individual freedom of action within defined rule sets. You want to know what makes
our military so scary to the rest of the world? Our noncommissioned
officers wield more combat decision-making power on the battlefield
than basically every other nation's admirals and generals. When you
fight Americans, you face the worst of all enemies: disciplined cre-
ativity. When Art Cebrowski and I published an article in *Proceedings*
in January 2003 called "The American Way of War," we wrote,

> The ultimate attribute of the emerging American Way of War
> is the super-empowerment of the war fighter—whether on the
> ground, in the air, or at sea. As network-centric warfare empowers
> individual servicemen and -women, and as we increasingly face an
> international security environment where rogue individuals, be
> they leaders of "evil states" or "evil networks," pose the toughest
> challenges, eventually the application of our military power will
> mirror the dominant threat to a significant degree. In other words,
> we morph into a military of super-empowered individuals fighting
> wars against super-empowered individuals. In this manner, the
> American Way of War moves the military toward an embrace of a
> more sharply focused global cop role: we increasingly specialize in
> neutralizing bad people who do bad things. Adding these new re-
> sponsibilities to the U.S. military is not only a natural develop-

ment but a positive one, for it is the United States' continued success in deterring global war and obsolescing state-on-state war
that now allows us to begin tackling the far thornier issues
of transnational threats and subnational conflicts—the battle-
grounds on which this global war on terrorism will be won.

What Americans need to remember when they hear all this nonsense about "empire," and "perpetual war," and "World War IV" is
how far we have come as a military power in the last quarter-
century. As we wage this global war against terrorism, which is neither "global" nor a "war" by traditional definition, remember this:
our nation is most responsible for guiding the world past the threat
of global nuclear war; our government fashioned a global economic and political order in which great-power war has become a
thing of the past; and our military's current mission involves extending security to individuals throughout the Gap. The American
way of war *defines* the moral dimension embedded in the grand
strategic goal of shrinking the Gap.

How America chooses to wage war defines the nature of peace in
the twenty-first century. Our rule sets are as clear as our actions, although we have not described them sufficiently in the explanations
we have offered to date for our wars. Here is how I choose to define them:

America stands ready for any type of war, because we know our
enemies cannot defeat us in extended conflicts, only damage our
will by striking with the advantage of surprise. So we train year-
round at levels other militaries can only dream of, covering a
universal range of scenarios. We practice contingency planning because our wars are long-distance wars, so we never plan to fight in
place. We expect to conduct war on the fly. In fact, we prefer it in
network-centric warfare (think soccer, not football).

The United States brings war only in very specific circumstances,
but when it does, it employs all elements of our national power. We
bring war to any state or nonstate actor that threatens or actually
attacks our homeland. This will be a war of destruction so as to de-

ter the like-minded. America brings war to any entity that attacks our forces or other agencies of the U.S. Government, because we know such attacks—even when committed abroad—are designed to attack global stability itself by diminishing our stature as its ultimate guarantor. When all other reasonable measures fail, we bring war preemptively to entities seeking weapons of mass destruction for use against us or our allies. We also bring war preemptively to states that harbor or actively support terrorist groups with a transnational reach. We bring war against any entities that threaten or wage war against our strongest allies. These include NATO, Israel, Taiwan, South Korea, Japan, Australia, and any state close to our borders. Finally, we bring war against any entities that threaten global economic stability by threatening or waging war against key pillars of that economy, to include the Persian Gulf economies.

We are prepared to bring war anywhere in the world, but our focus in terms of frequency lies inside the Gap. In the Western Hemisphere, we are prepared to wage war anywhere in the Caribbean Rim and the Andes portion of South America. In Europe, we have no compelling need to prepare for war, and that definition includes the Russian Federation, because security problems located within Core great powers remain their own to solve. America is prepared to wage war in Southwest Asia, defined as Central Asia and the Persian Gulf, because the energy that flows out of these regions is a global connectivity worth protecting. In Asia, we are ready to bring war against North Korea, and to deter Chinese aggression against Taiwan. Because of the global war on terrorism, America now stands ready to bring war as required anywhere inside sub-Saharan Africa, although we will seek to limit our exposure there until our efforts to export security to the Persian Gulf bring about lasting change not just for Iraq, but for Iran, Syria, Lebanon, and Saudi Arabia itself.

America begins war under a variety of circumstances. We retaliate automatically to any direct attack against our homeland, although our timing may be delayed whenever the identity of our attacker is in question. We immediately come to the aid of key allies under attack, no questions asked. Outside of such automatic responses, we prefer extensive domestic political debate regarding any decision to go to war. The American public wishes to see several boxes checked before the decision to go to war is reached by the White House. These include consultation with Congress, making a case to the American people via public speeches, seeking UN approval and support for the resulting operations, and enlisting as many allies as possible. America also conducts covert operations as part of our global war on terrorism. These are not subject to public debate, so long as the numbers of personnel remain small and the goals are both limited and well focused. Because of the strategic focus imposed by this global war on terrorism, the United States is likely to pursue more peace-enforcement operations in regions that rim the Non-Integrating Gap, although we will do so with an eye to enlisting the support of regional security organizations. Deeper inside the Gap (read, Africa), America is more likely to strike preemptively with less concern for what may follow, although, over time, our goal of shrinking the Gap will eventually center on sub-Saharan Africa.

America's goals in conducting war are broad. Beyond preserving U.S. national security, we seek to bolster global norms against mass violence, so we target only those actors who perpetrate or seek to commit such acts. But in order to effectively "criminalize" such activity, we must encourage the spread of legal rule sets, which, over time, establish the conditions under which economic development and—later—democracy can flourish. We also seek to protect the global economy from disruptions to its functioning, because we know deaths ensue from such disruptions just as surely as they do from war. When we wage war, we place special emphasis on limiting both enemy casualties (military and civilian) and damage to national economies, because we know that later integration of these same societies into the global economy is greatly facilitated when excessive force is avoided. Naturally, we balance these goals with the need to protect the lives of U.S. soldiers, because if our losses seem out of proportion to the enemies we fight and the goals we seek, then the American people will stop supporting such wars overseas.

The United States seeks the aid of all like-minded members of the Core and Gap whenever it needs to wage war. We desire the approval of international organizations such as the United Nations, but if the stakes are high enough, such approval is not crucial. More important to us is the approval and support of our closest military allies (NATO, Japan, Australia), as well as the support of—or at least nonobstruction from—the newest pillars of the Core (China, South Korea, Russia, India, Brazil, Argentina, Chile, Mexico). But there are no set rules in terms of the allies we enlist for any war, so "coalitions of the willing" are the norm, with no apology demanded from, or offered to, states declining to participate.

When America wages war, it mobilizes its resources on every possible front. We seek to destroy our enemy's ability to wage war. We seek to isolate him from all possible allies, denying him both resources and sympathy from others. When we engage in war overseas, we activate all manner of airlift and sealift networks (both military and civilian contractors) to move all required personnel and supplies into position as quickly as possible. Before firing a single shot, the United States mobilizes a global information grid to achieve the maximum possible information advantage over opponents, so that when our firepower is brought to bear, our targeting will be as precise as possible while that of our opponents will be as degraded as possible. Finally, the Pentagon mobilizes the world's best combat medical system for each war, spending more on the goal of preserving our soldiers' lives than most nations spend on their entire military.

America can access battlefields around the world as no other military can. We have the world's only blue-water navy, so the majority of our supplies and forces can transit the world's oceans in great safety. When strategic speed is required, the United States can tap the world's largest military airlift fleet, which comes with extensive midair refueling capacity. We can also, if need be, strike anywhere in the world directly from U.S. air bases within our borders. In general, though, the United States has many friends around the world, so we are able to effectively pre-position supplies for rapid use in the vast majority of crisis situations.

When America wages war, it brings everything it has in terms of forces. We utilize overseas bases as close to the war zone as possible, and typically are able to reach new agreements for such access in rapid order when the stakes of any conflict are high enough. But we do not need close-in air bases per se, because we have the ability to move carriers within range and can operate Air Force aircraft from great distances, thanks to our extensive fleet of midair refueling tankers. Before the United States starts a war, Special Forces will typically engage in a wide variety of special pre-invasion tasks designed to degrade enemy capabilities and enlist whatever indigenous support is possible. When the war begins in earnest, America typically "prepares the battlefield" through an opening salvo of air strikes that may last for days or even weeks. Once an enemy is damaged in this manner, we use ground forces to conquer territory and roll up enemy ground forces. The U.S. military employs the Navy, Marines, Army, and Air Force in a highly synergistic fashion known as "jointness," in order to overwhelm opponents quickly while putting the fewest number of ground troops in harm's way.

In general, the application of overwhelming force is the hallmark of the American way of war, as past experience has taught us that committing forces in a piecemeal fashion puts U.S. personnel unnecessarily at risk. So once the battle is begun, we seek "rapid domination" of the battlefield (both on the ground and in any surrounding littoral waters), staying consistently on the offensive, or as much as reasonable circumstances allow. We seek to avoid static front lines. As Art Cebrowski likes to say, we seek to turn each engagement with the enemy into an ambush across a "noncontiguous battlefield." In short, our enemy is safe nowhere on the battlefield because there are no rear areas. The same is true for U.S. forces. Since we know our enemies will seek to defeat us asymmetrically, we disperse our personnel as much as possible while taking advantage of all our network capabilities. When we seek to destroy an enemy, we typically target his air defenses first, especially airfields.

Then we go after his command-and-control facilities, or his communication networks. Then and only then do we go after his ground forces in a concentrated fashion. In short, we work to degrade our enemy's ability to see and understand what is going on in the battlefield as early in the process as possible.

America will go to every effort possible to avoid using weapons of mass destruction, but that does not include promising never to use them, otherwise we lose their essential deterrence value. Naturally, when we have evidence that an opponent possesses such resources and has the will to use them, we seek to neutralize its ability to employ WMD as preemptively as possible, either prior to or during the immediate onset of war. Special Forces play a key role here.

Once the enemy is defeated, the United States makes a strong effort to track down and incapacitate all remaining resistance. We also engage in what are known as psychological operations to convince the civilian population that our goals in conducting any war will serve their long-term interests. We focus great attention on tapping all available social and political leaders to reconstruct a functioning government authority that can begin to oversee a return to normal life. U.S. forces are prepared to conduct emergency relief operations on their own, but prefer to yield to international relief organizations as quickly as possible so their focus on providing security throughout the country can be maximized. To facilitate the legal recovery of the country, we will do everything within our power to facilitate the identification, capture, and imprisonment of individuals suspected of war crimes or human rights abuses. Ideally, this effort will be followed up by trials in internationally sanctioned courts.

Before the United States leaves any battlefield, the capital city must be under firm control by friendly forces, and the countryside must be settled enough so that UN peacekeeping troops or the successor regime can manage the situation with reasonable use of force. We do not leave until all the major players involved in the conflict sign up to the war-termination agreements that have been concluded, or until any resulting humanitarian crisis has been brought under control to the point where international relief organizations can handle the situation on their own.

What the United States often leaves behind following any war are the resources that we hope will prevent future instability. These may include military trainers to help the country restore its military or police functions, or to train existing state forces to combat rebels still fighting; a small "trip wire" force of American troops to signal our commitment to responding to future security situations; military supplies that we can utilize rapidly if we need to return to the country on short notice; and other assets and personnel deemed appropriate to long-term cooperation between our military and that of the country.

Currently, these are the basic rule sets of the American way of war. These rules are constantly evolving as the Pentagon moves progressively toward focusing on disabling, capturing, and killing individual targets as part of the global war on terrorism, and away from planning for major wars with great powers. But there will always be a broad spectrum of capabilities-based planning, meaning the Pentagon will always seek to maintain its ability to do just about anything anywhere, because any holes in our capabilities to wage war invite attack in precisely those functional areas. Having said that, there is a huge distinction between those low-probability scenarios we hedge against and those high-probability scenarios we focus on. The Core defines low probability, the Gap *near certainty*.

Over time, the American way of war will be comprehensively shaped by the continuing and emerging military tasks involved in eliminating specific security targets within the Gap, not defending against all possibilities of attack from fellow Core members. Otherwise, all America would be doing in taking up the security challenges of shrinking the Gap would be to overburden the U.S. military by refusing to acknowledge, much less exploit, its past and current successes in encouraging collective security throughout the Core. In short, the American way of war must reflect the world as we find it, not past fears of near-peers or future fantasies of American empire.

Chapter 7

THE MYTHS
WE MAKE

(*I Will Now Dispel*)

THERE ARE A LOT of myths floating around about America's security role in global affairs. You see them constantly cited in op-eds and on TV talk shows, and they are employed indiscriminately by average citizens and experts alike. People who listen to talk radio on a daily basis can probably recite them in their sleep. These myths survive primarily because no coherent vision has yet emerged about U.S. national security policy since the end of the Cold War, other than this seemingly open-ended global war on terrorism. So these misguided exaggerations become a sort of shorthand for expressing our deepest fears about futures we hope desperately to avoid.

Repeat after me: global chaos . . . perpetual war . . . global policeman . . . empire. . . .

These myths kill honest debates in a heartbeat. You know how it goes: you're at some gathering or party and the conversation turns to the war on terrorism, and you try to make some point you think makes sense about how all these efforts should—in some better world—come together in some logical fashion. It's not like you're apologizing for one political party or the other; you just want to state something hopeful about tomorrow—something not so tragically cynical. You know real people who are dying in this war, and you want their sacrifices to prompt something more meaningful than just a caustic put-down in some campaign debate.

And then some blowhard leans over from the conversation going on next door and simply slaps you down with, "Hell, everyone knows it's all about running our empire. If you can't admit we're playing globocop, then you're just blind to all the chaos that really exists out there. Better get used to it, because it's World War IV from here on out!"

Then the blowhard retracts his index finger from your chest and goes back to pontificating on why everything sucks in this world, and you're left wondering why these high-voltage phrases seem to short-circuit every intelligent conversation you try to pursue on this subject. I mean, are we all supposed to just lie down every time some "realist" throws these buzzwords in our face? Worse still are the *über*-realists who prattle on about war giving meaning to our lives and how we should all adopt a warrior spirit for the battles ahead. God save us all from the "wisdom" of these national *insecurity* experts.

This chapter focuses on how to dispel the worst of these myths. Consider it a sort of cocktail party primer on how to body-slam blowhards.

And whatever you do, *please try this at home.* Teach your children well, because when parents skip that effort, the next generation is left with nothing more than the myths we make.

THE MYTH OF GLOBAL CHAOS

I've had a Top Secret or higher clearance all of my professional career. It was something I looked forward to getting while I was in college, because it would mean I was "in the club" and that I was privy to the serious, insider dope. The "unclean," or anyone without a clearance, tend to assume that having one gives you access to some alternative universe where you finally find out how the world really works, what your parents were lying to you about all these years, and why Oliver Stone's movies are all *completely true*.

Truth be told, entering the world of classified material does not bring you any closer to reality, but rather farther away. You start talking primarily to others like yourself—the clean. You engage in conversations that cannot be repeated anywhere else, except with those likewise cleared, so you lose your ability to engage in reality checks with outsiders ("Does that make any sense to you?"). Not surprisingly, as external influences wane, your confidence level soars with regard to your secrets. You just know they must be true, because they are secrets. You have access to them because you are smarter and better than others—you can be trusted. Moreover, you are surrounded by other smart, better, trustworthy people, and so your discussions about the material are immensely self-reinforcing. These are not simply secrets, they begin to become absolute truths. As a bearer of such, you are empowered beyond normal people. You live on a higher plane, and are able to discuss concepts that would simply freak out ordinary people if they were exposed to them. Intellectually, you have become an *übermensch,* a superman of sorts. Like Neo, you have broken out of the Matrix of lies and false perceptions—*welcome to the real world.*

Don't get me wrong. I'm not saying everyone with a clearance is a head case, just that the more clearance you have and the more you really use it, the more you're at risk of falling into the head trip I just described. Of course, all of these perceptions are wrong. Being admitted to the world of secrets does not send your IQ skyrocketing or elevate your consciousness above that of mortal men. You just know one version of the dirt that exists throughout life, and because many security types tend to lead fairly closed lives outside of work (the business attracts intense, workaholic types), far too many assume that this version of the dirt allows them to understand life and humanity far better than others—doctors, lawyers, business leaders, and so on. But in reality, every profession has its insider information, and all of it involves dirt. What's different about my business is how that skewed belief in insider information emboldens so many of us to spend our lives scaring the hell out of people.

The classic way to scare ordinary people is that sly, if-you-only-knew-what-I-know confidence that lets you fearlessly prognosticate concerning all matters of future security. Since what most people fear is unpredictable bad stuff happening in the future, this is an intoxicating sort of power. Plus, since no one can ever really fact-check your *nudge-nudge-wink-wink—Say no more*'s because, of course, you can't reveal your sources, it's almost impossible to catch you in either a lie or a mistake. The result? You can say the most outrageous things that scare people in the worst way and basically never be called on the carpet. Since most people do fret about the future, you can play to their worst fears. The real-world data is, by and large, completely meaningless to the conversation. When you speak the unspeakable about either the present or the future, people *just know* you're telling the truth.

So far, I'm just talking about an open society like the United States. If you transplant this argument to an authoritarian state like the old Soviet Union or Saddam Hussein's regime in Iraq, then you move into a far more serious realm of mind control. In the United States, of course, we have an entire industry called the press, which is devoted to punching holes in the fear factoring done by the defense and intelligence communities, and that's what keeps us healthy and sane as a society.

I learned just how effective such fearmongering can be in an authoritarian state the summer I lived in the Soviet Union in the mid-1980s. One afternoon, while my student group was visiting a Communist youth camp out in the woods, I broke off from the main meeting to go have a smoke with one Russian teenager in a cabin that stood on the edge of the camp. In reality, this kid had asked around my group to discover which of us had the strongest background in security studies, and once he had decided I was the man, he talked me into leaving with him for smokes and some shots of vodka. Being the adventurous type, I went along, figuring we'd get slightly smashed and talk all sorts of trash about the relative ease of having sex with American girls versus Russian girls.

To my complete surprise, when my new friend opened the door to the cabin it was crammed full of teenagers, all sitting around a chair in seemingly tense anticipation. I was led to the chair, offered the standard small tumbler of vodka and a *papyrosa* (a gawdawful Soviet cigarette), and once I'd emptied the glass and lit up, the questions started flying. Basically, what these kids wanted to know was whether or not they'd all die in a nuclear war with the United States. At first I thought they were joking, but after a while I understood how completely serious they were, and so I spent close to an hour telling them—in my childlike Russian—all the reasons I was certain nuclear war would never happen between our two countries. In that brief moment, I liberated several dozen young minds from the paranoid grip of living in a society of secrets, and it was one of the most satisfying things I've ever done.

The first time I ever really got to test out my Top Secret clearance at CNA was relatively soon after I got it in 1991. I was invited to the "vault," the special facility within CNA's headquarters where analysts had access to Top Secret material and could conduct Top Secret discussions—thanks to all the extraordinary precautions taken within this secure mini-facility. I was pretty psyched going in. I mean, who knew what I'd learn?

Well, the discussion was pretty amazing, largely because it was so divorced from reality as to seem a dream. I had been brought in to help brainstorm a new study that was reviewing U.S. nuclear strategy in light of the Soviet Union's demise. That alone didn't make it a Top Secret discussion, because analysts write unclassified reports on this sort of thing all the time, as this one ended up being. What made it classified was the exact numbers we'd be discussing and the analysis we'd use in generating those numbers, because there you start moving into matters of actual military capabilities, and that's the stuff you really do want to keep secret. Naturally, whenever you're talking nuclear weapons, you're talking high body counts. There's just no two ways about it.

About fifteen minutes into the discussion, I found myself staring at the wall. None of this seemed real. It was all just so preposterously impossible to contemplate, not because it made me want to get all moralistic, but because the political scientist in me simply rejected the logic other analysts were assuming would let an American president actually engage in this sort of warfare. I made a requisite number of analytic protests regarding the approach, but I could see I wasn't going to get anywhere with these guys. They had that classified glow about them that told me they had already gone over to the dark side, and nothing I could say would bring them back. In the end, I didn't begrudge them this. They were, after all, just doing their jobs.

Anyway, I left the meeting early and drove over to my wife's obstetrician's office down the street. Vonne was three months pregnant with our first child, Emily, and today we'd be doing an ultrasound. The magical moment for me was not seeing Em's fuzzy outline on the monitor, but rather listening to her heartbeat. It was so incredibly real, that sound. I suddenly realized that I'd need to protect that single heartbeat for the rest of her life. And, yes, it was a bit intimidating and it did make me think of all the bad things out there in the real world that could end this life in a heartbeat. But it also filled me with an immense sense of hope. I was in this business to save single heartbeats, not contemplate immolating them by the millions.

Hunched over Vonne's prostrate body in that doctor's office, I suddenly realized that despite the allure of the world of secrets and my long anticipation at being admitted to that society, I needed to avoid classified work for the rest of my career. I just knew I wasn't cut out for the business of scaring people half to death.

It was a very good decision on my part because it played naturally to my personality. I love to be the skeptic in the room, or the smart-ass who's always poking holes in other people's grand schemes. It's the nastier, more sarcastic side of my personality. But it's also where many of my analytic skills come from, because the wary eye is the discerning eye, and seeing through all the bullshit is a relatively rare skill in a business where so many swallow it without blinking.

Again, I don't so much begrudge analysts their tendency for worst-case groupthink, because somebody's got to do it. What angers me is when that sort of analysis is authoritatively inflicted on the public in published reports or, worse, by talking-head experts on television—whether it's a fire-breathing senator, a gravel-voiced retired general, or just your all-purpose intense-looking "national security expert." My pet peeve for years now has been the tendency of national security experts to describe the post–Cold War international security environment as one of unremitting "chaos" and "perpetual war." Naturally, this sort of rhetoric has only increased since 9/11. Not because it's any more true but simply because the public's more receptive.

Let me poke some holes in this myth, which many security analysts will use to tell you why my "future worth creating" will never come about.

First reality check: If the world was full of chaos and perpetual war, then wouldn't the global economy be hurting on some level? There is simply no evidence of that. According to the World Bank, the global economy has grown approximately 30 percent since 1990. Wouldn't there be more poverty from all that conflict? There's not. Global poverty rates (the percentage living on less than $1 a day) have declined by 20 percent since 1990. Certainly countries would integrate less with one another economically with all that rising conflict. Again, no. Trade in goods as a percent of gross domestic product has increased significantly since 1989. Same for gross private capital flows and gross foreign direct investment. Apparently, despite all this conflict and perpetual war, the world is trading and investing money overseas far more than it did at the end of the Cold War.

Second reality check: Certainly we can track a growing number of conflicts around the world since 1990, right? Wrong again. According to the University of Maryland's Center for International Development and Conflict, "the general magnitude of global warfare has decreased by over fifty percent since peaking in the mid-1980s, falling by the end of 2002 to its lowest level since the early 1960s."

Third reality check: With all this perpetual warfare, wouldn't global military spending be increasing over time? I mean, wouldn't states become more fearful about the world outside as the chaos spread? Well, global military expenditures are up 14 percent in real terms since 1998. *Aha!* Then again, today's level is still 16 percent less than it was in the late 1980s, the peak of the Cold War. And who's doing much of the spending since 1998? That would be us—the United States.

Fourth reality check: With all this conflict, wouldn't at least U.S. military crisis responses have increased since the end of the Cold War? There you have me. The U.S. military responded to international crises 230 times across the 1980s and 280 times across the 1990s, or an increase of roughly one-fifth. But the vast bulk of that increase was focused on just four situations in the 1990s: Somalia, Haiti, the former Yugoslavia (Bosnia and Kosovo), and Iraq. So busy, yes, but all over the planet? Not exactly.

Fifth reality check: Certainly U.S. forces have engaged in far more combat operations over time, correct? When measured as a percent of total days involved in crisis response, U.S. forces engaged in combat operations just under 10 percent of the time in the 1980s, but almost 20 percent of the time in the 1990s. So, yes, there has been an increase, but one that says that 80 percent of the time U.S. forces respond to crises around the world, they are not engaged in combat. So even for the United States, the 1990s was a decade of activity *other than war.*

So why, then, when you read a newspaper or watch TV news, are you constantly bombarded with these phrases? Why do experts talk so confidently of "chaos" and "perpetual war"?

In my opinion, a myth was born in the early years after the Cold War. Like most myths, this one began with actual truths: the magnitude of global ethnic conflicts and separatist movements exploded around the end of the Cold War. For example, there were five new separatist conflicts around the world in the first half of the 1980s. That number doubled to ten in the second half of the eighties, and then increased by half to fifteen in the first half of the 1990s. Amazingly, the global total of ongoing separatist conflicts did not rise much over that time period, jumping slightly from the early-eighties total of thirty-five to the late-eighties total of forty-one, but then declining to thirty-nine by the early 1990s and decreasing thereafter as more and more conflicts reached political settlements. Today, the total is just under two dozen worldwide, the lowest numbers since 1960.

So what happened was really a spurt of conflicts involving separatists and ethnic violence as the Soviet empire collapsed in the late 1980s, with eleven such conflicts beginning in the former Soviet Union and Yugoslavia between 1988 and 1994. This bulge of conflict corresponded perfectly to a new pet theory that many security analysts were touting at that time within the Pentagon: the breakdown of the bipolar order would unleash a prolonged period of global chaos, as many ethnic conflicts previously held in check by Moscow's military might would erupt and burn at length.

I can remember sitting through dozens of such briefings in the early 1990s, feeling as if I were Alice in some amazing Wonderland. The flip-flop on this subject was so fast it made my head spin; in just a few short months we abandoned the notion that the Soviets were behind most of the mischief and conflict in the world and jumped immediately to the notion that—noooo!—Moscow had really been a source of great stability around the planet, and now that the Red Army had pulled back, the world was entering an uncertain and dangerous era!

To someone who had just finished writing his Ph.D. dissertation on Soviet bloc security assistance to revolutionary movements around the world, this 180-degree turn was mind-boggling. In a nutshell, the Pentagon simply missed the Soviet threat, and in its intense longing for that longtime companion, it immediately began idealizing that now-dead relationship.

The Pentagon would spend much of the 1990s pining for its old rival, and the search for its replacement would become a driving force in its long-range strategic planning right up to 9/11. That mis-guided quest would blind the Defense Department to the emerging international security landscape that we "suddenly" found our-selves in as we launched this global war on terrorism.

THE MYTH OF AMERICA AS GLOBOCOP

Whenever I am a guest on a talk radio show, I always field at least one question from a caller clearly worried that America is becom-ing the world's policeman or globocop. Because they have heard about U.S. military activity in South America, Africa, Europe, the Middle East, and Asia, they have become convinced that the Penta-gon is waging war all over the planet.

You might be wondering by now if I am guilty of sending mixed messages. First I tell you that the world is not nearly as chaotic as the fearmongers would have it. Then I tell you that the old Big One scenario of global war has been replaced by an almost unlimited number of lesser includeds that the U.S. military needs to get better at dealing with. But now I am unwilling to admit the Pentagon is the world's policeman? What gives?

First, I do not object to the terms "policeman" and "cop," be-cause a focus on rule sets naturally brings such images to mind—the people who enforce the rules, catch the rule breakers, warn the rule benders, and so on. I also like the cop image because it suggests that it's not personal, it is simply business. America does not go to com-bat because we hate a certain religion, or people, or even a bad ruler. We intervene when the rule sets are being so badly broken that the offending parties need to be stopped and removed from power. So cop, policeman, and fireman are all good images that keep us focused on what really matters: extending rule sets to parts of the world where they are thin or absent. Rule sets encourage and protect connectivity, and growing connectivity is ultimately stabilizing.

Yes, you can find conflicts on every continent on the planet. But it is important to remember that good news is rarely news; bad news always is. For example, Colombia is a dangerous and persistently violent country where drug cartels, rebel groups, and the government routinely war over who gets to control particular regions. That fighting has, on occasion, spilled over into border clashes with neighboring Venezuela, which, under strongman Hugo Chávez, has had its own share of internal instability in recent years. Factor in the rebel activity that has ebbed and waned at times in Peru, plus the usual concerns about drug trafficking across the Andes region and throughout Central America and the Caribbean, and that seems like a fairly nasty mix. But you know what? That relatively minor amount of activity does not come anywhere close to describing Latin America, which includes a lot of countries that, frankly, the United States spends almost no time worrying about in a security sense.

Africa is an even better example of this. Liberia, Sierra Leone, and the Ivory Coast in West Africa have all experienced serious levels of internal violence in recent years, but it is important to remember that there are almost a dozen other countries in that subregion alone that are not prompting the world to the same level of worry. The same can be said for southern Africa, eastern Africa, and north Africa. In each instance we are usually talking about a handful of bad situations embedded within a larger array of far more stable situations. Central Africa is clearly the worst overall situation of Africa's subregions, but even there, it is important to remember, there is a lot of normal life going on amid the recurring violence. Clearly, what constitutes "normal life" in Africa is far different from normalcy in the United States, but it is important to realize that Africa—a huge continent containing hundreds of millions of people—is not completely awash in nonstop violence.

As for the frequency issue, or the notion that much of humanity is fighting at any given time, it is important to check the actual historical record. A good source for this is the University of Maryland's *Peace and Conflict Ledger 2003*, which lists every country in the world by region, and then details those that have engaged in or suffered from armed conflict at some point in the twenty-first century. The numbers are very revealing. In the North Atlantic region (North America and Western Europe), only one nation out of 18 is checked: the United States. In the former socialist bloc of 27 countries, only Russia (for Chechnya) and Yugoslavia are checked. In Latin America, only Colombia is checked out of a total of 24 states. In Asia, it is 8 out of 27, while North Africa and the Middle East feature 4 out of 21. Africa, by far the worst situation, has 17 nations checked for armed conflict, but 27 that are not. Add it all up, and we are talking about only 32 countries (not counting the U.S.) out of a total of 161 states monitored in the Maryland study, or one-sixth of 191 states currently belonging to the United Nations. If you prefer glass-half-full statements, you could say that over 80 percent of the countries in the world today have not recently experienced any significant levels of mass violence or organized combat.

I do not want to get too caught up in the sheer "numerology" of counting states in conflict, because we are really talking about societies experiencing violence from within, not states going to war with one another. My larger point is this: Whenever we start talking about the United States as a global policeman, or "rushing in" to deal with these incidents of mass conflict, there are—at any one point in history—probably at least three-quarters of the states about which we do not need to worry. So, yes, the United States gets involved with situations "all over the world" (but really only inside the Gap), but there are also all those states in the Core where we simply do not need to come calling. Within that pool of 32 recent or ongoing situations of armed conflict, America is involved in only a handful. In the former socialist bloc, we are definitely involved in Yugoslavia but not Russia. We are involved somewhat in Colombia, Latin America's sole situation. In Asia, we are involved in the Philippines, Afghanistan, Pakistan, and Indonesia, but not India, Nepal, Myanmar, or Sri Lanka. In the Middle East, we are deeply engaged in Iraq, but not in Algeria, Israel, or Turkey. Finally in sub-Saharan Africa, the United States can only be said to be involved in Liberia, but not Burundi, Congo, the Ivory Coast, Sudan, Angola, Chad, Comoros, Congo-Brazzaville, Ethiopia, Nigeria, Rwanda, Sierra

Leone, Somalia, Uganda, Eritrea, or Senegal. Add it up. That is only 8 out of 32 cases. So if we are a global cop, we are clearly quite choosy about which cases we take on.

Of course, as part of our global war on terrorism, you could argue that the United States is involved, security-wise, with a lot more countries than I have indicated here (e.g., our new mini-base in Djibouti). My goal here is simply to point out that being a policeman does not mean you visit every house every day looking for bad guys. It simply means you have to step into certain bad situations that need your attention—on a regular basis. But doing that means the rest of the world gets to sleep a whole lot easier.

No matter how you slice the threat definition, it is hard to make the case that the Pentagon's task in the era of globalization is much more than what I would call a 5 percent solution. Meaning that the U.S. military is currently actively involved in about 10 significant situations around the world, out of a worldwide population of almost 200 states—or about 5 percent of the total. When you talk about the role of police in any community, they are typically focused on about 5 percent of the population—or the outright rule breakers and rule benders. The other 95 percent of the population is not a target but something to be defended. The same holds true in the current international community. The Pentagon needs to focus on the roughly 5 percent of both states and transnational actors that tend to bend or break the security rule sets. By working that fraction consistently, it sends the right signals to the rest of the community that playing by the rules pays off.

When the New York Police Department successfully brought down crime rates throughout the five boroughs over the 1990s, one of the ways they did so was by concentrating on the small things—or what the Pentagon would call the lesser includeds. This theory of crime prevention is known as the "broken window" approach, because it says that when criminals pick up signs from the environment—such as broken windows that remain unfixed—that say rule sets are either lax or unenforced, they become emboldened and commit more crimes. So the answer is, you fix those windows, you enforce all those "petty laws," and you have your personnel out there, present in the community and sending that signal each and every day that *rules matter.* Of course, to really clean up an environment, you need to concentrate your police in exactly those neighborhoods where the rule sets are weakest. You need to define these areas where the rule sets are thinnest, and then you need to shrink them right out of existence. That is not just community policing, that is a genuine strategic vision for the world at large— exactly what the Pentagon has lacked in the era of globalization.

THE MYTH OF AMERICAN EMPIRE

As I sit down to write this, it is September 11, 2003. I wear a somber suit and tie, as today I will attend a memorial service at the Naval War College, where we will remember ten graduates who died in the attack on the Pentagon. In the background, President Bush gives speeches pushing for more stringent antiterrorism laws and defending the cost of occupying Iraq, Osama bin Laden has a new tape airing on Al Jazeera calling for the expulsion of the American "infidels," and national newspapers run articles describing the world's plummeting lack of respect for the United States. Some are calling this the Age of American Empire. If it seems odd that America should constitute many nations' definition of what is most wrong with the world since September 11, 2001, then we have nobody but ourselves to blame.

Where we needed to put forth vision, we have left the impression of vindictiveness. Where we needed to offer hope in a future worth creating, we have frightened needlessly with loose talk of "Who's next?" and "Bring it on" and "World War III" (or "IV," I lose count at times). Finally, where we needed to explain grand strategy, we have spoken menacingly of preemption and little else. We have defined the future in terms of what America fears and desires, not what the world fears and desires. We recognize a Core that is threatened, but not a Gap crying out in suffering. We have failed in our imagination, in our words, and in our deeds. It is time for this nation to grow beyond our sense of anger and humiliation over 9/11, and the first foolish notion we must discard is that the only way we can make the future safe is to partition it through "empire."

America does not shrink the Gap to conquer the Gap, but to invite two billion people to join something better and safer in the Core. Empires involve enforcing maximum rule sets, where the leader tells the led not just what they cannot do but what they must do. This has never been the American way of war or peace, and does not reflect our system of governance. We enforce minimum rule sets, carefully ruling out only the most obviously destructive behavior. We push connectivity above all else, letting people choose what to do with those ties, that communication, and all those possibilities. Many in the Gap, and not just a few in the Core, will choose to opt out.

That is not the problem we seek to address. We know that violence and injustice are universally associated with involuntary disconnectedness. We know those who seek those conditions do so with the worst of intentions, full of hatred for the world beyond their exclusionary dreams of the "good life." We were made to feel that hatred on 9/11, and our natural reaction has been to recoil in terror, strike out in anger, and build walls internally, around our nation, and between Core and Gap.

Some of that firewalling makes sense. Being open does not require being defenseless or tragically naïve. But it does mean avoiding strategies designed to keep *them* out, or down, or dispirited. The concept of empire stems from this language of exclusion. It speaks to burden, not liberation. It speaks to elites, not masses. It instills fear, not respect. Empire is the absence of strategy. It does not describe where we must take this world, only where some find it today. It defines U.S. power by a single dimension—the ability to destroy. It mirror-images Osama bin Laden's call for revolution by proposing we defend the status quo, when what America really needs to do is understand we are in a race with history, connecting the disconnected before globalization's spread grinds to a halt, which would ensure no escape from the Gap for hundreds of millions and thus provide the forces of disconnectedness with a captive population.

America needs to be the one willing to rush in when everyone else is running away. We need to rescue those trapped inside before they are crushed under the weight of their own diminished expectations. We need to feel their pain, and make it our own.

Talk of an "empire" of freedom, liberty, or democracy is oxymoronic, and demands that the recipients of our largesse somehow traverse difficult historical terrain that we ourselves took decades to cover. America has seen its society consumed by civil wars on a number of occasions over our history. We can no more command societies around the world to bypass these fault lines than we can summarily disarm the hatreds fueling these conflicts. All we can offer is choice, the connectivity to escape isolation, and the safety within which freedom finds practical expression. None of this can be imposed, only offered. *Globalization does not come with a ruler, but with rules.*

America's role in providing globalization's security is merely removing from the playing field those actors who willfully disregard its emerging rule sets. Just because those rule sets look an awful lot like America's highly evolved internal rule sets does not give us the authority to demand their immediate replication around the world. America has evolved dramatically over the course of its 228 years of experimentation as the world's melting pot of peoples, cultures, and ideas. We may blaze this historical trail, but we cannot force the rest of the planet to march behind us in lockstep precision.

We are historically empowered to defeat all threats to our quest for global connectivity, because we know all too well what price we may pay—as a nation and a world—for allowing the ideologies of disconnectedness to prevail. But offering connectivity is not the same as mandating content; the former involves enforcing minimal rule sets, the latter maximal rule sets. America seeks global adherence to protocols, nothing more.

Our model is the Internet, which we unleashed to revolutionary effect around the planet; we administer this system primarily to raise its collective standards for robustness and stability. Our global security strategy must be very similar in approach: not fixating on any single threat, but focusing on keeping the network of collective security itself up and running. America can and should provide that unique security service to the planet as a whole, because as the economic and social engine of this world-historical process, we enjoy the safety of lying farthest away from globalization's tumultuous frontiers.

The terrorist attacks of 9/11 tore through that sense of insulation, triggering the natural desire for isolation. But Americans recognize the self-destructiveness of that pathway, and so we search for strategies of advance versus retreat. Where talk of "empire" fails us is the temptation to define the future as open to *us,* but closed to *them,* therefore *they* must be ruled. So there are those who speak of "imperial garrisons" that must be "left in place for decades to ensure order and stability." But for whom? America cannot be in the business of serving as security guard to the Core's gated community. Our mobility as individuals has always defined our freedom as citizens of this union of states. As that model of basic human freedom replicates itself across the Core (NAFTA, the EU, and all that will ensue), now is not the time to set globalization's fixed borders.

In fact, just the opposite is required. The increasing perversity displayed by those entities seeking violent enforcement of mass disconnectedness reflects their awareness that time is not on their side. September 11 did not reveal globalization's failure to spread so much as its dizzying speed of advance. The world is not witnessing the clash of civilizations but their individual transformations from isolated rule sets to interdependent rule sets. In our national hubris, we assume that the mere massing of our troops in the Persian Gulf will trigger a transformation of the region, when all we did by removing Saddam Hussein's regime was simply loosen the floodgates of global connectivity on a society long trapped in isolation.

By triggering that profound transformation of Iraq, we have set off a perturbation of the Arab system as a whole. The order that ensues will be driven by the connectivity that takes hold between

Iraq and the outside world. The battle we wage inside Iraq now does not involve extending U.S. "imperial" power but simply negating the efforts of those who will kill to preserve that society's disconnectedness. To the extent we succeed in defeating those efforts, our "power" in Iraq will evaporate. No empire will result, just the extension of the Core's connectivity and the elimination of yet another pocket of disconnectedness inside the Gap. To pretend that this activity—this exporting of security—somehow constitutes the advance of American empire is like pretending the midwife inherits parental rights over the baby she delivers, or that Microsoft owns copyright to any e-mail passing through my Hotmail account.

Historical analogies to previous empires are not only useless, but they point us in the wrong directions. Those who cite them approvingly commit the sin of static reasoning. The "good life" they want America to protect is not sustainable in a world divided by barriers but is instead preserved by the increased flow of resources between Core and Gap. Those who cite historical analogies to shame us into returning to our "roots" ignore our nation's past and continuing triumphs in enabling globalization's spread by our willingness to export security.

Both views likewise underestimate how America's continued willingness to play both security Leviathan and System Administrator to globalization is crucial to furthering its advance. They simply refuse to own up to America's responsibility for a future beyond our narrowly defined "national interests." The same this-far-and-no-farther mentality that fixes *these* united states at the round total of fifty seeks to limit America's responsibility for global order to "the barbarians at the gate." We need more destiny made manifest and less love for this *home*land. We need to understand that, in grand historical terms, there are only two types of people in the world: those who now live in *states united* and those who someday will.

It is not nationalism that drives America to spread its ideals around the world but an innate need to share our belief in a better tomorrow. As Minxin Pei, a senior scholar at the Carnegie Endowment for International Peace, so aptly points out, American nationalism is unique for its focus on past achievements linked to future triumphs. Most nationalism around the world expresses itself as past tragedies linked to current grievances. In short, Americans own the most optimistic, forward-looking patriotism in the world.

Even more amazing, our government does almost nothing to encourage it; it springs from within. No one told Americans to raise flags after 9/11. No government agency distributed them. No public authority dictated their use. Citizens spontaneously spent their own money on this flood of U.S. flags, many of which are produced in China. (How's that for a portrait of globalization?)

That need to share a faith in the future with others is what drives America to become the only nation that worries about the security of strangers all over the world. Moreover, where the vast majority of states define finger-wagging and economic sanctions as the upper limit of their responses to mass violence unleashed far from their borders, America will send her sons and daughters into harm's way time and time again.

Perhaps the worst definitions of American "empire" describe it in terms of compulsion, or the mechanistic notion that America seeks empire simply because it is strong and desires to become stronger. The cynicism displayed in that diagnosis is almost as pathetic as the sterile academic reasoning that defines the most powerful player in the world system as its inevitable bully. What such finger-pointing fails to understand is that this country has willingly walked away from more global power than any empire in human history has ever achieved. Indeed, over time America has displayed a generosity toward its "empire" that renders the very word ludicrous.

America, for example, is consistently chastised within the economic development community of experts for not providing foreign aid to poor countries at a level commensurate with its wealth. We are told, "The whole developed world is more generous than the United States. America does not do its share!" Somehow, the fact that America performs virtually all the Core's combat interventions in the Gap counts far less than other countries simply sending money, or—better yet—peacekeepers after the fact. But we are told,

"America intervenes militarily only for selfish reasons!" Apparently, these selfish reasons drive us to intervene in the world's most disconnected and impoverished countries. Then we are criticized for not converting a higher percentage of them into overnight democracies, which is like wondering why the oncologist lets so many of his patients die compared with the ear specialist.

My point in citing these differences in Core-state efforts to shrink the Gap is not to rank one above the other, for all such state-based efforts are crucial, even as they inevitably pale in comparison with what the private sector ultimately must achieve to integrate any Gap economy into the Core. Rather, I seek only to point out the obvious specialization that has developed among the Core's states, with each doing what it feels most comfortable providing in terms of blood and treasure. That America favors the former over the latter reflects our commitment to fighting for ideals versus spoils. Simply put, Americans believe that wealth is created in a non–zero sum manner—that is, one person having more does not mean everyone else must have less. Thus we see no logic in waging war for economic gain; it is simply inefficient. Yet somehow Americans have fought time and time again for ideals not easily reduced to crass economic self-interest (although revisionist historians have tried mightily), such as freedom from tyranny, slavery, fascism, and communism.

Now, as America wages war against disconnectedness, spending both blood and treasure, we are told by scholars of international relations that we do this reflexively, unwittingly, or merely to bolster our self-esteem and "power" (whatever that is). All attempts to explain ourselves in unselfish terms are immediately dismissed by the isolationist wings of both the left and the right as either sheer hypocrisy or a betrayal of our historical roots. If we seek to explain ourselves in strategic terms, we are accused by cynical commentators both here and abroad of fatal hubris because we prefer action over inaction, and because we exhibit no slavish deference to Europe's "lessons learned" from corrupt colonial empires long since buried—and deservedly so.

We are also accused of racism by stone-throwing moralists for seeking to impose our value systems on other cultures, and we are told—as we have been told so many times in the past—that *these people* somehow lack a democracy gene, or a capitalism gene. Somehow, we are meant to understand this crude social Darwinism as a more sophisticated approach to viewing the world, thus allowing us to trade in our "misguided" revolutionary zeal for the familiar self-hatred that reflexively blames America first and foremost for 9/11.

America is likewise accused of all manner of perversity in disrespecting traditional societies, primarily because of the gender equality we demonstrate in our actions and encourage in our deeds. Our critics are completely correct on this score, for this is a war of perversity. Our enemies kill our countrymen in acts of mass murder, and we find it perverse. We topple the extremist regime in Afghanistan and then let girls return to school for the first time in years, and the Taliban finds it perverse. This is a charge we must simply admit to, because the connectivity we spread cannot be denied to any gender, any faith, or any ethnic category whatsoever.

The only place where accusations of "empire" draw blood is on the subject of America adding new global responsibilities while not shedding old ones. But that is changing. It is absolutely true that our government has, with little to no public debate, lured America into a vast new array of long-term responsibilities for managing the Gap's security. During the run-up to the war in Iraq, there was debate on the war itself, but none on the implied transformation of the Persian Gulf region. To many Americans, the global war on terrorism involves a few "bad" Muslim states, not shifting military bases from Europe to Central Asia or—God forbid!—sub-Saharan Africa itself.

Yet we will conduct such massive shifts in how we permanently position our military forces around the world, taking advantage of the Core's relative tranquillity while addressing the Gap's persistent instability. We will draw down our military presence in Western Europe and Northeast Asia, because it is becoming clear that neither

Russia nor China is the compelling threat to globalization's future. Instead, we will move bases into the Gap, where somewhere on the order of two dozen facilities have been added since the end of the Cold War to better access Central Asia and the Middle East. Within the Persian Gulf itself, the Pentagon has already made subtle, little-noticed shifts, effectively ending our significant military presence in Saudi Arabia, thus relieving that regime of the political complications of having nonbelievers in their sacred lands.

But clearly, the most radical change in our global force posture involves our progressive movement into Africa, although here we are likely to see a sort of "frontier fort" model, as Thomas Donnelly so aptly describes it. These Spartan bases will never come close to the Mall of America gigantism of a Ramstein Air Force Base in Germany, but that only speaks to the realities of the operational environment we face in this global war on terrorism; the more we hunt such terrorists, the more they will retreat to the deepest, most off-grid locations inside the Gap.

This radical repositioning of U.S. military bases around the world is the surest sign yet that the Pentagon is moving toward an appropriately deep embrace of the new strategic environment signaled by the Core-Gap divide. The Cold War–era basing structure across the Core is now yielding to a new focus on the Gap, plain and simple. This fundamental shift reflects the inevitable reorientation of Pentagon strategic planning from great-power wars within the Core to small wars inside the Gap that target rogue regimes and terrorism networks. Having said that, I will tell you that one of the big manias right now within Navy threat planning circles remains Chinese submarines. Why? Because al Qaeda has no submarines. If they did, our submarine community would be as happy as clams.

A more suitable example of good Navy planning is the new concept of Flexible Fleet Response, which speaks to an inside-the-Gap, Sys Admin form of near-continuous ship presence that moves away from the strict rotation of surface combatants in key Cold War–defined "hubs." The strategic environment America manages today does not have "hubs," because the forces we seek to defeat are not concentrated in traditional battle formations. When disconnectedness defines danger, you tend to focus on the dark spots.

Concerns over American "empire" can be traced, in most instances, to fears concerning "imperial overstretch," a notion voiced by Yale historian Paul Kennedy at the end of the Cold War. The most salient definition of this fear was that America would not adjust well to the emerging strategic realities of the post–Cold War era, and would lose itself in managing a New World Order while emerging powerhouses such as Japan and a united Europe passed us by as new economic superpowers. While Kennedy's suppositions regarding America's waning years as a superpower were clearly overblown, more generalized concerns about America's slowness in adjusting to the new strategic environment were right on. In my opinion, the Pentagon spent the nineties desperately clinging to the past while largely ignoring the emerging future, only to find itself in a brandnew strategic environment after 9/11.

Did that lapse in strategic vision cost America in terms of security lost? Not really. Traditionally, the military establishment in our country is easily overtaken by historical events for a lot of good reasons related to civilian control and our republic's general desire not to let the generals get too uppity with their civilian masters. This setup is essential, as it has kept America a vigorous democracy that has never even come close to a military takeover. I do not want to live in an America where the generals are thinking ten steps ahead of the politicians. Having said that, I will say also that there are significant institutional prices to pay for the Pentagon's tendency to stick with what it knows until history tells it otherwise.

But it is also clear that the Pentagon, and the Bush Administration in general, has not done a good job of explaining all these changes in strategic planning, and that is quite perplexing to me. Americans are smart enough to realize that it is a different world after 9/11, and that our military operations around the Gap reflect that new strategic environment. The shifts being pursued in our global basing posture alone tell me that this administration has moved smartly to deal with the potential dangers of "imperial overstretch" by trading past successes for future challenges. But the search for the happy ending has not found much expression in either the Pentagon or the Bush Administration.

The Bush Administration seems top-heavy in bold decision makers and short on visionaries, and while lacking the latter is not much of a hindrance to waging wars effectively (in fact, it probably helps), this is a troubling trend for an America that stands at a historical creation point between one era and the next. It may seem facile to say that this administration has made the right strategic moves only to tell its story poorly to the world, but perceptions matter plenty in this highly charged period of world history. If America offers a convincing case for its unique leadership role in global security management, we may not only secure the "unipolar moment" *ad infinitum* but also leverage Globalization III into a "Globalization IV" defined by the Gap's elimination. But if America's words and deeds project too much the frightening Leviathan and not enough the calm System Administrator, then Globalization III remains at risk of suffering some version of Globalization I's disastrous retreat.

Only time will tell if George W. Bush is more Harry Truman than Woodrow Wilson. Truman started the ball rolling on a multidecade grand strategic course that changed human history, whereas Wilson's attempt at forging a new rule set—namely, the League of Nations—died a quick death, only to rise a quarter-century later from the ashes of World War II. Both Wilson and Truman were ahead of their time, but only one set in motion a future worth creating. Perhaps it is telling that history records no "wise men" in Wilson's circle other than Wilson himself, whereas Truman, clearly the lesser of the two presidents in terms of intellect, proved a far shrewder judge of the talent that history was kind enough to provide.

The world needs a better effort from America in coming years, but just as important, it needs a better explanation of what that effort seeks to achieve. To that end, we need a better dialogue between the public and our nation's leadership on the strategic choices that lie ahead. Too often that entire process gets short-circuited by a chattering class of op-ed columnists and network television experts who insist on issuing scorecards on a daily basis instead of exploring the long-term issues that both shape and are shaped by the national security strategies this nation pursues. The zero-sum nature of partisan politics in this country is, in many ways, the biggest handicap America suffers when it tries to forge a coherent long-term security strategy. Yes, this partisanship will sell newspapers and books, and draw viewers to the show, but it generates more apathy than understanding, and that apathy is what lulls far too many Americans into swallowing these misguided myths about our country's role in international security.

Most Americans are constantly confronted with pointlessly hyperbolic media debates about tactics, but are exposed to almost no calm deliberations regarding strategy. Typically, if a high government official tries to engage the public or the media on that level, the immediate result is a flurry of speculation about "raging debates" within the administration (or, worse, that official's "imminent departure"), rather than any serious exploration of the issues raised. I will confess, as someone who does this for a living, I simply cannot watch most of these shows for more than a minute or two without sensing that my strategic IQ is dropping with each idiotic sound bite offered (often hurriedly so, lest the buzzer on the countdown clock drown them out). Most of these discussions focus on generating more questions than answers, because questions are what keep you tuning in. But the cumulative result of this flood of unanswered questions is a public that often feels overwhelmed by current international events, when—simply put—we need not be.

Our world is not beyond describing, nor our future beyond imagining. But when every strategy we debate has to be shrunk to accommodate a three-minute TV segment or an 800-word op-ed, it often seems that way. When you see me trying to explain this entire book in two minutes on a TV news program, you'll know exactly what I mean.

So people get overwhelmed by it all. They throw up their hands and say it's all simply too "chaotic" to take in, and do you know what happens when they do that? Only two possible pathways seem reasonable: either we *go all the way* or we *forget the whole damn thing*. Either we *kill all those bastards* or we *bring all the boys back home*. Either we must wage *perpetual war* or we *just give peace a chance*.

Absolute times breed absolute measures, and absolute judgments to justify them. The myths we make fuel this dialogue of the deaf. Do yourself and the world a favor the next time you hear one: simply ask, "Oh, really, what exactly do you mean by that?" You will be surprised what a show-stopping question that can be. I know. I've built an entire career around it.

Chapter 8

HOPE WITHOUT GUARANTEES

MY CAREER AS A political-military strategist has often felt like one long trek out of the darkness and into the light, mirroring the path I believe America has taken as it moved out from the shadow of the static Cold War into the harsh sunlight of this tumultuous Era of Globalization. That journey has been difficult for me personally, because as a natural top-down thinker, I spent much of the nineties deeply frustrated with my inability to get a firm grip on the "big picture" of how the world worked and how global change unfolded. So the first half of my career I played mostly the critic of other people's visions, not someone who generated his own. Then my firstborn's long struggle with cancer put my family on another trajectory, and as her match with a beast from hell segued into a life worth living, I felt compelled in my work to define a future worth creating. So the search began in earnest.

When I got myself out of the insular worldview of the Pentagon community, I began to understand, thanks to a trio of brilliant mentors (Hank Gaffney, Art Cebrowski, Bud Flanagan—all products of that insular world), the deep connections between security, the spread of information technology, and the financial underpinnings of globalization. At that point, I stopped quoting others and began to quote myself. I stopped criticizing other visions and began shaping my own. I stopped trying to fit the world into sterile academic models and began to see it for what it was. In my research of the late 1990s, this Core-Gap model slowly came into focus, only to be made imperative once the terrorist attacks of 9/11 made clear to me the strategic tasks that lie ahead. I end this phase of my career, then, with a tremendous sense of hope in the future, more than I have ever known across a life that began just before the Cuban missile crisis of 1962, and has seen nothing but great progress in global peace since. I know not everyone sees the same wonderful arc of progress since 1962, and so in describing this future, I offer—to use J.R.R. Tolkien's immortal phrase—"hope without guarantees."

But it is beyond argument that I have seen far more "good" history than anyone in his early forties has a right to claim. When I think of my parents, born in the early 1920s, only to live through the Great Depression, World War II, the nuclear fears of the 1950s, and then Vietnam, their dark fatalism about the future seems more reasonable to me now than when I was young. But I have traversed a far different world-historical arc. I live in a world that walked away from global nuclear Armageddon, that left behind a Cold War rivalry both spanning the globe and filling it with wars, and that moved beyond an East-West divide into a global economy of great connectivity. I grew up fearing nuclear war and fear it no longer. I grew up watching wars unfold between states and see them no longer. I grew up witnessing terrorism by desperate individuals trying to draw attention to their causes and I ignore them no longer. You may see a world coming apart at the seams, a clash of civilizations, or the end of Western civilization, but I see something very different.

I see a world in which wars have become obsolete, where dictators fear for their lives more than democratically elected leaders, and where the world's great armies no longer plan great wars but instead focus on stopping bad individuals from doing bad things. I see a world in which America's definition of the big threat has downshifted progressively from an "evil empire" to "evil states" to "evil leaders." I see a world clearly divided between the connected and the disconnected, and I see ways to fix that.

The Global Transaction Strategy that I propose is nothing more than a U.S. national security vision that recognizes the primacy of these four global flows: people, energy, investments, and security. That means America cannot pursue any national policy—such as the war on terrorism or the preemption strategy—in such a way as to weaken this fragile, interdependent balancing act across the globe as a whole. Instead, all security initiatives must be framed in such a way as to encourage and strengthen these system-level bonds. We will accomplish this best by being explicit with both friends and foes alike that U.S. national security policy will necessarily differentiate between the role we need to play within the Core's ever-strengthening security community and the one we must assume whenever we enter the Gap. In sum, the United States needs to play System Administrator to globalization's continued functioning and advance, periodically waging war across the Gap as its *de facto* Leviathan.

If that is the overarching principle of the Global Transaction Strategy, then its macro rule set on security can be summarized in three basic goals. First, we need to do everything feasible to nurture security relations across the Functioning Core by maintaining and expanding our historical alliances, and increasing the Core's immune-system response capacity to deal with System Perturbations of the sort we suffered on 9/11. Second, working bilaterally with key Seam States and multilaterally with the Core as a whole, we need to discretely firewall off the Core from the Gap's most destabilizing flows—namely, terrorism, drugs, and pandemic diseases—while working the immigration rule set to provide opportunities to all who can contribute. Third, America must commit itself to progressively shrinking the Gap by continuing to export security to its greatest trouble spots, while integrating any countries that are economic success stories as quickly as possible.

Is this a strategy for a second American Century? Yes, because it acknowledges that America is globalization's source code—the world's first great multinational state and economic union. And, yes, because it asserts that U.S. leadership is crucial to globalization's advance. But, no, in that it reflects the basic principles of "collective goods" theory, meaning the United States should expect to put in the lion's share of the security effort to support globalization's advance because we enjoy its benefits disproportionately— hence we pursue this transaction out of rational self-interest.

Before I tell you how I believe a Globalization IV (2002 and beyond) works out, let me offer a quick rundown of what I believe are the key challenges and dangers that we inevitably encounter as America pursues this Global Transaction Strategy.

In terms of strengthening the Core's ability to withstand and better manage System Perturbations, I think the biggest challenge America faces comes in accepting and advancing the inevitable bifurcation of its military into a warfighting-focused Leviathan force and a peacekeeping-oriented Sys Admin force. First, the continuing effort at transforming America's military machine from its industrial-era roots to its Information Age future received a huge boost from 9/11. Not a budgetary boost, which has mostly gone rightfully to operations and maintenance, but a strategic boost that allowed the advocates of transformation to pull back from distant dreams of a near-peer competitor and join a global war on terrorism that is very here and very now.

In the post-9/11 strategic environment, transformation is immensely incentivized to succeed, especially as the strain of the occupation of Iraq alerts the Pentagon to the need to elevate all those "military operations other than war" from lesser includeds to the greater inclusive. As Art Cebrowski likes to say, "warfare is bigger than combat and combat is bigger than shooting." But clearly, much work still needs to be done. My main advice in this regard is that the Secretary of Defense should shape transformation first and foremost by redefining career paths and what it means to become a flag officer. In my mind, the quickest way forward is to eliminate service identities once a senior officer reaches flag rank. Although I still believe in having the four services, I think all flags should be "purple," or the color that symbolizes the Joint Staff and service "jointness" in general. Once the uniformed leadership of the military is thus forged into a truly unified whole, I believe the heavy lifting can begin on bifurcating the force for real. Until then, there will be too many iron "rice bowls" to melt down.

I believe that bifurcation is crucial because I am certain America still needs the "big stick" force and will for decades to come. But I am also certain that fearsome warfighting capability often stands in the way of our being better able to interact with allies and win new ones. If we are going to move in the direction of better managing System Perturbations like 9/11, to include this new task of homeland security, the Sys Admin force must come to the fore and eventually define America's security relationships around the world. This is the cop-on-the-beat force that will assure globalization's smooth functioning as far as security crises are concerned, while the Leviathan force will largely remain in the shadows, only to be used as necessary within the global war on terrorism.

One key direction along which this Sys Admin force must evolve is toward better understanding of the full potential of cyberwarfare. Up to now, the Pentagon has treated cyberwar much as it has treated globalization—a complication to military operations rather than a serious operating domain. This needs to end and soon, but I am quite optimistic on this score for generational reasons. Frankly, all the dinosaurs who just do not "get" network-centric war are almost out of the ranks, free to sell their wisdom on television networks. The next generation that assumes control understands networks in ways the previous one never could. They do more than just read e-mail, they know how the Internet works.

The best question I ever received from an audience came from an *Esquire* staff writer named Tom Junod, who after seeing my brief asked, "If your vision of the future comes about, what changes more, America or the world?" In terms of dealing with this new form of crisis I call the System Perturbation, I believe the world changes far more than the United States. It is not about turning this country into "fortress America" but merely about raising the security practices throughout the rest of the Core. Beyond that, I think the private sector will change more than the public sector, because governments in general are far more used to thinking about collective goods like security, which business sees largely as a sunk cost. Here I cite the amazing amount of public-private cooperation that emerged during the preparations for Y2K. That sort of partnership needs to be resurrected on far grander scales if we are to manage the System Perturbations of the future.

Within the U.S. Government, I think the Defense Department will change less than the rest of the federal system. This is true because the Pentagon's challenge is simply to disaggregate largely existing skill sets, while the Department of Homeland Security and the rest of the federal agencies involved in the global war on terrorism need to integrate widely disparate skill sets. To that end, I think "interagency" cooperation between federal departments has superseded "jointness," or cooperation among the military services, as the key management challenge in national security in coming years. Finally, within the Pentagon itself, I believe the way we wage wars will change a lot more than the equipment we buy or how we buy it. For far too long, too many think-tank weenies have chosen to judge all transformation efforts in terms of what appears in the lines of the defense budget. This is myopic in the extreme, and misses the enormous amount of change that has flowed throughout the defense community since 9/11. Simply put, we all need to focus on war within the context of everything else.

In terms of the second great thrust of the Global Transaction Strategy, or working to firewall off the Core from the Gap's worst flows, here I will emphasize the need for more security alliances throughout the Core. NATO needs to keep growing and soon absorb the entirety of the former Soviet Union. America also needs to generate a Pacific Rim regional security alliance that binds our military future to that of Developing Asia's and especially China's. A strong strategic alliance between India and the United States needs to be the cornerstone of follow-on security alliances that encompass Central Asia and the Persian Gulf, and that pillar will serve as the third of three that will eventually rise up and thereby rule out all war on the Eurasian landmass.

Outside of military alliances, the United States needs to continue doing exactly what U.S. Trade Representative Robert Zoellick has advocated and pursued over the past several years: bilateral free-trade agreements, regional free-trade agreements, and global free-trade agreements. None should be prioritized over another, and all should be pursued to their earliest common denominators. Bilateral agreements like the one the United States cut with Jordan more than half a decade ago can have huge demonstrative effects, even when the politics of the agreement far outpaces its economic logic. Regional agreements like the Clinton Administration's proposed Free Trade Area of the Americas are not just crucial first steps in reducing economic barriers to development in emerging markets, they renew America's sense of political expansion. Because of NAFTA, both Canada and Mexico are closer to being part of the United States today than much of the Wild West was prior to the twentieth century. We need to keep that sense of growing America in our relations with Latin America, which will account for the bulk of our population growth in coming decades.

Finally, in terms of the strategic goal of shrinking the Gap, I do side with those who say that the State Department is in desperate need of its own transformation. Unlike a Treasury or a Justice that is forced to keep up with changes in the private sector, the State Department has become a seriously ossified culture operating in an ever-changing global landscape. Full of regional area experts, the State Department has developed the negative skill set of always being able to tell you why the change America seeks abroad is simply too hard to achieve, and then doing its best to fulfill that prophecy. While it is true that America can always become more cognizant of cultural differences around the world, we need a State Department that promotes a shrink-the-Gap strategy in ways Defense will never be able to pursue. At it stands today, the State Department stands for absolutely no strategic vision whatsoever within the U.S. national security establishment, and that is a crying shame. Here I agree with Newt Gingrich (six words I never expected to write): The State Department needs a complete overhaul and now.

The main foci of any shrink-the-Gap strategy should include the following: First, the Core needs a far more aggressive approach to closing down chronic civil war situations, which are driven primarily by wars of control over key natural resources. Here the Core needs to pursue ambitious peacekeeping goals, utilizing existing regional security institutions such as ECOWAS (the Economic Community of West African States) as launching pads. The model of this approach was seen in Sierra Leone, where Core military troops formed the structure of command and control, while the peacekeeping forces were locally derived. What must follow such efforts is internationally recognized war crimes courts (again, Sierra Leone's example is a good one) and new forms of deal making between multinational corporations and states dependent on the export of natural resources like energy. Here, the best example comes from Chad, where a new deal between an ExxonMobil-led consortium and the government promises that a significant portion of the proceeds from a newly developed oil field will be set aside, under World Bank supervision, for Chad's long-term economic development.

Another focus would be a far more ambitious approach from the Core as a whole to stemming the AIDS epidemic not just within the Gap but across such New Core states as Russia, India, China, and Brazil as well. Recent World Trade Organization agreements that allow New Core economies to begin mass production of AIDS drugs for discount sale throughout their own countries and the Gap are a huge step forward, but more must be done. AIDS in Africa is wiping out the very people that continent needs to keep producing if we are ever to integrate the continent into the Core—its professional middle class and its military officer corps.

Finally, the Core's foreign aid should focus on encouraging the widespread use of bio-engineered crops and increasing telecommunications connectivity throughout the Gap. The former is a no-brainer, while the latter is the simplest and most direct way to eliminate disconnectedness inside the Gap, allowing the locals to take advantage of global information networks to generate more income through more advantageous sales of their goods. These approaches, when combined with the micro-loans philosophy of putting modest-sized technologies directly in the hands of potential entrepreneurs (usually women), offer the best potential for freeing up the daily lives of children from manual labor and redirecting that time toward education. Our goal should be very simple here: keep young girls in school at all costs, delaying sex and pregnancies. Also along this line, the United States must eventually abandon its myopic focus on abstinence as the preferred prevention method of controlling sexually transmitted disease. And we should encourage all forms of birth control throughout the Gap. All women there need to be able to avail themselves of safe choices for controlling their biological futures. Simply put, America must stop holding the Gap's healthcare hostage to our long-running rule-set clash over abortion.

Perhaps the most important institutional challenge we face in shrinking the Gap is the lack of international mechanisms to encourage and manage much-needed regime change there. The Gap suffers numerous bad leaders who have greatly overstayed their welcome, and the Core needs a series of international institutions to guide this process, such as Sebastian Mallaby's excellent suggestion that an "International Reconstruction Fund" be created along the lines of the International Monetary Fund. This organization would focus on pooling expertise and resources, such as peacekeeping forces, to facilitate the processing of failed states once bad leadership has been removed. How to identify such leaders for removal? Here the example of the joint UN–Sierra Leone war crimes special court shows the way. Once the court indicted Liberia president Charles Taylor for his activities in Sierra Leone, his fall was predetermined. This is exactly the sort of approach we should use for the Castros, Mugabes, and Qaddafis of the Gap. Let their own regional neighbors hurl the first charges, and then let the Core step in and force their downfall.

If those are the main challenges I foresee in this Global Transaction Strategy, what are the main dangers?

First, America cannot have the Old Core on the sidelines. The Core networks that Europe extends into the former Soviet Union and North Africa are crucial to shrinking the Gap. With its population rapidly aging, Europe needs to move beyond "guest workers" and into American-style encouragement of significant immigration flows. The right-wing, anti-immigration politicians need to be shouted off the political stage and pronto. As for Japan, it moves beyond its long slump by accepting the fact that it has moved beyond its great manufacturing stage and into something more postindustrial like the United States. Over time, it will become the great economic patron of China, moving its production and even much of its design to that nation. It will also shed its now antiquated defense philosophy and join the Core in shrinking the Gap's security problems. Tokyo's historic decision to send peacekeeping troops to Iraq was a huge step forward in this regard.

Second, globalization cannot afford to see any New Core powers lost to the Gap in coming years through economic failure or the onset of conflicts. One way to avoid this is to make sure all New Core powers (Russia, China, India, South Korea, South Africa, Brazil, Chile, Argentina, and Mexico) feel welcome and well utilized in the Core-derived institutions that conduct most of globalization's key decision making. The Clinton Administration's push to expand the G-7 group into a far larger G-20 was a brilliant first step, but many more could be taken. For example, the UN Security Council permanent membership group should be expanded to include all these states, plus Germany, Australia, and Japan, and the practice of letting one permanent member's veto hold up all actions should be abolished, except in cases involving the permanent members themselves. The fact that UN Secretary General Kofi Annan has openly broached this subject is a sign that reform will alter that antiquated rule set before the decade ends.

A second key way to avoid the loss of any New Core economy is to develop some international system for processing state bankruptcy. Here the best hopes are centered on the IMF and its tortuous efforts to generate a "sovereign Chapter 11" program that would more effectively deal with the issues faced by a Russia, Argentina, and Brazil in recent years. The key player in this drive has been the IMF's second-in-command, Anne Krueger, whose simple goal is to formalize the now messy procedure by which private-sector lenders and public-sector borrowers interact during debt crises. One of the key complaints regarding past IMF handling of debt crises is that the banks were protected more than the states, leaving the masses with the short end of the stick. Handling this form of System Perturbation better is a key pathway to bolstering the New Core's standing within the Core as a whole.

A third task to focus on as we try not to let any New Core states fall off the wagon are a trio of chronic security scenarios: the Kashmir conflict between Pakistan and India, the Taiwan-China situation, and the decades-long division of Korea. Regarding Kashmir, the United States needs to focus on what is best described as a failed state in Pakistan, which barely controls much of its countryside outside of Islamabad. Since that dovetails nicely with the global war on terrorism, this ball is unlikely to be dropped. With Taiwan and China, we need only to manage Taiwan's security evolution so that it does nothing to trigger unnecessary responses from a China with far larger fish to fry. Beyond that, time itself will render this security situation moot, as Taiwan and the mainland continue to integrate with each other economically. The last of the trio, divided Korea, is clearly a question of removing Kim Jong Il from power. Following the disposal of Saddam Hussein, this issue will naturally rise to the top of the list for whatever presidential administration emerges from the 2004 election.

The third great danger faced by America in this Global Transaction Strategy is the potential for the Doha Development Round to stall, which would call into question the World Trade Organization's future as the great economic mediator between Core and Gap—or more specifically, between the Old and New Core economies. The outlines of the great compromise here are fairly straightforward: the Core needs to open its markets up considerably to the food exports of the Gap, and the Gap needs to develop better rule sets regarding patent protection and foreign direct investment. The key task in making this bargain occur is getting agreement within the Old Core of America, Europe, and Japan, so again, how we treat our oldest and best allies is crucial to expanding the Core over time. The key danger, however, is that the New Core will pit itself against the Old Core as champion of the Gap's economic needs, something we have already seen in the Cancún negotiations of September 2003, when the so-called Group of 20-plus staged a walkout to protest the Old Core's refusal to cut their enormous agricultural subsidies. This group was led by China, India, Brazil, South Korea, and Mexico—all key pillars of the New Core.

Probably the most important indicator of failure in this strategy would be signs that the world was no longer as willing to buy American sovereign debt. In many ways, these are the only polls that matter in the global war on terrorism, because—as always—money talks. Ten years ago, foreigners owned only about one-fifth of all outstanding Treasury bills, but today that figure is closer to two-fifths. This growth represents the world's enormous trust in the U.S. Government, not just as a sure economic bet but as the ultimate guarantor of globalization's overall security. When the United States needed to sell a whopping amount of debt to finance the invasion of Iraq, foreigners bought four-fifths of the sovereign bonds offered—or well over $100 billion. America dips into that well too frequently and at great risk, especially if the rest of the Core loses faith in our definition of collective security.

Finally, the last great danger to success in the Global Transaction Strategy comes from within, or basically America losing heart because of some catastrophic terrorist attack or the withdrawal under fire of the U.S. military from postwar Iraq. Here again, I think the Bush Administration and any that may follow it must make every effort to sell the American people on the long haul ahead in this global war on terrorism.

If those are the main challenges and dangers faced in this Global Transaction Strategy, then what is a possible story line for this future worth creating? Let me leave you with this hopeful image, albeit one with no guarantees.

I see ten steps toward this future worth creating:

1. Obviously, this all starts with our efforts to re-create Iraq as a functioning, connected society within the global economy. Progress here will be measured in the ability of the Iraqi people to assume control over their own destiny as quickly as possible, but likewise in the sheer amount of individual transactions that arise between that battered society and the outside world. Democracy is not the key bellwether, nor is the complete eradication of violent terrorism, which is likely to last for many years. But show me an Iraq that is as globally connected as an Israel in ten years and I will show you a Middle East that can never go back to what it has been these past two decades—overwhelmingly disconnected, populated with dispirited youth, and enraged beyond our capacity for understanding.

2. Kim Jong Il must be removed from power and Korea must be reunited. I think these dice should be rolled by whatever administration takes power in January 2005, and I believe it inevitable if President Bush is reelected. There is simply no good reason why Northeast Asia should put up with this nutcase any longer. He has treated his own people with a gross negligence that justifies numerous war crimes charges, as Kim presided over the deaths of several million of his citizens during a famine that decimated the countryside in the late 1990s. These deaths were completely preventable, but Kim decided otherwise. Why he must soon go is that he willfully seeks to spread weapons of mass destruction around the Gap, in addition to running an international crime syndicate to prop up his amazingly cruel regime. The world and not just Asia will be a far better place without Kim Jong Il, so he becomes globalization's enemy number one following Saddam Hussein's demise.

3. Iran will experience an overthrow of the mullahs' rule by 2010, and this still-talented and potentially vibrant pillar of a transformed Middle East will once again assume a position of serious standing in global society. The counterrevolution has already begun, and it will continue to flare up periodically until some trigger sets off the big explosion. Current president Mohammad Khatami is a would-be Gorbachev awaiting his Chernobyl-like spark, which America would do well to engineer by making Iraq the greatest reclamation project the world has ever seen. If that is not enough, then Iran must become the main focus of our pressure for change once Kim is dethroned in North Korea, if only for the regime's continued support of transnational terrorist groups in general and al Qaeda in particular.

4. There will be a negotiations breakthrough on the proposed Free Trade Area of the Americas, and this dream will become a reality by 2015. Once this happens, or as a precondition for this happening, the United States will stop its long-term policy of dithering on Colombia's slow disintegration as a state and finally commit itself to ending the nearly joint rule of the drug cartels and the rebel groups within that failed state. This will be an amazingly messy task, our embracing of which must go all the way if we are determined to succeed. My guess is that a 9/11-like trigger will have to occur to set the endgame in motion, something that the White House can rally support around (and, yes, I know that sounds like another Tom Clancy novel). Colombia will not rise to the top of the list, however, so long as North Korea and Iran sit at the top two positions.

5. The Middle East will be transformed over the next two decades. The rehabilitation of Iraq will be a major trigger, but a far greater one will be the world moving beyond oil and into natural gas and hydrogen. The shift to natural gas alone will increase connectivity between the region and the outside world, as we are already seeing in Saudi Arabia, but the shift to fuel cells powering

automobiles will mean the oil-rich states of the region will finally have to develop their economies and move off the "trust fund" model of nondevelopment. A key step in this process will be in the massive revamping and commensurate buildup of their educational systems, which right now do not produce enough young people with viable skills to succeed in a global economy. U.S. pressure in this regard should focus on the House of Saud, getting it to stop its significant support for religious schools that, in the words of Fareed Zakaria, specialize in churning out "half-educated, fanatical Muslims who view the modern world and non-Muslims with great suspicion."

6. China will almost certainly become the diplomatic near-peer of the United States in global affairs during the rule of the next generation of national leadership, in large part because most of that future crop of senior leaders (known as the "fifth generation") were educated in the United States, and thus possess a sophisticated understanding of how we operate in the world. Between now and this decade's end, when the current "fourth generation" will begin yielding power, the Middle Kingdom will continue to behave in this more responsible fashion primarily because Beijing's confidence will continue to rise as its national economy grows, but also because the United States will learn to treat China more like a serious strategic partner in managing global stability. How Kim Jong Il goes down will be a crucial turning point in U.S.-China relations, so making sure Beijing is comfortable with how this happens is a major determinant of that strategy's success. Beyond that flashpoint and the persistent issue of Taiwan, we should focus on bolstering military-to-military cooperation with China above all other New Core security relationships save India. The biggest danger China faces in its emergence as an economic superpower comes from within, or basically a collapse of its financial system. The Old Core must do all within its power to steer Beijing away from this danger, and encouraging China's further adjustment to WTO standards is the best mid-term strategy.

7. There will be an Asian counterpart to NATO by 2020. The embryonic form of this grand Pacific Rim alliance will be a China-centric free-trade area that appears over the next decade, one that includes India, Australia, and ultimately all of NAFTA. This free-trade zone will help to erase the emerging digital and FDI divide between East Asia and Southeast Asia, and will help India catch up in development to China.

8. The emergence of an NATO-like alliance in Asia will eventually lead to a Core-wide security alliance that cements Developing Asia's ties with an ever-enlarging NAFTA and the eastwardly expanding NATO. Once the Core is so explicitly united in security, shrinking the Gap moves beyond simply integrating Central and Southwest Asia and focuses on sub-Saharan Africa.

9. The United States will admit new members to its union in coming decades, and these will come first from the Western Hemisphere, but over time from outside as well. By 2050, the United States could include a dozen more states. The first president of Mexican heritage will be elected directly from a Mexican state. But this historical pathway will not be contiguous, as we have learned in the cases of Hawaii and Alaska, and there is nothing wrong with cherry-picking the best economies as an inducement for harmonizing economic policies throughout the Western Hemisphere.

10. Africa comes last because Africa offers least. Saying that does not diminish the suffering that will rage on in this part of the world over the coming decades. Nor should that stop the Core from doing everything it can in the near term to integrate Africa piecemeal into the global economy far more than it is today. But from a practical security standpoint, the only way America will focus on sub-Saharan Africa is if the global war on terrorism becomes centered on that part of the world. When a Middle East is transformed beyond recognition, radical Muslim groups dreaming of a chunk of humanity they can break off and isolate under strict *sharia* may

well turn to Central and East Africa out of desperation. To the extent that development pushes Africa to the top of the list, the Core is well served by moving ahead on all fronts to systematically transform the Middle East, for beyond that task Africa, in great pain, waits its turn.

Perhaps all this qualifies me as a dreamer, but I do believe that all meaningful borders can be erased, and all religious differences rendered harmless as sources of mass violence. I believe the end of war is within our historical grasp, and that I will live to witness this achievement. But nothing worth that much for so many can come without real sacrifice. America must convince itself and the rest of the Core that it is worthwhile shrinking the Gap, and that the leading edge of that effort must be extending the Core's collective security rule sets into those regions suffering the worst deficits.

America has made this effort before and changed the world. Now is the time to rededicate this nation to a new long-term strategy much as we did following World War II, when we began an exporting of security that has already made war only a memory for more than half the world's population, enabling hundreds of millions to lift themselves out of poverty in the last couple of decades alone. It is our responsibility and our obligation to give peace the same chance in the Gap.

ACKNOWLEDGMENTS

THIS BOOK SERVES AS an autobiography of a vision I have labored to articulate across a professional career extending fourteen years, and as such, it deeply reflects the influences of numerous mentors and colleagues along the way. It became my practice very early in my career not to push my ideas where they were not wanted, but to follow them wherever they took me, letting the "market" discover me at its own pace. As such, I delivered briefings only to those who asked, wrote articles only when colleagues urged me to do so, and penned this book only after all of my closest mentors advised me to take this great step. It is not that I am passive regarding the shaping of my career path, so much as it has been my experience that others judge my particular talents far better than I. So whatever this book accomplishes, the credit goes primarily to those who have shaped me as a strategic thinker. In many ways, I offer this work first and foremost as a thank-you for everything these individuals have given me over the years in terms of their wisdom, support, and affection.

Three great mentors, all of whom appear in this book, have done the most to shape the message it carries, although any fault in its articulation lies completely with me.

The first is Henry H. Gaffney, Jr., a national security expert whose wealth of knowledge on the subject surpasses that of any other I have either read or known. Hank's influence on my work is so profound that I could list him as coauthor on virtually everything I have ever produced as an analyst. The numerous articles we have cowritten remain my most cherished memories of my career in this field, and I feel very privileged to have worked at his side for so many years.

The second is Admiral William J. (Bud) Flanagan, U.S. Navy (retired), who introduced me to the world of global economics through the research partnership he established between the Wall Street broker-dealer firm Cantor Fitzgerald and the Naval War College in the mid-1990s. Through his brilliant descriptions of how the global economy works, Bud did nothing less than make globalization come alive for me as a world-historical process, imparting to my research a focus it previously lacked. It is no accident that my career effectively took off the moment Bud first took me under his wing.

The third is Vice Admiral Arthur K. Cebrowski, U.S. Navy (retired), who is probably most responsible for making all the seemingly disparate strands of my thinking come together in the vision presented in this book. Art's ability to connect the dots in my work enabled my successful articulation of the grand strategy that flows naturally from these concepts. Without his guiding hand, I simply never would have made it to this point. He has elevated my game immeasurably, doing so with a generosity that defines him as a person.

All three of these amazing individuals are so much more to me than just career mentors; they are genuine father figures who have shaped my life, both inspiring and comforting me in ways they will never know. It is my sincere hope that this book does justice to everything they have imparted to me.

Across my professional career, there have been a host of others who have, in various forms, likewise helped shape the vision presented here, either in word or deed. Of this number I would cite for special recognition and gratitude the following: Phil Ginsberg, David Granger, Fred Rainbow, Jeff Sands, Andrew Chaikivsky, Susan Haeg, Hank Kamradt, Lawrence Modisett, Bob Wood, Peter Long, John Petersen, Jerry Hultin, Jim Caverly, Mitzi Wertheim, Tony Pryor, Gary Federici, Jack Mayer, Ken Kennedy, Jim Blaker, Bob Murray, and Critt Jarvis.

Deserving special mention and thanks is my longtime colleague at the Naval War College, Bradd Hayes. Bradd played a crucial role in my original development of the many strategic concepts presented in this book, being my frequent collaborator in the major research projects I directed at the college from 1998 through 2003. Bradd likewise oversaw the publication of the government report entitled *A Future Worth Creating: Defense Transformation in the New Security Environment,* by the Office of Force Transformation (Office of the Secretary of Defense). This compendium of articles and essays written (or coauthored) by Bradd, Art Cebrowski, Hank Gaffney, and me served as a sort of testing ground for almost all of the strategic concepts I offer in this volume.

With specific reference to the production of this book, I would like to thank Neil Nyren and everyone else at Putnam who not only made it happen but approached the project from start to finish with an enormous amount of enthusiasm for the message contained within. It was a great experience to collaborate with such an amazingly professional outfit.

My agent, Jennifer Gates, of Zachary Shuster Harmsworth, is probably the one person most responsible for making this publication happen. Prior to her entering my life, I was dead set against ever writing another book, believing I was genetically unsuited for the long form. Many agents knocked on my door prior to Jennifer, but she alone convinced me that this book was not only possible but necessary, and I will remain eternally grateful to her on that score. Our working relationship has been one of the most satisfying of my career, and her steering of the proposal process was nothing less than masterful. I give her my highest compliment: she has taught me much.

The last person most clearly responsible for the creation of this book is Mark Warren, the Executive Editor of *Esquire*. It was Mark who hatched the original idea of my writing "The Pentagon's New Map" for his magazine back in the fall of 2002, selecting from among the myriad strategic concepts strewn across my wide-ranging brief the defining concept of the Core and the Gap as the centerpiece of my strategic worldview. He shaped—from start to finish—that original enunciation of the vision, including its bold title. Moreover, it was Mark who directed the production of the now-iconic map with William McNulty of the *New York Times*. When it came time to brainstorm the tone and approach of this book, I naturally turned to Mark, making him my intellectual partner in the process. He became my writing coach, my mentor, my sounding board, and so much more than my editor. I wrote this book, but Mark translated it for the reader, allowing me to move beyond the narrow academic confines of most discussions of U.S. national security. To whatever extent this vision speaks to people, connecting to their hopes and fears, the thanks goes first to Mark for guiding me toward the book that only I could write. For that, I will remain forever grateful to this now dear friend.

Moving closer in, I offer my great gratitude to my brother-in-law, Stephen Meussling, who, along with Mark, was my first reader. Steve's insights and encouragement throughout the writing process sustained me greatly, and improved the book considerably.

I would also like to thank my brother Jerome for all his magnificent career guidance over the years. Basically, every major step forward I have taken over the past two decades was first imagined by him. I cannot think how I would have ended up where I am today but for his wise counsel. Along the same lines, I acknowledge the wonderful support I have received from my mother-in-law, Professor Vonne Meussling, throughout many difficult moments in both my career and personal life, and, most recently, in the editing of this book.

It almost goes without saying that this book is yet another small down payment on the enormous debt I owe my parents, John and

Colleen, for everything they have done for me across my lifetime. All the great convictions expressed in this vision began originally with them, my life being but an extension of their own.

Finally, I offer my deepest gratitude to my spouse, Vonne, who towers above all others as *the* great mentor in my life, in addition to being the great love of my life. The optimism of this volume springs primarily from the joy that is our lives together lived, our family now created, and our future still unfolding.

NOTES

Preface: An Operating Theory of the World
6 When *Esquire* magazine named me . . . finance and information technology.
Andrew Chaikivsky, "The Strategist," *Esquire*, December 2002, p. 163.
6 After I then published an article . . . and private sectors skyrocketed.
Thomas P. M. Barnett, "The Pentagon's New Map," *Esquire*, March 2003, pp. 174–79, 227–28.

Chapter 1 **NEW RULE SETS**

PLAYING JACK RYAN
16 In it, on page 19 . . . expand cooperation with the Russian Navy
Thomas P. M. Barnett with Floyd D. Kennedy, contributor, *Redefining U.S.-Soviet Naval Ties in the 1990s: The Opportunity for Cooperative Engagement* (Alexandria, Va.: Center for Naval Analyses, 1991).
17 Only about half of the ideas . . . in the "Good" scenario.
I reviewed the state of U.S.-Russian naval cooperation in the mid-1990s, eventually interviewing a number of Russian naval leaders in Moscow as part of the process. For details, see Thomas P. M. Barnett with Henry H. Gaffney, Jr., and Floyd D. Kennedy, Jr., *Future Visions of U.S.-Russian Naval Cooperation: What Is to Be Done?* (Alexandria, Va.: Center for Naval Analyses, 1996).

New Rules for a New Era

21 I've long daydreamed . . . worst-case planning procedures.

No kidding, I've actually thought about this! See my *Nine Issues Concerning USAID's New OPS System: How Recent Institutional Experiences Within the U.S. Military Might Point to Some Useful Solutions* (Alexandria, Va.: Institute for Public Research, 1997).

24 I've been reading . . . eventually *everything will happen.*

One crucial exception in the intelligence community is the National Intelligence Council, or NIC. Their analysis is the best in the business and the most balanced by far. In general, the NIC attracts the best talent in the intelligence world.

31 But around 1980 . . . heavyweight of that class China.

The best single World Bank publication on this story is by Paul Collier and David Dollar, *Globalization, Growth, and Poverty* (copublication of Oxford University Press and the World Bank, 2002).

32 While the world's population . . . cut in half.

Cited in Andrew S. Natsios, administrator, U.S. Agency for International Development, in "Alleviating Poverty and Hunger in the 21st Century" (March 2002), found online at usinfo.state.gov/journals/ites/0901/ijee/natsios.htm.

34 So, yeah, global nuclear war . . . new era of dominant threats.

Fareed Zakaria, *The Future of Freedom: Liberal Democracy at Home and Abroad* (New York: W.W. Norton, 2003), pp. 15–16.

Present at the Creation

35 Present at the Creation.

I borrow this title from Dean Acheson's memoir of the immediate postwar era entitled *Present at the Creation: My Years in the State Department* (New York: W.W. Norton, 1969).

36 I wanted to become one of the "wise men."

The "wise men," as identified by Walter Isaacson and Evan Thomas in their book *The Wise Men: Six Friends and the World They Made* (1986), were Dean Acheson, Averell Harriman, George Kennan, John McCloy, Jr., Charles Bohlen, and Robert Lovettin. As profiled by the authors, the six served as behind-the-scenes architects of the Truman Doctrine, the Marshall Plan, and the strategy of containment.

39 The notion that . . . prior to the Cuban missile crisis.

As Lawrence Freedman points out, it was known in official circles in the late 1950s as the "stable balance of terror." See his *The Evolution of Nuclear Strategy* (New York: St. Martin's Press, 1981), pp. 247–49.

41 Again, why this story . . . between America and Islam.

Michael Vlahos, "Enemy Mine," *Tech Central Station,* 29 July 2003, found online at www.techcentralstation.com/1051/defensewrapper.jsp?PID=1051-350& CID=1051-072903A.

43 The most frightening form . . . "the age of sacred terror."
See Daniel Benjamin and Steven Simon, *The Age of Sacred Terror* (New York: Random House, 2002).

44 The eight-year period . . . the total jumped to 27,608.
See annual State Department reports entitled, *Patterns of Global Terrorism 2003* (p. 163), found online at www.state.gov/s/ct/rls/pgtrpt/; and the DCI Counterterrorism Center's March 1998 report, "International Terrorism in 1997: A Statistical View."

44 I won't even mention . . . predicting terrorist strikes.
See Reuters, "U.S. Army Seeks Hollywood Theories: Directors, Writers Asked for Their Ideas on Terrorist Scenarios, MSNBC, 9 October 2001, found online at www.msnbc/news/639928.asp; and Bradley Graham and Vernon Loeb, "Pentagon Drops Bid for Futures Market: Investors Could Bet on Terrorism, Coups," *Washington Post,* 30 July 2003.

44 We should do what . . . rule-set gaps as quickly as possible.
For a good example of this, see Kenneth D. Rose, "Bunker Mentality: Stock Up. And Remember, We Got Past It Before," *Washington Post,* 16 February 2003; and Nicholas Kulish, "Obscure U.S. Agency Seeks Novel Gizmos to Combat Terrorism: Air-Conditioned Undershirt, Dishwasher-Safe Laptop Get Government Funding," *Wall Street Journal,* 4 March 2003.

45 There's a reason . . . babies from former socialist states.
Ten of the top twenty source countries for international adoptions in 2002 were former socialist bloc states (China, Russia, Ukraine, Kazakhstan, Vietnam, Bulgaria, Cambodia, Belarus, Romania, and Poland). Together they accounted for just over two-thirds (68 percent) of all international adoptions (20,099) that year, according to the Office of Visa Processing, U.S. Department of State.

45 As U.S. Trade Representative . . . "No future is inevitable."
Quoted in David Wessel, "War Poses Risks for Globalization Trend," *Wall Street Journal,* 20 March 2003.

A FUTURE WORTH CREATING

51 In his seminal 1999 volume . . . that mountaintop).
Thomas L. Friedman, *The Lexus and the Olive Tree: Understanding Globalization* (New York: Farrar, Straus and Giroux, 1999).

51 At the other end . . . "fault line wars").
Samuel Huntington, *The Clash of Civilizations and the Remaking of World Order* (New York: Simon & Schuster, 1996).

52 His 2003 book . . . or even that they occupy the same world."
Robert Kagan, *Of Paradise and Power: America and Europe in the New World Order* (New York: Knopf, 2003), p. 3.

53 So when I hear journalist . . . I get more than a little nervous.
Robert D. Kaplan, *Warrior Politics: Why Leadership Demands a Pagan Ethos* (New York: Random House, 2002).

53 Let's not kid ourselves . . . the military management of "empire."

For examples, see Robert D. Kaplan, "Supremacy by Stealth: Ten Rules for Managing the World," *The Atlantic,* July/August 2003, pp. 66–83; Andrew J. Bacevich, *American Empire: The Realities and Consequences of U.S. Diplomacy* (Cambridge, Mass.: Harvard University Press, 2002); and Max Boot, *The Savage Wars of Peace: Small Wars and the Rise of American Power* (New York: Basic Books, 2002).

55 So when China, India, and Brazil . . . that is a bad sign.

For example, see John Kifner, "India Decides Not to Send Troops to Iraq Now: A Preference for Medical Aid; An Eye on Local Politics," *New York Times,* 15 July 2003.

55 According to the National Intelligence . . . India, China, Brazil, and Russia.

David F. Gordon, *The Next Wave of HIV/AIDS: Nigeria, Ethiopia, Russia, India, and China* (National Intelligence Council Intelligence Community Assessment 2002-04D, September 2002), found online at www.cia.gov/nic/pubs/index.htm.

55 Not surprisingly . . . stem this rising tide without bankrupting themselves.

For details on the tenuous agreement finally reached on this subject, see Scott Miller, "WTO Drug Pact Lifts Trade Talks," *Wall Street Journal,* 2 September 2003.

Chapter 2. **THE RISE OF THE "LESSER INCLUDEDS"**

THE MANTHORPE CURVE

63 This group of "flags," . . . strategic naval vision for the post–Cold War era.

The five members of the flag-level working group were Rear Admiral E. B. "Ted" Baker, Rear Admiral R. C. "Sweetpea" Allen, Rear Admiral D. R. "Dave" Oliver, Major General M. P. "Matt" Caulfield, and Brigadier General C. E. "Chuck" Wilhelm. The three-star cochairs were Vice Admiral L. W. "Snuffy" Smith and Lieutenant General H. C. "Hank" Stackpole.

67 The chart featured two axes . . . threat, gauged from low to high.

The original chart was entitled "ASSUMPTIONS." The vertical axis was labeled, "INTENTIONS/CAPABILITIES TO CHALLENGE U.S. NATIONAL INTERESTS," and the horizontal axis was labeled, "U.S. PLANNING HORIZON" (with the three tics being just as I have displayed in my re-creation: 1990, 2000, and 2010). The exact label for the left-hand side of the curve was "GLOBAL (SOVIET) THREAT—COLLAPSE," and for the right-hand it was "GLOBAL THREAT—20 YR REVIVAL." The Rest of the World line was labeled, "ROW CHALLENGES—GRADUALLY INCREASING CAPABILITIES/LESS RE-

STRAINED INTENTIONS." It was the Pentagon standard at that time to put all bullets and labels in ALL CAPS!

72 Oliver had previously warned . . . with his bare teeth (which he did).

Admiral Oliver was not only a colorful figure and major strategic thinker within the Navy, he also served as technical consultant to director John Mc-Tiernan during the filming of the Paramount Studios film *Hunt for Red October*. Oliver kept a framed movie poster, signed by the director, in his Pentagon office.

73 In 1992, the idea seemed sacrilegious . . . implemented by the Navy today.

Four Ohio-class SSBNs, or ballistic-missile submarines, are currently being re-fitted as SSGNs, or guided-missile submarines. Each submarine will feature the capacity to launch 154 Tomahawk cruise missiles and deploy five dozen to six dozen Navy SEALs, or Special Operation forces. For details on this experiment, see David Nagle, "*Giant Shadow* Experiment Tests New SSGN Capabilities," *Navy Newsstand: The Source for Navy News,* 28 January 2003, found online at www.news.navy.mil/search/display.asp?story_id=5559.

74 In the final version, . . . to *use* command of the seas."

That slide is found in Enclosure 2, "The Strategic Concept of the Naval Service: A New Era—A New Course," in Thomas P. M. Barnett and Ferd V. Neider, Center for Naval Analyses Memorandum for the Record 92-0527 (Final Report of the Naval Force Capabilities Planning Effort [Phases I & II]), 23 March 1992.

The Fracturing of the Security Market

83 In my career, I have found . . . transnational terrorists).

I came across these three levels of perspective first in Kenneth Waltz's seminal volume *Man, the State and War: A Theoretical Analysis* (New York: Columbia University Press, 1954) and have employed it ever since.

84 Despite the fact that the Cold War . . . paradigm is one of my-army-against-your-army.

I have long called this tendency of the military to focus their gaze on the nation-state level the "Willie Sutton effect," after the famous bandit who, when asked why he robbed banks, replied, "Because that's where the money is." In other words, nation-states have long served as the preeminent collection point (i.e., taxes) for collective security efforts (militaries).

86 State-to-state arms transfers . . . backward states.

For the story on the ballooning global trade in small arms in the early 1990s, see *Lethal Commerce: The Global Trade in Small Arms and Light Weapons,* Jeffrey Boutwell, Michael T. Klare, and Laura W. Reed, eds. (Cambridge, Mass.: American Academy of Arts and Sciences, 1995). For analysis of its cost in lives, see the working paper entitled "Global Trade in Small Arms: Health Effects and Interventions," jointly published by the International Physicians for the Prevention of Nuclear War and the Small-Arms/Firearms Education and Research Network (SAFER-Net), found online at www.guncontrol.ca/Content/Temp/IPPNW-Global_health_.PDF.

86 According to the Small Arms Survey . . . of military small arms.

For more details, see their *Small Arms Survey 2003* found online at www.smallarmssurvey.org/publications/yb_2003.htm.

86 Factor in the growth . . . their security needs in the post–Cold War era.

For example, in the United States alone, the private sector is estimated to spend somewhere in the range of $50 billion to $60 billion annually on security, according to the Federal Reserve Bank of New York; see Roy Harris, "What Price Security?," *CFO Magazine,* 1 July 2003, found online at www.cfo.com/article/1,5309,9859%7C%7CM%7C626,00.html. What could logically be added to that is all the spending by individuals for home security systems, personal firearms, etc.

How 9/11 Saved the Pentagon from Itself

98 I reunited with . . . the Transitioneers, Big Sticks, and Cold Worriers.

Thomas P. M. Barnett and Henry H. Gaffney, Jr., "It's Going to Be a Bumpy Ride," *Proceedings of the U.S. Naval Institute,* January 1993, pp. 23–26. The article was cited in 1998 in *Proceedings'* 100th-anniversary issue as one of the best articles in the history of the journal.

98 By showing naval leaders . . . had to be made given budgetary constraints.

Thomas P. M. Barnett and Henry H. Gaffney, Jr., *Reconciling Strategy and Forces Across an Uncertain Future: Three Alternative Visions* (Alexandria, Va.: Center for Naval Analyses, 1993).

102 These long overseas deployments . . . greater workload for the same pay.

For recent overviews on this growing issue, see Kevin Sullivan, " 'Weekend Warriors' No More: National Guard's Expanded Role in Iraq Means More Combat Time, Greater Risks," *Washington Post,* 19 July 2003; Christine Dugas, "When Duty Calls, They Suffer: Self-Employed Reservists Can Return to Fiscal Devastation," *USA Today,* 17 April 2003; and Steven Greenhouse, "Balancing Their Duty to Family and Nation: For Some, Overseas and Overextended," *New York Times,* 22 June 2003.

104 As Secretary of Defense . . . regarding a transformation that "cannot wait."

Donald H. Rumsfeld, "Beyond This War on Terrorism," *Washington Post,* 1 November 2001.

104 In effect, 9/11 signaled . . . long-term desires and near-term realities.

Bill Keller, "The Fighting Next Time: Why Reformers Believe That Preparing the Military for Next-Generation Warfare Is Radical and Crucial—and One More Casualty of 9/11," *New York Times Magazine,* 10 March 2002, pp. 32–36.

105 As *Washington Post* columnist . . . well-motivated boots on the ground.

David Ignatius, "Standoffish Soldiering," *Washington Post,* 5 August 2003.

105 As author Max Boot points out . . . two world wars in rapid succession.
Max Boot, *Savage Wars of Peace,* p. 351.

Chapter 3. DISCONNECTEDNESS DEFINES DANGER

HOW I LEARNED TO THINK HORIZONTALLY

112 For example, in my Ph.D. dissertation . . . foreign policy independence.
My dissertation, which was overseen by Professors Adam Ulam, Joseph Nye, and Houchang Chehabi, was later published as *Romanian and East German Policies in the Third World: Comparing the Strategies of Ceauşescu and Honecker* (Westport, Conn.: Praeger Publishing, 1992).

118 Then the military would rapidly . . . virtually no warning time.
In reality, studies of such crisis responses indicates that "warning time" is substantial as a rule. For details, see H. H. Gaffney, *Warning Time for U.S. Forces' Responses to Situations: A Selective Study* (Alexandria, Va.: Center for Strategic Studies, 2002).

119 Think about our secretaries of state . . . aid package in return.
For a good example of this, see Peter Baker, "Iraq's Neighborhood Thick with U.S. Arms: Weapons and Technology Traded for Support," *Washington Post,* 5 February 2003.

MAPPING GLOBALIZATION'S FRONTIER

125 If you are one of . . . escape the mullahs' censorship.
Nazila Fathi, "Taboo Surfing: Click Here for Iran . . . ," *New York Times,* 4 August 2002.

126 Barbie has become a doll on the run.
Associated Press, "Barbie Dolls Confiscated in Iran," 22 May 2002.

126 By the time the wave of violence . . . people lay dead in the streets.
Marc Lacey, "Fiery Zealotry Leaves Nigeria in Ashes Again," *New York Times,* 29 November 2002.

126 Soon after, the Miss World . . . from the Functioning Core of globalization.
Alan Cowell, "Religious Violence in Nigeria Drives Out Miss World Event," *New York Times,* 23 November 2002.

126 But most modernizing societies . . . boomlet among international investors.
Matt Krantz, "Internet Investors Go All the Way to China for Latest Boom," *USA Today,* 21 July 2003.

126 By that I mean deny . . . sites that criticize the Communist leadership.
Erik Eckholm, ". . . And Click Here for China," *New York Times,* 4 August

2002; and Peter S. Goodman and Mike Musgrove, "China Blocks Web Search Engines: Country Fears Doors to Commerce Also Open Weak Spots," *Washington Post,* 12 September 2002.

127 Then came President Vladimir Putin's . . . because it was now safe for it to do so.

James Brooke, "Russia's Economy Building on 3 Solid Years of Solid Growth," *New York Times,* 25 June 2003. See also Gregory L. White, "Russia Wins Nod From Moody's: Investment Grade: Rater's Two-Tick Revision on Foreign-Currency Debt Marks Dramatic Turnabout," *Wall Street Journal,* 9 October 2003.

128 Thus, the second-quarter capital inflow . . . outflow of almost $8 billion.

Figures cited in David Ignatius, "Loot Turned Legitimate," *Washington Post,* 4 November 2003.

128 It happened because the Soviet Union's first great technocratic . . . comrade China.

I first explored the notion of a rising technocracy in the Soviet Union and its potential impact on political and economic reforms in a graduate paper I wrote for Professor Loren Graham of M.I.T. in his "History of Russian and Soviet Science" class in 1986. The paper, entitled "The Concept of Technocracy and the Soviet Politburo," earned me an A grade and later citation in one of Prof. Graham's published articles ("Toward a New Era in U.S.-Soviet Relations," *Issues in Science and Technology,* Fall 1989, pp. 36–42) as "recommended reading." Alas, I could not get my own article published because, as one editor (*Problems of Communism*) told me, the field of Soviet studies had already examined that issue during the Brezhnev era, so there was no need to revisit the concept! Obviously history turned out a little differrent in the Gorbachev era, thus leaving us with no more "problems of communism."

129 In terms of economic freedom . . . the same in terms of its legal rule sets.

Erik Eckholm, "Petitioners Urge China to Enforce Legal Rights," *New York Times,* 2 June 2003; Peter Wonacott, "Poisoned at Plant, Mr. Wu Became a Labor Crusader: Legal Reforms in China Have Created an Army of Self-Taught Attorneys," *Wall Street Journal,* 21 July 2003; and Chris Buckley, "Capitalists in Chinese Legislature Speak Out for Property Rights," *New York Times,* 12 March 2003.

131 As Dani Rodrik points out . . . protectionist economies until quite recently.

Dani Rodrik, "Globalization for Whom: Time to Change the Rules—and Focus on Poor Workers," *Harvard Magazine,* July–August 2002, p. 30.

132 Good evidence of a lack . . . or a recent state bankruptcy.

Using historical data, Jeffrey D. Sachs argues that state financial failures are a very strong predictor of subsequent U.S. military interventions; see his "The Strategic Significance of Global Inequality," *Washington Quarterly,* Summer 2001, pp. 187–98.

133 In Africa, this is known . . . Taylor being just the latest in a very long line.

Wil Haygood, "A Big Man Fails Another African Nation," *Washington Post,* 13 July 2003; and Tim Weiner, "Ex-Leader Stole $100 Million from Liberia, Records Show," *New York Times,* 18 September 2003.

133 North Korea's Kim Jong Il . . . down the path toward hereditary succession.

Peter Carlson, "Sins of the Son: Kim Jong Il's North Korea Is in Ruins, but Why Should That Spoil His Fun?" *Washington Post,* 11 May 2003; Steve Levine, "Odd Family Drama in Kazakhstan Dims Democratic Hopes," *Wall Street Journal,* 12 September 2002; Susan B. Glasser, "Ailing Azerbaijani's Son Named Premier: Stage Set for the Handover of Power; Democratic Opposition Denounces Move as 'Illegal,'" *Washington Post,* 5 August 2003; and Seth Mydans, "Free of Marx, but Now in the Grip of a Dynasty," *New York Times,* 15 October 2003.

133 Historically speaking, countries . . . least connected states in the world.

For an excellent summary, see Daphne Eviatar, "Striking It Poor: Oil as a Curse," *New York Times,* 7 June 2003.

134 In several sub-Saharan African . . . battles between various rebel factions.

Paul Collier, "The Market for Civil War," *Foreign Policy,* May–June 2003, pp. 38–45.

134 For example, lacking . . . retard integration into the global economy.

Ricardo Hausmann, "Prisoners of Geography," *Foreign Policy,* January–February 2001, pp. 45–53

134 It is estimated that . . . porous borders with Argentina, Brazil, and Bolivia.

Tony Smith, "Contraband Is Big Business in Paraguay," *New York Times,* 10 June 2003.

134 Under normal circumstances . . . loose rule set regarding shipping registries.

Marc Lifsher, "Landlocked Bolivia Is Making Waves on the High Seas," *Wall Street Journal,* 23 October 2002.

135 States that engage in smuggling . . . addition to selling counterfeit currencies.

Jay Solomon and Hae Won Choi, "In North Korea, Secret Cash Hoard Props Up Regime: Defectors, Intelligence Sources Say Division 39 Supplies Billions to Kim Jong Il: Ginseng and Counterfeit Bills," *Wall Street Journal,* 14 July 2003; and Doug Struck, "Heroin Trail Leads to North Korea," *Washington Post,* 12 May 2003.

135 A recent World Values Survey . . . divorce, abortion, and homosexuality.

Ronald Inglehart and Pippa Norris, "The True Clash of Civilizations," *Foreign Policy,* March–April 2003, pp. 63–70.

136 The men took over . . . women were struggling to find customers.

Simon Romero, "Weavers Go Dot-Com, and Elders Move In," *New York Times,* 28 March 2000.

136 Based on that sort of success . . . a global high-tech hub.

G. Pascal Zachary, "Searching for a Dial Tone in Africa: Internet Makes Telephone Service Less Expensive and More Reliable," *New York Times,* 5 July 2003.

137 Since Iraq had simply been passed over . . . wireline industry was antiquated.

Yuki Noguchi, "With War, Satellite Industry Is Born Again," *Washington Post,* 17 April 2003.

137 Based on cell phone penetration . . . out of a total population of twenty million.

Chip Cummins, "Business Mobilizes for Iraq: Kuwaiti Entrepreneurs Say Millions of Iraqis Will Want Cars, Cellphones, Refrigerators," *Wall Street Journal,* 24 March 2003.

MINDING THE GAP

138 A colleague of mine at CNA . . . presidential administrations (1977–1991).

Adam Siegel, *The Use of Naval Forces in the Post-War Era: U.S. Navy and U.S. Marine Corps Crisis Response Activity 1946–1989* (Alexandria, Va.: Center for Naval Analyses, 1991).

139 Competing think tanks . . . service-specific crisis responses.

Air Staff Historical Office, U.S. Air Force, *The United States Air Force and U.S. National Security: A Historical Perspective 1947–1990* (1991); and Special Assistant for Model Validation of the Concepts Analysis Agency, U.S. Army, *Force Employment Study* (1991).

139 When I began building this all-service database . . . to the end of the Cold War.

Thomas P. M. Barnett and Linda D. Lancaster, L.Cdr., USN, *Answering the 9-1-1 Call: U.S. Military and Naval Crisis Response Activity, 1977–1991* (Alexandria, Va.: Center for Naval Analyses, 1992).

143 If America seems to be acting . . . presence in Central and Southwest Asia.

For an example of this possible pathway, see Jeanne Whalen, "Vying for Dominance in Georgia: U.S.-Russian Frictions Surface Amid Delicate Alliance on Terror," *Wall Street Journal,* 8 October 2002.

146 And that is exactly what I thought . . . Gaffney at the Center for Naval Analyses.

For details on these trends, see W. Eugene Cobble, H. H. Gaffney, and Dimitry Gorenburg, *For the Record: All U.S. Forces' Responses to Situations, 1970–2000* (Alexandria, Va.: Center for Strategic Studies, June 2003).

To Live and Die in the Gap

155 Hussein's regime was . . . much less identify the remains.

Eric Schmitt, "Wolfowitz Visits Mass Graveyards of Hussein's Victims and Promises Help in Hunting Killers: Allied Investigators Have Discovered 62 Killing Fields," *New York Times,* 20 July 2003.

161 When the philosopher Thomas Hobbes . . . nasty, brutish, and short."

Thomas Hobbes, *Leviathan,* chap. 13, p. 62, in the original edition published in 1651.

162 In numerous African states, the poverty rates rise as high as 60 to 70 percent.

Data culled from the 2003 edition of the World Bank's *World Development Indicators.*

162 In contrast . . . close to two-thirds are located within the Core.

Freedom House's annual survey is found online at www.freedomhouse.org.

163 In contrast, nine out of every ten states . . . every four to six years.

The CIA's *World Factbook* is found online at www.cia.gov/cia/publications/factbook. I am indebted to LCDR Thad J. Dobbert, U.S. Navy, for conducting this research.

163 However, if we are to look at the 50 states . . . but one (South Africa) lie within the Gap.

Demographic data culled from the CIA's *World Factbook.*

163 All of the countries in the world . . . thirty-five years old are located in the Core.

Demographic data culled from the CIA's *World Factbook.* Life expectancy inside the Gap averages 61 years (averaging by country totals), and inside the Core 74 years. The global average is 63 years.

163 It is a general rule . . . by young males under the age of thirty.

Criminal data supporting this observation, both in terms of single-offender and multiple-offender victimizations, can be culled from the U.S. Department of Justice's Bureau of Justice Statistics, found online at www.ojp.usdoj.gov/bjs.

163 Right now the Middle East . . . rates combined with deaths from AIDS.

Data culled from U.S. Bureau of the Census and compiled by the National Intelligence Council.

164 No matter what list of "current conflicts" . . . squarely inside the Gap.

See the conflict databases posted at www.cidcm.umd.edu, www.globalsecurity.org, and www.fas.org.

164 Virtually all originate in the Gap . . . actually makes it into the Core.

Data culled from United Nations databases, found online at www.un.org. I am indebted to CDR Alan L. Boyer for conducting this research.

164 In the recent long-running war in the Congo . . . recruiting child soldiers.

Cited in Somini Sengupta, "Innocence of Youth Is Victim of Congo War," *New*

York Times, 23 June 2003; see also Emily Wax, "Toting AK-47s Instead of Book Bags: Liberia Faces Challenge of Disarming Children," *Washington Post,* 25 August 2003.

165 Of the sixteen current United Nations peacekeeping . . . fall inside the Gap.

Data culled from United Nations Web site (www.un.org). As of October 2003, the sixteen missions were to Afghanistan, Cyprus, Democratic Republic of Congo, East Timor, Ethiopia-Eritrea, Georgia, India-Pakistan, Iraq-Kuwait, Israel-Egypt, Israel-Syria, Ivory Coast, Kosovo, Lebanon, Liberia, Middle East, Sierra Leone, and Western Sahara.

165 Of the eighteen countries . . . from unexploded bombs, all lie within the Gap.

Data obtained from U.S. Department of State, Humanitarian Demining Program. The countries listed are Afghanistan, Angola, Bosnia and Herzegovina, Cambodia, Chad, Croatia, Egypt, Eritrea, Ethiopia, Iran, Iraq, Laos, Mozambique, Myanmar, Somalia, Thailand, Vietnam, and Zimbabwe.

165 Of the three dozen groups . . . 31 operate primarily inside the Gap.

Information gathered from U.S. State Department's annual report, *Patterns of Global Terrorism 2002,* found online at www.state.gov/s/ct/rls/pgtrpt/2002/. The 31 groups are Abu Nidal, Abu Sayyaf Group (Philippines), Al-Aqsa Martyrs Brigade (West Bank), Al-Gama'a al-Islamiyya (Egypt), Armed Islamic Group (Algeria), Asbat al-Ansar (Lebanon), Communist Party of Philippines/New People's Army, Hamas (West Bank), Harakat ul-Mujahidin (Pakistan), Hizballah (Lebanon), Islamic Movement of Uzbekistan, Jaish-e-Mohammed (Pakistan), Jemaah Islamiya (Southeast Asia) , Al-Jihad (Egypt), Kahane Chai (Israel), Kurdistan Workers' Party (Turkey), Lashkar-e-Tayyiba (Pakistan), Lashkar I Jhangvi (Pakistan), Liberation Tigers of Tamil Eelam (Sri Lanka), Mujahedin-eKhalq Organization (Iran), National Liberation Army—Colombia, The Palestine Islamic Jihad, Palestine Liberation Front, Popular Front for the Liberation of Palestine, Popular Front for the Liberation of Palestine—General Command, Al-Qaida, Revolutionary Armed Forces of Colombia, Revolutionary People's Liberation Party/Front (Turkey), the Salafist Group for Call and Combat (Algeria), Sendero Luminoso (Peru), United Self-Defense Forces/Group of Colombia.

165 Likewise, 19 of the 23 . . . "major drug producers" are found inside the Gap.

Information gathered from U.S. State Department's "Fact Sheet: President's Report on Illicit Drug Producing Countries," found online at www.usinfo.state.gov/regional/ar/mexico/bushdrug25.htm. The nineteen states are Afghanistan, the Bahamas, Boliva, Colombia, Dominican Republic, Ecuador, Guatemala, Haiti, Jamaica, Laos, Nigeria, Myanmar, Pakistan, Panama, Paraguay, Peru, Thailand, Venezuela, and Vietnam. The four Core states listed are Brazil, China, India, and Mexico.

165 Not surprisingly, 20 of Harris's . . . China being the exception.
 John R. Harris, "Redrawing the Pentagon's New Map," 9 April 2003, found online at www.virtualtravelog.net/entries/000020.html. The twenty Gap countries
 listed as "reluctantly connected" include: Algeria, Angola, Cameroon, Congo,
 Egypt, El Salvador, Ghana, Iran, Jordan, Kuwait, Lebanon, Morocco, Mozambique, Peru, Saudi Arabia, Tunisia, Uzbekistan, Venezuela, Vietnam, and Yemen.

DIFFERENT WORLDS, DIFFERENT RULE SETS

170 George W. Bush is making . . . road ahead is both long and challenging.
 For an example of this skepticism regarding the Bush Administration's pro-
 posal for a free-trade area encompassing the Middle East, see Paul Blustein,
 "Bush's Trade Carrot Brings High Hopes, Hearty Skepticism," *Washington
 Post,* 10 May 2003.

176 In many ways, that is the . . . all the way back to the Clinton Adminis-
 tration.
 See Serge Schmemann, "U.S. Links Peacekeeing to Immunity from New
 Court," *New York Times,* 19 June 2002; and Glenn Kessler, "War Crimes
 Court Fears Not New: U.S. Accused of Giving Up Chance to Ease Clinton Era
 Concerns," *Washington Post,* 2 July 2002.

176 Over seventy countries have already signed . . . all of them are Gap states.
 The 68 Gap states that have signed the so-called Article 98 Agreements as of
 October 2003 include Afghanistan, Albania, Antigua and Barbuda, Azerbai-
 jan, Bahrain, Bangladesh, Bhutan, Bolivia, Bosnia and Herzegovina, Botswana,
 Burkina Faso, Burundi, Cambodia, Chad, Colombia, Democratic Republic of
 the Congo, Djibouti, Dominican Republic, East Timor, Egypt, El Salvador,
 Equatorial Guinea, Gabon, the Gambia, Georgia, Guinea, Honduras, Israel,
 Ivory Coast, Kazakhstan, Kuwait, Liberia, Macedonia, Madagascar, Malawi,
 Maldives, Marshall Islands, Mauritania, Mauritius, Micronesia, Morocco,
 Mozambique, Nauru, Nepal, Nicaragua, Nigeria, Pakistan, Palau, Panama,
 Philippines, Romania, Rwanda, Senegal, Seychelles, Sierra Leone, Singapore,
 Solomon Islands, Sri Lanka, Tajikistan, Thailand, Togo, Tonga, Tunisia, Tu-
 valu, Uganda, Uzbekistan, and Zambia. The two Core states that have signed
 are India and Mongolia.

WHY I HATE THE "ARC OF INSTABILITY"

180 Now, the reporter who wrote . . . particular plans for permanent
 bases."
 Nathan Hodge, "Pentagon Strategist: Central Asia Bases Are Long-Term," *Defense Week,* 19 August 2002.

182 Jaffe went on to say . . . what it buys and where it puts forces."
 Greg Jaffe, "Pentagon Prepares to Scatter Soldiers in Remote Corners," *Wall
 Street Journal,* 27 May 2003.

182 Now, the story caused . . . strategy changes described in the article.

National Public Radio's *On Point,* "The New American Way of War," airdate 10 June 2003.

183 In October of 2003, *U.S. News . . .* the World's Most Dangerous Places."

See the "Special Report" by Mark Mazzetti, "Pax Americana: Dispatched to Distant Outposts, U.S. Forces Confront the Perils of an Unruly World," *U.S. News & World Report,* 6 October 2003.

183 First, the arc concept is old . . . the Horn of Africa up into Afghanistan.

National Security Adviser Zbigniew Brzezinski is credited with coining the phrase "arc of crisis" to describe the Middle East and South Asia.

184 So it's no surprise today . . . looks suspiciously like an encircling strategy.

As Chu Shulong, a military analyst at Tsinghua University, argues, "These developments give [Chinese hard-liners] stronger evidence to argue that the war in Afghanistan is part of a plot, a strategic ploy, aimed at encircling China." Quoted in John Pomfret, "China Sees Interests Tied to U.S.: Change Made Clear in Wake of Sept. 11," *Washington Post,* 2 February 2002.

184 When the German daily *Die Zeit* . . . comes wearing a military outfit."

Thomas Assheuer, "Der Babysitter kommt im Kampfanzug," *Die Zeit,* 22 May 2003.

186 Now, I know the Bush Administration . . . Africa being a "bridge too far."

Eric Schmitt, "Pentagon Seeking New Access Pacts for Africa Bases," *New York Times,* 5 July 2003; and Mike Allen and Bradley Graham, "Bush Emphasizes Humanitarian Role in Liberia," *Washington Post,* 7 August 2003.

187 As Daniel Pipes repeats . . . moderate Islam is the solution."

Daniel Pipes and Graham Fuller, "Combating the Ideology of Radical Islam," *Washington Institute for Near East Policy,* 10 April 2003.

188 Since security tends . . . through security at JFK Airport in New York City

For an example of this growing concern within the Organization of American States, see Associated Press, "Islands Fear Becoming a Route for Travelers with Terror Plans," *New York Times,* 9 January 2003.

188 This is what gets . . . rebels across its far-flung archipelago.

Larry Rohter, "Brazil Employs Tools of Spying to Guard Itself," *New York Times,* 27 July 2002; Robert Block, "Spreading Influence: In South Africa, Mounting Evidence of al Qaeda Links: Officials Cite Smuggling Cases and a Deadly Bombing; 'Perfect Place to Regroup,'" *Wall Street Journal,* 10 December 2002; Karen DeYoung, "Powell Says U.S. to Resume Training Indonesia's Forces," *Washington Post,* 3 August 2002.

188 Other countries where the Pentagon . . . Djibouti, Pakistan, and India.

For details see Arms Trade Oversight Project, "Changes in U.S. Arms Transfers Policy Since September 11, 2001," found online at www.clw.org/atop/911_list. html; see also James Hookway and Christopher Cooper, "U.S. to Send 3,000

Troops to Aid Philippines," *Wall Street Journal,* 21 February 2003; Steven R. Weisman, "U.S. to Sell Military Gear to Algeria to Help It Fight Militants," *New York Times,* 10 December 2002; Michael R. Gordon, "Millions for Defense, Barely a Penny for Djibouti," *New York Times,* 1 December 2002; and Celia W. Dugger, "Wider Military Ties with India Offer U.S. Diplomatic Leverage," *New York Times,* 10 June 2002.

189 A transnational terrorist organization . . . increasingly—Southeast Asia.
Douglas Farah, "Al Qaeda Gold Moved to Sudan," *Washington Post,* 3 September 2002; Douglas Farah, "Report Says African Harbored Al Qaeda," *Washington Post,* 29 December 2002; Raymond Bonner, "Philippine Camps Are Training Al Qaeda's Allies, Officials Say," *New York Times,* 31 May 2003; Ellen Nkashima, "Terrorists Find Easy Passage into Thailand: Experts Say Lax Border Controls Are Opportunity for Al Qaeda, Regional Militants," *Washington Post,* 27 January 2003; Ed Blanche, "Colombia Gun-Running Scandal Links Shady Israelis, Al-Qaeda," *The Daily Star On Line,* 13 August 2003, found online at www.dailystar.com.lb/13_08_03/art22.asp; Linda Robinson, "Terror Close to Home: In Oil-Rich Venezuela, a Volatile Leader Befriends Bad Actors from the Mideast, Colombia, and Cuba," *U.S. News & World Report,* 6 October 2003; Timothy L. O'Brien, "U.S. Officials Focus on Dubai as Terrorists Financial Center," *New York Times,* 5 October 2003; Zachary Abuza, "The Forgotten Front: Southeast Asia Is Now More Important to al Qaeda Than Ever," *Wall Street Journal,* 3 October 2003; Timothy L. O'Brien, "U.S. Officials Focus on Dubai as Terrorist Financial Center," *New York Times,* 5 October 2003; and Timothy L. O'Brien, "South American Area Is Cited as Haven of Terrorist Training," *New York Times,* 7 October 2003.

Chapter 4. THE CORE AND THE GAP

THE MILITARY-MARKET LINK

196 If anything, it had merely resumed . . . the world wake up from history."
From the song "Right Here, Right Now," by Jesus Jones, from the album entitled *Doubt* (Nettwerk Records, 1991).

199 Being so Catholic . . . sort of a Ten Commandments for globalization.
A version of this Decalogue appeared in my "Asia: The Military-Market Link," *Proceedings of the U.S. Naval Institute,* January 2002, pp. 53–56.

200 Our best estimates on coal . . . enough for the next two centuries.
Data culled from the Department of Energy's *International Energy Outlook, 2003.* For a good treatment of what he calls "The Chimera of Resource Scarcity," see Jerry Taylor, *Sustainable Development: A Dubious Solution in Search of a Problem,* Cato Institute "Policy Analysis" No. 449 (26 August 2002), pp. 6–14.

200 Big increases in income . . . other, less material factors kick in.

Survey data presented by Don Peck and Ross Douthat, "Does Money Buy Happiness?" *The Atlantic Monthly,* January–February 2003, pp. 42–43.

201 As Fareed Zakaria has noted . . . no such state has ever collapsed.

Updating (by adjusting for inflation) the pioneering work by political scientists Adam Przeworski and Fernando Limongi, Zakaria summarizes their arguments in his *Future of Freedom,* pp. 69–70. For the original article, see Przeworski and Limongi, "Modernization: Theories and Facts," *World Politics* (January 1997), pp. 155–83.

201 The same will be true . . . for oil in coming years quite dramatically.

According to the Energy Information Agency's 2003 *International Energy Outlook,* oil demand among developing economies will come close to doubling between 2001 and 2025, or from 27.9 million barrels per day to 50.7, while global oil demand will rise just over 50 percent.

202 As DOE warns . . . plans may prove feasible and others not."

Quoted from the chapter on "Electricity" in the 2003 *International Energy Outlook.* A 2003 report from the Organization for Economic Cooperation and Development (OECD) estimates that the world as a whole will need to make $16 trillion worth of investments by 2030 to maintain and expand its energy infrastructure as global demand for energy grows. OECD estimates that 60 percent of those investments will focus on electricity. For details, see the International Energy Agency's *World Energy Investment Outlook—2003,* found online at www.worldenergyoutlook.org/weo/pubs/gio2003.asp.

202 For example, while official developmental aid . . . four to one.

Data drawn from the UN Conference on Trade and Development's (UNCTAD) *World Investment Report* (1999 and 2002 editions), and from OECD databases found online at www.oecd.org. OECD aid flows to developing economies at the end of the Cold War averaged in the $55 billion to $60 billion range, while global FDI to emerging markets stood in the $25 billion to $35 billion range. At the turn of the century, FDI flows topped $200 billion, while ODA had decreased slightly to the range of $50 billion to $55 billion.

203 Not surprisingly, Singapore . . . as a percentage of GDP in the world.

For example, in 2000, Singapore's inward stock of FDI as a percentage of GDP stood at 104 percent, compared with a global average of 20 percent. Its outward stock percentage was also outsized at 58 percent, compared with the global average of 20 percent. Data drawn from UNCTAD's *World Investment Report,* 2002.

203 "Right now we're just pushing concepts into rules."

Andreas Kluth, "In Praise of Rules: A Survey of Asian Business," *The Economist,* 7 April 2001, p. 1.

203 The country came to a standstill . . . less well off in the process.

According to a Heritage Foundation report, civil unrest following the disputed December 2001 presidential election "virtually froze economic activity in

Madagascar's capital city of Antananarivo for the first half of 2002." As the IMF later noted, the political crisis "entailed substantial economic costs," but that once foreign investor confidence was restored, the future outlook brightened considerably. For more details on this story, see the Heritage Foundation's entry for Madagascar in its online *2003 Index of Economic Freedom,* found online at www.heritage.org/research/features/index/2003/index.html; and the International Monetary Fund's Public Information Notice No. 03/07 entitled, "IMF Concludes 2002 Article IV Consultation with Madagascar," found online at www.imf.org/external/np/sec/pn/2003/pn0307. htm.

204 According to polling expert . . . whether they think it's succeeding."
Quoted in William Schneider, "In War, the Mission Matters," *National Journal,* 19 October 2002.

204 On the eve of the war with Iraq . . . continuing threat to his own people.
According to a Time/CNN poll three weeks before the war, 83 percent of Americans said "the most compelling reason to disarm Hussein is that he has wantonly killed his own citizens." It was the top reason cited, with second place (at 72 percent) going to the cause of "eliminating weapons of mass destruction." Cited in Jim Hoagland, "Clarity: The Best Weapon," *Washington Post,* 1 June 2003.

205 Osama bin Laden understood this connection . . . and the Pentagon for his targets.
I first explored this concept in Thomas P. M. Barnett, "Globalization Gets Tested," *Proceedings of the U.S. Naval Institute,* October 2001, p. 57.

THE FLOW OF PEOPLE, OR HOW I LEARNED TO STOP WORRYING AND LOVE THE POPULATION BOMB

206 The UN calculates PSRs by national populations.
For details, see the UN Population Division's *Populating Ageing 2002* "wall chart," found online at www.un.org/population/publications.

206 My wife, Vonne, and I are . . . poorer, interior provinces of China.
Not surprisingly, the United States adopts more foreign-born children than the rest of the world combined. For details, see Jeff D. Opdyke, "Adoption's New Geography: Changes in Global Rules Make Process Even Tougher, Costlier; Bolivia, Brazil May Open Up," *Wall Street Journal,* 14 October 2003.

208 Right now, the best "medium" . . . nine billion by the year 2050.
The population projection data presented here, unless otherwise specified, can be found in the UN Population Division's *World Population Prospects: The 2002 Revision* (26 February 2003), found online at www.un.org/esa/population/publications. See also the division's *World Population 2002* "wall chart" for details.

209 The Census Bureau predicts . . . from Central and South America.
Jennifer Cheeseman Day, "National Population Projections," *U.S. Census Bureau,* found online at www.census.gov/population/www/pop-profile/natproj.html.

210 Because we're a relatively young nation . . . their peaks almost a decade ago.

All replacement migration data are culled from the UN Population Division's *Replacement Migration: Is It a Solution to Declining and Ageing Population?* (March 2000), found online at www.un.org/esa/population/publications/ migration/migration.htm.

212 Instead of paying more . . . service outside of their day jobs.

Mike Mills, "In the Modem World, White-Collar Jobs Go Overseas," *Washington Post,* 17 September 1996.

212 It's not just the back office–type . . . Nishara working in Bangalore.

Mark Landler, "Hi, I'm in Bangalore (But I Dare Not Tell)," *Washington Post,* 21 March 2001.

212 It is often said that Indian . . . write half the world's software.

According to Gartner, India now accounts for 60 percent of the offshore information-technology services market, as cited by Reuters, "Linux, Microsoft Face Off in India," 11 August 2003, found online at news.com.com/2100-1016_3-5062158.html.

212 Factor in the multiplier effect . . . their domestic market demand.

This multiplier effect comes from Susan Martin of Georgetown University, as cited in "Making the Most of an Exodus," *The Economist,* 23 February 2002, p. 42.

212 The rest are rich Gulf states . . . the most Core-like states in the Gap.

David Diamond, "One Nation, Overseas," *Wired,* June 2002, p. 143.

213 The difference in wage-earning . . . nursing shortage in the Philippines.

Cris Prystay, "U.S. Solution Is Philippine Dilemma: As Recruiters Snap Up More Nurses, Hospitals in Manila Are Scrambling," *Wall Street Journal,* 18 July 2002; and Saritha Rai, "Indian Nurses Sought to Staff U.S. Hospitals: Exams Cover Medicine and U.S. Culture," *New York Times,* 10 February 2003.

213 As the Philippines' secretary of labor . . . they'll come to us."

Wayne Arnold, "The Postwar Invasion of Iraq: Philippines Likely to Supply Many Workers to Rebuild," *New York Times,* 9 April 2003.

213 *Wired* magazine has described . . . so far-flung it boggles the mind."

Diamond, "One Nation, Overseas," pp. 140, 142.

213 Latin American workers toiling . . . foreign aid from the Core.

"Making the Most of an Exodus," *The Economist,* 23 February 2002, p. 41.

213 Conversely, any restrictions placed . . . can ever hope to achieve.

For details of new antiterrorist rules that threaten the ability of immigrants to send remittances out of the United States, see Susan Sachs, "Immigrants Facing Strict New Controls on Cash Sent Home," *New York Times,* 12 November 2002.

The Flow of Energy, or Whose
Blood for Whose Oil?

216 As Nicholas Kristof . . . "What did you do during the African Holocaust?"
Nicholas D. Kristof, "What Did You Do During the African Holocaust?" *New York Times,* 27 May 2003.

216 According to Scott Atran . . . you are more likely to back a radical policy."
Don Van Natta, "The Terror Industry Finds Its Ultimate Weapon," *New York Times,* 24 August 2003.

218 Worse still, eight of the largest eleven . . . economic rule sets is not occurring.
Charlene Barshefsky, "The Middle East Belongs in the World Economy," *New York Times,* 22 February 2003.

218 The value of U.S. imports . . . from the entire Arab League.
Barshefsky, "Middle East Belongs."

218 It is estimated that Muslim countries . . . trillion dollars in personal savings.
Phillip Day and S. Jayasankaran, "Learning Islamic Finance: Banks Consult Muslim Experts in Bid to Tap Growing Market," *Wall Street Journal,* 12 March 2003.

218 After all, Muslims long ago . . . reclassify interest payments as "rent."
CNN, "Financing Alternatives Devisee for Muslim Home Buyers," CNN.com, 2 August 2003, found online at www.cnn.com/2003/US/Northeast/08/02/muslim.mortgages.ap/.

219 Strict Muslim scholars . . . debt acceptable to Islamic religious law.
Day and Jayasankaran, "Islamic Finance."

219 As Fareed Zakaria . . . institutions that generate national wealth."
Zakaria, *Future of Freedom,* p. 75.

219 In 2001 the planet burned . . . 40 percent of that total was supplied by oil.
All data presented here is culled from the Department of Energy, Energy Information Administration's *International Energy Outlook 2003,* found online at www.eia.doe.gov/oiaf/ieo/index.html.

221 Six OPEC members located . . . excess productive capacity in the system.
"Conventional" oil reserves basically refers to readily accessible or fluid oil, versus oil trapped in shale rock or tar sand, which Canada possesses in abundance. For details, see the Department of Energy's "Persian Gulf Oil and Gas Exports Fact Sheet" (April 2003), found online at www.eia.doe.gov/emeu/cabs/pgulfhtml.

221 As one DOE security expert once told me . . . down on the other end, too."
I attribute that remark to James Caverly, now at the Department of Homeland Security.

223 I mean, we're right on the verge of the hydrogen age!

For a well-balanced look at the challenge of moving toward a fuel-cell auto fleet, see Jeffrey Ball, "Hydrogen Fuel May Be Clean, but Getting It Here Looks Messy," *Wall Street Journal*, 7 March 2003.

223 I want fuel cells because . . . and that's got to be good for America!

Frank Swoboda, "Engines of Change: GM's Work on Fuel-Cell Cars Could Cause Major Design Shift," *Washington Post*, 8 January 2002.

THE FLOW OF MONEY, OR WHY WE WON'T BE GOING TO WAR WITH CHINA

226 The Defense Department may . . . deep into planning the next Cold War.

For a good review of this phenomenon, see Thomas E. Ricks, "For Pentagon, Asia Moving to Forefront," *Washington Post*, 26 May 2000.

226 Every Pentagon review was saying . . . counter China's military power.

For a good example, see Michael R. Gordon, "Pentagon Review Puts Emphasis on Long-Range Arms in Pacific," *New York Times*, 17 May 2001.

228 In our workshop, participants . . . to at least 40 to 45 percent.

Thomas P. M. Barnett et al., *Foreign Direct Investment: 3 + x(Asia) = Triad Squared?: Decision Event Report II of the NewRuleSets.Project*, Center for Naval Warfare Studies, Naval War College, 9 April 2001, found online at www.nwc.navy.mil/newrulesets/FDIreport.htm.

229 Let's talk some numbers.

All data culled or calculated from United Nations Conference on Trade and Development (UNCTAD), *World Investment Report 2003*.

THE FLOW OF SECURITY, OR HOW AMERICA MUST KEEP GLOBALIZATION IN BALANCE

232 But when I ascended . . . and gave my usual brief.

Thomas P. M. Barnett, *Alternative Global Futures and Naval Security: A Briefing and Associated Essays Presented at the Indian Navy's International Fleet Review 2001*, Center for Naval Warfare Studies, Naval War College, March 2001; found online at www.nwc.navy.mil/newrulesets/AltGlobalFutures& NavalSecurity.htm.

233 Contrary to my colleagues' fears . . . their extremely intelligent counterpoints.

This exchange became the basis for a later article; see Thomas P. M. Barnett, "India's 12 Steps to a World-Class Navy," *Proceedings of the U.S. Naval Institute*, July 2001, pp. 41–45.

236 Thomas Friedman . . . and I think he's absolutely right.

Thomas L. Friedman, "India, Pakistan and GE," *New York Times*, 11 August 2002.

237 These two officials conducted . . . move beyond the moment of insecurity.

For details of this story, see Glenn Kessler, "A Defining Moment in Islamabad: U.S.-Brokered 'Yes' Pulled India, Pakistan from Brink of War," *Washington Post*, 22 June 2002.

238 But look what happens . . . jumps fourfold, to 66,930 days.

See Cobble, Gaffney, and Gorenburg, *For the Record*, "Appendix II: Further Discussion of Days: The Expansion in Combined Service Response Days in the 1990s: What Does It Represent?" As a consultant to the CNA Corporation, I generated the original "cumulative days" data and wrote the first draft of this section.

239 Of the thirty-seven major conflicts . . . per capita GDP totals of less than $2,936.

Twenty-one conflicts occurred in one or more countries described as "low-income" ($736 or less) by the World Bank (Afghanistan, Angola, Burundi, Cambodia, Chad, Democratic Republic of Congo, East Timor, Ethiopia-Eritrea, Georgia, Haiti, Indonesia, Liberia, Mozambique, Myanmar, Pakistan-India, Rwanda, Sierra Leone, Somalia, Sudan, Tajikistan, and Yemen); thirteen involved one or more "lower-mid-income" ($736 to $2,935) states (Algeria, Chechnya/Russia, China-Taiwan, Colombia, El Salvador, Guatemala, Iraq, Kurds/Turkey, Nagorno-Karabakh/Russia, Peru, Peru-Ecuador, Sri Lanka, and the former Yugoslavia). The total list of 37 conflicts (to include Lebanon-Israel, Northern Ireland/United Kingdom, and Chiapas/Mexico) was generated for the author by Henry H. Gaffney, Jr., of the CNA Corporation. The per capita GDP categories are taken from the World Bank's annual publication, *World Development Indicators 2003*.

241 Historically, the global economy has expanded . . . more risks to achieve them.

Michael Pettis, "Will Globalization Go Bankrupt?," *Foreign Policy*, September–October 2001, pp. 52–59.

241 The Party is also bribing the military . . . search for an enemy worth creating.

A wonderful example of how little things have changed in the Pentagon comes in the January 2004 Air Force "tabletop war game" in Maxwell Air Force Base, Alabama. The war game was designed to test future "transformational" force options. The "secret" scenario involved, according to a colonel who plotted it, "a near-peer who is not directly agitated by us, or us by them. But there is a third-party action that takes effect that creates movement and forces actions on the side of the near-peer that we eventually have to respond to, by nature of a third party." The scenario takes place in Asia in 2020. Not knowing the secret myself, I'm going to take a wild guess and say this game focused on China and Taiwan. But that's just my opinion. For the full coverage, see Elaine M. Grossman, "New Tech vs. Asian Threat Scenario: Air Force War Game Tests Options for Directed Energy, UAVs," *Inside the Pentagon*, 15 January 2004, pp. 3–4.

242 India, as UN diplomat Shashi Tharoor . . . future of the world."

Shashi Tharoor, *India: From Midnight to the Millennium* (New York: Harper-Collins, 1998), p. 3. Tharoor actually quotes British historian E. P. Thompson with this phrase.

243 So far, human connectivity . . . slowed or been redirected since 9/11.

For just a few from among numerous stories on this, see Scott Neuman et al., "Already Battered by Terror, Tourism Gets Double Blow," *Wall Street Journal*, 8 April 2003; Thomas B. Edsall, "Attacks Alter Politics, Shift Focus of Immigration Debate," *Washington Post*, 15 October 2001; Howard Schneider, "Ties Weakened That Bound U.S. to Arab World: Education, Tourism and Trade Hurt by Sept. 11, Mideast Strife," *Washington Post*, 8 July 2002; Nurith C. Aizenman and Edward Walsh, "Immigrants Fear Deportation After Registration: Number of Mideast, Muslim Men Expelled Rises Sharply," *Washington Post*, 28 July 2003; Keith B. Richburg, "Security Curtain Raised Along EU's New Eastern Front," *Washington Post*, 31 July 2003; Edward Walsh, "Effects of 9/11 Reduce Flow of Refugees to U.S.," *Washington Post*, 21 August 2002; and Joel Millman and Carlta Vitzthum, "Changing Tide: Europe Becomes New Destination for Latino Workers: With the U.S. Cracking Down, Jobs and Porous Borders Beckon Across the Atlantic," *Wall Street Journal*, 12 September 2003.

243 Clearly, few informed observers . . . rebuilding/occupation process.

Neil King, Jr., "Bush Has an Audacious Plan to Rebuild Iraq Within a Year," *Wall Street Journal*, 17 March 2003; and David E. Sanger and James Dao, "U.S. Is Completing Plan to Promote a Democratic Iraq: An 18-Month Occupation," *New York Times*, 6 January 2003.

243 This is a full-body transformation . . . the Middle East as a whole.

Condoleezza Rice, "Transforming the Middle East," *Washington Post*, 7 August 2003.

244 Over the longer run, an East Asian . . . and South Korea's won.

For an overview of such speculation regarding global currencies of the future, see Robert L. Bartley, "World Money at the Palazzo Mundell," *Wall Street Journal*, 30 June 2003.

244 The share of total investment . . . share rarely rose above 5 percent.

Daniel Altman, "First, the War; Now, Investor Consequences," *New York Times*, 30 April 2003.

Chapter 5. THE NEW ORDERING PRINCIPLE

248 As I later wrote of Emily, "she is the girl that lived."

My wife and I kept a diary of our daughter's medical treatments called "The Emily Updates: A Year in the Life of a Three-Year-Old Struggling with Cancer." The unpublished manuscript is still used for educational purposes at Georgetown University Hospital.

OVERTAKEN BY EVENTS

251 In fact, we spent almost no time . . . International Security Dimension Project."

Materials relating to all aspects of the project, including the final report, can be found online at www.nwc.navy.mi/y2k.

253 Then an article was posted . . . muckraking journalist Jack Anderson.

Jack Anderson and Jan Moller, "The Government's Secret Y2K Plans," *Deseret News,* 3 May 1999, found online at www.deseretnews.com.

254 In the end, plots to attack . . . were likewise discovered and derailed.

For good coverage of this trial and the associated plot, go to PBS.org and the coverage provided by *Frontline,* found online at www.pbs.org/wgbh/pages/frontline/shows/trail/.

256 It was not just Vice President . . . sent away to "undisclosed locations."

Barton Gellman and Susan Schmidt, "Shadow Government Is at Work in Secret: After Attacks, Bush Ordered 100 Officials to Bunkers Away from Capital to Ensure Federal Survival," *Washington Post,* 1 March 2002.

256 Americans did buy more guns.

Al Baker, "Steep Rise in Gun Sales Reflects Post-Attack Fears," *New York Times,* 16 December 2001; Al Baker, "Fed Feeds a New Bull Market in Private Security Services," *New York Times,* 27 October 2001; Michael McCarthy, "Fear Industry Booms as Uneasy Citizens Seek Safety," *USA Today,* 8 August 2002; and Barnaby J. Feder, "A Surge in Demand to Use Biometrics," *New York Times,* 17 December 2002.

256 Many people could not sleep . . . medication at significantly higher rates.

Linda Carroll, "Sleepless Nation: What Can You Do to Put Terrorism Fears and Anthrax Anxiety to Rest at Night?," MSNBC.com, 24 October 2001, found online at www.msnbc.com/news/646055.asp; MSNBC News Services, "Six in 10 Take Bioterror Precautions: Poll Suggest Anthrax Worries Affect Most Americans," MSNBC.com, 8 November 2001, found online at www.msnbc.com/news/654679.asp; Abigail Trafford, "Terror Attacks the Mentally Ill," *Washington Post,* 23 October 2001; and Tamar Levin, "Bioterrorism and Anxiety Are Swelling Prescriptions," *New York Times,* 1 November 2001.

256 Civil rights groups reported . . . Muslims in both America and Europe.

Darryl Fears, "Hate Crimes Against Arabs Surge, FBI Finds," *Washington Post,* 26 November 2002; Craig S. Smith, "Racism Up After 9/11, European Monitor Says," *New York Times,* 11 December 2002; and Mary Beth Sheridan, "Muslims in U.S. Feel Targeted by Anti-Terror Business Policies," *Washington Post,* 9 July 2003.

256 Governments all over the world . . . (Russia's struggle with Chechnya's rebels).

For examples of this phenomenon, see Craig S. Smith, "China, in Harsh Crackdown, Executes Muslim Separatists," *New York Times,* 16 December 2001;

Tim Golden, "Buoyed by World's Focus on Terror, Spain Cracks Down in Basque Region," *New York Times*, 29 August 2002; "For Whom the Liberty Bell Tolls: Almost Everywhere, Governments Have Taken September 11th as an Opportunity to Restrict Their Citizens' Freedom," *The Economist*, 31 August 2002; Associated Press, "One Effect of 9/11: Less Privacy (New Surveillance Laws Passed Worldwide, Report Says)," MSNBC.com, found online at www.msnbc.com/news/802878.asp; Michael Wines, "War on Terror Casts Chechen Conflict in New Light: Ties Are Seen Between Rebels and Foreign Extremists, Bolstering Claims by Russia," *New York Times*, 9 December 2001; and Serge Schmemann, "Antiterror Actions Can Be Too Harsh," *New York Times*, 12 January 2002.

256 Insurance companies suddenly . . . from just in time to just in case.

Dean Starkman, "Moody's Downgrades Securities on Lack of Terrorism Insurance," *Wall Street Journal*, 30 September 2002; Jackie Spinner, "Firms Rejecting Terror Coverage: Insurers Say Few Companies Feel Risk, Accepts Costs," *Washington Post*, 25 February 2003; Christopher Oster, "War Would Test Statute Governing Terror Insurance," *Wall Street Journal*, 18 March 2003; Richard Karpinski, "Web Supply Chains Revised," *InternetWeek.com*, 28 September 2001, found online at www.internetweek.com/newslead01/lead092801.htm; "9/11 Insurance Crisis Could Cause Major Property Foreclosures Across the United States," *Business Facilities: The Location Advisor*, May 2002, found online at www.facilitycity.com/busfac/bf_02_05_statenews.asp.

256 All that remains now . . . un-American activities in the age of global terrorism.

Adam Liptak, Neil A. Lewis, and Benjamin Wesier, "After Sept. 11, a Legal Battle on the Limits of Civil Liberty," *New York Times*, 4 August 2002.

257 There will be other 9/11s until . . . defense establishment around it.

As far as the Core as a whole is concerned, progress on this front is slow. For an example of a critical assessment of the Core's ability to withstand future bioterrorism, see Shankar Vedantam, "WHO Assails Wealth Nations on Bioterror: Coordination of Defenses Poor in Simulation; U.S. Support for Agency Questioned," *Washington Post*, 5 November 2003.

THE RISE OF SYSTEM PERTURBATIONS

259 They had backup facilities . . . business Thursday morning, September 13.

For the details behind this story, see Tom Barbash, *On Top of the World: Cantor Fitzgerald, Howard Lutnick, and 9/11: A Story of Loss and Renewal* (New York: HarperCollins, 2003), pp. 29–44.

260 When the United States took down . . . afforded unprecedented prominence.

For details, see Thom Shanker, "Conduct of War Is Redefined by Success of Special Forces," *New York Times*, 21 January 2002.

261 When the Arab world saw Marines . . . world was turned upside down.
For a description of this phenomenon, see Neil MacFarquhar, "Humiliation and Rage Stalk the Arab World," *New York Times,* 13 April 2003.

262 This is what Thomas Homer-Dixon calls "complex terrorism."
Thomas Homer-Dixon, "The Rise of Complex Terrorism," *Foreign Policy,* January–February 2002, pp. 52–62.

263 One baby in China . . . all the follow-on cases he generated.
Donald G. McNeil, Jr., and Lawrence K. Altman, "How One Person Can Fuel an Epidemic," *New York Times,* 15 April 2003.

263 It is quite possible that just one . . . China's sizzling GDP growth for the year.
For the story of the physician who is believed to have triggered many of the cases in Hong Kong, see Ellen Nakashima, "SARS Signals Missed in Hong Kong: Physician's Visit May Have Led to Most Known Cases," *Washington Post,* 20 May 2003.

263 China tried its usual . . . want to avoid even more bans on travel!"
For details, see Rob Stein, "WHO Tells Travelers to Avoid Hong Kong, China: U.N. Group Takes Unprecedented Step to Stem Epidemic," *Washington Post,* 3 April 2003.

263 Political leaders in China . . . SARS cases would be punished most severely.
See John Pomfret, "Underreporting, Secrecy Fuel SARS in Beijing, WHO Says," *Washington Post,* 17 April 2003; Peter Wonacott, Norihiko Shirouzu, and Jon E. Hilsenrath, "Foreign Firms Face Setbacks as SARS Cases Mount in China," *Wall Street Journal,* 23 May 2003; and John Pomfret, "China Orders End to SARS Coverup: Belated Campaign Against Disease Begins," *Washington Post,* 19 April 2003.

264 A Chinese news media outlet . . . senior party corruption anytime soon.
For details, see Geoffrey York, "SARS Crisis Emboldens China's Media," *The Globe & Mail,* 14 June 2002; and John Pomfret, "China's Crisis Has a Political Edge: Leaders Use SARS to Challenge Recalcitrant Parts of Government," *Washington Post,* 27 April 2003.

265 But because 9/11 begat anthrax mania . . . launching the Doha Round.
For some great coverage of this fascinating story line, see Louis Uchitelle, "Globalization Marches On, as U.S. Eases Up on the Reins," *New York Times,* 17 December 2001; "Dealing with Anthrax: Patent Problems Pending: The Rich World Should Apply the Same Rules to Drugs in Poor Countries as at Home," *The Economist,* 27 October 2001; "World Trade Organization: A Deal at Doha?: The Launch of a Round of Global Trade Talks Is Close, If Politicians Compromise," *The Economist,* 3 November 2001; and Joseph Kahn, "Nations Back Freer Trade, Hoping to Aid Global Growth," *New York Times,* 15 November 2001.

266 At that point, the Core's . . . said in effect, "Over our dead bodies!"

Tom Hamburger, "U.S. Flip on Patents Shows Drug Makers' Growing Clout: Political Donors Get Help in Reversing Policy on Poor Nations' Access to Cheaper Medicine," *Wall Street Journal,* 6 February 2003.

266 So, needless to say . . . as they crank out AIDS cocktail drugs cut-rate.

Geoff Winestock and Neil King, Jr., "Patent Restraints on AIDS Drugs to Be Eased for Developing World," *Wall Street Journal,* 25 June 2002.

266 More progress on many such fronts . . . quite frankly—too Gap-oriented.

Andrew Pollack, "Drug Makers Wrestle with World's New Rules: A Delicate Balance: Patriotism vs. Business," *New York Times,* 21 October 2001.

THE GREATER INCLUSIVE

268 The signs are all around . . . assassinations of terrorist targets upon sighting.

David Johnston and David E. Sanger, "Yemen Killing Based on Rules Set Out by Bush," *Washington Post,* 6 November 2002.

268 The Justice Department . . . priorities before 9/11, and a new one afterward.

Adam Clymer, "How Sept. 11 Changed Goals of Justice Dept.: Fighting Terror Didn't Lead Ashcroft's List," *New York Times,* 28 February 2002.

268 That changes not just the . . . cops get left holding the bag on everything else.

Susan Schmidt, "Counterterrorism, Cybercrime Are Focus of FBI's Overhaul," *Washington Post,* 4 December 2001; and Gary Fields and John R. Wilke, "The Ex-Files: FBI's New Focus Places Big Burden on Local Police: With Terror Its Top Priority, Bureau Pulls Resources from Core Crime Fighting: Little Time for Bank Heists," *Wall Street Journal,* 20 June 2003.

268 When the Attorney General says . . . that is a new rule set.

Dan Eggen, "Neighborhood Watch Enlisted in Terror War: Citizens Urged to Step Up in $2 Million Expansion," *Washington Post,* 7 March 2002.

268 When three out of every four mayors . . . screaming out for a new rule set.

Jodi Wilgoren, "At One of 1,000 Front Lines in U.S., Local Officials Try to Plan for War," *New York Times,* 19 June 2002.

268 When the FBI Director opens a new office in Beijing, that is a new rule set.

Elisabeth Rosenthal, "The F.B.I.: Ashcroft Says U.S. Will Place Agents in China," *Washington Post,* 25 October 2002.

268 When the Coast Guard revamps . . . that is a new rule set.

Edward Walsh, "For Coast Guard, Priorities Shifted on September 11: Focus Is on Defense Against Terrorism," *Washington Post,* 26 November 2001; and William Booth, "Where Seas Meet Shore, Scenarios for Terrorists: Nation's Vulnerable Ports Revamp Defenses," *Washington Post,* 3 June 2002.

268 When Washington, D.C., gets sensors . . . scream out "WE ARE HERE!"

Spencer S. Hsu, "In Wind, a Reply to Terror: Region Gets First Fallout Sensors," *Washington Post,* 2 June 2003; Philip Shenon, "Missile Threat Is Bringing Stricter Rules for Airports," *New York Times,* 30 March 2003; James Dao, "With Rise in Foreign Aid, Plans for a New Way to Give It," *New York Times,* 3 February 2003; Jessica T. Mathews, "September 11, One Year Later: A World of Change," *Carnegie Endowment for International Peace* (Policy Brief Special Edition), August 2002; Dana Priest and Dan Eggen, "Bush Aides Consider Domestic Spy Agency: Concerns on FBI's Performance Spur Debate of Options," *Washington Post,* 16 November 2002; and Dana Priest, "CIA Is Expanding Domestic Operations: More Offices, More Agents with FBI," *Washington Post,* 23 October 2002.

272 Within a short time . . . within eight to nine minutes—all at the push of a button.

For details, see David A. Fulghum, "Huge Promise, Nagging Concerns," *Aviation Week & Space Technology,* 18 August 2003.

274 It turns out this particular go-fast . . . big numbers only that time of year.

But since al Qaeda–linked terrorists have posed as fishermen in the past, there is no simple way to discount any ship our Navy comes across. For an example, see Marc Lacey, "Kenya Terrorists Posed as Fishermen, Report Says," *New York Times,* 6 November 2003.

THE BIG BANG AS STRATEGY

281 Of course, there are always plenty . . . nutty views to only the fringe types.

For some great examples of conspiracy theories, see Josh Tyrangiel, "Did You Hear About . . . The Search for Answers and a Blizzard of Information Have Made WTC Rumors as Ubiquitous as Flags," *Time,* 8 October 2001; and Kevin Sack, "Apocalyptic Theology Revitalized by Attacks: Calling 9/11 a Harbinger of the End Times," *New York Times,* 23 November 2001.

281 But then you get the Prime Minister . . . for very cynical purposes.

Recently retired Mahathir Mohamad, the longtime Prime Minister of Malaysia, made this controversial statement in a speech opening the summit of the fifty-seven-nation Organization of the Islamic Conference in Kuala Lumpur; for details, see Alan Sipress, "Malaysian Calls on Muslims to Resist Jewish Influence," *Washington Post,* 17 October 2003.

283 Nonetheless, conspiracy theories abound . . . staged the 9/11 terrorist attacks.

For details, see Ian Johnson, "Conspiracy Theories About Sept. 11 Get Hearing in Germany: Distrust of U.S. Fuels Stories About Source of Attacks; Videos, Hot-Selling Books," *Wall Street Journal,* 29 September 2003.

284 It is a task we face throughout the Gap . . . and a deficit of security.

The magnificent inaugural report from the UN Development Programme entitled *Arab Human Developmen\t Report 2002* notes that, "Out of seven world
regions, the Arab countries had the lowest freedom score in the late 1990s." The
report cites the "three deficits" as defining the Arab world's lack of development: "the freedom deficit; the women's empowerment deficit; and the human
capabilities/knowledge deficit relative to income"; cited from p. 27.

285 As a 2002 UN report noted . . . even lower than Sub-Saharan Africa."
Arab Human Development Report 2002, p. 29.

285 Recent opinion polls . . . people wish to emigrate to other countries—
half!
Arab Human Development Report 2002, p. 30; see also Afshin Molavi, "Iranian Youths Seeking to Escape: Bleak Prospects Lead Some Toward Border; Others to Drugs," *Washington Post,* 7 September 2003. Not surprisingly, the second
Arab Human Development Report (2003) highlighted the Bush Administration's tightening of visa restrictions as a major hindrance to social progress in
the Arab world. Arab students studying in the United States dropped by
roughly one-third in 9/11's aftermath.

285 The bin Ladens of that region . . . moving away from all that Westoxification.
For the origins and use of this term, see "The Curse of Westoxification: And
the Roots of Discontent," *The Economist,* 18 January 2003.

291 These disenfranchised urban youth . . . recruits for terrorist groups.
Craig S. Smith, "Saudi Idlers Attract Radicals and Worry Royals," *New York
Times,* 17 December 2002.

291 As Paul Wolfowitz has said . . . that this effort once made so much sense.
Paul Wolfowitz, "Support Our Troops," *Wall Street Journal,* 2 September 2002.

293 Israel's population agrees to this wall . . . from a youth-bulging Pales-
tine.
For details on the long-term population-growth issues that complicate any
Israel-Palestinian peace agreement, see Guy Chazan, "An Old Heresy Haunts
Israel: What If the Palestinians Reject a State of Their Own?" *Wall Street Jour-
nal,* 21 July 2003.

Chapter 6. THE GLOBAL TRANSACTION STRATEGY

298 It is merely to serve as globalization's bodyguard . . . throughout the
Gap.
I first explored this concept in Thomas P. M. Barnett and Henry H. Gaffney, Jr.,
"Globalization Gets a Bodyguard," *Proceedings of the U.S. Naval Institute,*
November 2001, pp. 50–53.

The Essential Transaction

304 Besides strengthening its ability . . . arms, money, and intellectual property.

Moises Naim explores the last five flows (drugs, people, arms, money and intellectual property) in his "The Five Wars of Globalization," *Foreign Policy,* January–February 2003, pp. 28–37.

305 Historical data demonstrate . . . reduce your attractiveness to foreign investors.

For example, see *OECD Economic Outlook No. 7,* June 2003.

306 Even South Korea . . . suffers from its proximity to its evil twin.

James Brooke, "Unwanted Attention for Korea: Worry Over the North Hurts the South's Economy," *New York Times,* 15 April 2003.

311 The same can be said for Japan . . . sports the world's largest bond market.

Phred Dvorak and Todd Zaun, "Japan's Bond Market: Too Big?" *Wall Street Journal,* 16 July 2003.

311 As the recent Core-wide . . . (U.S., EU, Japan) now rise and fall together.

Joseph Kahn, "The World's Economies Slide Together into Recession," *New York Times,* 25 November 2001.

311 One day China suffers SARS . . . and a collapse in tourism.

Renowned expert on the Chinese economy Andy Xie of Morgan Stanley was quoted early in the crisis as saying, "The economy has come to a standstill." Cited in Keith Bradsher, "Outbreak of Disease Forces Steep Plunge in Chinese Economy," *New York Times,* 28 April 2003.

311 The Chinese leadership . . . despite all those canceled business trips.

Peter Wonacott and Karby Leggett, "Despite SARS, China's Economy Bounces Back," *Wall Street Journal,* 14 July 2003. Interestingly enough, Morgan Stanley withdrew its forecasts of lower GDP for China for the year once the crisis was seen as abating due to the government's positive response.

312 As Krugman argues . . . but it's not an experiment anyone wants to try."

Paul Krugman, "The China Syndrome," *New York Times,* 5 September 2003.

314 In fact, we do well to encourage specialization . . . and peacekeeping.

For the best example of a country whose military is embracing that sort of specialization, see Matthew Brzezinski, "Who's Afraid of Norway?: She May Look Like G.I. Jane, but Defense Minister Kristin Krohn Devold Has Made Her Country's Military the Model for Small Nations That Want a Meaningful Role in World Affairs," *New York Times Magazine,* 24 August 2003, pp. 24–28.

The System Administrator

315 He wanted a copy of an article I had written immediately following Y2K.

Thomas P. M. Barnett, "Life After DoDth or: How the Evernet Changes Everything," *Proceedings of the U.S. Naval Institute,* May 2000, pp. 48–53.

317 The Coast Guard is essentially lost . . . tasks the U.S. Navy is keen to avoid.

For a good description of this, see John Mintz and Vernon Loeb, "Coast Guard Fights to Retain War Role: 'Slack-Jawed' over Criticism from Rumsfeld, Service Cites Its Battle Capabilities," *Washington Post,* 31 August 2003.

318 But this time, many were used . . . military installations around the world.

For a good overview of what eventually unfolded, see Thom Shanker and Eric Schmitt, "Reserve Call-Up for an Iraqi War May Equal 1991's: To Guard Against Terror: Activation of Around 265,000 Would Help Protect Sites in U.S. and Overseas," *New York Times,* 28 October 2002.

318 Then came the hard part . . . manage the transition and eager as hell to leave.

See Steven Lee Myers, "Anxious and Weary of War, G.I.'s Face a New Iraq Mission," *New York Times,* 15 June 2003.

318 The warrior force was . . . into an occupation force.

Some of the best immediate coverage of this turn of events is found in Rajiv Chandrasekaran, "Inexperienced Hands Guide Iraq Rebuilding," *Washington Post,* 25 June 2003; William Booth, "Ad-Libbing Iraq's Infrastructure: U.S. Troops Face Daily Scramble in 'Bringing Order to Chaos,'" *Washington Post,* 21 May 2003; and David Luhnow, "Amid Shortages, New U.S. Agency Tries to Run Iraq: Miscues on Advance Planning Draw Fire, but Electricity and Police Patrols Are Up," *Wall Street Journal,* 5 June 2003. For a Bush Administration reply to such criticism, see Donald H. Rumsfeld, "Beyond Nation-Building," *Washington Post,* 25 September 2003.

319 "Military operations other than war" . . . *country's entire defense budget.*

The President's request of 7 September 2003 included approximately $65 billion for defense and intelligence requirements related to the occupation of Iraq. By comparison, the highest credible estimates of Chinese defense spending are in the $60 billion to $70 billion range, or severalfold above the official Chinese figure of approximately $15 billion.

319 Outside of Vietnam . . . way below .500, and that has to end.

A Carnegie Endowment study on U.S. nation-building efforts following invasions across the twentieth century estimated that in only four of sixteen cases did the U.S. effort leave behind a functioning democracy ten years later. See Minxin Pei and Sara Kasper, *Lessons from the Past: The American Record of Nation Building,* Carnegie Endowment for International Peace Policy Brief No. 24, May 2003.

320 The Leviathan's speed of command . . . to mount coherent defenses.

My earliest descriptions of the Leviathan force are found in my article "The Seven Deadly Sins of Network-Centric Warfare," *Proceedings of the U.S. Naval Institute,* January 1999, pp. 36–39.

321 These groups . . . in any postwar or disaster environment but safe as well.

This was not the case in the early months of the U.S. military occupation of postwar Iraq. For details, see Ian Fisher and Elizabeth Becker, "The Reconstruction: Aid Workers Leaving Iraq, Fearing They Are Targets," *New York Times,* 12 October 2003.

321 The Sys Admin's decision loops . . . live with each other over the long haul.

For an excellent overview of this troubled relationship, see Adam Siegel, "Civil-Military Marriage Counseling: Can This Union Be Saved?" *Special Warfare,* December 2002, pp. 28–34.

321 All the broken windows will be fixed . . . *after* we "bring the boys home."

The best single exploration of this subject is by Bradd C. Hayes and Jeffrey I. Sands, *Doing Windows: Non-Traditional Military Responses to Complex Emergencies* (Washington, D.C.: National Defense University, 1997). As a side note, the Defense Department continues to rethink the use of certain ammunition so as to diminish the postconflict dangers not only to civilians but also to its own troops. For a good example, see Michael M. Phillips and Greg Jaffe, "Pentagon Rethinks Use of Cluster Bombs: Thousands of Unexploded Bomblets Impede Military Movement, Kill Civilians," *Wall Street Journal,* 25 August 2003.

321 It will remain a secret society . . . military operations within the homeland.

The Posse Comitatus Act of 1878 basically prohibits U.S. military forces from acting as a domestic police force, except when allowed by Congress.

322 Moreover, as the world's largest . . . a moneymaker for developing nations.

UN peacekeeping missions pay approximately $1,100 per soldier per month to governments supplying troops. According to Michael Sheehan, former UN Assistant Secretary General for Peacekeeping, "The cash flow has a huge impact on budgets, so there is enormous incentive to be involved." For details, see Alix M. Freedman, "First World Nations in Effect Pay Those of Third to Handle Missions: U.N. Peacekeeping Allowance Can Add Up to Real Money for Developing Countries," *Wall Street Journal,* 1 October 2003.

323 The Sys Admin force will be civil affairs–oriented . . . international protocols?

For an example of what the U.S. military was missing in its approach to occupying postwar Iraq, see Christopher Cooper, "As U.S. Tries to Bring Order to Iraq, Need for Military Policy Is Rising," *Wall Street Journal,* 21 August 2003.

325 Nuclear weapons will not be sanitized . . . sources of existential deterrence.

For some background on this issue and the current efforts within the Defense Department to rethink the utility of nuclear weapons, see Michael R. Gordon,

"Nuclear Arms: For Deterrence or Fighting?" *New York Times,* 11 March 2002; and Walter Pincus, "Future of U.S. Nuclear Arsenal Debated: Arms Control Experts Worry Pentagon's Restructuring Plan Means More Weapons," *Washington Post,* 4 May 2003.

THE AMERICAN WAY OF WAR

327 In January 1998 . . . "Network-Centric Warfare: Its Origins and Future."
Arthur K. Cebrowski, Vice Admiral, U.S. Navy, and John J. Gartska, "Network-Centric Warfare: Its Origins and Future," *Proceedings of the U.S. Naval Institute,* January 1998, pp. 28–35.

327 So much so that my first act . . . where Art's article had been published.
Barnett, "The Seven Deadly Sins," *Proceedings of the U.S. Naval Institute,* January 1999.

332 When Art Cebrowski and I . . . war on terrorism will be won.
Arthur K. Cebrowski and Thomas P. M. Barnett, "The American Way of War," *Proceedings of the U.S. Naval Institute,* January 2003, pp. 42–43.

333 Here is how I choose to define them:
This section is based on a list of such rules ("The Top 100 Rules of the New American Way of War") that I published with Henry H. Gaffney, Jr., in the *British Army Review* (Spring 2003), pp. 40–45. I acknowledge this list is, at times, more prescriptive than descriptive.

Chapter 7. THE MYTHS WE MAKE
(*I Will Now Dispel*)

THE MYTH OF GLOBAL CHAOS

347 Apparently, despite all this conflict . . . at the end of the Cold War.
For World Bank figures, see most recent edition of *World Development Indicators.*

347 According to the University of Maryland's . . . since the early 1960s."
Monty G. Marshall and Ted Robert Gurr, *Peace and Conflicts 2003: A Global Survey of Armed Conflicts, Self-Determination Movements, and Democracy* (College Park, Md.: University of Maryland, 2003), found online at www.cidcm.umd.edu/peace_and_conflict_2003.asp, p. 12. This annual report is hands down the best of its kind.

348 That would be us—the United States.
Data compiled by SIPRI. For details, see Web site of Stockholm International Peace Research Institute at www.sipri.se/.

348 So busy, yes, but all over the planet? Not exactly.
Data drawn from Cobble et al., *For the Record,* p. 33 and Appendix 1.

348 When measured as a percent . . . 20 percent of the time in the 1990s.
Cobble et al., *For the Record,* pp. 40–41.

349 Today, the total is . . . the lowest numbers since 1960.
Marshall and Gurr, *Peace and Conflict 2003*, p. 30.

THE MYTH OF AMERICA AS GLOBOCOP

351 For example, Colombia is a dangerous . . . who gets to control particular regions.
For a description, see Scott Wilson, "Venezuela Becomes Embroiled in Columbian War: Reports of Bombed Villages on Northeastern Frontier Point to Military Support for Guerillas," *Washington Post,* 10 April 2003.

352 Add it all up . . . of 191 states currently belonging to the United Nations.
Marshall and Gurr, *Peace and Conflict 2003*, pp. 9–11.

353 This theory of crime prevention . . . emboldened and commit more crimes.
For one of the earliest and best descriptions of this crime-prevention strategy, see James Q. Wilson and George L. Kelling, "Broken Windows: The Police and Neighborhood Safety," *The Atlantic Monthly,* March 1982, pp. 29–38.

THE MYTH OF AMERICAN EMPIRE

357 So there are those who speak of . . . to ensure order and stability."
Stephen Peter Rosen, "The Future of War and the American Military: Demography, Technology and the Politics of Modern Empire," *Harvard Magazine,* May–June 2002, pp. 29–39.

359 Most nationalism around the world . . . linked to current grievances.
Minxin Pei, "The Paradoxes of American Nationalism," *Foreign Policy,* May–June 2003, pp. 31–37.

359 Perhaps the worst definitions . . . and desires to become stronger.
The most thoughtful version of this frequent argument comes from Robert Jervis, "The Compulsive Empire," *Foreign Policy,* July–August 2003, pp. 83–87.

359 Somehow, the fact that America . . . peacekeepers after the fact.
For a glorious example of how these sorts of data calculations can be pursued to absurd conclusions, see the Center for Global Development and the Carnegie Endowment for International Peace's "Commitment to Development Index" in *Foreign Policy,* May–June 2003, pp. 56–66.

361 We topple the extremist regime . . . and the Taliban finds it perverse.
Erik Eckholm, "In Kandahar, a Top School Reopens, and Girls Are Welcome," *New York Times,* 23 December 2001; Carlotta Gall, "Long in Dark, Afghan Women Say to Read Is Finally to See," *New York Times,* 22 September 2002; and Pamela Constable, "Afghan Women Take Radio Liberties: Tiny Station Transmitting Message of Support to a Largely Illiterate Female Populace," *Washington Post,* 3 November 2003.

362 But clearly, the most radical change . . . Donnelly so aptly describes it.
Thomas Donnelly and Vance Serchuk, "Toward a Global Cavalry: Overseas

Rebasing and Defense Transformation," *American Enterprise Institute Online*, 20 June 2003, found online at www.aei.org/publications..

362 This radical repositioning of U.S. military bases . . . Core-Gap divide.

For a good overview of how the distribution of U.S. military bases around the world has changed since the end of the Cold War, see Bruce Falconer, "The World in Numbers: U.S. Military Logistics," *The Atlantic Monthly*, May 2003, pp. 50–51.

363 Concerns over American "empire" . . . Kennedy at the end of the Cold War.

Paul Kennedy, *The Rise and Fall of the Great Powers: Economic Change and Military Conflict from 1500 to 2000* (New York: Random House, 1987).

364 If America offers a convincing case . . . defined by the Gap's elimination.

The "unipolar moment" concept originates with Charles Krauthammer, "The Unipolar Moment," *Foreign Affairs*, Winter 1990/91, pp. 23–33.

Chapter 8. HOPE WITHOUT GUARANTEES

368 I know not everyone . . . "hope without guarantees."

J.R.R. Tolkien used this phrase when describing his treatment of the character "Gandalf" (*Lord of the Rings*) in a letter to Michael Straight, *New Republic* editor, January 1956, found online at www.tolkienonline.com.

369 We will accomplish this best by being explicit . . . we enter the Gap.

I first explored this concept in Thomas P. M. Barnett, "The 'Core' and 'Gap': Defining Rules in a Dangerous World," *Providence Journal*, 7 November 2002.

370 As Art Cebrowski likes to say . . . combat is bigger than shooting."

Quoted in John T. Bennett, "Cebrowski Calls for New Training Methods for Combat, Postwar Ops," *Inside the Pentagon*, 11 September 2003.

373 Full of regional area experts . . . then doing its best to fulfill that prophecy.

True to form, the State Department "foresaw" all the difficulties of the postwar occupation of Iraq, and just as true to form, the Defense Department ignored their concerns because State *always* tells Defense that what they are trying to achieve is virtually impossible. For details on this case, see Eric Schmitt and Joel Brinkley, "State Dept. Study Foresaw Trouble Now Plaguing Iraq: Some Say Pentagon First Ignored Warnings on Security, Utilities and Civil Rule," *New York Times*, 19 October 2003.

374 Here I agree with Newt Gingrich . . . complete overhaul and now.

See Newt Gingrich, "Rogue State Department," *Foreign Policy*, July–August 2003, pp. 42–48.

374 The model of this approach . . . peacekeeping forces were locally derived.

For a good overview, see Alex de Waal, "S.O.S. Africa," *Wall Street Journal,* 6 August 2003.

374 Here, the best example comes from Chad . . . economic development.

Roger Thurow and Susan Warren, "In War on Poverty, Chad's Pipeline Plays Unusual Role: To Unlock Buried Wealth, Nation Gives Up Control over Spending Its Cash," *Wall Street Journal,* 24 June 2003.

374 Finally, the Core's foreign aid . . . connectivity throughout the Gap.

For examples of this general trend, see David Barboza, "Development of Biotech Crops Is Booming in Asia," *New York Times,* 21 February 2003; and Justin Gillis, "To Feed Hungry Africans, Firms Plant Seeds of Science," *Washington Post,* 11 March 2003.

375 These approaches, when combined . . . redirecting that time toward education.

For a good example, see Roger Thurow, "Makeshift 'Cuisinart' Makes a Lot Possible in Impoverished Mali: It Can Do Work in a Flash, Leaving Time for Literacy and Entrepreneurship," *Wall Street Journal,* 26 July 2002.

375 This organization would focus . . . once bad leadership has been removed.

Sebastian Mallaby, "The Lesson in MacArthur," *Washington Post,* 21 October 2002.

376 The fact that UN Secretary General . . . before the decade ends.

Annan broached the subject in his annual report to the General Assembly, delivered 8 September 2003; see Felicity Barringer, "Annan Wants Security Council to Grow to Better Reflect World," *New York Times,* 9 September 2003.

377 The outlines of the great compromise . . . and foreign direct investment.

Some commentators, like Thomas Friedman, go so far as to say that the U.S. government's continued subsidization of U.S. farmers indirectly fuels terrorism around the world; see his "Connect the Dots," *New York Times,* 25 September 2003.

378 This group was led by China, India . . . all key pillars of the New Core.

For details, see Steven Pearlstein, "Trade and Trade-Offs," *Washington Post,* 10 September 2003; Elizabeth Becker, "Coming U.S. Vote Figures in Walkout at Trade Talks: American Farm Provisions Are a Key Issue," *New York Times,* 16 September 2003; Pascal Lamy, "Post-Cancun Primer: My WTO 'Q & A,'" *Wall Street Journal,* 23 September 2003; and Larry Rohter, "New Global Trade Lineup: Haves, Have-Nots, Have-Somes," *New York Times,* 2 November 2003.

378 When the United States needed to sell . . . or well over $100 billion.

Details come from Floyd Norris, "Foreigners May Not Have Liked This War, But They Financed It," *New York Times,* 12 September 2003; and Peter S. Goodman, "U.S. Debt to Asia Swelling: Japan, China Lead Buyers of Treasuries," *Washington Post,* 13 September 2003.

379 He has treated his own people . . . countryside in the late 1990s.

For descriptions, see Carl Gersham, "North Korea's Human Catastrophe," *Washington Post,* 17 April 2003; Robert Windrem, "Death, Terror in N. Korea Gulag," MSNBC, 15 January 2003, found online at www.msnbc.com/news/859191.asp; Doug Struck, "Opening a Window on North Korea's Horrors: Defectors Haunted by Guilt for the Loved Ones Left Behind," *Washington Post,* 4 October, 2003; and Peter Maass, "The Last Emperor Kim Jong Il," *New York Times Magazine,* 19 October 2003, pp. 36–47.

380 If that is not enough, then Iran . . . and al Qaeda in particular.

For details on the Iranian government's "Jerusalem Force," which trains, arms, and collaborates with foreign terrorist groups in the region, including al Qaeda, see Dana Priest and Douglas Farah, "Iranian Force Has Long Ties to Al Qaeda," *Washington Post,* 14 October 2003.

380 Once this happens . . . rebel groups within that failed state.

For a description of the most recent American effort to effect a "Colombian-ization" of the war effort there, see Scott Wilson, "U.S. Makes Plans to Give War Back to Colombia: Involvement Will Decline After Hunt Ends for Americans," *Washington Post,* 9 March 2003.

380 The shift to natural gas alone . . . "trust fund" model of nondevelopment.

For examples of how the Saudis are rethinking foreign investment with regard to natural gas, see Heather Timmons, "Saudis Trying to Drum Up Investment in Gas Fields," *New York Times,* 22 July 2003.

381 U.S. pressure in this regard . . . and non-Muslims with great suspicion."

Zakaria, *Future of Freedom,* p. 145.

381 The biggest danger China faces . . . a collapse of its financial system.

For details, see Kathy Chen, "Surge in Lending in China Stokes Economic Worries: Spending Investment Sprees Point to Overheating; Bad Debts Are on the Rise," *Wall Street Journal,* 3 October 2003.

INDEX

THE PENTAGON'S NEW MAP

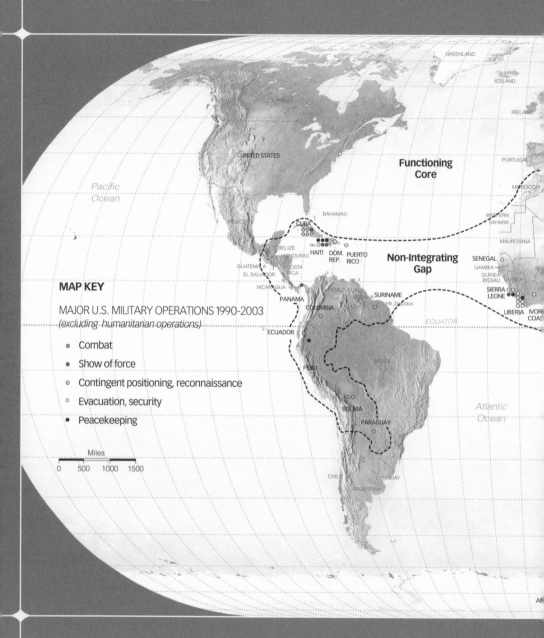

Functioning Core

Non-Integrating Gap

MAP KEY

MAJOR U.S. MILITARY OPERATIONS 1990-2003
(excluding humanitarian operations)

- Combat
- Show of force
- Contingent positioning, reconnaissance
- Evacuation, security
- Peacekeeping

Miles
0   500   1000   1500